CAMBRIDGE TEXTS IN THE
HISTORY OF POLITICAL THOUGHT

WEBER
Political Writings

CAMBRIDGE TEXTS IN THE HISTORY OF POLITICAL THOUGHT

Series editors

RAYMOND GEUSS
Reader in Philosophy, University of Cambridge

QUENTIN SKINNER
Regius Professor of Modern History, University of Cambridge

Cambridge Texts in the History of Political Thought is now firmly established as the major student textbook series in political theory. It aims to make available to students all the most important texts in the history of western political thought, from ancient Greece to the early twentieth century. All the familiar classic texts will be included, but the series seeks at the same time to enlarge the conventional canon by incorporating an extensive range of less well-known works, many of them never before available in a modern English edition. Wherever possible, texts are published in complete and unabridged form, and translations are specially commissioned for the series. Each volume contains a critical introduction together with chronologies, biographical sketches, a guide to further reading and any necessary glossaries and textual apparatus. When completed the series will aim to offer an outline of the entire evolution of western political thought.

For a list of titles published in the series, please see end of book.

WEBER

Political Writings

EDITED BY
PETER LASSMAN
University of Birmingham

AND
RONALD SPEIRS
University of Birmingham

PUBLISHED BY THE PRESS SYNDICATE OF THE UNIVERSITY OF CAMBRIDGE
The Pitt Building, Trumpington Street, Cambridge, United Kingdom

CAMBRIDGE UNIVERSITY PRESS
The Edinburgh Building, Cambridge CB2 2RU, UK
40 West 20th Street, New York, NY 10011–4211, USA
477 Williamstown Road, Port Melbourne, VIC 3207, Australia
Ruiz de Alarcón 13, 28014 Madrid, Spain
Dock House, The Waterfront, Cape Town 8001, South Africa

http://www.cambridge.org

First published 1994
Reprinted 2002

Printed in the United Kingdom at the University Press, Cambridge

A catalogue record for this book is available from the British Library

Library of Congress Cataloguing in Publication data
Weber, Max, 1864–1920.
[Selections. English. 1994]
Weber: Political Writings / edited by Peter Lassman and Ronald
Speirs.
p.   cm. – (Cambridge texts in the history of political
thought)
Translated from the German.
Includes bibliographical references and index.
ISBN 0 521 39312 4 (hardback). – ISBN 0 521 39719 7 (pbk.)
1. Political science.   I. Title.   II. Series.
JC263.W38213 1994
306′.2–dc20   93–5718   CIP

ISBN 0 521 39312 4 hardback
ISBN 0 521 39719 7 paperback

WV

Contents

Acknowledgements

To work on the writings of someone as wide-ranging in his scholarship as Max Weber is quickly to be reminded of the limits of one's own knowledge and to appeal to better informed colleagues for assistance. We gladly acknowledge the detailed help received from Harro Höpfl, Department of Politics, University of Lancaster, Maureen Perrie of the Centre for Russian and East European Studies, Jens Röhrkasten of the School of History and Bernard Standring of the Department of German, and the general support, advice and criticism of colleagues in the Departments of German and Political Science and International Studies at the University of Birmingham. The advice of Irving Velody, University of Durham, in the early stages of the project is also acknowledged with gratitude.

Introduction

Karl Emil Maximilian Weber was born in Erfurt in 1864. His father, Max Weber Sr, was a lawyer and a deputy in the Prussian Chamber of Deputies for the National Liberal Party from 1868 to 1882 and from 1884 to 1897. He was also a member of the Reichstag from 1872 until 1884. Weber's mother, Helene Fallenstein Weber, had an interest in questions of religion and social reform which she did not share with her husband.

The Weber household in Berlin attracted a large number of academics and politicians, including von Bennigsen, Dilthey, Theodor Mommsen and Treitschke. The discussions which took place there must have made a strong impression on the young Weber. In 1882 Weber began his studies at Heidelberg University. His main subject was law but he also attended courses in political economy, history, philosophy and theology. He moved to Strasbourg in 1883 where he combined his year of national service with study at the university. In 1884 Weber continued his studies in Berlin. Here he attended courses in law, including Gierke's course on German legal history. Weber was not impressed by the lectures of Treitschke which, because of their extreme nationalism, he considered to be little more than demagogy and propaganda. After graduation Weber did not find the practice of law sufficiently stimulating and continued his studies in the field of political science (*Staatswissenschaft*) as well as in legal and economic history.

In 1889 Weber submitted a doctoral dissertation with the somewhat lengthy title 'Development of the Principle of Joint Liability and the Separate Fund in the Public Trading Company out of Household and Trade Communities in the Italian Cities'. This essay then formed a chapter in a longer work entitled 'On the History of Trading Companies in the Middle Ages, based on South-European Sources' and was published in the same year. Weber subsequently published his *Habilitationschrift* (the higher degree necessary to acquire professorial status in a German University) in 1891 on 'Roman Agrarian History and its Importance for Constitutional and Civil Law'. During this period Weber became involved with the activities of the Evangelical–Social Congress, forming a friendship with Friedrich Naumann, a leader of the Christian–Social Movement and founder of the National Social Union (*Nationalsozialer Verein*).

In 1892 Weber published the results of an inquiry sponsored by the *Verein für Sozialpolitik* into 'The Conditions of the Agricultural Workers in the East Elbian regions of Germany'. This bulky study had considerable political significance. Its subject was the highly controversial one of the defence of German culture from Slav, mainly Polish, 'infiltration'. In the same year Weber became a lecturer in Roman and commercial law, and in the following year Althoff, the Prussian Minister of Culture, directed that Weber be made Professor of Commercial and German Law in Berlin. Nevertheless, in 1894 Weber moved to the University of Freiburg where he accepted a Chair of Political Economy (*Nationalökonomie*). The essay published here, 'The Nation State and Economic Policy', is his inaugural lecture. This lecture was highly controversial, as Weber intended it to be. He referred, with pleasure, to the horror aroused by 'the brutality' of his views.

Weber left Freiburg in 1896 to become Professor of Political Science at Heidelberg where he succeeded the eminent political economist Karl Knies. Although Weber was highly critical of the work of Knies, his own academic work followed in the same tradition represented by the 'Historical School' of German political economy. Among Weber's colleagues at Heidelberg were Georg Jellinek, Professor of Constitutional Law, whose *Allgemeine Staatslehre* (General Theory of the State) was published in 1900, and Ernst Troeltsch, the theologian and philosopher. Both were highly significant influences upon the direction of Weber's thought. (In passing it may be noted that, while at Heidelberg, Weber supported the introduction of the first female students, one of whom was Else von Richthofen, whose sister, Frieda, married D. H. Lawrence in 1912.)

Following the death of his father in 1897, Weber entered a period of mental illness marked by periods of deep depression. The antidote for this condition was extensive travel, especially in Italy, as a result of which Weber was eventually able to recover his ability for sustained and wide-ranging reading. Unable to carry out his professional obligations, Weber resigned from Heidelberg in 1903. Nevertheless, at this time he entered into a renewed period of creativity in which he began a series of writings on methodological themes as well as the essays which were later collected and published as *The Protestant Ethic and the Spirit of Capitalism.*

In 1904 Weber, with Edgar Jaffé and Werner Sombart, became an editor of the *Archiv für Sozialwissenschaft und Sozialpolitik* (Archive for Social Science and Social Policy). This journal declared that one of its aims was to explore the 'cultural significance of capitalist development'. Weber acquired first-hand knowledge of the cultural and political consequences of rapid industrial development when he visited America in the same year. He had responded to an invitation to deliver a lecture at the World Exhibition in St Louis, but he made use of this trip to travel widely in the United States.

The outbreak of revolution in 1905 focused Weber's attention sharply on Russia. He learnt to read the language in three months and was able to follow the course of events as reported in the Russian language newspapers and journals. In the long essay 'On the Situation of Constitutional Democracy in Russia' (most of which is reprinted here) and in a further essay published in the same year, *Russia's Transition to Sham-Constitutionalism*, he discussed the probable political consequences of the late development of capitalist industry within the Russian social, political and cultural context.

In 1909 Weber became editor of a projected encyclopedia of 'social economics' (*Grundriß der Sozialökonomik)* in which his own contribution, 'The Economy and the Social Orders and Powers', was to be one of the volumes. It was given the title 'Economy and Society' (*Wirtschaft und Gesellschaft*), with the original title as subtitle, when published after his death in 1921. During the First World War and in the years immediately preceding it Weber worked both on this project and on the comparative studies which focus on the economic ethics of the major world religions. During these years Weber continued to live in Heidelberg, where his home became a centre for intellectual debate. Among those who were frequent visitors were

Karl Jaspers, Werner Sombart, Ernst Troeltsch, Georg Jellinek, Georg Simmel and Georg Lukacs.

In 1914 Weber, despite his strong reservations about the direction of German foreign policy, was initially swept along by the general enthusiasm. As the war progressed, he recovered his more characteristic sense of detachment. He argued publicly against the professed war aims of the German government and opposed all suggestions for a policy of territorial annexation in Europe. The irresponsible nature of German policy was, in Weber's opinion, exemplified by the decision to intensify submarine warfare. The most likely effect of this policy would be to draw America into the war and, as a consequence, ensure the defeat of Germany. During this period Weber continued his academic work. He completed and published his essays on the world religions and accepted a Chair of Political Economy at the University of Vienna in 1918.

Returning to Munich in late 1918, Weber observed the revolution in Germany with dismay. The 'bloody carnival', as he called it, simply weakened Germany in its moment of defeat. In 1919 Weber made an unsuccessful entry into the political arena. His nomination as a Democratic Party candidate for the National Assembly was rejected by party officials. Nevertheless, Weber did contribute in an unofficial capacity to the deliberations on the nature of the future constitution and he participated briefly in the peace delegation at Versailles. Plans to make Weber Secretary of the Interior came to nothing. He had reservations about the new republic but, as the essays in this volume show, he was determined that it must be made to work for the sake of the nation's future.

Following an invitation from the students of Munich University, Weber delivered his two famous lectures 'Wissenschaft als Beruf' (usually translated as 'Science as a Vocation') in November 1917 and 'Politik als Beruf' (translated here as 'The Profession and Vocation of Politics') in January 1919. His lectures at the university were the object of demonstrations by organisations of right-wing students. In the summer of 1920 Weber died from pneumonia.

Max Weber once wrote that 'the political' was his 'secret love'. He was concerned with political affairs throughout his life. Weber himself often felt torn by the conflicting demands of scholarship and political involvement. It can be argued that political concerns run through all his academic work and that these concerns alone endow it with the unifying theme so many interpreters have sought in vain. The importance and originality of Weber's political thought have at times been obscured by commentaries which have presented his work as a relatively straightforward contribution to a version of modern social science which eschews political controversy.

The essays and lectures collected here possess a dual character. Although they were occasioned by current events and problems, they also point beyond their immediate context towards much wider considerations. The political writings are essential reading for anyone who wishes to understand Weber's vision of the modern world. Concern with the political fate of Germany is a reference point for all of these essays. Even the discussion of the situation in Russia is shaped by an implicit comparison with the state of affairs in Germany. Conversely, Weber's discussion of the fate of politics in Germany, however intense its immediate engagement, always has implications for our fundamental understanding of the politics of the modern western state.

As Weber's political writings span a period of some twenty-five years, it is only to be expected that they show some development and change of ideas. For example, the references to racial differences made in his inaugural lecture were abandoned in his later work, where he made it clear that the concept of race had no explanatory value. On the other hand, the central point of that lecture, the inescapability of politics as conflict (*Kampf*), remains a constant theme in all his work.

The important question for Weber is not the material wellbeing of the people, but the quality of human being in any given economic and social order. All work in political economy, he argues, aims at producing 'those characteristics which we think of as constituting the human greatness and nobility of our nature' (p. 15). We must not lose sight of the fact that the central question of political economy is concerned with *human beings* and the quality of their existence. Weber's forceful manner of expression shows that the discipline of political economy, in his view, is a political science in the classical sense: 'It is a servant of politics, not the day-to-day politics of the persons and classes who happen to be ruling at any given time, but the enduring power-political interests of the nation' (p. 16). Weber's thought and expression combines, distinctively, elements of Darwin, Nietzsche and Marx to stress the inescapability and necessity of conflict and selection between states, peoples and classes. Although Weber shows here that he can be as 'materialistic' in his analysis as any Marxist, the decisive difference between Weber and Marx is that for him there is no future utopia where this struggle can come to an end. Endless struggle is fate, and our strength of character is measured in terms of our ability to face up to this fact without consoling illusions.

Weber's view of political life is deeply pessimistic. 'We do not have peace and happiness to hand down to our descendants, but rather the *eternal struggle* to preserve and raise the quality of our national species' (p. 16). Weber had immersed himself in the study of political economy in order to carry out the academic duties associated with his Chair at Freiburg which was in a discipline of which he had in 1895 only a limited knowledge. He accepted the prevailing view of the economic arena as one of unending struggle against scarcity. But, as Weber sees it, economic competition is also '*power* struggle'. The state is the 'worldly organisation of the nation's power' (p. 17) and the preservation of the nation's power provides the ultimate criterion for economic policy.

Weber is reported (how accurately, one cannot tell) to have said that Marx and Nietzsche were the key intellectual figures of the modern age. While Weber was neither a disciple of Nietzsche nor of Marx, he was impressed by both thinkers. The originality of his own thought emerges from dialogue with these contending voices, from a combination of intense engagement with and critical distancing from them. Although they were certainly not the only influences on his thinking (the philosophical work of Dilthey, Rickert and Simmel on the nature of historical and cultural knowledge is of central importance, while the presence of Luther's Bible is palpable), many of his central themes would have been unthinkable without their influence. The problem of the late and extraordinarily rapid industrialisation of a recently united Germany put questions about the nature of the capitalist economy at the centre of concern for Weber's generation. The emergence of socialism as a political movement forced society at large and the academic world in particular to take stock, not only of 'the social problem' but also of the intellectual claims of Marxism. Simultaneously, the radical elitism of Nietzsche was felt as the 'earthquake of the epoch' by many of Weber's generation. Nietzsche was the most important of those thinkers who saw the transformation of European society and culture in terms of decline and decadence. Seen in this perspective, socialism was a symptom rather than a cure for the modern malaise and its commitment to an idea of progress no more than a delusion on the part of a debilitated civilisation.

'The Nation State and Economic Policy' contains many of the themes which will recur throughout Weber's later work. Here, as so often, Weber begins with a consideration of the 'dry facts'. He then enlarges the scope of his discussion so that his topic reveals implications which lead far beyond the immediate occasion of his reflections. The lecture begins with a summary of the findings of surveys recently conducted on the situation of agricultural labour in the eastern provinces of Prussia during the years 1892 to 1895. The agrarian problem carried a high political charge and Weber did not hesitate to throw himself into the debate. The result was immediate and intense controversy. Weber portrays Germany as a nation state which is faced by other nation states in an 'economic struggle for life' in which 'there is no peace to be had' (p. 14). The conditions and migration of German and Polish agricultural labourers in the eastern provinces is the immediate problem. Weber argues that economic problems of this kind must be viewed in political terms. If, as Weber sees it, there is a blatant contradiction between the economic class interests of the Prussian landed aristocracy, (the *Junker*), and the political interests of the nation in the eastern provinces, these latter interests must unequivocally take precedence.

To appreciate Weber's argument, one must see it in relation to contemporary debates on the question of Germany's future as an industrial state. Weber accepts that there is no alternative path for Germany's future development other than industrialisation. Yet the industrial future carries certain costs. It means that the character of social relations will be transformed, especially, at first, in the countryside. They will shift away from the more personal and patriarchal towards the impersonal relations of production organised on the basis of capitalist principles. Weber neither joins the ranks of the opponents of industrialisation, nor does he welcome unreservedly the development of a capitalist economy. His point is that the future of Germany as a 'world power' requires that it embrace industrialisation without nostalgic longings for a lost 'communal' past. Furthermore, and more fundamentally, everything depends on the nation's ability to feed its rapidly growing population.

Neither agricultural policy as such nor the details of the economic situation are Weber's prime concern, however. The focus of his interest is on the consequences of these developments for the interests of the nation. Yet it would be wrong to see Weber as merely putting forward the conventional nationalist ideas of the time. His concern is not with the power of the state as an end in itself but rather with the fate of the nation. The central question for Weber is one of political leadership. Which class or stratum (*Schicht*) could provide national leadership? Weber was pessimistic. At this stage, it appeared that none of the classes in Germany possessed the political maturity to take on this role.

In his inaugural lecture Weber describes a relentless process of selection at work between nations. Most worryingly, however, there is no guarantee that the economically most developed nations nor the most highly developed 'form of human being' will emerge as the victors from this process. In presenting this argument, Weber, who had been appointed to a Chair of Political Economy, was also participating in a debate about the nature and limits of economic thinking which had divided the Historical School of Political Economy in Germany. The question of the nature and value of the economic explanation of human affairs had become a central preoccupation of contemporary German historiography. Weber attacks what he terms the 'vulgar conception of political economy' which devises 'recipes for universal happiness'. While recognising the general value of economic concepts to explain human conduct, Weber also insists on their limitations. Politics must not be reduced to economics. The sphere of the political is autonomous.

Weber's account of the nature of politics is bound up with his view of the place of Germany in a world of *Machtstaaten*. In his earlier writings Weber shared the view common at the time among political economists that the world of industrial states was entering a phase of brutal struggle for resources and markets. Although he moderated his nationalism in later years, Weber continued to argue that the modern state cannot be defined in terms of 'the content of its activities'. It is 'in the last analysis' to be defined in terms of the specific means it employs. The means specific to the state and to all other forms of political association is, ultimately, physical violence. The specific character of the modern state is that it and it alone 'lays claim to the *monopoly of legitimate physical violence* within a certain territory' (pp. 300–311). Politics, according to this account, is to be defined in terms of the struggle for 'a share of power or for influence on the distribution of power, whether it be between states or between the groups of people contained within a single state' (p. 311).

If Germany was to be a powerful nation state, a *Machtstaat*, then, inevitably, it would experience what Burckhardt had called the 'diabolical character of power'. The possession and use of such power entailed decisions and actions which would be evil or immoral. Yet it is an essential component of Weber's tragic vision of politics and of history that, unless we withdraw from the world completely, into pacifism, for example, such actions are unavoidable. As a result of the facts of European history and geography, it was Germany's fate to have no choice other than to accept its '*responsibility before history*'. In Weber's view the position of Germany was entirely different from that of small states such as Switzerland or Denmark. Nevertheless, Weber did not resolve the Nietzschean problem of the relation between the nation state and national culture. Unlike the 'vulgar' nationalists, Weber does not agree that political greatness and cultural achievements necessarily go hand in hand. He rejects the view that smaller states must in any sense be 'less valuable' from a cultural point of view. Indeed, he is thankful that there are German communities outside the Reich. In such small states (Switzerland is an example here), 'other virtues may flourish: not only the simple, bourgeois virtues (*Bürgertugenden*) of citizenship and true democracy' but 'much more intimate and yet eternal values' (p. 76). It seems inevitable that Germany, as a *Machtstaat*, cannot provide the best ground for the flourishing of culture within its own borders, although the prestige of that culture may well depend upon such national power. Germany has a national responsibility to defend the culture of Central Europe against the dual threat of future Russian and Anglo-American hegemony. Writing during the First World War, it seems obvious to Weber that a powerless German state would be useless in the defence not only of German culture both within and outside the Reich, but also of the cultural autonomy of Central Europe.

The 1905 revolution in Russia provided Weber with the occasion to look at a state other than Germany where the liberal tradition was fragile. Although Weber accepted that Marx had made an important contribution to the understanding of social and political issues, he was not prepared to endorse his claims to scientific status. Marxian ideas, as far as Weber was concerned, were suggestive 'ideal types', no more and no less. Thus, he makes use of ideas derived in part from Marx both in the essay on the situation in Russia and in other writings. He discusses the class basis of the various parties and movements and attempts to assess the overall balance of conflicting interests, material and ideal. Furthermore, he includes an analysis of the role of Marx's ideas and of Marxist parties. However, the limits of Marx's philosophy of history are clear for Weber. We cannot count upon the 'laws of economic development' to produce conditions favourable either to democracy or to individualist values. Politics can never be a mere 'superstructural' reflection of the underlying material base. Economic or material development can just as clearly point in the opposite direction. The future is more likely to be one of cultural stagnation in which mankind is imprisoned in the *'housing for the new serfdom'* (p. 68). Weber's image of the bleak future of 'a polar night of icy darkness and hardness' (p. 368) is not simply one in which a bureaucratic 'benevolent feudalism' (p. 68) would limit the sphere of human freedom and sap the will to pursue it. This vision is also supported by contemporary political economic theory which argued that there was a definite propensity for industrial capitalism to lose its entrepreneurial dynamism and degenerate into a rentier state as markets and land were exhausted: the 'victory of "dividends" (*Rente*) over "profits" (*Gewinn*)' (p. 68). The 'anarchy of production' described by Marx and Engels was being supplanted by a bureaucratically administered regime comparable to the static empires of the ancient Mediterranean. Socialism would complete this development by strengthening the bureaucratic apparatus which would come to rule in all spheres of life. The alienation of every type of producer in the modern economy would be complete. The socialist project was inherently self-destructive.

In his lecture on socialism Weber considers various versions of this doctrine but takes the *Communist Manifesto* of Marx and Engels as his paradigm text. He does so because it reveals clearly a central contradiction in Marxist theory. This resides in its claim to be a science that reveals the determining laws of historical development while simultaneously prophesying the emancipation and renewal of mankind. Writing in 1918, Weber observed that the revolutionary regime in Russia was dependent on the services of Tsarist officers and officials and that, in reality, economic production was still based upon capitalist principles. In fact the revolutionary regime was importing the newest ideas of managerial organisation from the West. Weber was aware of the argument that the Russian revolution was taking place under exceptional conditions, so that it might be wrong to generalise from this particular 'experiment'. Nevertheless he pointed out that West European syndicalist movements, which could be considered to be the most revolutionary 'direct action' form of socialism, were also obliged to rely on the support of non-workers, the intellectuals. The intellectuals themselves were often inclined to support syndicalism because they were attracted by the romanticism inherent in the idea of the general strike. They saw the hope for revolution as a source of 'enchantment' within a world whose 'disenchantment' they felt acutely. This is an extension of the observation Weber had first made in 1905 when discussing the, at first glance, strange fact that there was an 'affinity' between revolutionary intellectuals and authoritarian bureaucracy in pre-revolutionary Russia.

In the inaugural lecture Weber had been unable to identify a class or estate (*Stand*) capable of representing the interest of the nation. His criticism of Bismarck was directed at the failure of his rule to create a responsible political leadership and to provide the German nation with the political education it sorely needed. Weber was impressed by the work of those contemporary writers, especially Moisie Ostrogorski and James Bryce, who had described the rise of the modern form of the bureaucratic political party machine, the 'caucus', first in America and then in England, and the way in which this development had changed the character of democratic politics. The first half of the lecture on 'The Profession and Vocation of Politics' relies heavily, as Weber acknowledges, upon Ostrogorski's *Democracy and the Organisation of Political Parties* (1902). The transformation of political parties, which are 'acknowledged by no constitution and by no law' (p. 149), from associations of notables into bureaucratic machines organised both inside and outside parliament is an 'unstoppable process'. Ostrogorski's and Bryce's accounts of the evolution of mass democracy as a competition for power between highly organised parties complemented Weber's view of 'universal rationalisation' and his perception that traditional liberalism was now outmoded. Given such conditions, the immediate question becomes: how can individual freedom survive? These developments produce a new kind of professional politician who lives 'from politics' rather than 'for politics'. The spread of bureaucracy readily gives rise to rule by officials and this Weber sees as inimical to genuine political leadership, essential for Germany's survival as a world power as well as to accountable government and the political education of the public. There is a tension here between Weber's 'liberalism' and his 'nationalism'. He does not indicate in a clear fashion which of these he considers to be the more important. It is consistent with his general way of thinking, in fact, to say that a tension between these two principles is desirable and must indeed be maintained because such tensions between competing values are essential in order to prevent cultural stagnation.

Writing during the last years of the First World War, Weber's overriding concern was with the survival of the German state and nation. Repeating a central theme of the inaugural lecture, Weber stresses the fact that Germany is a nation lacking political education and 'political will'. The policies of the wartime government had made this fact only too clear. The central issue was how to prevent the bureaucratic elimination of genuine political activity. In the modern mass state this placed the question of the nature and role of parliament at the top of the agenda: '*How is parliament to be made capable of assuming power?* Anything else is a side-issue' (p. 190). This raises a difficult problem of interpretation. Does Weber value the political work of parliament for its own sake, or does he value it simply because the survival of the nation, and its power, depend on it? In the last resort, he argues that 'the historical tasks of the German nation (. . .) take *precedence*, as a matter of principle, over all questions of the *form* the state should assume' (p. 130), but it is also essential for the nation to take responsibility for its own fate and, under the modern conditions of large states, where direct democracy is technically impossible, this can only occur through the representatives of the people.

Weber's discussion of the fate of Germany as a nation state must be placed in the context of his diagnosis of the emerging unique character of modern western society. The main trend identified by Weber was one of growing rationalisation in all spheres of social life. Symptoms of this were to be seen in secularisation, the growth of bureaucratic administration, the general advance of formalism and calculability as the bases of economic and legal institutions, and the fragmentation of value: in other words, 'the disenchantment of the world'. In political terms the problem was one of the future of liberal constitutionalism within states which were being transformed into mass democracies. The nature of such states was radically different from those in which the philosophical justification for liberalism had first been propounded. Furthermore the 'disenchantment' Weber described did not stop with liberalism. The traditional philosophical foundations of all political ideologies and doctrines were threatened by a relentless undermining of their own presuppositions. This created a problem for Weber which he was unable to resolve in a satisfactory manner. He was committed to the existence of the institutions of the western constitutional state which served as the necessary framework within which personal freedom and individualism were most likely to flourish, even if only for a minority. Yet his scepticism about the traditional justifications of the constitutional state, in terms of natural right, for example, meant that he was, in effect, defending liberal institutions without the fully elaborated liberal philosophy which, in the past, had supported them.

During the war years Weber advocated a strong parliament for Germany as the proper arena for national politics. Parliamentary politics, as opposed to mere bureaucratic rule, is important for two reasons. Political activity for and within a parliament, which for Weber means 'conflict, the recruitment of allies, and a voluntary following' is essential because, despite the power of the party machines, it can act as a barrier against all those pressures pushing towards social stagnation. Parliament is also important because it provides the arena in which genuine leaders can be selected. These points are especially important for Weber because, in his view, there is a close affinity between modern democracy and bureaucracy. The policy demands typically generated within democratic states can only be met by large-scale bureaucratic administration. This, in turn, will tend to usurp the role of political leadership if the bureaucracy is not controlled and scrutinised. Political leadership and the rule of officialdom are antithetical. The distinction between them is especially important for the conduct of foreign policy. Weber argued that the combination of a weak parliament, an interfering monarch and rule by officials in the post-Bismarckian era had produced extremely incompetent foreign policy, if it could be called policy at all. In contrast, Weber looked to the example of Britain where, he believed, a strong parliament with political leaders who were masters of a political machine had been successful, with popular support, in creating and maintaining a world empire.

The modern politician and, especially, the party leader is superior to the official in one fundamental respect: 'the only persons with the training needed for political leadership are those who have been selected in political *struggle*' (p. 219). An essential component of the struggle between parties in mass democracy is demagogy. As soon as 'the masses can no longer be treated purely as passive objects of administration' then 'democratisation and demagogy belong together' (p. 220). Modern democracy means that the political leader 'uses the means of mass demagogy to gain the confidence of the masses and their belief in his person, and thereby gains power' (p. 220). In other words, there is an inescapable element of 'Caesarism' in modern mass democracy. In fact, Weber sees this as a characteristic of all democratic regimes: 'the major decisions in politics, particularly in democracies, are made by *individuals*, and this inevitable circumstance means that mass democracy, ever since Pericles, has always had to pay for its positive successes with major concessions to the Caesarist principle of leadership selection' (p. 222). This introduces another problem for the interpretation of Weber's account of democracy in the modern state. Although he argues that a strong parliament is necessary as a place where political leaders are to be selected, he also argues in favour of the Caesarist element, whereby it is both inevitable and desirable that political leaders should appeal directly to the masses and, in this sense, bypass parliament. The national political leader is, in Weber's well-known terminology, a charismatic leader who relies upon faith and devotion to his personal character for the maintenance of his rule. In 'Parliament and Government' Weber argues that the opposition between the plebiscitary and parliamentary selection of leaders does not mean, as many of his contemporaries argued, that parliaments are worthless. The existence of parliament guarantees stability, controls the nature of positions of power, preserves civil and legal safeguards against the power of the national leader, provides a 'proving ground' for potential leaders, and, very importantly, provides a peaceful way to eliminate a 'Caesarist dictator' who has lost the support of the masses.

One of the threats to stable political life comes from the possibility that 'emotional elements', 'the politics of the street', will become predominant. In 1918 Weber believed that 'neither the Caesarist character and mass demagogy, nor the bureaucratisation and stereo-typing of the parties are in themselves a rigid barrier to the rise of leaders' (p. 230). The organisation of the modern party and the 'train-ing ground' of parliamentary committee work will ensure that 'Caes-arist representatives of the masses' will 'submit to the established legal forms of political life'. The leaders Weber has in mind here are not selected for their demagogic qualities 'in the bad sense of the word' (p. 230). One of the main functions of the existence of ration-ally organised parties and of a parliament with real power is that they will curtail the influence of the irrational 'democracy of the street' (p. 231). Weber's analysis, in effect, turns Ostrogorski and the other critics of mass democracy upside down. He interprets the rise of the disciplined party and demagogic leaders as an advantage of the modern state, whereas they had seen these features as signs of a crisis of democracy and liberalism.

The tension between parliament and the plebiscitary leader becomes more pronounced in Weber's post-war writings. The situ-ation in Germany is now one which holds out little promise for the creation of a strong parliament. The choice is stark: 'the only choice lies between a leadership democracy with a "machine" and demo-cracy without a leader' (p. 351). Germany has leaderless democracy, which is to say 'rule by the professional politician who has no voca-tion' and who lacks 'those inner, charismatic qualities which make a leader'. Furthermore, the system of proportional representation that has been accepted for the new Republic will have the effect of 'creat-ing an unpolitical parliament in which there is no room for genuine leadership' (p. 351). The only possible counterweight to an 'unpolit-ical parliament' would be a directly elected President of the Reich who would provide the necessary element of leadership which an 'unpolitical parliament' could not deliver. Weber argued forcefully that the President, as head of state, must be elected directly by the people and that his position must rest '*unquestionably on the will of the whole people*' (p. 304). It is important to note that Weber's argument is a response to the particular and extreme circumstances in which Germany found itself in 1918–19. Conceivably, if the tradition of party politics had been stronger, Weber would not have put forward this controversial proposal. The power of the plebiscitary President is to be strictly limited. He must see 'the prospect of the gallows as the reward awaiting any attempt to interfere with the laws or to rule autocratically' (p. 305). The President will also serve to introduce a more appropriate form of party organisation and, hence, strengthen parliament. The President, because he is directly elected, will provide the possibility of a political leader who is able to transcend party political and particularist divisions and represent the *'unity of the Reich'*. Nevertheless, Weber wanted to give the President considerable power. He must be able to intervene by dissolving parliament and be able to call a referendum (a measure which he had previously condemned) to resolve a political crisis.

In 'The Profession and Vocation of Politics' Weber turned to the question of the 'inner' qualities required of those who live 'for politics' rather than merely 'from politics'. Passion, a sense of responsibility and judgement are the three qualities he identifies. The decisive quality is judgement. In language which recalls Nietzsche's 'pathos of distance', but without the connotation of an attitude of condescension, Weber refers to 'the ability to maintain one's inner composure and calm while being receptive to realities, in other words *distance* from things and people' (p. 353). But there must also be passionate commitment to a cause. This alone gives meaning to the conduct of the politician in a world that is increasingly 'disenchanted'. The genuine political leader is, for Weber, constrained, ultimately, not by the institutions of government but by those powerful inner commitments which give direction to his calling. Despite Weber's use of the now familiar Nietzschean terminology, the educated German reader would have recognised that he was referring to an ethic of duty to one's calling which transcended the 'will to power' in any crude sense. 'Power politics' for its own sake, without commitment to a cause, was for Weber empty and absurd. He retained the traditional ethical values of the patrician: *Vornehmheit* ('chivalry'), *Anstand* ('decency') and abhorrence of *Gemeinheit* ('baseness'). A practical consequence of this was his insistence that the returning soldiers should be granted equal suffrage in Prussia immediately.

In Weber's view the distinguishing characteristic of politics is that, 'within the overall moral economy of our conduct of life' (p. 355), it alone operates through the medium of power 'backed up by the use of *violence*' (p. 357). This fact gives politics its distinctive ethical burden. The political leader is faced with a choice between two distinct ethical principles: 'the ethic of principled conviction' and 'the ethic of responsibility'. Weber gives the example of the syndicalist dedicated to the ethic of conviction who acts despite his awareness of the likely harmful consequences of his actions for the class whose cause he seeks to promote. A politician guided by the ethic of responsibility accepts that he must be guided by consideration of the consequences of his conduct. Furthermore, he is acutely aware of the 'ethical irrationality of the world' (p. 361). By this Weber wishes to say that the politician is typically faced with the problem of making use of 'morally suspect' means to achieve an end he believes to be good. There is no ethical authority, in Weber's view, for the politician to consult. He must rely on his own judgements and, ultimately, seek to reconcile, as best he can, the demands of principle and the likely consequences.

A central component of Weber's vision of the modern world is his belief that there is no longer any possibility of an objective ranking of ultimate values or moral principles. We are confronted by a pluralism of conflicting ultimate values. Yet Weber also argues that in the organised, bureaucratic and disenchanted world he has described, the most important channel for the expression of individuality is conscious commitment to just such a value or cause. His own scholarly investigations and political essays have the purpose of making clear, in as objective a manner as possible, the realities and possibilities given in any particular situation. The aim is to strive for clarity and to practise politics without illusions. Weber is probably alluding to Nietzsche's account of 'honesty' and 'hardness' as intellectual virtues. Many of Weber's readers find a fundamental problem here. Weber argues that, despite, or because of, the tragic nature of politics, in which 'the eventual outcome of political action frequently, indeed regularly, stands in a quite inadequate, even paradoxical relation to its original, intended meaning and purpose (*Sinn*)' (p. 355), the politician must be committed to a cause. The problem is that Weber feels that no cause can be 'proved', simply by intellectual means, to be superior to any other. All that seems to matter is that there must be a cause to supply the inner meaning essential for genuine political conduct. 'The *nature* of the cause the politician seeks to serve by striving for and using power is a question of faith' (p. 355). At the same time, Weber's own political essays and actions sought to demonstrate the worth of the values to which he was attached. Here he stood, he could do no other. In other words, although Weber believed that values could not be given any form of 'ultimate' foundation, it was possible and indeed necessary that we argue for them. Even more importantly, one's own life and work could serve as an example of their worth.

Weber respected those who were genuinely guided by the ethic of conviction. In fact, he recognised that the ethic of responsibility itself rested on an undemonstrable conviction: 'In this respect, the ethics of conviction and the ethics of responsibility are not absolute opposites. They are complementary to one another, and only in combination do they produce the true human being who is *capable* of having a "vocation for politics" ' (p. 368).

Max Weber is difficult to classify as a political thinker. He has been called a liberal by some, while others have denied any connection with liberalism. Certainly, Weber's political thought transcends the boundaries of the German National Liberal tradition where its roots lie. Furthermore, his vision of politics as endless conflict is in direct opposition to any dreams of 'perpetual peace'. Weber's fundamental commitment was to the ideal of individual liberty. Liberty is valued because it makes possible the fullest development of the human personality. The political problem arises because the modern democratic state contains forces that threaten rather than enhance liberty. Democracy is accepted as a fact; it is not an absolute value for him. Modern democracy, although it can lead to the 'spiritual proletarianisation' of the masses, also creates the conditions for the emergence of creative personalities, the plebiscitarian leaders who appeal directly to the people, most of whom tend to be politically passive. A model of democracy which sees it as a competition between parties for votes, and which ignores the charismatic component in Weber's account, has been highly influential in post-war political science. Weber would not have agreed with this view. While Weber's own conclusions are stamped by his time, his work remains important because it reveals the intractable problems involved in any attempt to understand the nature and possibilities of modern liberal democracy. For Weber the *Herrenvolk* conjured up by Nietzsche was to be most fully realised, not in a society where an elite ruled the 'slavish' masses, but in a 'nation of masters' in which each individual has the 'chance' and education to determine his own and the nation's fate. At the same time, he feared the reality of the party machine which cast the ordinary citizen in the role of election fodder. He wanted to defend the institutions of the liberal constitutional state, but his own intellectual principles prevented him from justifying them in terms of a fully elaborated political philosophy. These are the unresolved tensions in his work.

Bibliographical Note

The most comprehensive account of Weber's political thought which also places it within its historical context is W. J. Mommsen, *Max Weber and German Politics 1890–1920* (Chicago, 1984). This book was highly controversial when it first appeared in Germany in 1959 because it challenged most of the prevailing interpretations of Weber. Some of Mommsen's later essays, in which he modifies some of his earlier interpretations, can be found in his *The Age of Bureaucracy. Perspectives on the Political Sociology of Max Weber* (Oxford, 1974). Mommsen's *The Political and Social Theory of Max Weber. Collected Essays* (Oxford, 1989) discusses a wide range of topics and includes the important paper 'The Antinomian Structure of Max Weber's Political Thought'.

D. Beetham, *Max Weber and the Theory of Modern Politics* (London, 1974) is less historical in approach and deals with Weber's essays on Russia as well as his writings on Germany. It is critical of Mommsen's interpretation. A much shorter account is to be found in A. Giddens, *Politics and Sociology in the Thought of Max Weber* (London, 1972). S. S. Wolin, 'Max Weber. Legitimation, Method, and the Politics of Theory', in *Political Theory*, 9 (1981), pp. 401–24 is a breathtaking critical essay on Weber's place in the political tradition. D. Beetham, 'Max Weber and the Liberal Political Tradition' in *Archives Européennes de Sociologie*, 30 (1989), pp. 311–23 looks at Weber as a problem 'of' and as a problem 'for' liberalism. Surprisingly, very little has been written on Weber's views of Russia. R. Pipes, 'Max Weber and Russia' in *World Politics*, 7 (1955), pp. 371–401 is critical and very useful. L. Scaff and T. C. Arnold, 'Class and the Theory of

History: Marx on France and Weber on Russia' in R. J. Antonio and
R. M. Glassman (eds.) *A Marx – Dialogue* (Lawrence, 1985) is an
interesting comparison of the two theorists.

The postwar controversy over Weber's political ideas and their
bearing upon his reception as a 'founding father' of modern sociology
erupted into a public confrontation at a conference held to mark the
centenary of his birth in 1964. The papers are collected in *Max Weber
and Sociology Today* (edited by O. Stammer) (Oxford, 1971). Included
are the lectures by Raymond Aron, 'Max Weber and Power Politics'
and Herbert Marcuse, 'Industrialisation and Capitalism' as well as
the contribution by Jürgen Habermas to the debate on 'Value-
freedom and Objectivity' where he made the infamous statement
(subsequently modified) that Carl Schmitt, who had supported the
Nazi regime, was a 'legitimate pupil' of Weber. K. Loewenstein, *Max
Weber's Political Ideas in the Perspective of Our Time* (Massachusetts,
1966) is a defence of Weber against such accusations and includes
personal recollections of the 'Weber circle'. H. H. Bruun, *Science,
Values and Politics in Max Weber's Methodology* (Copenhagen, 1972) is
a very detailed textual analysis which investigates the difficult problem
of the relationship between Weber's ideas on the nature of values
both in scholarship and in politics. Two important attempts to rein-
terpret Weber's place in the history of ideas are W. Hennis, *Max
Weber. Essays in Reconstruction* (London, 1988) and L. A. Scaff, *Fleeing
the Iron Cage. Culture, Politics, and Modernity in the Thought of Max
Weber* (Berkeley, 1989). Hennis argues that Weber is best understood
as a late representative of a tradition of political theory which includes
Rousseau, Machiavelli and Tocqueville among its members. Scaff
places Weber's political thought within the context of the cultural
criticism of his time. Hennis and Scaff are both returning to themes
which were more common in the pre-1933 literature on Weber. An
important example of these earlier works is K. Löwith, *Max Weber
and Karl Marx* (London, 1982. First published in Germany in 1932).

Max Weber and Contemporaries edited by W. J. Mommsen and
J. Osterhammel (London, 1987), contains thirty-seven papers on this
theme. C. Antoni, *From History to Sociology* (London, 1959) places
Weber within the tradition of German historicism. F. Ringer, *The
Decline of the German Mandarins. The German Academic Community
1890–1933* (Cambridge, Mass., 1969) provides an account of the
tradition and fate of the 'cultivated middle strata' to which Weber

belonged. *Max Weber. A Biography* by Marianne Weber (New York, 1975) contains much useful information although it is not always completely accurate. K. D. Barkin. 'Conflict and Concord in Wilhelmian Social Thought' in *Central European History*, vol. v (1972), pp. 55–71 is a useful discussion of the political and intellectual context.

The nature of the relationship between Weber and Nietzsche has been revived as a topic. R. Eden, *Political Leadership and Nihilism. A Study of Weber and Nietzsche* (Tampa, 1983) is an interpretation written under the influence of the political philosophy of Leo Strauss, whose own controversial but influential critique of Weber is to be found in his *Natural Right and History* (Chicago, 1950). R. Aron's 'Max Weber and Modern Social Science' in *History, Truth, Liberty. Selected Writings of Raymond Aron* (Chicago, 1985) contains a criticism of Strauss's interpretation. Weber's relationship to Carl Schmitt is explored in R. Slagstad, 'Liberal Constitutionalism and its Critics: Carl Schmitt and Max Weber' in J. Elster and R. Slagstad (eds.), *Constitutionalism and Democracy* (Cambridge, 1988). D. Käsler, *Max Weber. An Introduction to his Life and Work* (Oxford, 1988) is a survey of Weber's work. Written from a sociological standpoint it ignores his political writings. R. Bendix, *Max Weber. An Intellectual Portrait* (London, 1960) is a descriptive account. Most useful for an introduction to reading Weber's own texts is H. H. Gerth and C. W. Mills (eds.), *From Max Weber. Essays in Sociology* (London, 1948). This contains 'Science as a Vocation' which is the companion lecture to 'Politik als Beruf'. An alternative translation is in P. Lassman and I. Velody (eds.) *Max Weber. 'Science as a Vocation'* (London, 1989). Weber's *Economy and Society* (New York, 1968) contains his definitions of political and social concepts.

Chronology

1908	Participates in the conference of the National Liberal Party
1909	Editorship of the 'Grundriß der Sozialökonomik'
1909	Weber active in the foundation of the German Sociological Society
1913	Resigns from the German Sociological Society after intense disagreement over questions of value and objectivity
1914	Beginning of the First World War
1914–15	Organises nine military hospitals
1916–18	War Journalism. Opposes the extension of submarine warfare and the policy of annexation
1917	Participates in the two (May and October) Burg Lauenstein conferences. His audience mainly socialist and pacifist youth
1917	Revolution in Russia
1917	Lecture on 'Science as a Vocation' ('Wissenschaft als Beruf') in Munich (November)
1918	Chair of Political Economy at the University of Vienna. Lectures on 'A Positive Critique of the Materialist Conception of History'
1918	Germany requests ceasefire (October)
1918	Joins the newly formed German Democratic Party
1918	Revolutionary uprisings in Germany begin (November)
1919	Lecture on 'The Profession and Vocation of Politics' ('Politik als Beruf') (January)
1919	Participates in the peace negotiations at Versailles
1919	Chair in Munich
1920	Dies of pneumonia
1921	*Economy and Society* published

Note on the Translation

The translations are based on the original printings (in brochure form) of the essays in question but take account, wherever possible, both of later alterations (as in the second printing of *Wahlrecht und Demokratie*) and of the invaluable textual and other commentaries in the new historical-critical edition.

Wherever earlier translations exist I have consulted them as a check on the accuracy of my own versions and have gratefully adopted some of their solutions. Where this translation differs from earlier versions, particularly American ones, is mainly in the attempt to follow the German as closely as is consistent with readable English, and hence in the decision not to 'domesticate' Weber by substituting a familiar equivalent in English where this would have obscured characteristic features of his diction or of the German cultural context. An explanatory glossary is provided to elaborate on the translation of a number of key or difficult terms. Further comments are to be found in the editors' footnotes.

Ronald Speirs

The Nation State and Economic Policy (Inaugural lecture)[1]

Preface

I was prompted to publish the following arguments by the opposition rather than the assent which they elicited from my audience. They offer colleagues in the same discipline, and others, new information only on points of detail, and the occasion that gave rise to them explains the special sense in which alone they lay claim to the name of 'science'. Essentially, an inaugural lecture is an opportunity to present and justify openly the personal and, in this sense, 'subjective' standpoint from which one *judges* economic phenomena. The exposition on pages 17–20 was omitted for reasons of time and in view of the audience, while other parts of the argument may have assumed a different form when I was actually delivering them. It should be noted that the opening remarks give a very simplified account of events which were naturally a good deal more complicated in reality. During the period 1871–85 the population movements in individual districts and communities in West Prussia were not uniform, although they changed in characteristic ways, and they are much less transparent than the examples selected here. In other instances the tendency I have tried to illustrate from these examples is subject to the influence of other factors. I shall return to a fuller consideration of this topic in another context in the near future.[2] It is obvious that the

---

[1] Translation of *Der Nationalstaat und die Volkswirtschaftspolitik. Akademische Antrittsrede* (Freiburg and Leipzig, 1895). The inaugural lecture was delivered in May 1895 and published in July.

[2] Weber did not in the event produce any more work in this area on a comparable scale to the investigations into rural conditions (see Max Weber *Gesamtausgabe*, I, 3) which had led to his appointment to the Chair at Freiburg, possibly because he suffered a breakdown in the years 1897–1904. He did, however, write a number of essays on

results which can be derived from these statistics stand on less steady feet than those provided by the admirable publications of several of Neumann's[3] pupils on the relations between the nationalities in Posnania and West Prussia. In the absence of correct material, however, we shall have to make do with them for the time being, especially as the main features of the phenomena they illustrate are already familiar from the rural enquiries of recent years.[4]

The title I have chosen promises much more than I can or will fulfil today. What I intend is firstly to illustrate, from just *one example*, the role played by physical and psychological racial differences between nationalities in the economic struggle for existence.[5] I should then like to add some reflections on the situation of states which rest on national foundations – as ours does – in the framework of a consideration of economic policy. I have chosen as my example a set of events which are taking place far away from here but which have caught the attention of the public repeatedly in the last ten years. I therefore ask you to follow me to the eastern marches of the Reich, into the flat landscape of the Prussian province of *West Prussia*. This setting combines the characteristics of a national frontier area with unusually abrupt differences in the economic and social conditions of existence, and this makes it suitable for our purposes. I am afraid I must begin by asking you to be patient while I rehearse a series of dry facts.

related subjects which are contained in volume 4 of the *Gesamtausgabe*, as well as a piece in 1904 on 'Agrarstatistische und sozialpolitische Betrachtungen zur Fideikommißfrage in Preußen', *Gesammelte Aufsätze zur Soziologie und Sozialpolitik* (Tübingen, 1924), pp. 323–93.
[3] Friedrich Julius von Neumann (1835–1910), economist, former holder of Chairs of Political Economy at Freiburg University and Tübingen University. Neumann's *Grundlagen der Volkswirtschaftslehre* (Tübingen, 1889) was included in Weber's reading list for his introductory lectures on economics, *Grundriß zu den Vorlesungen über Allgemeine ('theoretische') Nationalökonomie* (1898), re-published Tübingen, 1990.
[4] The *Enquêten* to which Weber refers were investigations into specific social problems carried out by the 'Verein für Socialpolitik' with the aim of influencing government policy. Weber's own study of the East Elbian provinces was part of one such larger investigation into agricultural labour.
[5] The phrase used by Weber, *Kampf ums Dasein* (struggle for existence), belongs, like *Ausleseprozeß* (process of selection), to the vocabulary of Darwinian arguments about the 'survival of the fittest' in the inevitable competition for the resources of the environment. Weber draws on such vocabulary (e. g. *Verdrängung*, supplantation) at a number of points in this lecture, although pointing out, in his footnote 'D', that he does not approve of the uncritical application of the findings of the natural sciences

In its rural districts the province contains three different types of contrast.

Firstly, extraordinary differences exist in the *quality of arable land*: from the sugar-beet soils of the Vistula plain to the sandy uplands of Cassubia the estimates of the net tax yield differ by a multiple of between ten and twenty. Even at district level the average values fluctuate between 4.75 and 33.66 marks per hectare.

Then there are contrasts in the *social stratification* of the population cultivating this land. As usual throughout eastern Germany, official records refer, alongside the 'rural parish' (*Landgemeinde*), to a second form of communal unit unknown in southern Germany, the 'estate district' (*Gutsbezirk*). Correspondingly, the estates of the nobility stand out in the landscape in visible contrast to the villages of the peasants. These estates are the seats of the Junkers, the class which gives eastern Germany its particular social stamp. Their manorial farmhouses are surrounded by the single-storey cottages which, along with some parcels of land for crops and grazing, the lord of the manor (*Gutsherr*)[6] allots to the day-labourers who are obliged to work on the manor farm all year. The area of the province as a whole is divided roughly equally between the peasants and the Junkers, but in individual regions the share of the manorial estates varies from a few per cent up to two-thirds of the entire area of the administrative districts.

Finally, within this population with its double social stratification, there exists a third opposition, that between the *nationalities*. Again, the national composition of the population in individual communities differs from region to region. This is the difference which interests us here. Firstly, of course, the density of the Polish population (*Polentum*)[7] increases the nearer you get to the border. However, as any language map will show, it also increases as the quality of the

---

to the human sciences. 'Selection' ('Auslese') remained an important concept for Weber; see, for example, his *Economy and Society*, ch. 1, section 8.

[6] A term like 'lord of the manor' corresponds only approximately to the German *Gutsherr*, so it should not be assumed that each occupies exactly the same position within the hierarchy of feudal relations.

[7] The word *Polentum* is both a collective noun, referring to the body of the Polish people and a term of characterisation, corresponding roughly to English 'Polishness'. Weber repeatedly switches from the one sense to the other, as he does with the, in this context, antithetical term *Deutschtum*, indicating thereby that the competition between these two population groups is also a competition between different sets of national characteristics and cultural values.

soil deteriorates. One's first reaction, which is not entirely wrong, is to want to explain this historically from the fact that the Germans first occupied the area by flooding across the fertile plain of the Vistula. However, if one goes on to ask which *social strata* are the bearers of German and Polish nationality (*Deutschtum* and *Polentum*) in the country districts, the figures of the most recently published population census (1885)[A] present an odd picture. Admittedly we cannot derive the national composition of parishes directly from these figures, but we can do so indirectly (if we are prepared to make do with the only approximate accuracy of the figures) by using as a link in the equation the figures for religious affiliation which coincides with nationality to within a few per cent in this region of mixed nationalities. If we separate out the economic categories of the peasant village and the manorial estate in each district, by identifying them – again only approximately – with the local administrative units of the rural parish or the estate district,[B] it emerges that their national composition varies in *opposite* ways when taken in relation to the quality of the soil. In the fertile districts the Catholics (i.e. the *Poles*) are relatively most numerous on the *estates*, while the Protestants (that is the *Germans*) are to be found in greater proportion in the *villages*. In districts with poor soil precisely the opposite situation prevails. For example, if one aggregates all districts with an average net tax yield of under 5 marks per hectare, there are only 35.5 per cent Protestants in the villages and 50.2 per cent on the estates; if, by contrast, one takes the group of districts with an average net tax yield of 10 to 15 marks per hectare, the proportion of Protestants in the villages is 60.7 per cent and only 42.1 per cent on the estates. How does this come about? Why do the Poles gather on the estates on the plain and in the villages in the uplands? It strikes one immediately that *the Poles tend to congregate in the economically and socially lowest stratum of the population*. On good soils, particularly that of the Vistula plain, the peasant's standard of living has always been higher than that of the day-labourer on an estate; on poor soils, by contrast, which could only be cultivated rationally by large-scale farming, the knightly

---

[A] *Gemeindelexikon* (Berlin, 1887).
[B] This administrative division nevertheless characterises social stratification better than if one uses as a basis the distribution of the different types of enterprise. In the plains manorial farms of less than 100 hectares are not uncommon, nor, conversely, are peasant farms of more than 200 hectares on the high ground.

estate was the bearer of culture[8] and hence of the German population (*Deutschtum*). Even today, the poorest of the small peasants there still enjoy a quality of life *inferior* to that of the day-labourers on the estates. If we did not know that already, the age structure of the population would lead us to suspect it. If one climbs from the *villages* on the plains to those on the uplands, the proportion of children under fourteen rises from 35/36 per cent to 40/41 per cent as the soil gets poorer. If the *estates* are brought into the comparison, the proportion of children is higher in them than in the villages on the plain, increasing as the height above sea-level rises, though more slowly than in the villages, while on the highest ground the proportion is *lower* than that of the children in the villages there. As usual, a large number of children follows hard on the heels of a low standard of living, since the latter stifles any thought of providing for the future. A high level of economic sophistication (*Kultur*) and a relatively high standard of living are identical with the *German people and character* (*Deutschtum*) in West Prussia.

Yet the two nationalities have competed for centuries on the same soil, and with essentially the same chances. What is it, then, that distinguishes them? One is immediately tempted to believe that psychological and physical racial characteristics make the two nationalities differ in their *ability to adapt* to the varying economic and social conditions of existence. This is indeed the explanation and the proof of it is to be found in the trend made apparent by a *shift* in the population and its nationality structure. This tendency also makes clear just how fateful that difference in adaptability has proved to be for the German race in the east.

Admittedly, we only have at our disposal the figures from 1871 to 1885 as a basis for observing the population shifts in individual parishes, and these figures allow us to perceive only the indistinct beginnings of a trend which, according to everything we know, has now become extraordinarily pronounced. Apart from this, the clarity of the statistical picture naturally suffers in consequence of the inevitable, but not entirely correct, equation of religious affiliation with nationality on the one hand, and local administrative units with social

[8] Here and at other points in this lecture Weber applies the very broad term *Kultur* specifically to the question of agri*cultural* development. The implication is that sophistication in one particular area, even a technical and practical one, is symptomatic of the general cultural attainment or character of the people concerned.

stratification on the other. Nevertheless, it is still possible to gain a clear enough view of the important issues. The rural population of the province, like that of large parts of the east generally, tended to *decline* between 1880 and 1885. In West Prussia this fall amounted to 12,700 persons, that is a decline of 1.25 per cent during a period when the population of the Reich grew by about 3.5 per cent. However, this phenomenon, like those we have already discussed, was unevenly distributed, for in some districts there was a contrasting *increase* in the rural population. And indeed the *way* in which growth and decline were distributed is highly characteristic. To begin with the different soil qualities, anyone would expect the decline to have affected the districts with the *poorest* soil most severely, since that is where the margin of subsistence would first become too narrow as a result of failing prices. If one looks at the figures, however, one sees that the *reverse* is the case: precisely the most well-favoured districts, such as Stuhm and Marienwerder, with an average net tax yield of around 15 to 17 marks, saw the greatest emigration (of 7–8 per cent), whereas on the higher ground the districts of Konitz and Tuchel, with a net yield of 5–6 marks, experienced the greatest *increase*, and one which had remained constant since 1871. One looks for an explanation and one asks first, from which social strata the population loss came, and which social strata benefited from an increase? If one looks at the districts with high numerical losses (Stuhm, Marienwerder, Rosenberg), these are without exception districts where *large scale landownership* predominates particularly strongly. If one then aggregates the *estate districts* of the whole province, one finds that, although they in any case contained a population two-thirds smaller than that of the villages (for the same area of land) in 1880, they alone account for almost three-quarters of the drop in the rural population, or over 9,000 persons. Their population has fallen by about 3.75 per cent. But, again, this fall in population is also distributed unevenly *within* the estates, for in some places an increase took place, and if one isolates the areas where the estate population decreased sharply, it emerges that it was precisely the estates on *good* soil which experienced particularly high emigration.

In contrast to this, the population *growth* which took place on the poor soils of the uplands mainly benefited the villages, and particularly the villages on poor soils, as opposed to the villages of the plain. The tendency is therefore towards a *decrease* in the numbers of day-labourers on the estates with the *best* soils and an *increase among the peasants* on *poor* land. What this implies, and how the phenomenon is to be explained, becomes clear when one again asks how the *nationalities* relate to these shifts in population.

In the first half of the century the Polish element in the east appeared to be being pushed back slowly but steadily. However, since the 1860s, as is well known, it has been advancing just as steadily and just as slowly. Despite their inadequate basis, the language censuses for West Prussia make the latter point extremely plain. Now a shift in the boundary between two nationalities can occur in two fundamentally distinct ways. The first is when the language and customs of the majority are gradually imposed on national minorities in a nationally mixed region, so that these minorities become 'absorbed'. This phenomenon, too, can be found in eastern Germany, as can be demonstrated statistically in the case of Germans belonging to the Catholic Church. Here the bond of the church is stronger than that of the nation, memories of the *Kulturkampf*[9] also play their part, and the lack of a German educated clergy means that the German Catholics are lost to the cultural community of the nation. But more important, and of greater interest for our purpose, is the second form of nationality shift, namely *economic supplantation*. This is what we are dealing with here. If one examines the shifts in the numbers belonging to each religion in the rural parish units between 1871 and 1885, it emerges that on the plain the migration of day-labourers away from the estates is regularly associated with a relative decline of Protestantism, whereas the increase of the village population in the uplands is associated with a relative increase of Catholicism.[c] *It is chiefly German day-labourers who move out of the districts with a high level of culture; it is chiefly Polish peasants who multiply in the districts with a poor standard of cultivation (Kulturstand).*

---

[c] For example, the manorial estates in the district of Stuhm had a decline in population of 6.7 per cent between 1871 and 1885, while the proportion of Protestants in the Christian population fell from 33.4 per cent to 31.3 per cent. The villages in the districts of Konitz and Tuchel grew by 8 per cent, while the proportion of Catholics rose from 84.7 per cent to 86.0 per cent.

[9] The term *Kulturkampf* refers to Bismarck's hostile policies towards the Catholic Church and its political voice, the Centre Party, between 1872 and 1878. This was a misguided attempt to enforce loyalty to the new Reich.

Yet both processes – emigration in the one area, population growth in the other – lead back ultimately to one and the same reason, *namely lower expectations of the standard of living*, both in a material and an ideal sense, something which is either natural to the Slav race or has been bred into it in the course of its history. It is these lower expectations which have helped the Slavs to victory.

Why do the German day-labourers move away? The reasons are not material, since the emigration is not from districts with a low level of pay or from the categories of poorly paid workers. There is hardly a more secure material situation than that of a cottager on the eastern estates. Nor is it the much talked-of longing for the amusements of the big city. This may explain the unsystematic wandering off of the younger generation, but not the departure of long-serving families of day-labourers; and why should that craving particularly affect people from areas where large landownership is predominant? Why is it demonstrably the case that the emigration of day-labourers decreases, the more the *peasant village* dominates the face of the landscape? The reason is this: amongst the estate complexes of his homeland the world of the day-labourer contains only masters and servants (*Herren und Knechte*),[10] and his descendants will be faced for ever after only with the prospect of toiling away on someone else's land to the tolling of the estate bell. In this inarticulate, half-conscious urge[11] towards far off places there lies hidden an element of primitive idealism. Anyone who cannot decipher this does not know the magic of *freedom*. Indeed, its spirit seldom touches us today in the stillness of the library. The naive libertarian ideals of our early youth have faded, and those of us who have grown prematurely old and all too prudent even believe that one of the most elemental drives in the human breast has been laid to rest along with the slogans of a political and economic philosophy that has now gone into historical decline.

[10] The terms used by Weber are *Herr* and *Knecht*, the same ones as Hegel used for this relationship. In this context *Knecht* also has the particular sense of 'farm servant' or 'farm labourer'. In addition to the designation of social role, however, these terms can connote differences of character or personal quality: a capacity for masterfulness or subservience.

[11] Weber's formulation, 'in dem dumpfen, halbbewußten Drang in die Ferne' is reminiscent of lines 328–9 from Goethe's *Faust*: 'ein guter Mensch in seinem dunklen Drange/ Ist sich des rechten Weges wohl bewußt'. The Faustian characteristic of restless 'striving' was for long held by many Germans to be a central quality of 'Germanness'. Weber's mention of the library and the passing of youth in the following lines reinforce the presence of *Faust* in his text.

The process is a mass-psychological one: the German agricultural labourers can no longer adapt to the *social* conditions of life in their homeland. We have reports of West Prussian estate owners complaining about their labourers' 'self-assertiveness'. There is a decline in the old patriarchal relationship to the smallholders on the estates which once linked the day-labourer directly to the interests in agricultural production, in that he was a small cultivator with a right to a share in the produce. Seasonal labour in the beet-growing districts requires seasonal workers and payment in money. They are faced with the prospect of a purely proletarian existence, but one without the possibility of that vigorous rise to economic independence which gives self-confidence to the industrial proletariat gathered in the cities. The people who are replacing the Germans on the estates of the east are better able to submit to these conditions of existence – the itinerant Polish workers, troops of nomads recruited by agents in Russia, who cross the frontier in tens of thousands in spring and leave again in autumn. They first emerge in association with sugar-beet, a crop which turns agriculture into a seasonal trade, then they become generally established, because employing them means savings on workers' dwellings, on taxes to support the poor, on social obligations, and further because their precarious situation as foreigners puts them in the hands of the landowner. These are side effects of the economic death throes of the old Prussian Junkerdom. On the sugar-beet estates a stratum of industrial businessmen is taking the place of the lord of the manor with his patriarchal dispensations. In the uplands the lands of the manorial estates are crumbling away from outside under the pressure of the crisis in agriculture, as colonies of small peasants and tenants renting small parcels of land spring up on their outfields. The economic foundations on which the power of the old landed nobility rested are disappearing, and the nobility itself is becoming something other than it once was.

Why is it the *Polish* peasants who are gaining ground? Is it because of their superior economic intelligence or capital resources? It is rather the opposite of both of these things. Under a climate, and on a soil, which essentially permit the production of cereals and potatoes, alongside extensive cattle-raising, the person who is least threatened by an unfavourable market is the one who takes his products to the place where they are least devalued by a collapse in prices – his own stomach; in other words the person producing for his own needs.

Again, it is the person who can *minimise* his own requirements, the person who makes the fewest physical and ideal demands on the quality of life, who is in the most favourable position. The small Polish peasant in the east is a very different type from the industrious peasants cultivating tiny patches of land whom one may see here in the well-favoured valley of the Rhine, attaching themselves to the urban economy via market-gardening and horticulture. The small Polish peasant gains more land because he is prepared even to eat grass, as it were – in other words not *despite* but rather *because of* his habitually low physical and intellectual standard of living.

Thus what we see taking place seems to be a *process of selection*. Over a long period both nationalities have been placed in the same conditions of existence. The consequence of this has *not* been, as vulgar materialists imagine, that they have acquired the same physical and psychological qualities, but rather that one group yields to the other, that the victorious nationality is the one possessing the greater ability to adapt itself to the given economic and social conditions of life.

The two races seem to have had this difference in adaptability from the very outset, as a fixed element in their make-up. It could perhaps shift again as a result of further generations of breeding of the kind which may have produced the difference in the first place, but at present it simply has to be taken account of as a fixed given for the purposes of analysis.ᴰ

ᴰ I think I hardly need to observe that the disputes in natural science over the signific-ance of the principles of selection, or over the general application *in natural science* of the concept of 'selective breeding' (*Züchtung*), and all the discussions relating to it in this area (with which I am not familiar), have no relevance to these remarks. However, the *concept* of 'selection' is as much of a commonplace today as, say, the heliocentric hypothesis, and the idea of 'breeding' human beings is already to be found in Plato's *Republic*. Both these concepts are employed by F. A. Lange, for example, in his *Arbeiterfrage*,[12] and they have long been so well established here that it is not possible for anyone who knows our literature to misunderstand their meaning. More difficult to answer is the question of how much lasting value should be attached to the latest attempts of anthropologists to extend the principle of selection, as understood by Darwin and Weismann, to the field of economic investigation. They are ingenious, but arouse considerable reservations as to method and factual results, and are no doubt mistaken in a number of exaggerated claims. Nevertheless, the writings of Otto Ammon (*Natural Selection in Man, The Social Order and its Natural Basis*),[13] for example, deserve more attention than they have been given, irrespective of all the reservations that have to be made. An error made by most attempts by natural scientists to throw light on the problems of our science consists in their misdirected ambition to 'dis-prove' socialism. In their enthusiasm to attain this goal, they involuntarily turn what

As we have seen, the free play of the forces of selection does not always operate, as the optimists among us believe, in favour of the nationality which is economically the more highly developed or better endowed. Human history contains examples both of the victory of less developed types of human being and the disappearance of fine flowers of intellectual and emotional life when the human community that gave rise to them lost its ability to adapt to the conditions of its existence, either because of its social organisation or its racial qualities. In our case the economically less developed nationality is being helped to achieve victory by the transformation of the forms of agricultural enterprise and the tremendous crisis in agriculture. The forced growth of sugar-beet cultivation and the unprofitability of cereal production for the market are parallel developments pulling in the same direction: the former breeds the Polish seasonal worker and the latter the small Polish peasant.

If we look back over the facts discussed so far, I freely confess that I am quite unable to develop theoretically the full implications of the various general points which may be extrapolated from them. The immensely difficult question, certainly insoluble at present, of *where* the limit of variation lies for the physical and psychological qualities in a population as they become subject to the influence of the conditions of existence in which they are placed, is a problem I do not even dare to touch on.

On the other hand, the question one cannot help asking is, above all, this: what can and should be done in this situation?

With your permission, however, I shall not discuss these questions at length on this occasion. Instead I will restrict myself to a brief indication of the two demands which, in my view, ought to be made

---

was intended to be a 'natural-scientific theory' of the social order into an apologia for it.

[12] F. A. Lange (1828–75), *Die Arbeiterfrage in ihrer Bedeutung für Gegenwart und Zukunft* (Duisburg, 1865).

[13] Otto Ammon (1842–1916) was an anthropologist who carried out studies, such as the measurement of head size and shape, on military recruits in Baden. He was an opponent of socialism, arguing that social differences were grounded in natural differences. Weber included both of these works by Ammon in his reading list for his lectures in 1898 (see above, note 3). In later essays Weber distances himself from such views, remarking scathingly on the power of the purse to produce social difference regardless of an individual's natural gifts. See below, p. 103.

from the standpoint of the German people, and are in fact being made with growing unanimity. The first is the closing of the eastern frontier. This was accomplished under Prince Bismarck and then undone again after his resignation in 1890; permanent settlement remained forbidden to the foreigners, but they were admitted as migratory workers. A 'class-conscious' large landowner at the head of the Prussian government excluded the Poles in the interests of preserving our nationality, and the hated opponent of the Agrarians[14] admitted them in the interests of the big landowners, who are the *only* people to gain from this influx. Clearly, the 'standpoint of economic class' is not always decisive in matters of economic policy; *in this case*, it was the circumstance that a weaker hand took over the helm of the ship of state from a strong one.[15] The other demand which needs to be made is for the state to buy up land systematically, that is the extension of the crown demesne lands on the one hand, and systematic colonisation by German peasants on suitable soils, especially on suitable demesne land, on the other. From the standpoint of the nation, large-scale enterprises which can only be preserved at the expense of the German race deserve to go down to destruction.[16] To leave them to their own devices means permitting unviable colonies of starving Slavs to come into existence by way of the gradual parcelling-off of the estates. Nor is it only our interest in stemming the tide of Slavs which demands the transfer of significant tracts of eastern Germany into the hands of the state; it is also called for by the annihilating criticism of the continued existence of their private property that is implicit in the landowners' own demand that the government should relieve them of the risks they bear by introducing a corn monopoly and state subsidies of 500 million marks a year. In other words, they are asking to be relieved of their personal responsibility for their own property, despite the fact that this is the only justification for their owning it at all.[E]

[14] This is a reference to Bismarck's successor, General Leo Count von Caprivi (1831–99), as Reich Chancellor (1890–4) and Prime Minister of Prussia (1890–2).

[15] When Bismarck was forced to resign the Chancellorship in 1890 *Punch* published a cartoon showing him in pilot's uniform leaving a mighty ship. The German translation of the caption, 'Der Lotse verläßt das Schiff', gained wide currency, as Weber's allusion to it indicates.

[16] Another allusion to Goethe's *Faust*, this time to lines 1339–40 spoken by Mephistopheles: 'denn alles, was entsteht/ Ist wert, daß es zugrunde geht'.

Yet, as I say, it is not this practical question of Prussian agrarian policy I want to discuss today. I would prefer to return to the fact that such a question arises at all in all our minds, to the fact that we consider that the German race should be protected in the east of the country, and that the state's economic policies *ought to* rise to the challenge of defending it. What makes us feel we have a right to make this demand is the circumstance that our state is a *nation state*.

Yet what does the economic way of looking at things have to say on this question? Does it regard such nationalist value judgements as prejudices, of which it must be careful to rid itself so that it can apply its own specific criterion of value to the economic facts, free

---

[E] In the same context Professor Schmoller[17] in particular has also been prompted to make the same demand for state purchase of land in his journal (*Schmollers Jahrbuch*, 19, 1895, pp. 625ff.). In fact that part of the stratum of large landowners whose retention as agricultural managers is desirable from the state's point of view can in most cases be retained as tenants of the crown demesne rather than as owners in their own right. Admittedly, I believe that the purchase of land only makes sense in the long term if organically combined with the colonisation of suitable crown lands; in other words, if a part of the land in the east passes through the hands of the state and while it is thus held undergoes an energetic course of improvement with the assistance of state credits. Quite apart from the fact that it is burdened with the 'recuperation period', in the shape of the colonists who have been planted and who ought preferably to be handed over after a while to the more hard-hearted normal taxation authority, along with their requests to postpone repayment, the Settlement Commission is faced with the difficulty that the estates which have been purchased have mostly been in the hands of crown tenants for over a decade. The improvement must now be carried out at breakneck speed by administrative means and with great losses, whereas a large number of crown lands would certainly be suitable for immediate colonisation. However, the consequent slowness of the procedure does not by any means justify Hans Delbrück's[18] verdict on the national-political impact, delivered in his many well-known articles in the *Preußische Jahrbücher*. A merely mechanical calculation, comparing the number of farms founded with the numbers of Poles, is not conclusive proof for anyone who has observed the civilising effect of colonisation on the spot: a few villages with a dozen German farms each will eventually *Germanise* many square miles, always provided that the flood of proletarian reinforcements from the east is stemmed, and that we do not kill the goose that lays the golden eggs by leaving the big estates to the free play of the forces which are leading to their fragmentation and ruin – forces which are now operating even more freely thanks to the laws on renting land in perpetuity.

[17] Gustav von Schmoller (1838–1917), professor of economics, president of the 'Verein für Socialpolitik' (1890–1917), founder of the 'younger' German historical school of economics, several of whose works figure in Weber's *Grundriß* (see note 3 above).

[18] Hans von Delbrück (1848–1929), professor of history, editor of the *Preußische Jahrbücher*, 1883–1919.

of any influence from emotional reflexes? And *what is* this criterion of value 'peculiar' to economic policy? I should like to try to approach this question via some wider reflections.

As we have seen, the economic struggle (*Kampf*) between the nationalities runs its course even under the semblance of 'peace'. The German peasants and day-labourers in the east are not being driven off the soil by politically superior enemies in open conflict. Rather they are coming off worse in a silent and bleak struggle for everyday economic existence in competition with an inferior race; they are leaving their homeland and are about to submerge themselves in a dark future. In the economic struggle for life, too, there is no peace to be had. Only if one takes the semblance of peace for its reality can one believe that the future holds peace and a happy life for our descendants. As we know, the vulgar conception of political economy is that it consists in devising recipes for universal happiness; in this view, adding to the 'balance of pleasure'[19] in human existence is the only comprehensible purpose our work has. Yet the sombre gravity of the population problem[20] alone is enough to prevent us from being eudaemonists, from imagining that peace and happiness lie waiting in the womb of the future, and from believing that anything other than the hard struggle of man with man can create any elbow-room in this earthly life.

Certainly, only on the basis of altruism is any work in political economy possible. Overwhelmingly, what is produced by the economic, social and political endeavours of the present benefits future generations rather than the present one. If our work is to have any meaning, it lies, and can only lie, in providing for the *future*, for our *descendants*. But there can also be no work in political economy on the basis of optimistic hopes of happiness. As far as the dream of

[19] The term *Lustbilanz* (balance of pleasure) presumably refers to Jeremy Bentham's doctrine of utility which advocated that actions should be judged in the light of the pain or pleasure they produced in different people: 'Take the *balance*; which, if on the side of *pleasure*, will give the general *good tendency* of the act, with respect to the total number or community of individuals concerned; if on the side of pain, the general *evil tendency*, with respect to the same community.' *An Introduction to the Principles of Morals and Legislation*, ch. 5, para. 6.

[20] Interest in the teachings of Malthus on population growth had been revived by the debates on Darwinism. Malthus was mentioned in Weber's reading list for his lectures, *Grundriß zu den Vorlesungen*, section 5 II (see note 3 above).

peace and human happiness is concerned, the words written over the portal into the unknown future of human history are: 'lasciate ogni speranza'.[21]

The question which stirs us as we think beyond the grave of our own generation is not the *well-being* human beings will enjoy in the future but what kind of people they will *be*, and it is this same question which underlies all work in political economy. We do not want to breed well-being in people, but rather those characteristics which we think of as constituting the human greatness and nobility of our nature.

The criteria of value which political economists have naively identified or given prominence to have alternated between the technical economic problem of the production of goods and the problem of their distribution ('social justice'). Yet, again and again both these criteria have been overshadowed by the recognition, in part unconscious, but nevertheless all-dominating, that a science (*Wissenschaft*) concerned with *human beings* – and that is what political economy is – is concerned above all else with the *quality of the human beings* reared under those economic and social conditions of existence. Here we should be on our guard against one particular illusion.

As an explanatory and analytic science, political economy is *international*, but as soon as it makes *value judgements* it is tied to the particular strain of humankind (*Menschentum*) we find within our own nature. Often these ties are strongest precisely when we think we have escaped our personal limitations most completely. If – to use a somewhat fanciful image – we could arise from the grave thousands of years hence, it would be the distant traces of our own nature that we would search for in the countenance of that future race. Even our highest, our ultimate ideals in this life change and pass away. It cannot be our ambition to impose them on the future. But we *can* want the future to recognise the character *of its own ancestors* in us. Through our work and our nature we want to be the forerunners of that future race.

The economic policy of a German state, and, equally, the criterion of value used by a German economic theorist, can therefore only be a German policy or criterion.

Have things perhaps become different in this regard since economic development began to extend beyond national frontiers,

---

[21] 'Abandon all hope' (. . . 'all ye who enter here'), Dante's *Inferno*, iii, 9.

creating an all-embracing economic community of nations? Is the 'nationalistic' criterion of evaluation to be thrown on the scrapheap along with 'national egoism' in economic policy? Has indeed the struggle for one's own economic interests, for one's own wife and children, become a thing of the past, now that the family has been divested of its original functions as a productive community and become woven into the circle of the national economic community? We know that this is not the case. The struggle has assumed *other forms*, and it is an open question whether these new forms can be said to have mitigated the severity of the struggle or internalised and exacerbated it. Equally, the expanded economic community is just another form of the struggle of the nations with each other, one which has not eased the struggle to defend one's own culture but made it more *difficult*, because this enlarged economic community summons material interests within the body of the nation to ally themselves with it in the fight *against* the future of the nation.

We do not have peace and human happiness to hand down to our descendants, but rather the *eternal struggle* to preserve and raise the quality of our national species.[22] Nor should we indulge in the optimistic expectation that we shall have completed our task once we have made our economic culture as advanced as it can be, and that the process of selection through free and 'peaceful' economic competition will then automatically bring victory to the more highly developed type.

Our successors will hold us answerable to history not primarily for the kind of economic organisation we hand down to them, but for the amount of elbow-room in the world which we conquer and bequeath to them. In the final analysis, processes of economic development are *power* struggles too, and the ultimate and decisive interests which economic policy must serve are the interests of national *power*, whenever these interests are in question. The science of political economy is a *political* science. It is a servant of politics, not the day-to-day politics of the persons and classes who happen to be ruling at any given time, but the enduring power-political interests of the nation. For us the *nation state* is not something vague which, as some believe, is elevated ever higher, the more its nature is shrouded in

---

[22] Again, Weber's choice of words reflects the influence of Darwinism: 'die Erhaltung und Emporzüchtung der nationalen *Art*'. The German for 'Origin of Species' is 'Entstehung der *Arten*'.

mystical obscurity. Rather, it is the worldly organisation of the nation's power. In this nation state the ultimate criterion for economic policy, as for all others, is in our view *'reason of state'*. By this we do not mean, as some strange misunderstanding would have it, 'help from the state' rather than 'self-help', state regulation of economic life rather than the free play of economic forces. In using this slogan of 'reason of state' we wish to present the demand that the economic and political power-interests of our nation and their bearer, the German nation-state, should have the final and decisive say in all questions of German economic policy, including the questions of whether, and how far, the state should intervene in economic life, or of whether and when it is better for it to free the economic forces of the nation from their fetters and to tear down the barriers in the way of their autonomous development.

Was there no need for me to remind you of these apparently self-evident things? Was it particularly unnecessary for one of the younger representatives of economic science to do so? I think not, for our generation in particular seems frequently to lose sight of these very simple foundations of judgement more easily than most. We have witnessed a quite unexpected growth of its interest in the issues of concern to our science. In every sphere we find that the economic way of looking at things is on the advance. Social policy has super-seded politics at the forefront of thinking, just as economic power-relations have replaced legal relations, and cultural and economic history have ousted political history. In the outstanding works of our colleagues in history we find that, where once they told us about the warlike deeds of our ancestors, they expatiate today on the monstrous notion of 'matriarchy',[23] while relegating to a subordinate clause the victory over the Huns on the Catalaunian Plain.[24] One of our most ingenious theorists was so full of his own importance that he thought he could characterise jurisprudence as a 'handmaiden of national

---

[23] Weber is referring to the theories of *Mutterrecht* (matriarchy) which were current at the time. Elsewhere he refers to J. Bachofen's *Das Mutterrecht* (Stuttgart, 1861), a work he included in his reading list for his lectures (p. 7/11, see note 3 above). Weber's own discussion of this issue is to be found in his posthumously published *General Economic History* (New York, 1961).

[24] At the battle of the Catalaunian Fields, or Catalaunian Plain (AD 451), Attila, King of the Huns, was defeated by the Roman general Aetius.

economics'. One thing is certainly true: the economic way of looking at things has penetrated into jurisprudence itself, so that even in its innermost sanctum, the manuals of the Pandect Jurists,[25] the spectre of economic thinking is beginning to stir. In the verdicts of the courts one quite frequently finds so-called 'economic considerations' being cited once the limit of legal concepts has been reached. In short, to adopt the half-reproachful phrase of a legal colleague, we economists have 'come into fashion'. When a way of looking at things breaks new ground so confidently, it is in danger of falling prey to certain illusions and of overestimating the significance of its own point of view, particularly in one, quite specific direction. The broadening of the subject-matter of *philosophical* reflection – outwardly evident in the very fact that nowadays we find many of the old Chairs of Philosophy being given to outstanding physiologists (for example) – has led many of us laymen to believe that the old questions about the nature of human understanding are no longer the ultimate and central questions of philosophy. Similarly, not only has the notion sprung up in the minds of the rising generation that the work of national economics has greatly extended our *understanding* ('Erkenntnis') of the nature of human communities, but they also believe that there exists a completely new criterion by which these phenomena can ultimately be *evaluated*. They think that political economy is able to derive ideals of its 'own' from its subject matter. The notion that there are such things as independent economic or 'socio-political' ideals shows itself clearly to be an optical illusion as soon as one tries to discover from the literature produced by our science just what its 'own' bases for evaluation are. What we find is a *chaos* of different evaluative criteria, some eudaemonistic, some ethical; often both are present together in an obscure identification of one with the other. One finds value judgements being made everywhere without compunction. In fact, to refrain from *evaluating* economic phenomena would mean refraining from doing the very thing people expect of us. But it is the exception rather than the rule for the person making a judgement to clarify *in his own mind*, and for others, the ultimate subjective core of his judgements, by which I mean the *ideals* on the basis of which he

---

[25] Weber is referring to contemporary legal arguments based on the Pandect or Digest of Roman Law published by the Emperor Justinian in AD 533. He discusses the codification of Roman law and the contemporary debate between Romanists and Germanists in his *Economy and Society*, vol. 2, ch. 8.

proceeds to judge the events he is observing. There is a lack of conscious self-scrutiny, the writer is unaware of the internal contradictions in his judgement, and where he seeks to formulate his specifically 'economic' principle of judgement in general terms he becomes vague and unspecific. The truth is that the ideals we introduce into the subject matter of our science are *not* peculiar to it, nor are they produced by this science itself; rather they are *the old, general types of human ideals*. Only someone basing himself exclusively on the pure, Platonic interest of the technologist, or, conversely, on the current interests of a particular class, whether ruling or ruled, can believe himself capable of deriving an inherent criterion of evaluation from the subject matter itself.

Is it so unnecessary for us, the disciples of the German Historical School,[26] to remind ourselves of these very simple truths? We in particular succumb readily to a special kind of illusion, namely that we are able to *refrain entirely* from making conscious value judgments of our own. As anyone can easily verify for himself, the result is, of course, that we do not remain true to any intention we may have of acting in accordance with this principle. Rather, we fall prey to unexamined instincts, sympathies and antipathies. An even more likely consequence is that we unconsciously allow the starting point for our analyses and explanations of economic events to determine our *judgement* of those events. Perhaps we more than most must be on our guard lest the very qualities which made the scholarship of the dead and living masters of our school so successful should turn into faults in our hands. In practice we have to consider, broadly speaking, two different points of departure for economic analysis.

Either we view economic development chiefly from above, looking down from the heights of the administrative history of the larger German states, and pursuing the genesis of the way they have viewed and administered economic and social affairs. In this case we involuntarily become their apologists. If (to stay with this example) the government decides to close the eastern border, we are inclined and prepared to view the decision as the culmination of a sequence of historical developments, which, in the wake of powerful memories

---

[26] The German Historical School of political economy (of which there was an 'older' and a 'younger' branch) was committed to the view that economic enquiry is best undertaken from a national and historical point of view rather than attempting to construct transhistorical and transnational laws and abstractions.

from the past, presents today's state with lofty tasks it must perform in order to safeguard our national culture. If that decision is not taken, we are more inclined to agree that such radical interventions are in part unnecessary and in part no longer correspond to present-day views.

Alternatively, we may prefer to view economic development from below, seeing the great spectacle of the emancipatory struggles of rising classes emerging from the chaos of conflicts of economic interest; we may observe the way in which the balance of economic power shifts in their favour – in which case we unconsciously take sides with the rising classes, because they are the stronger, or are beginning to be so. They seem to prove, precisely because they are victorious, that they represent a type of humankind that stands on a *higher* level 'economically'. It is all too easy for the historian to be ruled by the idea that the victory of the more *highly* developed elements in the struggle goes without saying, and that defeat in the struggle for existence is a symptom of 'backwardness'. As each of the many symptoms of the shift of power appears for the first time, the historian feels gratified, not only because the new fact confirms his observations, but because, half unconsciously, he feels it as a personal triumph: history is honouring the promissory notes he has drawn on it. Unwittingly, he looks on anything which resists that development with a certain hostility; it strikes him as being not simply a natural consequence of the different interests which of course demand to be represented, but to some extent as a rebellion against the 'verdict of history' as he, the historian, has formulated it. Our duty to criticise even events which we regard as the unconsidered outcome of historical tendencies abandons us at the very moment when we have most need of it. In any case, we historians are all too strongly tempted to join the camp-following of the victor in the economic struggle for power, *forgetting in the process that economic power and the vocation for political leadership of the nation do not always coincide.*

This brings us to some concluding reflections of a more practical-political nature. We economic nationalists measure the classes who lead the nation or aspire to do so with the one *political criterion* we regard as sovereign. What concerns us is their *political maturity*, which is to say their grasp of the nation's enduring economic and political *power* interests and their ability, in any given situation, to place these interests above all other considerations. A nation is favoured by fate if naive identification of the interests of one's own class with the general interest also corresponds to the enduring interests of national power. On the other hand, it is one of the delusions which arise from the modern over-estimation of the 'economic' in the usual sense of the word when people assert that feelings of political community would be stretched beyond breaking point by temporary divergences of economic interest, indeed that such feelings *merely* reflect the economic base underlying that shifting constellation of interests. Only at times when the structure of society is changing fundamentally is this approximately accurate. One thing is certainly true: where nations are not reminded daily of the dependence of their economic success on their position of political power (as happens in England), the instinct for these specifically political interests does *not*, or at least not as a rule, dwell in the broad *masses* of the nation as they struggle with daily necessity, nor would it be fair to expect it of them. At great moments, in time of war, for example, their souls too become aware of the significance of national power, and at such times it becomes evident that the nation state rests on deeply rooted psychological foundations in the broad, economically subordinate strata of the nation as well, and that it is far from being a mere 'superstructure', the organisation of the ruling economic classes.[27] It is just that in normal times this political instinct sinks below the level of consciousness amongst the masses. Then it is the specific function of the leading economic and political strata to be the bearers of the nation's sense of political purpose (*Sinn*). In fact this is the *only* political justification for their existence.

Throughout history it has been the *attainment of economic power* which has led any given class to believe it *is a candidate for political leadership*. It is dangerous, and in the long term incompatible with the interests of the nation, for an economically declining class to exercise political rule (*Herrschaft*). But it is more dangerous still when classes which are moving *towards* economic power, and therefore expect to take over political rule, do not yet have the political maturity to assume the direction of the state. Germany is currently threatened

[27] This is a critical reference to the Marxist notion that the 'mode of production' is constituted by a 'material base' and an 'ideological superstructure'. When mentioning Marxist ideas Weber refers mainly to *Das Kapital* (all three volumes) and to the *Communist Manifesto*.

by both of these things, and this is in truth the key to understanding the present dangers of our situation. The changes in the social structure of eastern Germany, with which the phenomena discussed at the beginning of this lecture are connected, also need to be placed in this larger context.

Right up to the present, the dynasty has drawn its political support in the Prussian state from the social estate of the Prussian *Junker*. Although it created the Prussian state in opposition to them, it was only possible with their support. I know full well that the name of the Junkers has a hostile ring in south German ears. It will perhaps be thought that I am speaking with a 'Prussian' voice if I now say a word in their favour. I cannot see why. Even in today's Prussia many paths to influence and power and many ways to the ear of the monarch are open to the Junkers but not to every citizen. Nor have they always used this power in historically defensible ways, and I see no reason why a bourgeois (*bürgerlich*) scholar like myself should love them. Despite all this, however, the strength of their political instincts was one of the most powerful assets which could possibly have been invested in the service of the state's power-interests. They have done their work, and today they are in the throes of an economic death-struggle from which no kind of economic policy on the part of the state could rescue them and restore to them their former social standing. The tasks of the present are also quite different in kind from those they could accomplish. The last and greatest of the Junkers[28] stood at the head of Germany for a quarter of a century, and the future will probably consider that his incomparably great career as a statesman also contained an element of tragedy, one which even today remains hidden to many people. This lies in the fact that the work of his hands, the nation to which he gave unity, gradually and irresistibly altered its economic structure even while he was still in office, becoming something different, a people which was bound to demand other ways of ordering things than those he could give them, or to which his Caesarist nature could accommodate itself. In the final analysis it was precisely this process which brought about the partial failure of his life's work. For this life's work was meant to lead not merely to the external, but also to the inner unification of the nation, and, as every one of us knows, that has not been achieved.

---

[28] The reference is, of course, to Bismarck.

Nor could it be achieved with his means. When, last winter, ensnared by his monarch's favour, he made his entry into the decked-out capital of the Reich, there were many people who felt – as I well know – as if the Sachsenwald had opened up like the Kyffhaüser of old.[29] Yet this feeling was not shared by everyone. For it seemed as if the cold breath of historical transience could be felt in the air of that January day. We felt a strange tightening of the breast, as if a ghost had stepped down from a great era of the past and was moving about among a new generation, and through a world that had become alien to it.[30]

The manors of the east were the bases for the ruling class of Prussia, which was dislocated and scattered over the countryside, and they were the social point of contact for the officials. With the decay of these estates, however, with the disappearance of the social character of the old landed nobility, the centre of gravity of the political intelligentsia is shifting irresistibly into the cities. *This* shift is the decisive *political* factor in the agrarian development of eastern Germany.

But into whose hands is the political function of the Junkers passing, and what are we to make of the political vocation of those who take it over?

I am a member of the bourgeois (*bürgerlich*) classes. I feel myself to be a bourgeois, and I have been brought up to share their views and ideals. Yet it is precisely the vocation of our science to say things people do not like to hear – to those above us, to those below us, and also to our own class – and if I ask myself whether the German bourgeoisie has the maturity today to be the leading political class of the nation, I cannot answer this question in the affirmative *today*. The bourgeoisie did not create the German state by its own efforts, and when it had been created, there stood at the head of the nation that Caesarist figure made of distinctly un-bourgeois stuff. The nation was set no other great power-political tasks again; only much later on, timidly, and half unwillingly, did an overseas 'power policy' (*Machtpolitik*) begin, one which does not even deserve the name.

---

[29] The *Sachsenwald* is (or was) a large area of forest to the north-east of Hamburg given to Bismarck by Kaiser Wilhelm I in 1871. The *Kyffhäuser* is a castellated, wooded hill in the Harz Mountains where, according to legend, Frederick I, Barbarossa, lives on, ready to come to the help of his Germans at a time of great national danger.

[30] The reference is to the Kaiser's attempted reconciliation with Bismarck in that year.

After the struggle for the nation's unity had been won, and its political 'satiation' was an established fact, a peculiarly 'unhistorical' and unpolitical spirit seized the rising generation of the German bourgeoisie, drunk as it was with success and thirsty for peace. German history appeared to be over. The present was the complete fulfilment of the past thousands of years. Who was inclined to ask whether the future might judge otherwise? Indeed it seemed as if modesty forbade world history to pass over these successes of the German nation and return to its normal daily agenda. Today we are more sober, and it behoves us to try to lift the veil of illusions which hides from us the position of our generation within the historical development of the fatherland. Under these circumstances, it seems to me, we judge things differently. At our cradle stood the most frightful curse history can give any generation as a baptismal-gift: the hard fate of the political *epigone*.[31]

Do we not see his miserable countenance staring at us wherever we look in the fatherland? Those of us who have retained the capacity to hate pettiness have recognised, with passionate and angry sorrow, the petty manoeuvring of political epigones in the events of recent months (for which bourgeois politicians are primarily responsible), in far too much of what has been said recently *in* the German parliament, and in some of what has been said *to* it. The mighty sun which stood at Germany's zenith and caused the name of Germany to shine into the furthest corners of the earth almost seems to have been too strong for us, scorching the bourgeoisie's slowly developing capacity for political judgement. For how do we see this class conducting itself at present?

One section of the upper bourgeoisie longs all too clearly for the coming of a new Caesar to protect it, both against the masses of the people rising from below, and against the threat from above, in the socio-political impulses which they suspect the German dynasties of harbouring.

Another section sank back long ago into that political philistinism from which broad strata of the lower middle classes have never yet

---

[31] The term 'epigone' is much less rare in German usage than in English. Perhaps most familiar from the title of a novel by Karl Immermann, *Die Epigonen* (1836), it expresses a fear amongst German middle-class intellectuals in the nineteenth century that they were condemned to mere imitation and debility after the passing of a period of cultural greatness (the Age of Goethe).

awakened. When, after the wars leading to unification, the nation was confronted with the first signs of positive political tasks, namely the idea of overseas expansion, these philistines lacked even the most rudimentary *economic* understanding needed to grasp what it would mean for Germany's trade in far-off oceans if the German flag were to be seen flying on the surrounding coasts.

The political immaturity of broad strata of the German bourgeoisie does not have economic causes, nor is it due to the frequently cited 'politics of interest' which affects other nations just as much as it does the Germans. The reason is to be found in its unpolitical past, in the fact that it was not possible to catch up on a century of missed political education in a single decade, and in the fact that rule by a great man is not always a means of educating the people politically. The vital question for the political future of the German bourgeoisie now is whether it is too *late* for it to make up the lost ground. No *economic* factor can substitute for such education.

Will other classes be the bearers of a greater political future? The modern proletariat is self-confidently announcing that it is heir to the ideals of the middle classes. What is one to make of its candidacy for the political leadership of the nation?

Anyone who tells the German working class today that it is politically mature, or on the road to political maturity, could only be a flatterer seeking the dubious laurels of popularity.

The highest strata of the German working class are far more mature *economically* than the self-centred propertied classes would like to admit, and this class also has the right to demand the freedom to stand up for its interests in the shape of the openly organised economic struggle for power. *Politically*, the German working class is infinitely less mature than a clique of journalists who would like to monopolise its leadership would have it believe. In the circles of these déclassé bourgeois they like to toy with reminiscences of the way things were a hundred years ago and in some cases they have even succeeded in making some anxious souls regard them as the spiritual successors of the men of the Convention.[32] Yet they are infinitely more harmless than they think they are, for there is not a spark of that Catilinarian energy to *act* in them, nor the slightest trace

---

[32] Weber is referring to the National Convention in France (1792–5) which proclaimed a Republic and passed a number of revolutionary measures.

of that mighty *nationalist* passion, both of which could be felt in the halls of the Convention. They are wretched minor political talents, lacking the great *power* instincts of a class with a vocation for political leadership. Contrary to what is being said to the workers, it is not only those with a vested interest in capitalism who are politically opposed to their having a share in the government of the state. They would find very few traces of a community of interest with capital in the studies of us scholars in Germany, but we question *them too* about their *political maturity*. We oppose them politically because there is nothing more destructive of a great nation than for it to be led by a body of *politically* uneducated *philistines* – and because the German proletariat has not yet sloughed off this characteristic. Why are some of the proletariat in England and France different in this respect? The reason is not only that they have been educated *economically* for a longer period by the English workers' organised fight for their interests. Once again there is above all a *political* factor involved, namely the *reverberations of a position of world power* which constantly confronts the state with great power-political tasks and exposes the individual to 'chronic' political schooling, whereas he receives such training here only when our borders are threatened, that is in 'acute' cases. The question of whether politics on the grand scale can make us aware once more of the significance of the great political issues of power is also decisive for *our* development. We have to understand the fact that the unification of Germany was a youthful prank carried out by the nation in its old age, and that it would have been better, on grounds of expense, to leave it undone if it was to have been the end rather than the beginning of Germany's involvement in world politics.

What is *threatening* about our situation is the fact that the bourgeois classes seem to be wilting as the bearers of the *power*-interests of the nation, while there is still no sign that the workers are beginning to become mature enough to take their place.

The danger does *not* lie with the *masses*, as is believed by people who stare as if hypnotised down into the depths of society. The deepest core of the *socio*-political problem is not the question of the *economic* situation of the *ruled* but of the *political* qualifications of the *ruling and rising* classes. The aim of our socio-political activity is not to make everybody happy but the *social unification* of the nation, which has been split apart by modern economic development, and to prepare it for the strenuous struggles of the future. Only if we were indeed successful in creating an 'aristocracy of labour' to be the bearer of the political sense of purpose (*Sinn*) which today's labour movement, in our view, lacks, could the spear of leadership, which the arm of the bourgeoisie is still too weak to bear, be transferred to the broader shoulders of the workers. But that moment still seems a long way off.

For the present, however, one thing is clear: there is an immense work of *political* education to be done, and there is no more serious duty for each of us in our narrow spheres of activity than to be aware of *this* task of contributing to the *political* education of our nation. This must also be the ultimate goal of our science in particular. In transitional periods economic developments threaten the natural political instincts with decay. It would be a misfortune if economic science were also to strive towards the same goal by breeding a soft, eudaemonistic outlook, in however spiritualised a form, behind the illusion of independent 'socio-political' ideals.

Of course, this means that we in particular are permitted to remind people that any attempt to formulate in legal paragraphs a vote of no confidence in the future social peace of the nation is the very opposite of political education. The same is true of attempts by the *bracchium saeculare*[33] to reach for the hand of the church to support temporal authorities. But the opposite of political education is also to be found in the hackneyed yelping of the ever-growing chorus of amateur social politicians (if I may be forgiven the expression). The same is also true of that unspeakably philistine softening of sensibility, however much it may command affection and respect in human terms, which believes it is possible to replace political with 'ethical' ideals, and ingenuously to identify these in turn with optimistic hopes of happiness.

Even in the face of the enormous misery among the masses of the nation which weighs so heavily on the sharpened social conscience of the new generation, we have to confess sincerely that it is our awareness of our responsibility *before history* that weighs even more heavily on us today. It is not given to our generation to see whether the fight we are engaged in will bear fruit, nor whether posterity will acknowledge *us as its forefathers*. We shall not succeed in exorcising

---

[33] 'Secular arm'.

the curse that hangs over us (that of being the belated offspring of a great, but past political epoch), unless we discover how to become something different: the precursors of an even greater epoch. Will that be our place in history? I do not know, and I will say only this: youth has the right to stand up for itself and for its ideals. Yet it is not years which make a man old. He is young as long as he is able to feel the *great* passions nature has implanted in us. Thus – allow me to conclude here – it is not the burden of thousands of years of glorious history that causes a great nation to grow old.[34] It will remain young as long as it has the capacity and the courage to keep faith with itself and with the great instincts it has been given, and if its leading strata are able to raise themselves into the hard, clear air in which the sober work of German politics flourishes, an atmosphere which, however, is also filled with the earnest grandeur of national sentiment.

---

[34] Nietzsche had blamed contemporary weakness on the 'excess of history' in the second chapter of his *Untimely Meditations*, entitled 'On the Uses and Disadvantages of History for Life'.

On the Situation of Constitutional Democracy in Russia[1]

May I be permitted to add to the above account, which has kindly been made available to us,[2] some remarks about the political current in which the draft originated. The question of the extent to which the draft might assume practical importance in forthcoming political discussions is one we shall leave aside. For our purposes it suffices that the draft is symptomatic of a particular mode of political thought amongst outstandingly able and idealistic Russian patriots for whom

---

[1] 'Zur Lage der bürgerlichen Demokratie in Rußland' appeared in the *Archiv für Sozial-wissenschaft und Sozialpolitik*, 22; 1 (1906). This is the only essay by Weber in this collection to have been substantially abridged. Asterisks will mark omissions and, where these are lengthy, a footnote will indicate the topics dealt with in these sections.

Weber's title, 'Zur Lage der bürgerlichen Demokratie in Rußland', creates diffi-culties of translation, since there is no English equivalent for *bürgerlich* (see the glossary) which will convey the full sense of the German term. In the course of his argument Weber himself expressly points out that *bürgerlich* must not be confused with the *German* word *Bourgeois*, a term recently imported from French; it was used to denote capitalist money-makers and carried with it distasteful connotations of the materialistic philistinism and ruthlessness of the French Second Empire. A further complication arises from the ambiguity of the phrase *bürgerliche Demokratie* which means both a *form* of democracy (constitutional and liberal) as well as the parties and social groups fighting to achieve it. Here we have rendered *bürgerlich* freely as 'constitutional', firstly because the group responsible for publishing the draft under discussion called itself 'constitutional-democratic' and secondly in order to highlight the unifying aspirations of the movement in question in preference to defining it too narrowly in terms of class.

[2] Weber is referring to the report by S. Zhivago on the 'Loi fondamentale de l'Empire Russe. Projet d'une constitution russe elaboré par un groupe de la Ligue de l'Affran-chissement (constitutionalistes-démocrates russes)' (Paris 1905) which appeared in the same volume of the *Archiv* as Weber's essay (pp. 81–5). The two papers appear together under the title 'Zur Beurteilung der gegenwärtigen politischen Entwicklung Rußlands' ('Towards an assessment of Russia's present political development').

we have complete personal sympathy, regardless of any success, given the enormous difficulties in their situation, their work ultimately has. The fact that they are generally no friends of German culture – indeed often its bitter enemies on Russian soil – and the fact that they are predominantly hostile to Germany in political matters does nothing to change my attitude.

The draft has been worked out by members of the 'Union of Liberation' (*Soyuz Osvobozhdeniya*) and is formally one of the projects debated at the congresses of the members of the *zemstvos*[3] and the *Duma*.[4] Let me say a few words about both organisations which are the bearers of the liberal and democratic movement. Although its official constitution did not take place until January 1904 in Petersburg, the 'Union of Liberation' was founded in the summer of 1903 during an ostensible group holiday in the Black Forest under the chairmanship of the estate-owner Petrunkevich who, along with the zemstvo of Tver, had been disciplined by Plehve.[5] The participants belonged to very different camps, ranging from the Zemstvo Constitutionalists to the 'Social Revolutionaries'; only the official Social Democrats had excluded themselves. About one third were members of zemstvos. The remainder came from various groups of the 'intelligentsia'. The movement's main organ, supported financially by the League, was Peter Struve's[6] fortnightly journal *Osvobozhdenie*, which initially (from 1902) appeared in Stuttgart, then in Paris after the German police had served, regrettably, as Tsarist agents. During the years of persecution it is estimated to have had roughly 4,000 subscribers abroad and perhaps twice (?) as many in Russia. The costs, particularly those of smuggling it into Russia, must have been very considerable. It exercised its influence consistently on behalf of 'bourgeois' (in the broadest sense of the term) 'democracy' and must be credited with doing so very effectively, particularly in driving 'populist' romanticism out of the heads of the social reform-

---

[3] Units of local self-government established by statute in 1864.

[4] From 1870 the *duma* was the consultative council in a town, elected on the basis of a 'census' or property franchise. From 1906 the term *Duma* also applied to the Russian parliament.

[5] W. K. von Plehve (1846–1904), Director of Police 1881–4, Minister of the Interior 1902–4.

[6] P. Struve (1870–1944), economist, political thinker and politician. Originally a 'legal Marxist', he became a member of the central committee of the Constitutional Democrats.

ists. The fight against these romantic illusions has provided Peter Struve himself with his chief task in life. Struve, who has a thorough knowledge of capitalism, one which was initially strongly oriented on Marx, is well known to the readers of this journal from earlier years. The Union did not have the capital to found its own daily newspaper. On the other hand, it gave moral support, and doubtless subventions too, to existing press institutions. The heterogeneity of its elements and its necessarily 'conspiratorial' organisation undoubtedly led to a dissipation of its energies. However, this would probably have been even greater without the cohesion it provided. From Autumn 1904 the organisation of the zemstvos and dumas, in its final form, existed alongside the Union. As is generally known, the membership of both types of body is nowadays produced by periodic (triennial) elections based on social estates and graded according to property classes. These bodies are representative assemblies of the propertied classes in town and country and are organised in two tiers, as district (*uezd*-) and, above this, as regional zemstvos. With the exception of the *uprava*[7] (the equivalent of our magistrates' offices) or permanent bureau (a chairman and between two and five salaried members) elected by the assembly of the zemstvo, all of these bodies are run by honorary officers. Despite the fact that it was of course legally prohibited to do so, they began to organise, from Autumn 1904 onwards, the 'All-Russian Congresses' of the regional zemstvos and the dumas of the larger cities which up till now have been the bearers of the constitutional-democratic movement that has increasingly come to dominate the congresses. With just twenty regions participating, the first zemstvo congress was held in November 1904 in Petersburg because Svyatopolk-Mirskii's[8] vacillating government had initially given permission for it to conduct its business if it met there, under the eyes of the government, rather than in Moscow. At the last moment the government nevertheless prohibited the congress, but to no avail because on this occasion, as with subsequent congresses in Moscow, the participants assembled in defiance of the prohibition, refusing to disperse and requiring the police to take the minutes of the meeting. Just how insecure the liberal movement still felt at that time and how enormously the congresses have developed

---

[7] The executive organ, at both district and regional level, of the zemstvo.
[8] Prince P. D. Svyatopolk-Mirskii (1857–1914), Minister of the Interior 1904–5.

since then, is demonstrated by the fact that, before the first congress, they did not dare to hope for more than fourteen votes in support of a resolution demanding a constitution. In fact the 'eleven points',[A] including the demand for a popular assembly, were accepted, with only Count Stenbok-Fermor (Kherson) opposing; the only exception was the demand of the minority led by Shipov for it to be designated merely as an assembly 'participating in legislation'. The resolution was not sent directly to the Tsar but to the minister (Svyatopolk-Mirskii), and was passed on, since the congress itself was illegal, from the regional zemstvos to whom the congress had transmitted it for discussion. The corresponding resolution from the regional zemstvo of Chernigov was then, as we know, dubbed 'impudent' by the Tsar. A further zemstvo congress took place in February 1905 and another in April (to which two-thirds of the regions sent representatives). Both parties – the Constitutional Democrats and the Slavophiles – had summoned special congresses of their groups for May of that year. The impact of the battle of Tsushima[9] was to unite them in a 'coalition congress' (24 and 25 May by the old style calendar) which sent the well-known deputation to Peterhof on 6 June. The Tsar in person dubbed the participants at the July congress as 'prattlers' and this was also the last of the congresses to be treated as in some sense 'illegal' by the police. The subsequent zemstvo congress called to discuss Bulygin's[10] Duma project met unmolested in September, as did, after the publication of the October manifesto, the congress of 6–13 November which made its 'confidence' in Count Witte[11] dependent on certain general 'conditions' and which has been reported thoroughly in the German press. The first congresses were purely assemblies of the zemstvos.

[A] Freedom of the person, of association and of assembly, the equality of citizens, particularly for the peasants (point 8). The abolition of the estate element from the zemstvo constitution, of the limits to its areas of responsibility and independence and the creation of smaller zemstvo districts (point 9). The appointment of freely elected representatives (point 11) who, in the view of the majority, are to participate (point 10) in the legislature (60 votes to 38), in the determination of the budget (91 votes to 7) and the scrutiny of the administration (95 votes to 3). The minority version – 'participation in legislation' – gained 27 votes.

[9] The destruction of the Russian fleet in the war with Japan in May 1905.
[10] A. G. Bulygin (1851–1919), Minister of the Interior from January to October 1905.
[11] Count S. J. Witte (1849–1915), Finance Minister 1892–1903; Chairman of the Council of Ministers 1905–6, proponent of a policy of industrialisation.

The representatives of the towns had held separate congresses for a time, and it was not until the July congress that their representation was general (with the exception of some reactionary dumas). The constitutional-democratic group of the zemstvo representatives regularly held its meetings before the congress – and only in 1905 after it. Attachment to the organisation of the zemstvos had the major advantage for the liberal movement of providing them firstly with a secure legal base which the government (after the experiences of the Moscow zemstvo which will be mentioned below) would assuredly not dare to eliminate entirely, at least not for the time being. Secondly, it put at their constant disposal a permanent organ in the shape of the standing committee (*uprava*) of the zemstvo which was preparing the congress, for which there was legal provision and which continued to exist outside the assemblies (which usually met annually in the autumn), its function being to act as a bureau both for the congresses and during the period between the congresses, preparing and introducing the resolutions of the assemblies. This was all the more important because the legal chairmen of the official assemblies of the regional and district zemstvos, the Marshals of the Nobility who were elected by the nobility, were generally of a reactionary persuasion. The leadership of the 'All-Russian Congresses' was taken over by the Moscow uprava which, under Shipov,[12] had already brokered the as yet unpolitical discussions between the zemstvos in 1902–3. Unintentionally, Plehve had ensured that the Moscow uprava would be outstandingly well equipped to take over the leadership of the political movement when he sacked the 'moderate liberal' Slavophile Shipov because of the resistance of the zemstvos to absolutist rule. Shipov's temporary popularity rested on his dismissal. The man elected to replace him, however, was the radical Golovin, and Plehve did not dare at that point to intervene since he had just recently broken up the zemstvo of Tver on account of similar acts of resistance on the part of its leading members (Petrunkevich, de Roberti and others). Participants assume that, if Shipov had been leader of the uprava, the great radical zemstvo congresses in Moscow would not have been possible in the way they were under Golovin. As far as the social composition of this zemstvo liberalism is concerned, the

---

[12] A. N. Shipov (1851–1920), Chairman of the Moscow Regional zemstvo, 1893–1904, leader of the right wing of the zemstvo movement.

members of the zemstvos and dumas entitled to vote are elected partly according to their property and partly according to a classification of voters based on social estates, and they themselves must have the property qualification to vote. Yet just as the Social Democrats in Berlin learned to create the house-ownership qualification artificially by granting individuals a hundredth share in a house, say, the passive franchise[13] has regularly been created for members of the 'intelligentsia' by fictitious property transfers, as, for example, when the active involvement of an academic specialist in specific reforms of urban administration was desired. We therefore find the cream of the (liberally inclined) Russian academic intelligentsia and political writers represented at the zemstvo congresses alongside the liberal landowners, and the composition of the congresses is reminiscent, inasmuch as such comparisons are possible, of the German pre-parliament in 1848 and the Frankfurt – not the Berlin – National Assembly.[14] Apart from the thirty-four regions in which the zemstvo organisation exists, *ad hoc* electoral bodies were created for the purpose of representation at the congresses via existing unions of agriculturists and others; how this was done I have been unable to ascertain in detail. At any rate, areas not organised on zemstvo lines, as well as Siberia and Transcaucasia, were also represented at the latest zemstvo congresses, and at the November congress the Poles too were represented. Admittedly, some gaps remained, as some zemstvos and dumas either refused to the very end to participate (Kiev) or were represented only on an individual basis (Petersburg). (Not a few of the *uezd*-zemstvos are actually downright reactionary.)

The honorary, elected members of the zemstvos (*deyateli*, officially referred to as *glasnye*) thus mainly represent the 'bourgeois' intelligentsia, provided this epithet is not taken to mean the economic class, but is understood in the sense of its general outlook on life and level of education. By contrast, the true 'bourgeoisie',[15] and in particular the large industrialists, are relatively lacking in influence in the zemstvos. That is why, as early as 11 March 1905, representatives of the Central Belt led by Morozov, of the large Petersburg capitalists

---

[13] 'Das passive Wahlrecht' means the entitlement to be elected.

[14] The 1848 Frankfurt Assembly was dominated by academics and the professions (the *Gelehrtenstand*).

[15] Here Weber uses *Bourgeoisie* rather than *Bürgertum* because he is referring to the status grouping of businessmen.

led by Nobel, and of the southern Russian mining industry led by Avdakov,[16] protested at an audience granted by Minister Bulygin about the competence of the zemstvo and duma representatives to represent 'public opinion'. From an economic point of view, the zemstvo liberals were generally 'non-interested parties', and thus bearers of a political and socio-political idealism of a kind which, at the moment, is not easy to organise as a force in public life here in Germany, as the fate of the National Social Union[17] has shown. To use the Russian expression, they represent the 'second element' of the zemstvos, in contradistinction to the officials employed by the zemstvos who are a proletaroid intelligentsia. From time to time Plehve has warned, in ill-tempered tones, that the latter are the 'third element' (hence the other term); most, if not all of them, are organised, along with other strata of similar social stamp, in the 'Union of Unions'. This 'third element' forms a very numerous bureaucracy (getting on for 50,000 people, so it is said), and it shares with the uprava the burden of regular work in the zemstvos. It is common to mock the tendency towards 'systematisation' which inspires the radical ideologues of this stratum, and the foreigner who sighs as he contemplates the ocean of zemstvo statistics will at times feel that the ability to distinguish between the important and the unimportant is lacking. Nevertheless, the idealism and readiness for sacrifice amongst this category of officials who truly live 'in and with the people' is one of the most pleasing and admirable ethical aspects of Russia today.

The Constitutional Democratic party grew out of the 'Union of Liberation' and the zemstvo constitutionalists. The July congress of the zemstvos accepted the suggestion that they should nominate forty members to negotiate with delegates from the 'Union of Liberation' and the 'Union of Unions'; the 'Union of Liberation' made a corresponding decision, and in the period 12–18 October (old style) of this year the party was constituted in Moscow. Unfortunately, as the city was cut off from the outside world at the time by strikes I have no more precise reports about what took place. It is certain that the 'Union of Unions' did not join the party, since it was too moderate for the views of their members. Although the 'Union of Liberation'

---

[16] In the original this name was misspelt as Ardakow.

[17] The 'Nationalsoziale Verein' (National Social Union) was founded in 1896 by Friedrich Naumann (1860–1919).

dissolved itself, the Petersburg group rejected the proposal made by Professor Milyukov and Struve to join the Constitutional Democratic party, accompanying this decision with vehement attacks on Struve as an 'aristocratic foreigner'. At first this group continued to exist as a rump, transforming itself in December into a socio-political club, in reply to which Struve is said (according to newspaper reports) to have founded a society modelled on the Fabians. Thus the elements which had been united in the 'Union of Liberation' up to that point now fell apart and the 'proletaroid intelligentsia' represented in the 'Union of Unions' went its own separate way from the 'bourgeois' (*bürgerlich*) intelligentsia which for the most part belonged to the zemstvo party.

The above-mentioned April congress of the zemstvos now accepted as a basis for discussion the draft of some *osvobozhdentsy* which is discussed here; at the same time a committee was charged by the bureau with revising the draft. The result of that revision now exists (in Russian) under the same title as the draft discussed here. Apart from some matters of detail, the deviations from the original relate to the removal of the 'highest court of law' and the exclusion of the Finnish question, which, like the Polish question, is not even mentioned. In this re-cast form the proposal was then accepted in principle at the July congress, subject to discussion in the local self-governing bodies, with seven votes against. So far a further constitutional proposal has not been presented by the liberals; one supposedly drawn up by the 'Party of Legal Order', which will be mentioned later, is not available to me at present.

The draft constitution discussed here will first attract the objection that it is thoroughly 'unhistorical', which is indeed true of the type of extract of modern international constitutional law it represents. Yet what is truly 'historical' in Russia today? With the exception of the church and the system of communal land tenure among the peasants, which will be discussed below, absolutely nothing, apart from the absolute power of the Tsar, a relic from the time of the Tartars which hangs in mid-air in quite unhistorical 'freedom', now that all those 'organic' institutions have crumbled away which gave Russia its characteristic stamp in the seventeenth and eighteenth centuries. A country which, in its most 'national' institutions, strongly resembled the monarchy of Diocletian until barely a century ago is indeed incapable of undertaking 'reforms' which are both viable and at the same time historically oriented. The most vital institution of Russian public

life, with the firmest roots in public opinion and of proven effectiveness, the zemstvo, is, at the same time, the most alien to the old
Muscovite idea of overall responsibility by the estates for the duties
distributed amongst the estates. It is a modern self-governing body
which, in the mere forty years of its existence, has already been
re-structured once, changing it from a body purely representing proprietors of land as such (including the peasants) into one with a
structure essentially based on the social estates. It is of course not
possible for me to judge its achievements. To measure it by the
condition of the roads and bridges, as Western European travellers
tend to do, is obviously just as inappropriate as it would be in America, and for the same economic reasons. As everyone knows, Russians
believe much more in the importance of the 'systematic' and of general theories than the Americans with whose local government the
zemstvos can best be compared. The self-governing bodies of both
countries share the same conviction about the fundamental importance of popular education, and the idealism of those belonging to
the circles of most zemstvos who accept the burden of financial sacrifices for 'ideal' goals of this kind deserves the highest respect (it is
certainly the equal of the conduct of the representatives of our East
Prussian estates in 1847).[18] Even in its present atrophied form, and
despite the difficulties of its situation, the zemstvo can still point to
achievements over a wide range of areas which ought to silence the
all too frequently heard verdict about the Russians' 'unreadiness' for
a free form of government; this is evident even from the information
available to the observer abroad, which reveals the unparalleled variety of activities undertaken by the zemstvos, from founding elementary schools through the gathering of statistics, the provision of medical and veterinary services, road building, tax distribution and
agricultural instruction, to the important area of emergency aid
(during famines). It is quite understandable that the central government, despite the 'technical'[B] superiority of its administration, should
seem, by comparison, to be a parasite serving only to preserve the

---

[18] The conflict in 1847 between the East Prussian estates and Friedrich Wilhelm IV
over the question of a loan for the construction of a railway demonstrated the conflict
between sectional and national interests.

[B] And, it may be expressly added, despite the fact that any unprejudiced consideration
must be at pains to avoid thinking of men like Plehve, say, in the roles of theatrical
villains or obscurantists. There is no question of this. The iron logic of the *system*
they served, the rationalist governmental pragmatism of this 'enlightened' bureaucracy

existing distribution of political power, with virtually no substantive (*sachlich*) interests other than in finance policy and for that reason deeply mistrustful of its rival. The zemstvo has therefore had to fight for its successes against constant obstruction from the state's police, on whose powers of coercion it has had to rely for the execution of its decisions. It achieved its successes despite the fact that a jealous government constrained its work ever more noticeably and in the end quite systematically, forbidding it to raise the level of local taxes (specifically the revenues for schooling), banning the charitable zemstvo organisation during the last war in favour of the utterly corrupt 'Red Cross' organisation of the state, and attempting to take its emergency relief system into state control. After the government had thereby compelled the zemstvo to become an increasingly passive, single-purpose organisation (*Zweckverband*), the task of which was to produce the revenues prescribed by the government for its own expenditure, and after it had sabotaged the extension of the zemstvo system to the provinces of Little Russia and Belorussia, Plehve was seriously bent on breaking up the zemstvos entirely during his last days in office and replacing them with the bureaucracy of the state.

*

The unconditional realisation of the principle of a 'four-point' *suffrage* (general, equal, direct and secret) distinguishes the Party of Constitutional Democrats, who are behind this proposal, from other constitutionalist groups on the right which stand for an indirect or property-based suffrage, as well as from Shipov's anti-bureaucratic, Slavophile group with its idea that a consultative popular assembly controlling finances should be developed from the existing zemstvos. In the first instance the demand for this form of suffrage, the most controversial point in the proposal, is for the democrats a consequence of the absence of other 'historical' points of departure, since the government had spent the last twenty-five years discrediting the zemstvos. Then

which quite naturally looked with anger on the 'inefficient routine' and the impractical 'stubbornness', the 'sectional interests', the 'lack of understanding' and egoism, the 'utopian dreams' of the 'intelligentsia' and the self-governing bodies, and the 'empty rhetoric' of the press, regarding them as elements which constantly hindered and obstructed the combination of utilitarian gratification of the people from above with the corresponding respect for authority demanded by the *raison d'état*. It was this system that 'made life Hell' and caused quiet, other-worldly scholars to fall into a frenzy of wild rejoicing when they heard the news of Plehve's assassination.

there is of course the further factor which makes it impossible for advocates of reforms of principle everywhere to argue with complete inner sincerity for a graduated franchise nowadays, namely the effect of capitalism with its power to create classes. The conflict of economic interests and the class character of the proletariat attack the specifically bourgeois (*bürgerlich*) reformers[19] from the rear; their work suffers the same fate here as it does everywhere else. Only for as long as the predominance of the craft system gave the masses of workers at least the theoretical opportunity to become 'independent' was it possible to believe with subjective sincerity that a form of electoral representation based on property taxation also represented those who had not yet become independent. Not only was the development of the urban 'middle class' (*Mittelstand*) in the Western European sense inherently very weak in Russia for historical reasons, but, quite apart from this, the effect of capitalism has been spreading there for a such long time now that any attempt to argue for a property franchise means that the reforming propagandist is left with officers but no army. For understandable reasons the workers in the cities would never dream of having anything to do with such a thing. In the countryside, moreover, a property franchise could hardly be established in the territories where *obshchina* (communal land tenure) exists without the greatest arbitrariness. Here in the village community *equal* voting by the heads of households is the 'historical' starting point. Nevertheless, if it had acted *at the right* time a hitherto autocratic government could have imposed some scheme of voting entitlement or other (one with an educational qualification, say, or with plural voting rights) – a party of reform could hardly draw different conclusions from the situation than those embodied in the proposal. If it were to do so, autocracy would have it in its power (and this is the ultimate, crucial reason) to play the workers off against the Duma the moment it became recalcitrant, just as the previous regime had done, with at least seeming success, in order to intimidate the propertied classes it suspected of liberalism. If the democratic party accepted a property-based franchise (that is the exclusion of the mass of the peasants from elections or blatant discrimination against them), the forces of reaction would immediately have the peasants solidly behind them as well, for it is precisely the owners of private, census-

---

[19] The original edition has *Reformen* where it should have read *Reformern*.

worthy property against whom the hatred of the masses in the countryside is directed – the estate owners, the kulaks above all (a word meaning "fists" – peasants and small rural capitalists who have grown rich), and the rest of the 'village bourgeoisie'. Under no circumstances do the peasants blame their misery on the Tsar. Just as they used to blame the officials in the past, the peasants would in future blame a Duma in which the great mass of them could not participate, since they would rank *below* all urban proletarians in the census. Already the representatives of the reactionary nobility and of state officialdom are assiduously spreading reports that the liberals' aim is to prevent any peasant from entering the Duma. The government's demagogic policy was strikingly evident above all in Bulygin's project for the Duma.[20] The assembly proposed in the manifesto of 6 (19) August, with powers to discuss legislation and to control the budget, is to be elected, according to the appended electoral regulations, in twenty-six major cities on the one hand and in provisional electoral assemblies on the other by delegated 'electors'.[21] What is more, candidates are to be chosen from the midst of the electors themselves, so as to limit as far as possible the candidacy of representatives of the 'intelligentsia'. In the provinces the election of these delegates is distributed across the three classes of (1) larger private landowners; (2) the cities; (3) the peasants; with the distribution varying in each province. However, whereas the first two classes have a property franchise of a fairly plutocratic kind (the workers always being completely excluded), the peasants' delegates are to be elected from the *volost*[22] assemblies which in turn rest on the equality of all the householders in the village. In other words, the only people for whom there is to be no property barrier are the largely illiterate peasants. Moreover, the peasant electors chosen in this way are to have the right (in contrast to the other classes) to nominate a deputy from their own midst before the election of the other deputies to the Duma, after which they elect the remaining deputies along with the others. In other words, the peasants' representatives have a privileged franchise,

---

[20] Bulygin proposed the creation of an advisory Duma on 6 August 1905. The date in brackets refers to the Julian calendar ('old style').

[21] The term used by Weber is *Wahlmänner*. These individuals were themselves elected in assemblies at one level, from which they were delegated to vote on behalf of their constituency at a higher level.

[22] A peasant administrative unit usually comprising several village communities.

restricted to their social group, for at least fifty-one deputies (the number of the European-Russian provinces), and, together with the census landowners, they usually provide more than two thirds of the electors for the remaining deputies. The manifesto of 17 (30) October which makes it an 'invariable rule' that no law shall henceforth come into force without the agreement of the Duma, added the general pledge that, as far as possible in the short time available, the franchise was to be given to those classes 'which had been deprived of it until now', while the 'further development' of the 'principle' of a 'common' franchise was to be left to the 'newly created legislative order'. After all this has happened, as Peter Struve quite correctly says in his introduction to the draft we are discussing, it is already 'too late' for any other liberal franchise programme in Russia today. What is more, it was the idea of 'human rights' and the demand for a 'four-step franchise' which had united the radical bourgeois intellectuals in the 'Union of Liberation' with the 'proletaroid' intellectuals, including even some in the Social Revolutionary camp. The only way to prevent splits amongst the intellectuals during the struggle seemed to lie in adhering unwaveringly to this conception.

If one were willing – and able – to disregard this situation, *then* of course even a democrat or social democrat, however convinced of his principles, could have very grave doubts about the question of introducing this precise form of franchise – as the first ever – in this particular country at *this* precise moment.

The Russian democrats themselves do not all share the same view on the crucial issue, namely the likely effect of this franchise. They are usually most ready to admit to having reservations about handing over the zemstvos to completely uneducated illiterates, no matter how much they stress the need for a far stronger representation of the peasants, who are at present condemned to the status of a minority with no influence. Complete bureaucratisation of the zemstvo administration would indeed be the immediate consequence, and with all due respect for the outstanding achievements of the zemstvo officials (the so-called 'third element' – *tretii element*), this could only be the precursor of centralisation along French lines. It was the 'economic independence' of the honorary members of the zemstvos that guaranteed the independence of the zemstvo in relation to those 'above them' and, under our economic order, this would remain just as necessary, if not more so, in order to guarantee their independence in relation to a central government in the hands of a parliamentary party, as long as the peasants remain shackled to the agrarian communism of their village communities. Opinions vary as to the likely effect of universal and equal suffrage for the Duma. I know Russian democrats whose position is roughly, ' "*Fiat justitia, pereat mundus*".[23] Even if the masses reject or destroy all cultural progress, we can only demand what is just, and we shall have done our duty if we give the masses the franchise and thus place the responsibility for their actions on their own shoulders.' At most they may add, 'Even the most extreme form of ochlocracy[24] can do no worse than the "Black Hundreds"[25] hired by the officials when their position of power was threatened. No matter, it is better to suffer cultural darkness for generations than to do what is politically unjust. Perhaps the educative effect of this suffrage will yield good results at some time in the future.' Such views probably also contain an unconscious element of Solov'ev's[26] belief in the peculiarly ethical-religious nature of the Russian people's political mission, as indeed one person of this persuasion pointed out to me directly. Here the absolute rejection of the 'ethics of consequentialism' in the area of politics too means that only the unconditional ethical imperative is valid as a possible lode-star of positive action. For them the only possibilities are *either* the fight for what is right *or* 'holy' self-abnegation. Because *all* values other than ethical ones have been excluded, when one has done what one perceives to be one's positive 'duty', then unconsciously those words from the Bible come into force again, words which have penetrated most deeply into the soul not only of Tolstoy but indeed of the whole Russian people, namely 'Resist not evil'.[27] The abrupt switch from tempestuous, energetic action to resigned acceptance of the situation results from a refusal to acknowledge that the morally indifferent exists or to accept that the morally indifferent is a possible 'value'. This is a trait which the pan-moralism of Solov'ev's notion of 'holiness' shares with a brand of democracy that is purely ethical in its orientation. Yet, alongside such extreme ideologues there are others (indeed doubtless the majority) who take a more favourable view of

---

[23] The motto of Kaiser Ferdinand I (1503–64).

[24] 'Ochlocracy' means mob rule.

[25] Officially approved terrorist groups. Weber also refers to them as 'Black Gangs'.

[26] V. S. Solov'ev (1853–1900). Philosopher, religious thinker, poet and literary critic.

[27] Weber is quoting freely from Matthew 5, 39.

the chances than most foreigners who tend to detect a degree of sincerity in the constitutional intentions of the present regime precisely in the fact that it is *not* placing an arithmetically equal franchise in the hands of the politically uneducated masses at the present moment. Firstly, the Russians cite certain *economic* reasons why the masses, with the franchise in their hands, would be *bound* to pursue liberal ideals in both politics and culture; we shall discuss these economic reasons in more detail later, since they are particularly important in the opinion of some democratic leaders. Even in the explanation offered for the proposal there are really just two purely political arguments. One is the general assertion that the franchise will perform an 'educative' function. Yet if this is claimed for *equal* franchise, surely certain 'developmental' pre-conditions would have to obtain. The other argument consists of pointing to what happened in Bulgaria after the introduction of universal suffrage there, consequences which the authors of the proposal view positively. Apart from anything else, this is surely to underestimate the difference between a small state and a great nation which – as even people like Struve accept – is obliged to engage in 'world politics', and even more so the difference between the traditional position of the religiously and nationally consecrated Tsar and that of a temporarily hired and imported minor monarch.[28]

Incidentally, it must be emphasised that the draft constitution is in other respects far from being 'radical' in its constitutional thinking. It is true that the authors rightly reject today's modish talk about the 'outdatedness' of parliamentarism.[c] Taken as a whole, however, their draft is at pains to spare the position of the Tsar. There is no mention

---

[c] This kind of empty talk is inappropriate at present because it invites critical comparisons between countries with a parliamentary-democratic regime and those with a 'personal' regime, and because even in the area in which it claims to be particularly effective, that of foreign policy, the personal type of regime tends to come off badly. One can only be justified in passing judgement on the achievements of German diplomacy if one knows the official papers. But anyone can see that consistent leadership and the achievement of lasting successes must have been made absolutely impossible for the diplomats if their work was constantly being interrupted by noisy intermezzi, speeches, telegrams and unexpected decisions on the part of the monarch, with the result that their entire energies were absorbed by the task of straightening out the mess thereby created, or even that the diplomats themselves finally had the idea of employing these theatrical means themselves.

[28] Weber uses the term *Duodezmonarch*. He is referring to Prince Ferdinand von Sachsen-Coburg-Gotha-Kohary, elected King of Bulgaria in 1887.

in it of elected officials, apart from the 'justices of the peace'. It mentions neither the sovereignty of parliament, as in the English model, nor the rule of the parliamentary majority on French lines. This respect for the position of the monarch distinguishes the supporters of the Constitutional Democratic group from the radical groups on their left which, if not republican, want to see the principle of popular sovereignty guaranteed by the summoning of a Constituent Assembly and to have it expressly laid down that parliament shall determine the course of politics. Clearly, the Constitutional Democrats were swayed not only by compelling considerations of Realpolitik but also by the thought that only the monarch can represent the unity of the empire effectively if a large measure of autonomy is to be granted to the different nationalities. Consideration of the position of the Tsar meant, therefore, that the draft was also unable to carry through the complete separation of the executive from the legislature, as in the American model. As mentioned above, this is why it attempted to create something which is in fact new in several respects, in the form of a 'supreme tribunal' standing outside the hierarchy of judicial authorities. Its functions should embrace the following: (1) Cassation[29] of any actions of the government and verdicts of the courts which infringe the constitution, including those resting on formally correct but materially unconstitutional laws, on appeal from private interested parties, from one of the two chambers or from one of the empire's highest constitutional authorities. Curiously enough, the authors of the draft believe that, in this function, the tribunal is a copy of the American Supreme Court, a surprising error in view of the Russians' intimate familiarity with James Bryce's well-known book.[30] (2) The scrutiny of the conduct of elections is to be part of the remit of the tribunal. (3) Augmented by the judges of the Court of Cassation, the tribunal should also be the authority which hears political complaints levelled against ministers by either of the chambers. According to the proposal, this political indictment, which is to exist independently of and in addition to the permissible prosecution of all officials in the normal courts, and which can lead only to dismissal and exclusion from office for five years, may be based on the following grounds: (a) intentional contravention of the constitution,

---

[29] 'Cassation' means the negation of a decision on the grounds of its invalidity.
[30] J. Bryce, *The American Commonwealth*, 3rd edn (2 vols., London, 1893).

or (b) 'grave damage to the interests of the state' as a result of the misuse of office, of exceeding the limits of official competence or of negligence. Clearly this procedure was also intended to lead from a parliamentary vote of no-confidence into a trial to be adjudicated on the basis of 'objective' criteria. Yet the substantive (*sachlich*) content of the 'interests of the state' cannot be established 'objectively', that is without regard to those ideals and interests, and hence those 'value judgements', on which the divisions between political and social parties rest. The strictly formal task of protecting the constitution and of handing down legally founded judgements about what 'is the case' would thus be put in the same hands as the task of pronouncing political sentiments about what 'ought to be the case'; inherently this is a very suspect notion. Admittedly, the authors could, for example, point out that in fact formal decisions on constitutional questions are usually reached in a similar way; it is well known that, when the judges in the American Federal Court ruled in favour of Hayes in a disputed presidential election, the votes were divided strictly along party lines. Today no-one doubts that the verdict was a crass misjudgement, but nevertheless it prevented a civil war. This institution has been deleted in the second draft and, in contrast to the Manifesto of 17 (30) October, the constituent congress of the Constitutional Democratic Party restricted itself to demanding the establishment of ministerial responsibility and the right of the Duma to discuss not only the legality but also the efficacy of ministerial actions.[31]

*

Inasmuch as its origins lay in the realm of ideas, the political 'individualism' of Western European 'human rights', which Struve, for example, has consistently advocated, was in part created out of religious convictions which rejected human authorities unconditionally as a blasphemous idolisation of God's creatures.[D] Today's form of

---

[31] A long section on the 'Nationality and Language Question' and on 'Church and State' has been omitted here.

[D] Cf. Jellinek's well-known work on 'Human and Civil Rights', *my* contributions to the *Archiv für Sozialwissenschaft*, vols. XX, 1 and XXI, 1, and E. Troeltsch's account of Protestantism in Hinneberg's *Die Kultur der Gegenwart* (I, 4, 1).[32] Struve has been influenced by Jellinek's writings which he cites repeatedly. The affinity between the economic and political ethics of Russian rationalistic sects and Puritanism (in the broad sense of the word) has already struck Leroy-Beaulieu and others. But at least in the numerically most significant section, the *raskol*[33] in the strict sense, this tendency 'enlightenment' ensures that such convictions no longer enjoy mass support. The other main source of the idea was an optimistic faith in the natural harmony of interests among free individuals, which nowadays has been destroyed forever by capitalism. Thus, even for 'intellectual' reasons it is not possible in today's Russia to run through these stages of development belatedly. Specifically bourgeois individualism is now a thing of the past even amongst the classes of 'education and property' and will certainly not now capture the minds of the '*petite bourgeoisie*'. As for the 'masses' who would, and according to the declared intention of the liberals, *should* be given power by universal suffrage – where are the impulses to come from to support a movement making demands that go beyond purely material goals, such as that launched by politicians of bourgeois democratic persuasion in the programme of the 'Union of Liberation' ? These goals include: (1) guaranteed rights of freedom for the individual; (2) a constitutional state under the rule of law and based on 'four-point' suffrage; (3) social reform along Western European lines; and (4) agrarian reform.[34]

*

In the large cities socialist agitation is flourishing at present. As is widely known, the Russian Social Democrats had already split into two groups before the events took place which permitted them to operate openly in Russia itself; these groups were led by Plekhanov, Axelrod, Martov and 'Starover' (A. Potresov) on the one side, and

---

is counterbalanced by deep differences in the character of its 'inner-worldly asceticism'.

[32] G. Jellinek, *Die Erklärung der Menschen- und Bürgerrechte. Ein Beitrag zur modernen Verfassungsgeschichte* (Leipzig, 1895); English translation *The Declaration of the Rights of Man and of Citizens. A Contribution to Modern Constitutional History* (New York, 1901). Weber's own essays are 'Die protestantische Ethik und der "Geist" des Kapitalismus. 1: Das Problem' in *Archiv für Sozialwissenschaft und Sozialpolitik*, 20 (1904), pp. 1–54 and 'Die protestantische Ethik und der "Geist" des Kapitalismus. 2: Die Berufsidee des asketischen Protestantismus' in the *Archiv*, 21 (1905), pp. 1–110; English translation, *The Protestant Ethic and the Spirit of Capitalism* (London, 1930). E. Troeltsch, 'Protestantisches Christentum und Kirche in der Neuzeit' in P. Hinneberg (ed.), *Die Kultur der Gegenwart* (Berlin and Leipzig, 1906). A. Leroy-Beaulieu *L'empire des Tsars et les Russes* (3 vols., Paris 1889–93); English translation, New York and London, 1905.

[33] The 'schismatics' who separated from the Orthodox Church in the second half of the seventeenth century.

[34] In the following section an account of the socialist and bourgeois (*bürgerlich*) parties has been abridged.

by 'Lenin' (Ulyanov) on the other. The former group remained in possession of the hitherto shared party organ *Iskra*, published in Geneva, and found its official representation in the 'All Russian Conference of Workers' Parties', held for the first time in 1905. At the time of the split at any rate this group rejected armed insurrection, at least for the present, and were equally opposed on principle to participation in any revolutionary government which might come about; instead they placed at the centre of their activities the development of trades unions. The other group, represented since 1903 by Lenin's *Vpered*, refused to acknowledge *Iskra* as the party organ any longer, and, as it contained the majority within the party as a whole, acted as if it were the continuation of the common organisation at the 'third Congress of the Russian Social Democratic Workers' Party', founding the journal *Proletarii* as its organ, replacing the formation of trades unions with the demand for the eight-hour day, preaching insurrection and participation in any revolutionary government that might be created, rejecting all legal forms of agitation and, in opposition to the followers of the *Iskra* group, demanding on behalf of the peasants the immediate 'confiscation' of all land not in the hands of the peasants. This last point runs strictly counter to the official programme of the Social Democrats who demanded on behalf of the peasants that the *obrezki* be handed over to them, that is to say that they be allocated the land taken from them at the time of the emancipation (about one fifth), and always poured scorn on the social revolutionary demand for the confiscation of all land as 'utopian', distancing themselves demonstratively, as late as Spring 1905, from the 'All Russian Congress of Engineers' when this demand was as much as discussed. 'While preserving its independence', Lenin's party, in contrast to Plekhanov's, also regarded 'occasional pacts' with the social revolutionaries as useful. Both groups, however, declare it to be the duty of the party to support the efforts of the liberals which are directed against autocracy while at the same time discrediting in the eyes of the workers all liberal groups, including the 'Union of Liberation' and the 'Union of Unions'. In contrast to this, the second congress, before the split, had agreed to a resolution of 'Starover' which declared that co-operation with the bourgeois democrats was possible and, in certain circumstances, useful. This resolution was expressly negated by Lenin's group, but Plekhanov's group, too, no longer takes any account of it in practice. As can be seen, the causes of the split are not issues of principle but rather are partly personal and partly tactical in nature. However, the reasons for it are also to be found in the particular spiritual or intellectual character of Russian socialism. At the moment it is only natural for it to have as one of its sources the opposition of the orthodox leaders, who have mainly been living abroad where they have been influenced by the Western European social democratic parties, to the 'putschism' that has now seized hold of the emerging mass organisations in Russia itself since the introduction of freedom of the press. This is why even Bebel's attempt at mediation failed: Lenin refused to accept any advice from non-expert foreigners. However, there is no doubt that this mood of putschism itself is not merely the result of the tempestuous hope, born of the immediate situation, that the great day has now arrived to bring about the final political overthrow of autocracy at all events and to enforce at least the immediate realisation of the 'minimal programme' of socialism. Rather, revolutionary action and opposition to the 'laws of development' have run deep in the blood of specifically Russian socialism since its founding fathers, Herzen and Lavrov, as an after-effect of certain Hegelian ideas.

*

Thus, both among the urban workers, who are also subject to the attentions of the Christian Social and the social revolutionary adherents of the most extreme kind of radicalism, and amongst the 'free professions', the chances of the bourgeois democrats, even by their own estimates, would probably be extremely doubtful if a democratic suffrage existed, despite the fact that their programme contains all the demands made by radical Western European social reformers.[E] On the other hand, as far as the thin stratum of the 'bourgeoisie' in the strict sense is concerned, the manufacturers – the old bearers of nationalism as described for German readers by von Schulze-Gävernitz[35] – have in part moved very close to the liberals and even

---

[E] Compulsory insurance, compulsory courts of arbitration, the eight-hour day (as a principle) etc.

[35] G. von Schulze-Gävernitz (1864–1943). Political economist, Reichstag deputy for the 'Fortschrittliche Volkspartei' and the 'Deutsche Demokratische Partei' 1912–20. Weber is referring to an essay by him on 'Nationalism in Russia' published in the *Preußische Jahrbücher* in 1894.

the democrats.[F] This is quite natural, given the conditions of recent years, when Plehve's government sought to win over the workers and to play them off against the 'intelligentsia'; indeed the eleven huts in which Gapon's[36] movement had its centre were built at government expense. Yet *all* the better-known names from this group are missing from the Constitutional Democratic party. They were opposed to the zemstvo movement, and the programme of the anti-protectionist 'Union of Liberation' held absolutely no attraction for them. In terms of social policy the majority of their representatives probably still took an essentially reactionary stance at the beginning of 1905 and hoped for repression, although they were far from unified in this attitude. Not a few petitions in favour of granting the right of coalition come from the manufacturers. Politically, many of them now seem to belong to the 'Party of Legal Order' or the 'League of 17 October' which is very close to it. At any rate, after what has happened so far, the government cannot simply use them against the liberals and in favour of reaction. When a representative of the 'Party of Legal Order' called on a meeting of the 'Union of Trade and Industry' to join forces with the government in the fight against the 'Soviet of Workers' Deputies', other speakers vigorously rejected the demand, saying that 'society' must conduct the struggle alone. If the Union were to seek the protection of the government now, it was pointed out, the day would come when others would turn to the government for help *against* the Union, and would be just as successful in doing so.

Finally, most of the lower middle classes whose likely attitude is, as usual, the hardest to predict, will probably be prevented from joining the liberals because of their anti-Semitism. At any rate, this is a conclusion one can draw from their growing participation in the movement of the 'Black Gangs'. Of course, it must not be forgotten that the organisation of police espionage in the major cities and some other 'suspect' places, which demands, for example, that every house

---

[F] The largest firms in Petersburg declared in a submission to the ministry on 31 January that only 'fundamental reforms of a general political character', but not administrative interference in work relations could bring the workers back onto 'the path of law'. The major industrialists in Moscow took the same view (*Pravo*, p. 588)

[36] G. A. Gapon (1870–1906). Priest and organiser of working class opposition. Organiser of the demonstration of 9 January 1905 ('Bloody Sunday') when the police opened fire on the crowd.

should have a caretaker (*dvornik*) charged with the surveillance of its occupants, and imposes such responsibilities and costs on landlords, and that obligatory passports, 'administrative' exile (that is not subject to legal process), and the lack of any security within one's home against searches which can take place at any time, preferably at night – all these things are creating such a degree of utterly loathed dependence on corrupt and capricious minor officials, that protests against these conditions will probably outweigh all other considerations for the next few years. In practice any *lasting* compromise with a system which needs to use such means has become impossible.

Yet it is the position of the *peasants* which is and will remain the decisive question for the future not only of the Constitutional Democratic movement, but more importantly of the fundamental points in its programme, and beyond this for the chances of liberal 'development' in the Western European sense. It will remain the decisive issue even if a franchise based on the property census were to give the liberals a majority. In this case, if the peasants are reactionary a reactionary government could use them at any time as a rod for the backs of a recalcitrant Duma. Accordingly, the programme of bourgeois democracy is in fact essentially designed to appeal to the peasants. Peter Struve would like to turn the peasant, too, into a 'person' by accustoming him not only to 'law' in the objective sense but also to 'rights', in the subjective sense, which for him mean the 'human rights' of English individualism. The greatest emphasis is constantly being placed on the fact that *agrarian reform* is the question central to all others, that political reforms will and must serve this aim and that it in turn will serve political reform. But, of course, that is not to say that the peasants themselves will become democratic. Like the authors of this draft, Peter Struve relies fundamentally on the economic interests of the peasants whose demands in this direction he believes *cannot* be satisfied by a reactionary government. One must therefore ask which demands are those of the peasants themselves, and which are being made by the democratic agrarian reformers on their behalf. The assembly of the zemstvos in February had already addressed itself to the agrarian question, and had promulgated the slogan of the 'supplementation' (*dopolnenie*) of the peasants' share of the land (*nadel*)[37] which has become characteristic of liberal agrarian

[37] *Nadel* normally refers to the share of land allocated to a family within a commune. Here Weber is using it to refer to the overall share of land held by the peasant

reform ever since. All further details were set aside for separate discussion. The programme of the 'Union of Liberation' then raised the following very considerable demands relating to agrarian policy: (1) Abolition of the peasants' redemption payments. (The government has in the meantime decided on this measure; half are to be abolished in 1906, complete abolition in 1907.) (2) Allocation of land to landless peasants and to those with an inadequate share of land by breaking up demesne, privy and appanage estates, and, where these do not exist, the *expropriation* of private landowners. (3) The creation of a state land-fund for the purpose of planned internal colonisation. (4) Reform of land rent law so that improvements are guaranteed to the tenant, and courts of arbitration will 'regulate rents in the interest of the workers' and settle disputes between tenant and landlord. (5) The extension of labour protection legislation to agricultural workers 'as far as it is appropriate to the fundamental conditions of agriculture'. These are augmented by further points in the programme of an evidently 'physiocratic' hue: the abolition by stages of indirect taxation and the development of direct taxes on the basis of progressive income tax; the abolition of protectionist preferential treatment of individual entrepreneurs while simultaneously 'protecting vigorously the productive forces of the people'. The staged reduction of excise duties, so it is said, will both 'improve the position of agriculture and help industry to flourish'. In a critique of the draft Peter Struve has rejected, as an 'editorial oversight', the complete abolition of indirect taxes, on the grounds of their budgetary importance. Yet precisely this point seems to be popular with those farmers who might support a liberal leadership. A seemingly genuine petition by fifty-six 'literate' and eighty-four illiterate 'middle-class' farmers from the district of Kherson, for example, also demanded the abolition of duties on tea, sugar, machines and matches, as do other, similar petitions from peasants, masses of which can be found in newspapers and journals. It should at least be said that, in Russia as it is today, progressive income tax can quite clearly be no financial substitute for duties on finance and consumption. Not only the economic but also the moral preconditions are lacking for truly effective taxation of this kind, which is not even possible in the United States today for the

---

communes as opposed to other landowners in Russia which must be 'supplemented' so that they can support themselves from it.

same reasons. It is also quite unclear, given such a taxation programme, where the finances are to come from to carry out the
momentous reforms demanded here. However, let us go back to the
reforms themselves.

German readers must have been struck straightaway by the fact
that there is no mention in all this of the *obshchina* (*mir*),[38] the most
characteristic institution of Russia's system of agrarian tenure. Now
it is far from being the case that the current peasant question only
exists in the districts where land is owned by the village communes,[G]
which is to say in the centre and in the eastern 'Black Earth' regions
and everything lying to the north and north-east of them. On the
contrary, the question runs through the whole, vast empire from the
Baltic to the Steppes, and is just as much of a burning issue in some
areas of Little Russia as it is, say, in the Moscow region. Admittedly,
the political problems of agriculture for the Great Russian people
which has been called to hegemony are all linked directly or indirectly
with the system of communal land tenure, and the territory in which
it is widespread embraces both the greatest density of peasants and
the main areas where there is widespread and chronic distress
amongst the masses. Above all, however, its area of distribution as
an *idea* is quite universal. The whole formation of socio-political
parties in Russia is intimately connected with decades of heated
debate about what should become of this system. It engages the
imagination of the masses as much as that of social politicians of all
shades of opinion and determines their attitudes to a degree far in
excess of its real and immediate importance. Of course, this very fact
throws some light on one of the reasons why the liberal programme
makes no mention of it. There is no doubt that the omission also
involves a concession to 'Populists' and Slavophiles who have turned
liberal on the one hand, and to Socialists, Social Revolutionaries and
land reformers on the other, who, for opposing reasons, would all be
unable to agree to an outright attack on the system of communal land
tenure. Conversely, the specifically economic liberals, and particularly
individualists like Struve who have been trained in a strictly Marxist

[G] Here the term 'communal land tenure' always and only refers to that system (of
so-called 'strict' communal land tenure) whereby the individual does not inherit his
share (of arable land etc.) from his family but has it allocated to him by the commune
(by repartition).

[38] A peasant land commune.

school, would be bound to oppose as 'utopian' any proposals for agrarian-political reform which took communal land tenure as their starting point.

The other explanation for this silence is of course the fact that the legislative treatment of the problem, whatever direction it takes, will take a decade, and practical politicians are faced today with much more urgent tasks in the area of agricultural policy. Nevertheless, even the first step towards any at all generous agrarian policy is bound to collide with the system of communal tenure.[39]

*

The 'Young Populists' are clearly quite right about this, and it also explains the democrats' reticence about the problem: there is no question but that the mass of the *peasants themselves* simply cannot be won over to an 'individualist' agrarian programme in the Western European sense. Firstly, there can be no doubt that the defence of communal land tenure – regardless of the fact that decisions on repartitioning can be the outcome of a most embittered class struggle – is by no means *only* an expression of economic class interests but also involves deeply rooted ideas of 'natural justice'. It is clearly the case that the decision required before land can be repartitioned is by no means usually reached only with the votes of people who stand to gain from it or who have been made malleable by beatings or a boycott. On the other hand, it is equally true that the repartitioning of land is frequently something which only happens on paper, at least inasmuch as its aim is 'socio-political', even if it does appear to be the most important element of agrarian democracy in this system of social relations. The wealthy peasants rent out, alienate and bequeath their land (only within the commune, of course) on the firm assumption that there will be no decision to repartition it; or conversely, other members of the commune are in their debt and hence in their power, so that the repartitioning in fact strengthens their dominance. Because the repartitioning applies only to land, but not to animals and working capital, it is quite compatible with the most ruthless exploitation of the weak. But of course it is precisely this discrepancy between the law and the facts that causes the angry radicalism of the masses to grow as the value of the land rises and

[39] A detailed discussion of the Agrarian Question has been omitted here.

differentiation increases accordingly. The crucial point appears to be that this communist radicalism is clearly bound to *intensify*, as far as one can see, precisely *if* or when the situation of the peasants is improved by reducing their burdens and increasing the land at the disposal of the commune. For, whereas the ownership of land is still regarded as a duty (which every member of the commune tries to evade) in districts where the burdens imposed on the share of land exceed its yield, in all areas where, conversely, the yield exceeds the burdens, repartitioning is sought by the masses. The districts with the best soil are therefore the districts where the masses have the most compelling interest in repartitioning and where the wealthy peasants have the strongest interest in opposing it. Thus, *if* the system of communal land tenure is preserved, every remission of taxes and burdens, such as the present remission of redemption payments, must *increase* these foci of communist interests and social conflict. It is also well known that the German peasants in Southern Russia, for example, did not, in many cases, introduce communal land tenure in the strict sense until the government increased the land they owned, and for very understandable reasons. Generally speaking, the effect of supplementing the *nadel* is unlikely to be any different: faith in communism is bound to expand enormously. As far as one is able to judge from outside, the Social Revolutionaries will have their hopes in this direction confirmed.

Nevertheless, this programme of adding to the *nadel* must be accepted *today* by any honest agrarian reformer. The Constitutional Democratic party has consequently committed itself in its agrarian programme (points 36–40) to the relevant demands of the Union of Liberation and the Liberal Agrarian Congress, in part with even more far-reaching concessions to the objections of the Social Revolutionaries. These concessions include: (1) the demand that compensation of the landowners who are to be dispossessed should be determined by a 'just price' *and not the market value* (point 36); (2) the express demand that the renewal of tenancy be legally guaranteed, possibly also the right of the tenant to be compensated for improvements, and above all the creation of *judicial authorities* (on the Irish model) for the reduction of 'disproportionately high' farm rents (point 39); and (3) the creation of a farming inspectorate to supervise the application of workers' protection legislation, as extended to agriculture. The principles according to which the expropriated land is to be allocated to the peasants (allocation for ownership or exploitation on the basis of personal or communal tenure) are to be laid down 'in accordance with the nature of land ownership and land use in the different regions of Russia'.

*

All in all, then, carrying out the reform programme of the bourgeois democrats would in all probability result in an enormous intensification in the 'spirit' of agrarian communism and social revolution amongst the peasants, which is already so strong today that the peasants, at least in the mass, could certainly not be won over to an individualist programme of the kind once championed by Struve and others. The peculiarity of the Russian situation seems to be that it is *possible* for 'un-modern' *agrarian* communism to intensify as a result of intensified 'capitalist' development and the concomitant rising values of land and agricultural products, *alongside* the further development of the industrial proletariat and hence of 'modern' socialism. In the area of the 'intellectual movement', too, the 'possibilities' of development do not yet seem fixed.

Although the atmosphere of the *narodnichestvo*[40] which still pervades all shades of the 'intelligentsia' in all classes and political programmes will be broken up, the question is: what will replace it? The very matter-of-fact (*sachlich*) view of things characteristic of social reformist liberalism would be hard put to it to capture the 'expansive' character of the Russian mind. For this romantic radicalism among the 'Social Revolutionary' intellectuals has another side to it. Because it is close in character to 'state socialism', despite all protests to the contrary, it is extremely easy to leap from this position into the authoritarian and reactionary camp. If the reports, particularly of foreign, but also of conscientious Russian[41] observers are correct, the relatively frequent, rapid transformation of extremely radical students into highly authoritarian officials certainly does not need to be the result of innate characteristics, as some have said, nor of base ambition to secure their own material interests. For there have also been many cases of the reverse process taking place in recent years: convinced adherents of the pragmatic rationalism advocated by Plehve

---

[40] The Populist (or *narodnik*) current amongst the intelligentsia.
[41] In the first edition the adjective 'Russian' was erroneously omitted.

55

and Pobedonostsev[42] have suddenly crossed over into the extreme Social Revolutionary camp. The explanation is rather that the pragmatic rationalism of this tendency *inherently* longs to 'act' in the service of some absolute social-ethical norm, and, given the intellectual background of still existent agrarian communism, tends therefore to oscillate back and forth between 'creative' actions from 'above' or from 'below', succumbing by turns to reactionary and to revolutionary romanticism.[43]

*

What, then, will the peasants do in the elections? The strength of their resistance to the influence of officials and conservative clerics is clearly variable, and appears, quite understandably, to be strongest, not in the districts suffering emergencies, but rather in the south, for example, in the Cossack villages, and in the provinces of Chernigov and Kursk. In these regions and also in some parts of the industrial belt the peasants, notwithstanding the presence either of supervisory officials of the state police or the Marshals of the Nobility, have often passed the most sharply worded resolutions and covered petitions with thousands of signatures demanding the removal of bureaucratic supervision and permission to elect representatives of the people who would deal *directly with the Tsar*, without the interference of paid officialdom. This is their central conception, *one that is admittedly in no way related to modern parliamentarism.* In other words, they want to see the disappearance of the bureaucracy of Tsarist autocracy, but – and here the Slavophiles are correct – they have no wish to see it replaced by a bureaucracy under the direction of parliament. At present the force of this anti-bureaucratic current is not inconsiderable. There have been quite a few cases where the peasants have rejected the 'loyal' resolutions prepared by officials for the *skhod*,[44] and other cases where they accepted them while the officials were present but subsequently recanted, or where they have returned publications sent to them by reactionary leagues. Yet it is not very likely that this mood would be strong enough to prevail against the authority and brutality of the officials during elections. Even in the version of 11 December,

---

[42] K. P. Pobedonostsev (1827–1907). Tutor to Alexander III and to Nicholas II. Jurist and conservative politician.

[43] Some more of the detailed discussion of the agrarian problem has been omitted here.

[44] Village assembly.

the electoral law seeks to exclude all forms of free electioneering. Although it permits assemblies of electors and delegated electors wishing to hold 'preparatory' discussions about the different candidates to take place without the police being present, permission to attend is restricted, on principle, to those entitled to vote in the district and to the delegated electors concerned, while the police are to control the admission of participants! In addition, an (incredible) exception to this principle is made in favour of the *official presiding* over the election (a Marshal of the Nobility or his representative), *even if he himself is not a voter or delegated voter*. At the same time, the law upholds the principle of election 'from the midst of one's own group' or 'from the numbers of those entitled to participate'. It is well known that the *de facto* application of this principle in elections in the United States greatly depresses the quality of the legislatures, which is doubtless one of the aims of this provision. All this is of more formal significance in the towns, but what the supervision of electoral meetings in the countryside means, especially amongst the peasants, is plain to everyone, and *above all* to the peasants themselves whose *cardinal demand* is the removal of official supervision. It is clear that the government cares *only* about the *immediate* effect of its measures, for thereby it has *permanently* given the radicals the most convenient (and most legitimate) argument for their campaigns of agitation. It is most probable that the government will 'succeed' in ensuring that the peasants' representatives are conservative, but every peasant will know that they do not represent *him*; and he will have one more reason to hate the bureaucracy.

In view of this, no one can say what the result of the peasant elections to the Duma will be. Generally, foreigners tend to expect the composition of the Duma to be extremely reactionary, as far as the peasant vote is concerned, whereas Russians, despite everything, expect its composition to be extremely revolutionary. Both could be right, and, more importantly, both could have exactly the same effect on the outcome. In modern European revolutions the peasants have generally swung from the most extreme radicalism imaginable to non-involvement or even to political reaction, once their immediate economic demands had been satisfied. Indeed there is probably no doubt that, *if* Russian autocracy were to issue a complete or partial edict to stuff the peasants' mouths with land, or if the peasants themselves seized the land during a period of anarchy and, one way or the other, were finally left in possession of it, the mass of the peasants would consider everything else settled and they would lose all interest in the form of government. In contrast to this view, the representatives of bourgeois democracy, and Struve in particular, take the view that a reactionary government would be *incapable* of meeting the peasants' demand for land, since this would entail the economic dispossession not only of the nobility but also of the Grand Princes and finally of the Tsar himself. According to this view, the interests of the peasants are incompatible with the interest of these powers in their own self-preservation. Yet, though the estates of the Imperial House have expanded enormously in absolute terms, they are not very extensive in comparison with the property in private ownership, and it is the latter which attracts the hatred of the peasants. In this case the question is: which and how many of the peasants' demands would democracy in its turn be able to satisfy? Naturally, Struve has declared his emphatic opposition to any simple confiscation of land. Equally naturally, however, the declaration in the Constitutional Democratic programme that the market value of land is *not* the price to be paid in compensation to its former owners, amounts to 'confiscation' from the 'bourgeois' point of view. Here the 'yield value principle' of our 'inheritance politicians' has been given a revolutionary twist.[45] Prince Trubetskoi was even afraid that Chuprov's proposal would drive the liberal nobility into Shipov's camp. Yet the nobility is a very heterogeneous stratum, reaching, as an Education Minister under Nicholas I once said, 'from the steps of the throne down into the ranks of the peasants' and it appears that some of them are not disinclined to hand over their land at the present time. Prince Dolgorukov said at the Liberal Agrarian Congress in Moscow that it was preferable to 'live at liberty in a country house without land than live, as now, in a fortress in the country'. However, the Congress of Agricultural Entrepreneurs, held behind closed doors in Moscow in December 1905, demanded ruthless repression. The land will at any rate cost any non-violent government enormous sums of *money*. Particularly in the south-east, but also in the north-east of this vast empire, there is land to be colonised if huge capital funds are made available for irrigation and (in Siberia) for forest clearing. Abolition of redemption

---

[45] Inheritance law (which Weber supported) was based an the taxable value of any land transferred by inheritance, whereas the price of land changing hands by sale was determined by the market rate.

payments, reduction of taxes on the peasants, the *Civil List* which would replace the land owned by the imperial family, the losses of demesne revenues, the capital funds for improvements, all these things amount to a huge reduction in state income and an equally huge increase in demand – all in all, therefore, much greater problems of financial procurement than the state has ever faced before. Ultimately, however, increased land will not in itself solve the agrarian problem. Indeed, if this is conceived as the *sole* measure to be adopted, it could very well threaten 'technical progress',[H] leaving peasants severely disappointed even after all their demands had been met. Finally and above all, the stage of development reached by the peasants today means that they can hardly be considered the 'bearers' or 'pillars' of agrarian policy; rather they must remain essentially the 'objects' of such a policy. In view of all this, any party seeking to carry out that reform by the *legal* route is not to be envied its task.

In contrast to all this, the government has so far merely agreed to the remission of redemption payments, to the extension (by new capital of 30 millions) of the activities of the rural bank for the transfer of manorial land into the hands of the peasants, and finally, in fairly vague terms, to initiate an agrarian reform that is to 'unite' the interests of the estate owners with those of the peasants. Despite all the 'committees' of recent years it is questionable whether the government has even the most general notions as to how this might be achieved. The question which will become one of prime and crucial importance, however, is how the government on the one hand and the peasants on the other will come to terms with the legal *right* of *every* peasant *to demand the allocation of his share as private property*, once redemption payments have been abolished.

The paths of the social reformist, liberal democrats in Russia are filled with renunciation. In the light both of their own understanding of their duty and of considerations determined by the demagogic

---

[H] Particularly in the regions exporting grain, the *operational* problem produced by the shortness of the growing season is quite unaffected by any specifically peasant policies. The decline of the *kustar*[46] and the domestic industry of the peasants as a result of capitalism and the satisfaction of needs in a money economy directly affect vital issues in peasant farms; on this point the 'Populists' are quite correct.

[46] A peasant who was also engaged in a cottage industry.

conduct of the old regime, they have no choice but to demand universal and equal suffrage unconditionally. Yet their own ideas could probably only achieve political influence if elections were held on a similar basis to the election of the zemstvo. Their duty requires them to join the support for a programme of agrarian reform which, in all probability, will greatly strengthen the essentially archaic communism of the peasants rather than voluntaristic socialism with all its economic and technical 'progress'. That programme will also promote the 'ethical' equalisation of life-chances as the economic practice and outlook of the masses rather than the economic selection of those who are 'commercially' most effective, thereby necessarily slowing down the development of the individualistic culture characteristic of Western Europe which most of the liberals regard as inevitable. The 'sated' type of German who cannot bear not to be on the side of the 'winning cause' (whichever it may be), his mind elated and his chest puffed up with his qualities as a practitioner of Realpolitik, can only look with pity on a movement like this. For the outward instruments of power of these people are of course slight, as the extremist Social Revolutionaries are constantly and scornfully pointing out. It is a fact that no one knows where they would be today if the deaths of Plehve and Grand Duke Sergei had not intimidated autocracy.[47] The only comparable weapon possessed by the liberals was the fact that the *officers* would not, in the long run, remain willing to act as the executioners of the families from which they themselves came for the most part. In fact the tactic recommended by the liberals has quite often been effective, namely to face the troops unarmed rather than provoke them into fighting by the use of bombs and armed resistance, as has repeatedly been done by a section of the Social Revolutionaries. Admittedly, this would have its limitations in dealing with a determined military leadership, and the insurrection in Moscow at the present moment will do *much* to promote discipline in the army. Apart from this there is another, specifically 'bourgeois' instrument of power which the Russian liberals do not, however, hold in their hands. If foreign financial powers had not indicated their own grave concern, not in so many words but through their actions, the Manifesto of 17 October[48] would perhaps not have come into being at all

---

[47] Plehve and Grand Duke Sergei Aleksandrovich were both assassinated by terrorists.
[48] In the 'Manifesto of 17 October 1905' Nicholas II proposed to widen the franchise and to give parliament a role in legislation.

or, if it had, would have been rescinded before long. Autocracy was *only* affected by fear of the fury of the masses, of mutiny amongst the troops and of the weakening effect on the authoritarian regime of the defeat in the east, because these things were linked to its dependence on the cool, hard hand of the banks and stock exchanges. The position of politicians like Witte and Timiryazev rests on this fact. When the Social Democratic newspaper *Nachalo*[49] described Count Witte as an 'agent of the stock exchange' there was of course a grain of truth in this primitive idea. It is unlikely that Witte has any definite convictions of any kind as far as the question of the constitution and internal government are concerned. At any rate, his various pronouncements on these matters flagrantly contradict one another and he also now habitually dissociates himself from the alleged 'misunderstandings' produced when statements attributed to him are recounted by people who are beyond suspicion, even when they were made during negotiations with party delegates, and not in confidential conversations. His interest is essentially directed at economic policy. Whatever else one may think of him, he has, for example, had the 'courage' (as he would see it) to endure the equally strong detestation of both the reactionary bureaucrats and the revolutionary [50] democrats for defending private property amongst the peasants, just as he is now attracting both the increased hatred of the Slavophiles and the personal dislike of the Tsar (which is in fact aggravated by the fact of his 'indispensability'). There is not the slightest doubt that he thinks along 'capitalist' lines, as do liberals in the mould of Struve. In place of Plehve's attempts to govern with the masses (under authoritarian leadership) against the middle classes, he would doubtless be very glad to see an understanding reached with the propertied classes against the masses. He, and perhaps he alone, is in a position to sustain Russia's credit and currency at the present moment, and he has certainly the will to do so. He is doubtless very well aware that it is an absolute requirement of this policy that Russia be transformed into a state under the rule of law (*Rechtsstaat*) with certain constitutional guarantees, and one may predict that, given the opportunity to do so, he would conduct domestic policy accordingly, so as to preserve Russia's position of financial power, since this has been

[49] 'The Beginning', an organ of the Russian Social Democratic Workers' Party.
[50] In the original edition the democrats were erroneously described as 'reactionary' rather than 'revolutionary'.

his life's work. Of course this is linked with the idea that a liberal regime which was to some extent 'sincere' would also strengthen the alliance with France politically. For Witte, however, and even more so for the Tsar and those around him, these motives for supporting a liberal policy are not infinitely strong. The only question is how large a burden these motives can be made to bear before they collapse, and before the notion of attempting a military dictatorship as the precursor of some form of sham constitutionalism gains the upper hand. Naturally, this idea is entirely feasible in the immediate future. Even if just a tenth of the officer corps and the troops remain at the disposal of the government – and the fraction would possibly be as high as nine-tenths – a revolt by even large numbers of people would not matter.[1] The stock exchange greeted the first blood on the streets of Moscow with a boom, and everything that has happened since then has shown how greatly this fact has strengthened the confidence of the forces of reaction and made Witte change his mind. Here, as elsewhere, the economic emergency that is bound to result from the terrible devastation of industry will paralyse the proletariat's fighting spirit once their political illusions have been dashed. Despite everything, the foreign observer is bound to consider it very possible that, for the time being, there will be a government which in practice will preserve the power of centralist *officialdom*, since this is what is really at stake. There is no doubt that the social powers which supported the previous regime are already more powerfully organised than appearances suggest. The chances of their resurgence were the greater, the more the sectarian small-mindedness of the 'professional socialists', even when faced with the gangs of murderers and arsonists employed by a body of police officials fighting for its life, directed the main attack of their supporters against the 'rival' bourgeois democratic parties whom they singled out for special abuse. However understandable it may be from a 'human' point of view, such behaviour is completely ineffectual in political terms and destroys all attempts to educate people in the ways of effective political action – as we in Germany know only too well. Their triumphant reward may well be to see the forces of reaction gain the upper hand entirely, or to watch broad sections of the propertied classes go over to the camp

---

[1] This is shown by the course of the Moscow uprising which is at its height now. Only an unfortunate *European* war would finally smash autocracy.

of the 'moderate' parties. They will thus have gained the right to indulge in bombastic phrase-mongering for yet another generation and – as is happening here – to enjoy the intoxicating thought that 'the world is full of such dreadfully bad people'.

*

On 20 November the Party of Legal Order offered Count Witte the help of strike-breakers if the threatened walk-out of post and telegraph workers were to take place. Such groups have been joined partly by the moderates from the Duma and zemstvo, partly by the bourgeoisie in the narrow sense (bankers and large industrialists), and partly by people who, like Krasovski, argued at the beginning of the zemstvo congresses that no constitution could be achieved but that they should demand legal guarantees of personal and press freedom – without, admittedly, being able to say what these freedoms would mean in practice if a constitution did not exist. Besides recognising the Manifesto of 17 October, to which the old conservative officials responded, notoriously, with the carnage of the Black Hundreds and which they perhaps hoped to sabotage, these categories share a more open indifference to religion. Otherwise the only definite thing one can say about all of them is that they are absolutely in favour of 'calm' and will assent to anything that will achieve this in any way. The Petersburg 'Union of Legal Order' supports Jewish suffrage, 'so that they calm down'; after a long debate the voters with the property franchise in Petersburg were in favour of Polish autonomy for the same reason; at other meetings of these voters it was claimed that maintaining instruction in the 'law of God' (the catechism) was indispensable for the maintenance of order, and the radical demand for the separation of state and church was rejected. Thus, in the end, they will all be content with any concessions the Tsar deigns to offer them. It is self-evident that their numbers would soar rapidly under pressure from revolts amongst the peasants and the soldiery, the threat of a general strike and the prevailing putschist tendency amongst Social Democrats. Quite naturally, the government (and Witte especially) also hoped that anarchy would have this effect and that, as Witte put it, 'society itself' would eventually demand the restoration of order (and, we may be permitted to add, that scope should be given to the slogan, '*Enrichessez vous!*') This is indeed what happened. Naturally, however, this development took place at the cost of constitutional zemstvo democracy. Prince Dolgorukov observed, in resigned tones, that the days of the zemstvo congresses were past. The hour of the ideological gentry was indeed past, and the power of material interests resumed its normal function. This process saw the elimination on the left of idealism that was capable of thinking politically, and on the right the elimination of the moderate Slavophiles whose aim was to extend the old *self-government* of the zemstvos. Neither of these things would cause Witte much pain. Yet, in effect, Witte's wait-and-see policy has probably served the interests of others, or rather it is likely that he did not have it in his power to do otherwise. Essentially, the Court probably regards him as a mere stop-gap who cannot be dispensed with at the moment because of the impression he makes abroad, particularly on the stock exchanges, and on account of his intelligence. For there has probably never been any doubt about the attitude of those elements in the government who are close to the *Court*. It is true that in some cases senior administrative officials were disciplined in those areas where the police took the initiative in organising the civil war after receiving seemingly quite genuine and wholly uncontested reports. Action was taken against them because of what people abroad might think, but the effect was 'to kick them upstairs' (as happened to our Prussian 'canal rebels').[51]

Yet Count Witte made no serious effort, or perhaps was unable to make any, to crush the ruthless obstruction by provincial officialdom which has not the slightest intention at present of believing that a constitutional regime will survive for long. It is understandable, but perhaps not quite accurate, that the liberals should feel there was a lack of 'honesty' in this – 'a rogue gives more than he has' – yet the obstacle lies at a higher level. Numerous measures by the Ministry of the Interior which were reported in the newspapers could have no other *effect* than alternately to incite the masses and then demonstratively to let go of the reins, until the Red Terror had intensified to the point where the time was ripe for the White Terror. It is *not* credible that this policy stemmed *exclusively* from weakness and confusion. What was wanted was 'revenge for 17 October'. There is no doubt that if the unrest was prolonged any further, the perhaps quite intentional and inevitable consequence of this would be to discredit

---

[51] An incident in 1899 in Prussia when twenty provincial officials protested against a plan of the Kaiser's to build a canal. They were paid off but many were later re-employed in higher positions.

all emancipatory movements, and above all the bourgeois-constitutional, *anti-centralist* liberalism which for decades has been hated equally by the reactionary and the rationalist state bureaucracy because of its importance for public opinion and because of its position in the self-governing bodies. If total anarchy set in for a while there would doubtless be even less hope for this type of liberalism than under the recrudescence of autocratic rule, the precursor of which, given prevailing conditions, would be a period of anarchy.

It is certainly correct that the congenital folly, not only of all radical politics, as some have said, but of all ideologically oriented politics of any kind, is the ability to 'miss opportunities'. When Vincke once refused to negotiate privately with the ministers of the 'New Era' in Prussia on the army bill that was to be introduced, on the grounds that this was not morally permissible for a representative of the people, and again in 1893, when the Liberals were a fraction of an hour too late in taking a decision which they did nevertheless take after the Reichstag had been dissolved – in both instances it was a fateful turning-point for the cause of liberalism. One tends to assume that a similar accusation can be levelled at the Russian liberals, judged from the standpoint of their own party policy; indeed some statements by Witte directly invite such a judgement. This was my *prima facie* impression in the autumn too. But the more closely one considers the situation, the more one is forced to suppose that the liberal politicians judged what was awaiting them more accurately than those remarks by Count Witte. In both the examples cited above the negotiations in question were undoubtedly 'sincerely' intended. In the present instance, however, absolutely *no* opportunity has been offered even to the 'most moderate' constitutional zemstvo liberalism, and it was therefore simply not in its power to alter the course of fate (just as it was not in Bennigsen's power in 1877 when he declined to enter Bismarck's ministry for better reasons than our historians usually assume).[52] Just as Louis XVI did not want, on any account, to be 'saved' by Lafayette of all people, nothing seems more certain than that Court circles and officialdom would rather make a pact with the devil than with zemstvo liberalism. Political antagonisms

---

[52] Bennigsen refused Bismarck's offer to appoint him as his Deputy and Prussian Minister in 1877. Bismarck could not accept Bennigsen's demand that two additional posts in the Prussian Ministry should be held by National Liberals.

within the same social stratum or between rival social strata are, after all, often the most keenly felt.

The furthest the government has gone towards 'meeting' the liberals was Count Witte's invitation to the Moscow *uprava* to send representatives of the zemstvo party to him for consultations. Their discussions took place on 27 October (old style) between Witte and the delegates Golovin, Prince L'vov and Kokoshkin. The crucial difference of opinion remaining between them at that time was that Count Witte wanted it left to the Imperial Duma, augmented by representatives of the working class, to carry out the introduction of a universal, equal and secret franchise, for which he gave an express assurance of his co-operation, whereas the delegates insisted that a Constituent Duma be convened on the basis of that franchise, as this was the only way public order could be secured. Yet underlying this ostensible difference, quite apart from the old distrust of the zemstvo people, was a set of historical circumstances clearly inimical to *any* understanding, namely the fact that Trepov[53] was still in possession of his powers; that he was later replaced by Durnovo,[54] whom respected individuals had accused in open letters to the press (citing the instances in detail) of taking money 'even in small sums' (of 12-15,000 roubles) for favours; that he was still in post; and that the demand for a precise declaration of the Manifesto of 17 October in a strictly constitutional sense *was not met*. Under these circumstances Witte's assurance that he 'felt closest' to the constitutional-democratic zemstvo party could not possibly command sufficient credence, particularly after his 'confidential memorandum' of 1899, in which he had stressed the incompatibility of the zemstvos with autocracy, thereby thwarting the general application of the zemstvo system which had been intended. Above all, despite the fact that Russia's situation 'cries out' for a 'statesman', the dynastic ambitions of 'personal rule' leave as little room for a great reformer there, even if one could be found, as they do elsewhere (in Germany, for example).

For the present this much seems certain: never for a single moment has the Tsar intended to reach a truly lasting and sincere understanding with these men, whom he described in the most unparliamentary

---

[53] D. F. Trepov (1855–1906). General Governor of St Petersburg and deputy Interior Minister in 1905.
[54] I. N. Durnovo (1830–1903). Interior Minister 1889–95. Chairman of the Committee of Ministers 1895–1903.

language just six months ago. If this 'factor' is included as an 'absolute given' in any calculations, then it is undoubtedly true that Russia is not 'ready' for sincere constitutional reform – but in this case the fault does not lie with the liberals. One is bound to reach the conclusion that, under these circumstances, it made no political sense at all for the zemstvo people to believe that any understanding favourable to liberalism could be reached with the government unless quite different guarantees were forthcoming. Its proponents could do no more than 'keep their shield bright' once they had completed their 'mission'[55] as far as the present moment allowed. It is quite possible, although not certain, that they must resign themselves for the immediate future to the thought that the movement of zemstvo liberalism has perhaps been 'consigned to history' for the time being, at least in the form it has taken hitherto, brilliant though it was in its way and although it was something of which Russia could be just as proud as we Germans are of the Frankfurt Parliament. This would probably be better for its future than a 'March Ministry'.[56] Only in this way can 'ideological' liberalism remain a 'force' in the realm of ideas, beyond the reach of outward coercion, and only in this way does it seem possible to restore the recently destroyed unity between 'bourgeois' intellectuals, whose power rests on property, broad education and political experience, and the 'proletaroid' intellectuals, whose importance rests on their numbers, their close contact with the 'masses' and their ruthless fighting spirit. This may happen once the proletarian intellectuals have been taught by the disappointments which await them to stop underestimating the real importance of the 'bourgeois' element, however much antipathy they may feel towards it on emotional grounds. The further development of capitalism will ensure the decay of 'populist' romanticism. There is no doubt that Marxism will generally take its place. But the work that needs to be done on the enormous and fundamental problem of agriculture simply cannot be carried out with the intellectual tools of Marxism, and it is precisely this problem which could re-unite these two strata of the 'intelligentsia'. It can clearly only be solved by the organs of self-government, and for this very reason it seems vitally important

---

[55] 'Mission' is in English.
[56] The King of Prussia's replacement of a Conservative minister by a Liberal in March 1848 was a compromise with the middle class which nevertheless preserved the Crown's prerogative of an absolute veto.

for liberalism to understand that its vocation still lies with the struggle against both bureaucratic and Jacobin *centralism*, and in working to spread the old, fundamental, individualist notion of 'inalienable human rights' amongst the masses, rights which have come to seem as 'trivial' to us in Western Europe as black bread is to a man who has enough to eat.

These axioms of 'natural justice' neither provide *unambiguous* instructions for a social and economic programme, nor are they themselves produced *solely* and *unambiguously* by any conditions, least of all by 'modern' ones.

The opposite is the case. Just as the fight for such 'individualist' values has to take account of the 'material' conditions of the surrounding world at every turn, equally the 'realisation' of such values simply could not be left to 'economic development'. The outlook for the chances of 'democracy' and 'individualism' would be very poor indeed if we had to rely for their development on the effects produced by the 'laws' of *material* interests. These interests point as clearly as can be in the opposite direction. The *housing for the new serfdom*[57] is ready everywhere: in America's 'benevolent feudalism',[58] in Germany's so-called 'welfare provisions', in the factory system in Russia, and it is just waiting for certain conditions to make the masses 'compliant' enough to enter it once and for all – a slow-down in the tempo of technical and economic 'progress', the victory of 'dividends' (*Rente*) over 'profits' (*Gewinn*), together with the exhaustion of the remaining 'free' land and markets. At the same time, the growing complexity of the economy, its partial takeover by the state or by municipalities, the territorial size of nations, all these things create ever more paper-

---

[57] '*Das Gehäuse für die neue Hörigkeit*' is one of the simpler instances of a complex and not always transparent metaphor ('*Gehäuse*') employed repeatedly by Weber throughout his writings. As the condition of '*Hörigkeit*' ('serfdom') meant that unfree peasants belonged to the estate of a feudal lord who protected them in return for their labour on the land, it is most likely that '*Gehäuse*' refers in this context to the primitive 'housing' of the serfs. Weber extends the sense of both terms metaphorically, however, by transferring them to the modern context where the individual worker gives up his freedom when he 'moves in' to the protective 'housing' of welfare provisions and factory labour.

[58] Weber is probably referring to T. Veblen, *The Theory of Business Enterprise* (New York, 1904), p. 176, who, in turn, is referring to W. J. Ghent, *Our Benevolent Feudalism* (New York and London, 1902). Veblen is discussing the trend towards the separation of the ownership of property and the management of the business enterprise. Veblen merely says that this gives 'a superficial resemblance to the feudal system'.

work, further division and specialisation of labour and specialist training for administrators, in other words: a caste. Those American
workers who were *opposed* to the Civil Service Reform knew what
they were doing. They preferred to be governed by upstarts of dubious morality rather than by a body of mandarins with a patent of
office; but their protest was in vain.

In view of all this, those people who live in constant fear that the
future will hold *too much* 'democracy' and 'individualism' and too
little 'authority', 'aristocracy' and 'respect for office' or such like,
really should put their minds at rest. The world will see to it, only
too certainly, that the trees of democratic individualism will not grow
up into the heavens.[59] All our experiences teach us that 'history' is
unremitting in spawning ever new 'aristocracies' and 'authorities' to
which anyone can cling if he feels he (or the 'people') needs to do
so. If the *only* things that mattered were 'material' conditions and the
constellations of interest directly or indirectly 'created' by them, any
sober observer would be bound to conclude that all *economic* auguries
point in the direction of a growing *loss* of freedom. It is quite ridiculous to attribute to today's high capitalism, as it exists in America and
is being imported into Russia, to this 'inevitability' of our economic
development, any 'elective affinity'[60] with 'democracy' or indeed
'freedom' (in *any* sense of the word), when the only question one can
ask is how all these things can 'possibly' survive at all in the long run
under the rule of capitalism. They are in fact only possible if they
are supported by the permanent, determined *will* of a nation not to
be governed like a flock of sheep. We are 'individualists' and partisans
of 'democratic' institutions 'against the tide' of material constellations. Anyone who wishes to be the weather-vane of a 'developmental
trend' should abandon these old-fashioned ideals as quickly as possible. The genesis of modern 'freedom' presupposed certain unique,
never-to-be-repeated historical constellations. Let us list the most
important of these. Firstly, expansion overseas; this wind from across
the seas blew through Cromwell's armies, through the French Constituent Assembly, and still blows today through our entire economic

---

[59] '*Es ist dafür gesorgt, daß die Bäume nicht in den Himmel wachsen*': a saying of Luther
adopted by Goethe as a motto for part 3 of his autobiography, *Dichtung und Wahrheit*.

[60] This was a term used in chemistry during the nineteenth century to describe the
propensity of certain chemicals to interact. Goethe used it as the title of his novel
Die Wahlverwandtschaften.

life. But now there is no new part of the world available. As in late antiquity, the main areas into which the population of Western culture is advancing unstoppably are great inland tracts, on the continent of America on the one hand and in Russia an the other – flat, monotonous spaces favourable to a schematic approach to life. Secondly, the peculiar economic and social structure of the 'early capitalist' epoch in Western Europe,[J] and thirdly the conquest of life by science, the 'coming-to-self of Mind'.[62] But the work of ordering our outward lives rationally has now been done, at least 'in principle', and doubtless after countless 'values' have been destroyed. The universal effect produced by the conditions of commercial life today is to make our outward lives uniform by 'standardising' production. Today 'science' (*Wissenschaft*) as such no longer creates a 'universal personality'. Finally, the specific 'ethical' character and 'cultural values' of modern man have been moulded by certain ideal notions of value which grew out of a particular set of religious ideas rooted in a concrete historical epoch, in conjunction with numerous other, equally specific, political constellations and the material preconditions mentioned above. One merely has to ask whether any material development, and particularly that of advanced capitalism today, is inherently capable of preserving these unique historical conditions or even of re-creating them, to know the answer immediately. It is not at all likely that taking the economy into social control (*Vergesellschaftung*) as such will necessarily bring about either the development of 'free' personalities or of 'altruistic' ideals. Do we find the seeds of anything like this in those people who, as they see it, are to be carried inevitably to victory by 'material developments'? 'Correct' Social Democracy is drilling the masses in intellectual parade-marching, directing their gaze, not to the paradise beyond (which, under the Puritans, performed very creditable services on behalf of 'freedom' in this world *too*), but towards paradise on earth, and turning this into a kind of vaccination against those

---

[J] A number of important features of early capitalism have been aptly characterised by Sombart.[61] Such things as 'conclusive' or 'final' historical concepts simply do not exist. However, I refuse to join in with the vanity of today's writers who take the same attitude to another person's terminology as they would to that person's toothbrush.

[61] W. Sombart, *Der moderne Kapitalismus*, vol. I (Leipzig, 1902) pp. 71f. and pp. 423ff.

[62] 'The development of Mind lies in the fact that its going forth and separation constitutes its coming to itself. The being-at-home-with self, or coming-to-self of Mind may be described as its complete and highest end', G. W. F. Hegel, *Lectures on the History of Philosophy*, vol. I, translated by E. S. Haldane (London, 1892), p. 23.

with vested interests in the prevailing order. It accustoms its pupils to submit to dogmas and party authorities, to the fruitless spectacles of mass strikes and to take inactive pleasure in the roars of rage from their prebendaries in the press, an enervating show which their opponents regard as being as harmless as it is laughable. It accustoms its followers, in other words, to a 'hysterical enjoyment of emotion' which displaces, and replaces, economic and political thought and action. The only thing which can grow on this barren soil, once the movement's 'eschatological epoch' has passed, and generation after generation have clenched their fists in their pockets or bared their teeth at the heavens, is intellectual stultification.

Yet time presses, and we 'must work while it is still day'.[63] An 'inalienable' sphere of freedom and personality must be won *now* for the individual who belongs to the great masses and who is thrown entirely on his own resources – *now*, in the course of the next few generations, while the economic and intellectual 'revolution', the much despised 'anarchy of production'[64] and equally despised 'subjectivism' are still at their height, since they, *and only they*, make it possible for the individual to attain these things. Once the world has become 'fully' developed economically and 'sated' intellectually, these spheres may *perhaps* never be conquered for the ordinary individual, at least as far as our weak eyes can see into the impenetrable mists of mankind's future.

No matter how severe her reverses in the immediate future prove to be, Russia is nevertheless irrevocably joining the trajectory of a specifically European development. The powerful influx of Western ideas is breaking down patriarchal and communist conservatism[65] there, just as a reverse process is at work in the United States where the mighty influx of Europeans and particularly of people from Eastern Europe is breaching the old democratic traditions. In both cases this is happening in concert with the powers of capitalism. As a later account may demonstrate more fully, there are certain respects in which, despite enormous differences, the economic peculiarity of capitalist development in the two 'communicating' reservoirs of popu-

---

[63] An approximate quotation from John 9, 4: 'I must work the works of him that sent me while it is day: the night cometh when no man can work.'

[64] 'Anarchy of production' is a phrase taken from Karl Marx, *Das Kapital*, vol. (Berlin, 1971), p. 502 and *passim*.

[65] Here Weber is referring to the traditional agrarian communism of the peasants.

lation is nevertheless comparable. In particular, it is inevitable that both should lack ties to 'history', something which works together with the 'continental' character of their almost limitless geographical territories. Even more important is the fact that a great deal depends on both developments; in a certain sense they are indeed perhaps the 'last' opportunities to build 'free' cultures 'from the bottom up'. 'Thousands of years had to pass before you entered life, and thousands more years wait in silence for what you will do with this life of yours'[66] – these words which Carlyle, a passionate believer in personality, wanted to cry out to every new individual can be applied equally and without exaggeration to the current situation in the United States and to that of Russia, partly as it is now and partly as it is likely to be after one more generation. This is why, regardless of all differences of national character and (let us admit it openly) probably also many differences of national interest, we cannot fail to be profoundly moved and affected as we watch the Russian struggle for liberation and the bearers of that struggle, whatever 'direction' and 'class' they may belong to.

The system of sham constitutionalism that is about to be introduced will in itself ensure that their work has not been in vain. For as far as the *negative* aspect of the problem is concerned, the view of the 'developmental theoreticians' will prove correct. In all probability, Russian autocracy, as it has existed until now, that is the centralist police bureaucracy, will have no choice but to dig its own grave, particularly if it now defeats its hated opponents. As far as its interest in self-preservation is concerned, there can be no such thing as 'enlightened' despotism. Yet for the sake of the prestige that is indispensable to it, it is obliged to join hands with precisely those economic powers which, under *Russian* conditions, are the bearers of irresistible 'enlightenment' – and decomposition. Struve and others appear to be right in saying that Russian autocracy is incapable of attempting to solve any of the great social problems without injuring itself fatally in the process.

By the time they appear in print, these lines will probably already be out of date. No one knows today what will then remain of the liberals' hopes that the foundations will be laid *now* for a libertarian reform that will break the hold of bureaucratic centralism, nor how

---

[66] Weber is probably quoting from memory. The source cannot be found.

many of these hopes will simply have disappeared into thin air like a mirage. This latter possibility need not take the form of an undisguised restoration of the old order. Rather, it is fairly certain that something like a 'constitution' will be created or preserved, along with greater latitude for the press and personal freedom of movement. Even the most convinced advocates of the old regime have probably realised that the bureaucracy will itself be reduced to stumbling in the dark if it blocks up every door and window. The experiences of others elsewhere could lead them to hope that a show of constitutionalism, in combination with some form of economically oriented 'policy of national solidarity',[67] could offer a much more suitable and effective tool with which to defend their position of power than crude, so-called 'autocracy'. At any rate one inevitable result of this would be a certain increase in freedom of movement, which does at least have some importance to modern people who have lived under a dictatorial regime notorious for having driven members of proverbially 'peaceable' sections of the population onto the streets in violent rage, where they then shot down, not one of the 'great', but any poor policeman they happened to find. In the process, however, the people with the most character and independence amongst the social reformist bourgeois intelligentsia would of course be pushed to the political sidelines, both personally and as far as their programme is concerned. In this respect the bureaucracy of the autocratic regime would indeed reap even now the fruits of the demagogic policies it has pursued for years, cultivating capitalism on the one hand while on the other hand suppressing any orderly development of bourgeois independence and playing the social classes off against one another. For *today* it would perhaps be difficult to involve liberal intellectuals in any constitutional, anti-centralist reform designed to last or to satisfy anybody, even if the monarch himself were to feel the vocation and inclination to play the role of liberal reformer. It is quite unlikely that a group so hated by the bureaucracy would be allowed to lay down the law. But it is equally true that a victory for those with vested interests in bureaucratic power, which, as things stand, *now* strikes the outside observer not merely as possible but as very likely (even if it takes place under constitutional forms), would not be the last word on the

---

[67] The *Sammlungspolitik* to which Weber refers was the policy formulated by Miquel in 1897 which aimed to stop the advance of the Social Democrats by creating an alliance of agrarian and industrial interests that would be able to dominate the Reichstag.

subject in Russia, just as the erstwhile Prussian *Landratskammer* was not the last word here.[68] No matter how pliable the 'popular assembly' produced by the elections is, it will mean nothing. It will simply feed the hatred felt by every peasant throughout the vast empire towards the *chinovniki*,[69] even if the silence of the graveyard descends on the whole country. For, whatever happens, it is unlikely that the events, promises and hopes of the last year will be forgotten. The movement will come to life again whenever this tightrope-walking machinery of state shows a moment of weakness. Despite the apparent refinement of its technique of government, the horrifying poverty of 'spirit' exhibited in public by this supposedly strong regime is bound to stick very firmly in the minds of the broad mass of the population. Yet, for the sake of its own security, the present system cannot make fundamental changes to its method of *government* either. Its political traditions, too, oblige it to permit the continued operation of the *political* forces – bureaucratisation of the administration and police demagogy – which are bringing about its own decomposition, and constantly driving its economic ally, the propertied classes, onto the side of its opponents. But the illusions and the nimbus with which it surrounded itself and which once obscured this development have now been utterly dispelled. After all that has taken place between the Tsar and his subjects, it will be difficult for the system not 'to lose face' and to start the old game over again in some new variant. There are now far too many who have seen its nakedness and who are bound to tell it to its face, with a smile, 'Conjurer! You will summon up no more spirits'.[70]

---

[68] *Landratskammer* was the name given to the Prussian House of Deputies during the era of Manteuffel, 1850–9, in which many seats were taken by officially favoured provincial superintendents.

[69] A derogatory term for officials.

[70] Friedrich Schiller, *Der Geisterseher*, *Sämtliche Werke*, vol. II (Stuttgart/Berlin, 1905),

Between Two Laws

The discussion (in *Die Frau*)[1] about the meaning and purpose (*Sinn*) of our war could perhaps be augmented by placing more emphasis on a point, the importance of which you in particular will readily appreciate, namely *our responsibility before history* – I can only put it in these rather pathetic terms. The facts themselves are plain enough.

Any numerically 'large' nation organised as a *Machtstaat* finds that, thanks to these very characteristics, it is confronted by tasks of a quite different order from those devolving on other nations such as the Swiss, the Danes, the Dutch or the Norwegians. There is of course a world of difference between this assertion and the view that a people which is 'small' in numbers and in terms of power is thereby less 'valuable' or less 'important' before the forum of history. It is simply that such nations, by their very nature, have different obligations and therefore other cultural possibilities. You are familiar with Jakob Burckhardt's arguments, which have caused so much astonishment, about the diabolical nature of power.[2] In fact this evaluation is a wholly consistent one, when considered from the standpoint of those cultural values which have been entrusted to a people, such as the Swiss, who are not able to bear the armour of great military states and who therefore have no historical obligation so to do. We too have every reason to be grateful for the fact that a branch of the German

---

[1] 'Zwischen zwei Gesetzen' appeared in *Die Frau. Monatschrift für das gesamte Frauenleben unserer Zeit*, February 1916. The piece was an 'open letter' to the editor of the journal. The title may not have been Weber's own.

[2] 'Now power is of its nature evil, whoever wields it', J. Burckhardt (1818–97), *Reflections on History* (Indianapolis, 1979), p. 139.

race (*ein Deutschtum*) exists outside the boundaries of the national *Machtstaat*. Only communities which renounce political power are able to provide the soil on which other virtues may flourish: not only the simple, bourgeois virtues (*Bürgertugenden*) of citizenship and true democracy, which has never yet been realised in any great *Machtstaat*, but also much more intimate and yet eternal values, including artistic ones. As true a German as Gottfried Keller[3] would never have become the quite particular, unique phenomenon he was, had he lived within a military encampment such as our state is obliged to be.

Conversely, the demands placed on a people organised as a *Machtstaat* are inescapable. Future generations, and particularly our own successors, would not hold the Danes, the Swiss, the Dutch or the Norwegians responsible if world power – which in the last analysis means the power to determine the character of culture in the future – were to be shared out, without a struggle, between the regulations of Russian officials on the one hand and the conventions of English-speaking 'society'[4] on the other, with perhaps a dash of Latin *raison* thrown in. They would hold *us* responsible, and quite rightly so, for we are a *Machtstaat* and can therefore, in contrast to those 'small' nations, throw our weight into the balance on this historical issue. That is why we, and not they, have the accursed duty and obligation to history and to the future to resist the inundation of the entire world by those two powers. If we were to refuse this duty, the German Reich would have proved to be an expensive and vain luxury, injurious to culture, a luxury which we ought not to have allowed ourselves and which we should get rid of as soon as possible by reshaping our state on the Swiss model,[5] dissolving it into small, politically impotent cantons, possibly with provincial courts well disposed to the arts. Then we should wait and see just how long our neighbours would permit us to continue cultivating at our leisure those cultural values of a small nation which were supposed to provide the meaning and purpose (*Sinn*) of our existence for ever more. It would be a grave error, however, to suppose that a political entity like the German Reich could simply decide, *voluntarily*, to embrace a pacifist policy of the kind adopted, say, in Switzerland, limiting itself, in other

---

[3] Gottfried Keller (1819–90), Swiss writer.
[4] Weber uses the English word.
[5] 'Verschweizerung', the term used by Weber, has a condescending tone, suggesting a reduction not only of scale but of importance.

words, to the maintenance of a sturdy militia to counter any violation of its borders. In principle at least, a political formation like Switzerland is not an obstacle to anyone's plans for political power – although she too would immediately be exposed to Italian ambitions for annexation if we were to be defeated. This results both from her powerlessness and her geographical situation. The very existence of a great power like Germany, however, is an obstacle in the path of other *Machtstaaten*, particularly of Russia with its peasants, hungry for land because of the lack of culture[6] there, and the power interests of the Russian state church and bureaucracy. It is absolutely impossible to conceive of any means whereby this state of affairs could have been altered. Of all the great powers, Austria was surely the one least affected by the urge to expand, and yet *precisely because of this* it was the most threatened – something that is all too easily overlooked. Our only choice was either to thrust our hands into the spokes of the wheel of history at the last possible moment before the destruction of Austria, or to stand by and watch this happen – and to allow ourselves to be crushed under the same wheel a few years later. And this is how things will remain in the future unless the Russian drive for expansion can be diverted in some other direction. That is fate, and no amount of pacifist talk will alter the fact. It is equally clear that, even if we wanted to, we could never again draw back, *without disgrace*, from the choice we made when we created the Reich, nor from the duties we assumed when we did so.

The pacifism of American 'ladies' (of both sexes) is truly the worst cant[7] ever to have been proclaimed – quite naively – from any teatable, combined as it is with the pharisaical attitude of the parasite who is making good profits from supplying war materials towards the barbarians in the trenches. The Swiss too, with their anti-militarist 'neutrality' and their rejection of the *Machtstaat*, exhibit on occasion a fair measure of pharisaical incomprehension of the tragic historical obligations incumbent on any nation organised as a *Machtstaat*. Nevertheless, we still remain objective enough to recognise the quite genuine kernel in their position; at the same time, however, it is one which we, as Germans living within the Reich, cannot adopt because of our particular fate.

---

[6] *Kultur* is used here, as it was in the 'The Nation State and Economic Policy' (p. 5 above), to include technical and agricultural progress.

[7] Weber uses the English word.

The New Testament, however, should either be left out of such discussions entirely or it must be taken *seriously*. In this case one has to be as consistent as Tolstoy. Nothing less will do. Anyone who has even a penny of investment income which others have to pay directly or indirectly, anyone who owns any durable goods or consumes any commodity produced not by his own sweat but by that of others, lives off the operation of that loveless and unpitying economic struggle for existence which bourgeois phraseology designates as 'peaceful cultural work'. This is just another form of man's struggle with man, one in which not millions but hundreds of millions of people, year after year, waste away in body or soul, sink without trace, or lead an existence truly much more bereft of any recognisable 'meaning' (*Sinn*) than the commitment of everybody (including women, for they too are 'fighting' the war if they do their duty) to the cause of honour, which means, simply, commitment to the historical obligations imposed on one's own nation by fate. The position of the Gospels is absolutely unambiguous on the decisive points. They are in opposition not just to war, of which they make no specific mention, but ultimately to each and every law of the social world, if this seeks to be a *place of worldly 'culture'*, one devoted to the beauty, dignity, honour and greatness of man as a creature of this earth. Anyone unwilling to go this far – and Tolstoy only did so as death was approaching – should know that he is bound by the laws of this earthly world, and that these include, for the foreseeable future, the possibility and inevitability of wars fought for power, and that he can only fulfil the 'demand of the day',[8] whatever it may be, *within* the limits of these laws. This demand was and is different for Germans living in Germany from that which is placed on Germans living in Switzerland, say. And so it will remain, for everything that shares in the goods of the *Machtstaat* is inextricably enmeshed in the law of the 'power pragma' that governs all political history.

That old sober empiricist, John Stuart Mill, once said that, simply on the basis of experience, no one would ever arrive at the existence of *one* god – and, it seems to me, certainly not a god of goodness – but at polytheism.[9] Indeed anyone living in the 'world' (in the

[8] An allusion to J. W. Goethe, *Maximen und Reflexionen*, No 442–3 (Weimar, 1907).
[9] Weber is referring to J. S. Mill *Three Essays on Religion*, first published in 1874 and translated into German in 1875. These essays can be found in the *Collected Works of John Stuart Mill*, vol 10, ed. J. M. Robson (Toronto and London, 1969).

Christian sense of the word) can only feel himself subject to the struggle between multiple sets of values, each of which, viewed separately, seems to impose an obligation on him. He has to choose which of these gods he will and should serve, or when he should serve the one and when the other. But at all times he will find himself engaged in a fight against one or other of the gods of this world, and above all he will always find that he is far from the God of Christianity – or at least from the God proclaimed in the Sermon on the Mount.

Suffrage and Democracy in Germany[1]

The complex and many-faceted problem of democracy will be dealt with in this paper only as it affects the situation at the present moment *here in Germany*. We shall go straight into the topic without further ado and without reflections of a general kind.

As is generally known, the present franchise for elections to the Reichstag was introduced by Bismarck for purely demagogic reasons in his famous ultimatum to the Frankfurt Federal Diet when he championed this principle in the face of grave reservations from the liberals of the time. His motives had to do partly with foreign policy objectives, and partly with the domestic political aim of realising his Caesarist ambitions in defiance of the (at that time) recalcitrant middle classes. Admittedly, his hopes that the masses would respond conservatively were disappointed, but the splitting of precisely those social strata which are so characteristic of the structure of modern society into two classes existing in close proximity and hence in hostility to one another (the bourgeoisie and the proletariat) later made it possible (as Prince Hohenlohe observed) to exploit the *cowardice* (Hohenlohe called it 'timidity') of the bourgeoisie in the face of 'democracy' and thereby preserve the rule of the bureaucracy.[2] This cowardice is still having its effects today. The fact that it was perfectly possible to be a democrat

---

[1] *Wahlrecht und Demokratie in Deutschland* (Berlin–Schöneberg, 1917). This was first published in brochure form as the second in a series entitled 'Der deutsche Volksstaat. Schriften zur inneren Politik' ('German Democracy. Writings on domestic politics').
[2] A reference to a remark made by Prince Chlodwig zu Hohenlohe-Schillingsfürst to Bismarck in 1878 concerning the draft of his anti-socialist legislation.

and yet to reject Lassalle's[3] enthusiasm for that form of franchise under the circumstances of the time, is evident, for example, from the position taken by Eduard Bernstein[4] in his introduction to Lassalle's writings. Considered purely in terms of national politics (*staatspolitisch*), one could very well ask whether there was not some advantage for the internal and external consolidation of the new Reich during the first few decades of its existence in having voting arrangements which gave rather more privileges to those sections of society which were economically and socially prominent and (at that time) politically educated, more or less along the lines of the previous franchise arrangements in England. In particular, this might have made it easier to accustom people to responsible participation in the work of parliament. We do not wish to engage here in doctrinaire 'suffrage orthodoxy', but the example of Austria under Count Taaffe shows that all bourgeois (*bürgerlich*) parties kept in power solely by electoral privileges can no longer leave the weapon of threatening equal suffrage in the hands of officialdom, without this weapon being turned against those parties whenever there is a serious threat to bureaucratic power interests. The German middle-class parties would have experienced exactly the same thing at Bismarck's hands if they had rejected equal suffrage. And the example of Hungary teaches us that even where a politically astute ruling nationality has the most powerful interests in opposing equal suffrage this will not permanently prevent the competing political parties of that nationality from using the slogan of equal suffrage in their struggle with one another, thereby giving currency to the idea and ultimately leading to its introduction. It is not by chance that political opportunities keep presenting themselves at which the topic gets raised. However things may be elsewhere, there can be no doubt that in Germany since Bismarck's day no other form of suffrage can ever again be the *outcome* of disputes about suffrage. Whereas other questions of suffrage (e.g. proportional representation), although of great political importance, are felt to be 'technicalities', the issue of equal suffrage is felt, subjectively, to be such a purely political one that it *must* be settled once and for all if we are to avoid sterile conflicts. This alone is crucial as far as national politics are concerned. Yet 4 August 1914 and the

---

[3] F. Lassalle (1825–64), one of the founders of German social democracy and of the labour movement.

[4] E. Bernstein (1850–1932), a leader of the 'revisionist' wing in German socialism.

days that followed it also demonstrated that this form of suffrage will prove its worth when put to a decisive political test, provided people understand how to govern with it and have the good will to do so. It would function just as well *permanently* if equal voting rights imposed on the elected the responsibility of *persons with a real share and say in the power of the state.* Democratic parties which *share in government* are bearers of nationalism everywhere.

It is only natural that nationalism should be spreading amongst the masses in particular in an age that is becoming increasingly democratic in the way it provides access to the goods of national culture, the bearer of which is, after all, the *language* of the nation. Even the truly modest measure of actual, and precarious, participation conceded to the representatives of radical democracy in Germany during the war was sufficient to persuade them to place themselves at the service of objective (*sachlich*) *national* politics – in stark contrast to the plutocrats in the Prussian Diet who could actually think of nothing better to do in the third year of the war than to discuss a bill proposing the *ennoblement of war profits.*[5] Instead of making available new agricultural land in the east of Germany – and we could supply the men for ten army corps from new peasant smallholdings – German soil was to be handed over, behind the backs of the fighting army, to feed the vanity of a new plutocracy grown rich from the war, by creating on it fee-entailed estates for men ambitious to attain the patent of nobility. This fact alone is sufficient criticism of the class-based franchise.[6]

The inner untenability of this form of franchise and of all those which operate in a similar manner is in any case perfectly obvious. If the Prussian three-class structure were to remain in operation the entire mass of the returning *fighting men* would find itself in the lowest class, bereft of influence, whereas membership of the privileged classes would fall to *those who stayed at home* – to those who had

---

[5] Weber had argued against this proposal in his article 'Die Nobilitierung der Kriegsgewinne' (itself the second part of 'Deutschlands äußere und Preußens innere Politik'), published in the *Frankfurter Zeitung*, 1 March 1917 and reprinted in Weber, *Gesamtausgabe* I15, pp. 206–14.

[6] A reference to the electoral system in operation for the Prussian House of Deputies since 1849. This divided the electorate into three classes on the basis of the amount of tax paid and distributed the suffrage accordingly, with each class electing one third of the delegates (*Wahlmänner*) for each electoral district. The intended result was to favour the interests of those with property. Given the dominant position of Prussia in the *Bundesrat* relative to other states, this arrangement had important consequences for the politics of the Reich.

meanwhile fallen heir to the jobs or clients of the fighting men, to those who had grown rich in or through the war or who had at least been spared by it, to those whose existing or newly acquired property had been defended with the blood of the men who had fought in the field and who had been politically declassed by the war. Certainly, politics is not an ethical business. But there does nevertheless exist a certain minimum of shame and obligation to behave decently which cannot be violated with impunity, even in politics.

What other form of suffrage could replace this class-based one? All manner of plural voting rights are very popular with the littérateurs. But which is it to be? Should people with families, say, be privileged by granting them additional votes? The lowest strata of the proletariat and peasants on the poorest soil, in fact all strata with the weakest economic prospects, marry earliest and have the greatest number of children. Or should 'education' – the fondest dream of the littérateurs – be the basis? There is no doubt that educational difference is nowadays the most important difference giving rise to true social '*estates*' (*Stände*), in contrast to the stratifying effect of possessions and economic function (which create differences of *class*). It is essentially the social prestige of education that enables the modern officer to assert his authority at the front or enables the modern official to do so within the social community. However much one may regret the fact, differences of 'education' are one of the very strongest social barriers which operate in a purely inward way. This is particularly true of Germany, where almost all privileged positions within and outside the public service are tied not only to a qualification in some *specialised* area of knowledge but also to 'general *education*' (*Bildung*), an objective served by the entire school and university system. All our examination diplomas attest above all to the fact that an individual is in possession of this important attribute of social *status*. Education could, then, be the basis for structuring the franchise. But which degree of education? Should political 'maturity' be attested by the university doctorate-factories or by the middle-school leaving certificate, or perhaps by the certificate reducing military service to just one year?[7] The numerical differences involved in each of these cases would be enormous, and politically quite peculiar results

---

[7] During the war it was possible to leave school with a leaving certificate after completing only part of the final course of study, provided one volunteered for one year's military service.

could flow from the third and numerically most significant option if it were used as the basis of an entitlement to multiple votes. Above all, however, we must ask whether further privileges ought really to be given to the *examination* diploma to which the bulk of all offices are handed over in any case, and thus to the stratum, with all its social pretensions, that is qualified thereby. Should power over the state be put in the hands of the certificated candidates for office with their hunger for prebends, whose numbers now greatly exceed demand thanks to competition amongst the universities for student numbers and the social ambitions of parents for their children? What does *political* 'maturity' have to do with a doctorate in physics or philosophy or philology? Every entrepreneur or trade union leader, men who are made acutely aware of the structure of the state every day through their participation in the free fight for economic life,[8] knows more about politics than a man for whom the state is simply the payments-office from which, thanks to his educational qualifications, he receives a secure, pensionable income commensurate with his social status.

Or should we introduce a '*middle-class franchise*' – one of the favourite intellectual offspring of all short-sighted 'law and order philistines' by privileging, say, the proprietors of 'independent' businesses and the like. Quite apart from the fact that this too would put *those who stayed at home* at an advantage over the fighting men, what would it mean for the 'spirit' of German politics in the future?

At present, only *three* of the economic determinants of Germany's future can be predicted with any certainty. Firstly, there is a need for economic work to be enormously *intensified* and *rationalised* – not so as to make German life rich and glittering, but simply in order to make life at all *possible* for the masses in our country. In view of the iron-hard spring that peace will bring us, it is a crime for the littérateurs, of whatever persuasion, to claim that the German 'will to work' is the nation's original sin and to propose a more 'easy-going' way of life as an ideal for the future. These are the *parasitic ideals* of a stratum of prebendaries and *rentiers* who have the impertinence to judge the hard daily struggle of their fellow citizens who are engaged in physical and mental work against standards dreamed up at their

---

[8] Weber is still using the Darwinian language of the 'struggle for existence' first found in his inaugural lecture (p. 2 above).

writing-desks. While these littérateurs may childishly imagine that Germany will enjoy as a fruit of the war the 'blessing' of a return to the contented work of the good old days, reality will look very different, as is clear from the second incontestable fact about the future, namely that the war will bestow on us *new rentiers* with capital amounting to 100,000 million marks. Even before the war the statistical rise in the relative numbers of pure *rentiers* had become worryingly large in a nation dependent on its ability to compete with the great working nations of the world. The citizens working in the economy will have to provide the unearned income for this enormously swollen stratum in society. In part, the transformation is evident from the growth of vast new paper fortunes, and partly from the way existing fortunes are being transformed by subscriptions to public bonds. For what does it *mean* when someone with a fortune now holds it in state securities in his bank deposit rather than in equities (that is shares in private enterprises)? Formally speaking, he is a '*rentier*' in both cases, someone whose income the banks provide when they snip off his dividend coupon. Formerly, however, when his income was produced by share certificates, it meant that hard, demanding *work* had been done somewhere, in a firm's accounts room or management office (places of intellectual work which is as good as, and often better than, that done in any academic's study), or in the machine-rooms of factories where commercial and technical managers, officer-workers, master-craftsmen and workmen are busy producing goods to satisfy an existing mass demand, creating men's pay and bread, all this as perfectly or imperfectly as the present economic order (which will be with us for a long time to come) permits. What the shares-dividend 'proves' is that men have fought and won a battle for a share of the market, a fight in which the managers' social and economic rank and power were at stake, as were the jobs at which the office and factory workers earned their bread. If, by contrast, the investor now receives his interest from state bonds this means that the tax-collector or exciseman or some such official has succeeded in extracting the money from the pockets of those obliged to pay taxes and has been paid for his efforts, and that the prescribed work in state offices has been duly performed in accordance with regulations and instructions. Of course *both* forms of work have to be done, work for the state and work in private industry. But it is as plain as can be that the whole economic and political future of Germany, the basic living standards of the masses *and* the provision of the means for 'cultural needs' depend *in the first instance* on there being no reduction in the intensity of productive *economic* work in Germany, and on the German nation experiencing no further expansion than has already taken place of what one might call the *rentier-mentality*, the typical mental attitude to economic life of the petit bourgeois and peasant strata in *France*. For this would mean the economic paralysis of Germany and an even more rapid spread than at present of the two-child family. It would also give rise to another feature of conditions in France, namely dependence on the *banks*. The ignorance of the littérateurs who do not recognise the difference between the *unearned fortune* of the coupon-cutting investor and the *productive capital* of the entrepreneur, and who show as much *ressentiment* towards the latter as they do covetous benevolence towards the former, have heard something of the role played in France's parliamentary regime by 'finance capital', both in regulations of a material kind (taxes) and in the selection of ministers, and they think of course that this is a consequence of the 'parliamentarism' they fear. In truth, however, it results from the fact that France is a nation of *rentiers*, that the *credit-worthiness of whatever government is in power*, as expressed in the stock-market value of government bonds, is the single most important question for the millions of small and medium-sized investors in assessing the worth of ministers, and that *this* is the reason why the banks are so often involved in, or are even consulted about, the selection of ministers. Every government would *be bound* to take account of their views, regardless of whether it was monarchic or parliamentary or plebiscitarian, in exactly the same way as did a debtor state such as Tsarist Russia in 1905, which first wrote its 'constitution' and then carried out a 'coup d'état', and did so in each case because these things were demanded by the mood on the foreign stock-exchanges supplying the state with credit. Any progressive extension here of state-financed activities[9] funded by issuing state bonds, and particularly any growth in the numbers of medium and small investors in such securities, would have exactly the same consequences here, regardless of whether we have 'democracy', 'parliamentarism' or 'monarchic' government. The relation of the *English*

---

[9] The word used by Weber is *Verstaatlichung* which often equates to the English 'nationalisation'. Here, however, Weber is referring to the various arguments current at the time for state direction of industry rather than for socialism in the strict sense.

state to capitalism, by contrast, was primarily a relation with *entrepren-eurial* capitalism (*Erwerbskapitalismus*) which served to spread Eng-land's power and people across the face of the earth. It is a weighty question in its own right to know which measures of financial policy could be introduced in Germany at present in order to shed the suffocating burden of *interest payments* on government issues while yet doing justice to the claims and expectations of subscribers. In the area of economic policy, at any rate, the maximum rationalisation of economic work, giving economic rewards to rational economies in production, in other words to 'progress' in this technical–economic sense – whether one loves it or hates it – is a question of vital import-ance, not only for the position of the nation in the world but simply to enable the nation to have any kind of tolerable existence at all. Thus it is a compelling political necessity for us to grant to those who are the bearers of this rational work at least that minimum level of political influence which only *equal* voting rights can give them. On this one essential issue, the *rationalisation* of the economy, the interests of the workers and those of the entrepreneurs occupying the *highest* organisational positions, despite all their social antagon-isms, are identical; and both sets of interests are identical with the political interest in maintaining the nation's position in the world, if not in every detail then at least *in principle*, and they are diametrically opposed to the interests of all those strata in society who live from prebends and all those spokesmen for economic stagnation who share the same outlook. It seems to be high time for the influence of those strata to be brought to bear on something which has perhaps already been so fundamentally mismanaged as to cast a shadow over our future. For the third, completely certain prospect for the future is that our economy will be a '*transitional*' one for years to come, with rationing of raw materials, the allocation of international currency, and possibly even of firms themselves and their clients. It is clear that this can be a unique opportunity *either* to *rationalise* the economy *or*, conversely, for a host of 'middle class' (*mittelständlerische*) experi-ments in the worst conceivable sense of this almost universally mis-used word. By using a system of state rationing and related devices it would be possible to subsidise all manner of 'independent' mendicant existences, a mass of beggarly but comfortable existences behind a *shop counter*, the ideal of every small capitalist. This would result in the very opposite of an intensified and rationalised economy. It would breed parasites and layabouts, bearers of that 'leisurely' way of life which our littérateurs regard as the ideal for the future. What would this mean? It would mean the *'Austrianisation' of Germany*, and would do so precisely in relation to the very thing that the Austrians themselves regard as the main source of everything they call 'slovenliness' in their own country. For, though we can learn much from them in the areas of good taste and social education, we would not have the slightest reason to be grateful if we were to emulate their 'policy on the middle classes', the wondrous fruits of which can be studied in fat volumes recording decisions on questions such as whether putting nails into a chair is the work of an upholsterer or a joiner. The danger that something similar might happen here is not inconsiderable, for there are undoubtedly politicians in influential circles today who are incorrigibly of the opinion that the foundations of what *they* call 'monarchic convictions' (*Gesinnung*) could best be laid on the stinking swamp of laziness and slovenliness that such a policy would create, that beery compliancy which would do nothing to challenge the power of the *bureaucracy* and the forces of economic reaction. If one imagines electoral privileges being granted to those strata which a policy of this kind would like to breed, the effects are easy to foresee: it would *paralyse Germany*, both politically and economically. If *anyone* wants to see this paralysis come about for some positive religious or ultimate metaphysical reason, let him confess it openly. One should *not*, however, want this simply out of craven *cowardice in the face of democracy*. Yet precisely this kind of cowardice, the fear that the legitimacy of existing property and social positions will be undermined, is the central motive for doing so at the moment.

To the amateurish pipe-dreams constantly being produced by the instincts of German littérateurs belong all those non-ideas which circulate under the label of an 'assembly based on *occupational corporations*' (*berufsständische Vertretung*).[10] These ideas are connected with all sorts of confused notions about the future of our economic organ-

---

[10] The idea of political representation based upon 'occupational corporations' (*berufsständische Vertretung*) as an alternative to parliamentary government had much support throughout the nineteenth and early part of the twentieth century both in Germany and in other parts of Europe, where it often went under the name of 'corporatism'. Weber is probably referring to the contemporary ideas of, among others, W. Rathenau and W. von Moellendorf.

isation. It will be recalled that even the way accident insurance was organised in occupational cooperatives gave rise to (and partly originated in) the expectation amongst influential circles of littérateurs that this was the first step towards an 'organically structured' national economy; the reader may also be aware of what became of this. Today some people even expect that the economic organisations of the future, which will be mainly governed by considerations of finance and currency policy, will slay the dragon of '*capitalism*', the father of everything evil and source of all unrest. Some people are childish enough to imagine that the 'communal economy', the 'economy based on solidarity', the 'cooperative economy', and such-like slogans, which emerged during the war and from the compulsory organisations to which it gave rise, will be the forerunners of a fundamental change of 'economic principle' (*Wirtschaftsgesinnung*) in the future that will resurrect the lost 'economic morality' of the past at some higher, 'organic' stage of development. What makes anyone who is familiar with the reality of these matters so impatient with these littérateurs is, above all, their profound ignorance of the nature of capitalism. The least offensive example of this is their failure, in their blissful ignorance, to see any difference between the war profits of the Krupp concern and those of some little black-marketeer in malt, since both, as they say, are products of 'capitalism' after all. Much more significant is the fact that they have not the faintest idea of the gulf of difference separating the kind of capitalism which lives from some momentary, purely *political* conjuncture – from government contracts, financing wars, black-market profiteering, from all the opportunities for profit and robbery, the gains and risks involved in adventurism, all of which increased enormously during the war – and the calculation of profitability that is characteristic of the bourgeois *rational conduct of business* (*Betrieb*) in peacetime. As far as the littérateurs are concerned, what actually happens in the accounts office of this type of business is a book with seven seals. They do not know that the underlying 'principles' – or 'ethics', if this term is preferred – of these two different types of capitalism are as mutually opposed as it is possible for two mental and moral forces to be. They have not the slightest inkling that one of them, the 'robber capitalism' tied completely to politics, is as ancient as all the military states known to us, while the other is a specific product of modern European man.

If one *wants* to make ethical distinctions (and that is at least possible here), the peculiar situation is as follows: the brazen[11] casing (*Gehaüse*) which gives economic work its present stamp and fate was created and is maintained precisely by the – in terms of personal business *ethics* (*Geschäftsethik*) highest *rational* – capitalist *operational ethics* (*Betriebsethik*) of this second type of 'capitalism', the ethics of professional duty and professional honour, which, generally speaking, stand far above the average economic ethics which have *really* existed in *any* historical age (as opposed to those which have merely been *preached* by philosophers and littérateurs). Of course, the fate and character of economic life will be determined increasingly and irrevocably by this rigid casing if the *opposition* between state bureaucracy and the bureaucracy of private capitalism is replaced by a system of bringing firms under 'communal control' by a *unitary* bureaucracy to which the workers will be subordinated and which would no longer be counterbalanced by anything outside itself. Let us consider this opposition further. The bearer of the specifically modern form of capitalism as an *inescapable system* ruling the economy and thereby people's everyday fate was *not* profits made on the infamous principle that, 'you can't make millions without your sleeve brushing against the prison wall'; rather, it was precisely that type of profitability which is achieved by adopting the maxim, 'honesty is the best policy'.[12] Has any of those prolix ideologues who dream of an ethic of economic solidarity ever looked behind the curtains of our 'communal wartime economy' and seen what effect it actually had on the 'instinct for gain' it was supposedly going to stifle. A wild dance around the Golden Calf, gamblers grabbing at every chance opportunity escaping

[11] Here the metaphor of *Gehäuse* (see 'Constitutional Democracy', note 57) has been complicated by the addition of the adjective *ehern*. As this means 'made of bronze or brass' or 'made of iron, it appears that *Gehäuse* is now being used in the sense of another kind of housing, that of the protective casing around a piece of machinery. Thus the metaphorical sense is that the rational conduct of modern business creates a rigid structure in which work is carried out in a mechanical fashion. Matters are complicated further by the fact that *ehern*, in its metaphorical use, has a number of connotations. In the sense of 'hard', 'unyielding' or 'merciless', ehern is frequently used in German in conjunction with *Gesetz* ('law'), *Notwendigkeit* ('necessity') and *Schicksal* ('fate'), while 'das eherne Zeitalter' of ancient tradition (Hesiod, Aratos) marked a decline from the Golden and Silver Ages of mankind. Both sets of connotations accord with Weber's analysis of the modern age as one in which rationality becomes men's fate, obliging them to live in a 'disenchanted' world.

[12] 'honesty is the best policy' is in English.

through the pores of that bureaucratic system, the loss of every standard for *any* kind of business-ethical distinctions and inhibitions, and
an iron compulsion forcing everybody, including even the most conscientious businessman, either to join in and howl with the hyenas
on this unique Golgotha of *all* economic ethics – or else be punished
with economic destruction. It was exactly as it has always been,
although on a much more monstrous scale, whenever the chances of
capitalist gain followed the footsteps of the god of war or of Blessed
Saint Bureaucracy. It will take generations before the after-effects of
this decay of the normal bourgeois-capitalist ethos have been *eradic-
ated* – yet this is supposed to be the basis of a new economic ethics?
It will take our best efforts to get back to the level of the *old* ethics
before we do anything else! But all this is just an aside.

The war economy will be followed by the formation of massive,
rational *single-purpose associations* (*Zweckverbände*).[13] But we shall certainly not see relationships of community (*Gemeinschaft*)[14] which have
grown 'organically' on the soil of natural or primary *inward* human
relations, nor shall we see social formations of that inward quality
which, to varying degrees, was characterisitic of the family, the clan,
the parish, feudal relationships or those with the local landlord, or
in guilds, corporations, even the fraternities of estates in the Middle
Ages. Anyone still unaware of the difference between these things
and *all* modern, rational purposive associations should learn his sociological ABC before troubling the book-market with the products of
his vanity. The fact that individuals would be bound to belong not
just to one but often to many such formations simultaneously would
admittedly mean that any system of voting rights based on such
groups could not have the character of a 'popular assembly'
(*Volksvertretung*), but this would not in itself condemn this form of

---

[13] *Zweckverbände* are organisations which bring together various groups or communities
to undertake major projects such as transport planning or the building of schools or
canals or to pursue common interests. The legislation governing such organisations
was being extended in Germany from 1910 onwards.
[14] Weber is ridiculing the idea of an emotionally cohesive national community and
strongly integrated economy, the possibility of which was thought to have been
demonstrated during the war. Weber mentions such terms as *Gemeinwirtschaft*,
Solidaritätswirtschaft, and *Genossenschaftswirtschaft*. The classic locus for the formulation of the contrast between *Gemeinschaft* (irrationally or 'organically' founded
community) and *Gesellschaft* (rationally or 'mechanically' constructed society) is the
work of F. Tönnies, *Gemeinschaft und Gesellschaft. Abhandlung des Communismus und
des Socialismus als empirischer Kulturformen* (Leipzig, 1887).

franchise to being sheer 'nonsense'. It would simply be an 'assembly representing interests' (*Interessenvertretung*); similar things have existed in the past. But you only have to begin to attempt a grouping of the typical figures of a modern economy along '*occupational*' lines, such that the groups produced thereby could be used as *electoral* bodies for a general assembly representing the *people*, in order to find yourself face to face with complete nonsense. Firstly, there would simply be no room at all for the actual 'leaders' of the economic system. To which of the dozens of available 'occupations' should one assign Messrs Stinnes, Thyssen, Krupp von Bohlen, Count Henckel-Donnersmarck, von Mendelssohn and Rathenau, the members of the *Discontogesellschaft*[15] who bear full personal liability – or should perhaps all of these people be brought together in a single electoral corporation of 'giant businessmen'? And what about general managers like Kirdorf, Hugenberg and the like – should they be distributed amongst the 'management officials' of the individual 'occupations', or what is to become of them? This is how things are from the very top of the capitalist system right down to the bottom. It is impossible to put into *materially* appropriate categories precisely those people who are really the most important helmsmen of economic life today, right down to the wholesaler and the works manager. One would have to find some universal, *formal* characteristic in order to draw dividing lines between the electoral corporations, which would however flatly contradict the material, economic *meaning* (*Sinn*) of the occupational position in question in hundreds of ways, given the economic conditions prevailing today. What distinguishes our modern economy from one tied to social 'estates' is precisely the fact that you can almost *never* deduce from the outward position a person holds the economic *function* he performs, so that not even the most detailed occupational statistics can tell us the slightest thing about the inner structure of the economy. Just as one cannot tell just by looking at a beautifully landscaped hereditary estate the extent to which it has been mortgaged, you cannot tell from appearances what the proprietor of a shop is in economic terms; he could be the owner of a shop which is a branch of a larger business, the employee or tied client of an economic power (such as a brewery), a genuinely independent

---

[15] The *Discontogesellschaft* was founded in 1851 in Berlin. It became an enormously powerful finance house supplying capital, often in conjunction with large banks, for the creation of new banks.

retailer or whatever. Nor can you tell whether an 'independent tradesman' is a homeworker, a sub-contractor, an independent small capitalist or a commissioned master craftsman. And these are just the simplest cases! It is sheer political infantilism for our littérateurs to keep indulging in the fond notion that this would be the way to give 'open' and hence 'honest' expression 'within the circle of one's professional colleagues'[16] to the power of material interests which today exercise their influence 'covertly' in parliamentary elections. There are thousands of strings which capitalist powers could pull in order to make not just 'independent' small traders and craftsmen, but also the independent manufacturer dance to their tune at elections – quite apart from the fact that every such attempt at drawing dividing-lines between different occupations would have to be undertaken on the shifting sands of constantly changing operational units, trends in production and workforce, all of which are radically restructured in response to every new machine or market opening. For these purely economic reasons there is nothing objectively more untruthful than the attempt to create '*organic*' structures (in the sense of the old social estates) as electoral corporations in the political sphere in an age of constant technical and commercial restructuring and the progressive growth of economic and social ties based on *single-purpose associations*. Wherever suffrage experiments on the basis of occupational 'estates' have been attempted – in Austria recently and in Bulygin's franchise for the Russian Duma – it was necessary to create quite crude, formal categories. In Austria this resulted in a deeply corrupt parliament which can claim as its only honour to have been the first to invent procedural obstruction; in Russia it produced the buds of revolution. Yet in neither case was political influence given to the representatives of the truly important powers in the economic world today, and certainly not 'openly'. In addition to the fact that such an institution is not adapted to the constantly changing structure of the modern economy, purely political interests would cut across occupational interests. Supposedly realistic but misconceived projects such as those we have just been considering always fail utterly to recognise the autonomous operation of political interests. The result would not be to base parliamentary representation on the 'open' per-

---

[16] The term Weber uses, *Berufsgenossen*, is emotionally more loaded than its English equivalent and carries the suggestion of precisely that type of comradely solidarity which, he claims, is no longer characteristic of modern society.

ception of the 'natural' interests of the various occupations, internally united in solidarity; rather, the result would be to fracture professional solidarity even further by introducing party-political divisions. Even now we can see political parties struggling for power in municipal authorities, cooperatives, sickness insurance schemes, and so on – in other words, in every possible kind of social formation. This has often been regretted. We do not wish to include in our discussion the various aspects of this far from simple problem of organisational politics. But one thing is apparent: wherever one finds the rule of ballot slips and electioneering, the *political* parties as such are already predisposed to become the bearers of the struggle, for the simple reason that they have at their disposal the necessary political apparatus. If one now imagines these corporations based on occupational interests having to cast their votes via their delegates on questions of national politics and culture, it is clear what the outcome would be. If, by raising such associations to the status of bodies electing the parliament, political divisions were to be carried over into organised interest groups (whose proper function is to deal with *substantive* issues on which all the members of the association share the same interest), the first, inevitable consequence would be this: the struggle of purely economic interests would be bound to create for itself new organs *alongside* the framework (*Gehäuse*) of these electoral corporations. The boxes into which votes were counted would strive in vain to encompass the reality of economic life. Of course the struggle of economic interests would have an impact on these corporations, as on all other electoral bodies. But it would be directed much more towards naked *individual* relationships based on force (indebtedness, clientele), as opposed to long-term class relations, than is the case today when vested interests finance and influence the electoral contest between the parties. At the same time this influence would be much more hidden. For if such a complicated voting structure were to exist, who could trace the relationships of dependence between a formally 'independent' small trader or craftsman and some capitalist power, or track down the influence exercised by the pressure of such capitalist powers on the political attitudes of those dependent on them? The severity of dependency as such would increase, since those affected could now be checked up on very reliably by their *rivals* in the electoral corporations. When herded together in such electoral corporations, the supposed bearers of 'professional solidarity' would be set at one another's throats by denunciations and boy-cotts. These occupational corporations would no longer only have *professional* interests to secure, for the result of electoral contests within the corporations would determine *how the prebends and offices of the state were to be filled*. Have the well-intentioned but technically incompetent people who advocate *this* system realised what the out-come would be? Enough of this. We have only mentioned these child-ish literary soap-bubbles here because they invite us to make clear our position on yet another general problem.

After all, organised interest groups as the bearers of rights of rep-resentation *already exist* at present, both here and elsewhere. Firstly, as advisers to the bureaucracy: agricultural, trade and craft chambers and in future probably workers' chambers,[17] as well as railway boards and the like. But these very examples can teach us what a formal occupational organisation nowadays does *not* achieve. Or does anyone imagine that these official corporations could ever *replace* the 'League of Agriculturists', the 'Central Confederation of Industrialists', or even the employers' organisations or the trades unions? Where does one *really* find the pulsing 'life' of occupationally organised common interests? Equally, we already *have* within our legislative machinery corporations which are at least partially constituted along occupa-tional lines – the 'Upper Chambers' (*Erste Kammern*). Predominantly it is the associations of landowners of a particular social stamp ('old established land-ownership') who send their representatives to them, as well as chambers of commerce, some particularly large municipal-ities and also universities; perhaps in the future even chambers of tradesmen and workers will also be represented there. This method of representing interests may be terribly rough-and-ready but it just about suffices for these political purposes. Our politically infantile littérateurs imagine that it must be possible, by increasing the num-bers and specialisation of such rights of representation, to turn these upper houses into parliaments in which every citizen would be repres-ented as a member of the organic circles in which he lives and works – as was (allegedly) once the case in the *Ständestaat*.[18] We shall say

---

[17] The 'chambers' referred to here were bodies elected by the members of some social group for its self-governance. A craft chamber, for example, supervised the appren-ticeship system, organised examinations and maintained specialist training colleges.

[18] The *Ständestaat* existed in German territories from the end of the Middle Ages until around 1800. It was based on a division of powers between the monarch and the 'estates' (clergy, nobility, burghers).

something about this *Ständestaat* later. At present the upper chambers, which we now want to consider briefly, are (in theory, but usually not in truth) places for the expression of the political views partly of notables, partly of those strata with interests which, for traditional reasons, are considered of particular importance purely from the point of view of national politics, and this means above all the views of propertied people and particular professions valued highly in society. Although this is not always the case in fact, the 'idea' is usually that such people are *not* selected in the light of party-political considerations. From this follows the crucial feature of the natural position of this kind of 'upper house' in the state. Wherever its position is correctly ordered in political terms, this body *lacks* at least the right to its own budget, this being the foundation on which the power of an assembly representing the *people* rests. In other respects its legal position, viewed politically, is as follows: it is an authority which may object to, criticise, return for further discussion, cancel and delay, or even amend decisions of the representatives of the people, but, regardless of whether it has the formal *right* to do so, it *cannot* permanently block the will of an unquestionably strong majority in the popular assembly on some important political question, on pain of losing its formal rights (as in England at present) or of an enlargement of the peerage (as in Prussia in 1873).[19] This latter provision is a safety-valve which can never be removed without political risk, although all upper houses protest against it out of a desire for power, and the Prussian House of Lords will undoubtedly seize the opportunity provided by electoral reform to attempt to have this right of the Crown abolished and possibly claim the right to a budget. This would lead to the most severe crises and dangers, for it would mean the *continuance of the class system of suffrage*, except that it would now be divided between *two* bodies whose conflicts would expand into crises for the state. Let us hope that this is not attempted.

The influence of upper houses can be very significant, even if their formal rights are restricted, or indeed precisely because this is so. But however their membership is composed, they have absolutely nothing to do with a representative assembly of the people. In theory they provide a counterbalance to party rule. In practice one has to

---

[19] Weber is referring to the Parliament Act of 1911 in England and to Bismarck's enlargement of the Prussian Upper House in 1873, designed to introduce to the peerage individuals more sympathetic to government policy.

admit that they are often of questionable political usefulness and lacking in intellectual distinction; the Prussian House of Lords is the only 'legislative' body that believes it needs a *criminal judge* to enforce the respect to which it lays claim. Upper houses nowadays could certainly be genuine forums for *individual* political eloquence. In fact they are all too often places of superfluous chatter. No doubt speeches in the Prussian House of Lords are much more polished and 'distinguished' pieces of oratory than one hears in the Reichstag, but who would want to spend his time reading those speeches? Yet a *council of state debating matters in public* – for this is what a properly constructed upper house is intended to do – could perform an undeniably valuable service, particularly in a parliamentary state, as a place where political thinking which is *not tied to any party*, and political intelligence which *holds no office* but has the experience of office behind it – the experience in office of *former statesmen* – address the party-political leadership of the day. Admittedly, very few such institutions in their present form actually fulfil this purpose.

In a democratic state (*Volksstaat*)[20] an upper chamber can either – as in the democracies overseas – be a body which is also elected on the basis of equal suffrage, but by a different electoral *procedure*, so that it acts as a corrective to the inevitable imperfections which all *electoral systems* have. Or it can be an assembly in which the *intelligentsia with proven abilities* in politics, administration, the economy, scholarship and technology are represented. In this case, however, it can only be a *consultative* body with powers to criticise and *cancel* legislation by means of a 'veto of suspension'. *Formally* it can therefore only be a chamber with *lesser* rights. It would be *politically* desirable for the representatives of occupational interest groups in any case only to have a place in such upper houses *alongside* the representatives, firstly of the *intelligentsia* in national political life and secondly of cultural political *education*. It would therefore include, for example, *all* retiring ministers and mayors of large cities, as well as the representatives of institutions which are important for cultural–political reasons (elected representatives of school teachers, university teachers, artists,[21] journalists). At all events the question of the future composition of such bodies is not so unimportant as people here tend

---

[20] *Volksstaat*, meaning a state ruled by the people, is modelled on the Greek *demokratia*.
[21] 'Artists'(*Künstler*) was added to this list in the second printing (1918). We have assumed that this and certain other small changes were made on Weber's authority.

to believe simply because, unfortunately, these bodies are mostly only constructed today to serve as a form of mechanical brake on the 'dangers' of democracy and in order to mollify cowardly philistines (*Spießbürger*) (whatever their social position).[22] However, we do not want to be sidetracked into a discussion of this problem here.

Our present question is simply *why* the corporations of interests organised by the state, like the chambers of commerce which Eugen Richter used to attack so vehemently, and all bodies constructed on similar lines, in fact *fail* so completely to function as channels for the living stream of economic interests, when compared with the vitality of the real economic *interest groups* (*Interessenverbände*). On the other hand, why are they also, when compared with the *parties*, so utterly incapable of encapsulating political life? Is this fortuitous? It certainly does not come about by chance: it is the *consequence* of the fact that the parties on the one hand and the interest groups on the other are both *based* on the legally *free* recruitment of their adherents, whereas the bodies formed by the state are *not*. *As a result* of this structure the parties and interest groups are suitable organisations for *fighting* and *compromise*, whereas the state bodies, *as a result* of their structure are suited to the *expression* of expert opinion on matters of fact or to purely 'routine' peaceful administration. Unfortunately, however, the German enthusiasm for 'organisation' always understands by this word only compulsory organisation regulated by the police in the name of authority. Our littérateurs like to regard organisations founded on free, independent initiative ('*voluntary*' organisations) as being actually illegitimate, or at best as merely provisional arrangements, destined to be subsumed at some point in an organisation under police regulation, regardless of the possibility that the essential character of such organisations makes them capable only of being structured on a voluntary basis. That is their central error.

One of the congenital follies of our amateur political littérateurs is the desire to 'prepare a system with words', that is with the paragraphs of a statute to be drawn up by them, even if all the preconditions for such a system are absent. From a political point of view, the official organisations representing occupational groups – right up to any upper house composed of representatives of occupations – are forma-

---

[22] By the time Weber was writing, *Spießbürger* had become widened to refer to small-minded people generally rather than simply to a particular class.

tions intended to have their utterances – expert opinions or resolutions or debates – *weighed* and *not counted*. More or less weight will be attached to them, depending on the *substantive* (*sachlich*) content of their utterances. By contrast, *political parties* in the modern state are organisations which have as their starting point the (legally) *'free'* recruitment of supporters, while their goal is to determine policy through the *numbers* of their supporters. The *ultima ratio* of all modern party politics is the voting or ballot slip. Similarly, in a capitalist economy associations representing *economic* interests are based on (legally) 'free' recruitment, their aim being to use the private economic power of their members, whether this takes the form of the ownership of goods, a market monopoly or a monopolistic union of economically indispensable workers, in order to force on others a *compromise* in line with their own interests regarding the conditions which determine the price of material goods or work. For both types of free formation the decisive, uniquely appropriate and hence 'organic' feature of their organisation is its characteristically *'voluntary'* basis. Any attempt to compel them to unite on the model of an official department of state would be a purely mechanical compulsion which would put an end to their inner life. It is not that they themselves are strangers to 'compulsion'. Quite the opposite. To achieve their purposes they employ boycott, outlawing and every material and mental means of enticement and force the human mind can devise on the basis of (formally) free recruitment – with the exception, however, of that form of force for maintaining the *'legitimate* outward order' of the state which is reserved exclusively and peculiarly to the apparatus of the state as a coercive association (*Zwangsverband*). For reasons of state it is also possible to lay down conditions governing party organisations which, depending on circumstance, can either protect the rights of the majority against a breach of trust by a minority clique, or, conversely, can protect the rights of a minority against coercion, as has happened in America. But this does not change their fundamentally voluntary character – a *membership* formed on the basis of legally free will. The same applies to government regulations on the conditions governing the foundation of trade unions. It is precisely the fact that the party leader depends on the formally *free* recruitment of his following that is the absolutely decisive feature distinguishing his position from the rule-governed promotion of officials. It is precisely the fact that the leaders of groups with shared

economic interests are obliged to organise their following in a formally *'free'* way that determines their character, and this fact in turn
is determined by the structure of the modern economy. Under the
conditions prevailing today this type of organisation is the irreconcilable antithesis of any amalgamation in this area carried out by the
state's police. Anyone who has failed to understand these things has
not yet grasped the most elementary facts of modern political and
economic life. These things are not 'eternal' truths, but it is how
things are today. Of course it is possible to construct on paper as
many electoral corporations based on occupational representation as
one likes. But even if one were to do so, the consequence, as we
have said, would be that the political parties on the one hand and
the economic interest groups on the other would carry on their *real*
lives *behind* any such bodies.

That must suffice for the moment. We have only mentioned all
these romantic fantasies, which no well-informed person will consider worth the honour of serious refutation, because these completely unhistorical constructions do harm by increasing the nervousness of the German philistines in all sections of society about
taking the plunge into specifically *modern* problems, thereby putting
our citizens even more out of touch with the real world and with
politics. I wonder if any of these scribbling romantics has a clear
perception of the true nature of the *real Ständestaat* of the past; a few
brief observations on the topic are called for. Confused ideas about
the 'articulation of society' according to the 'natural occupations' in
'communities of estates', about the bearers of 'a Christian fraternal
ethic', and a 'hierarchical structure' with the spiritual monarch of
the world at its apex, mask *total ignorance* of the realities behind an
image drawn partly from the ideologies of philosophical literature
and partly from very modern, rationalistic, organisational concepts.
The underlying realities were different. What was truly characteristic
of the so-called *Ständestaat* was not any 'organic' articulation of society according to 'natural economic occupational groups', nor indeed
an economy built on the 'principle of solidarity'. What distinguished
the economy of the *Ständestaat* from today's economy were features
which are to be found throughout the world under the most varied
political arrangements imaginable. Admittedly, these economic
forms, in contrast to the economic situation today, made the *Ständestaat possible*, whereas this type of state is not possible today; but,

equally, the same economic forms created the preconditions elsewhere for quite different forms of state which are also not possible
today. They did not, however, create the *Ständestaat*. Something else
entirely was peculiar to the *Ständestaat* (which only developed fully
in one part of Europe), namely the fact that individuals and corporations could acquire *political* rights in the same way as one acquires
private ownership of material goods, and the fact that these *proprietors
of privilege* (not always only them, but they were always the main
constituents) came together in joint congresses for the purpose of
ordering political matters by means of *compromise*. In those days individuals held as hereditary privileges the ownership of citadels and
militarily or politically or financially important powers of every conceivable kind, all of which were owned in exactly the same way,
whereas today only the king holds his crown in this way. The things
we are now accustomed to regard as the content of the unified
'supreme authority' (*Staatsgewalt*) fell apart under that system into a
bundle of individual entitlements in various hands. There was as yet
no question of a 'state' in the modern sense of the word. Any political
action necessitated agreement amongst these owners of prerogatives
who were autonomous in principle, and it was the purpose of the
assemblies of estates to produce just such a unified view. Originally
and in principle, however, they did not take votes, nor did they have
the concept of a decision which was binding even on those who
disagreed with it. The form in which business was concluded was
the 'settlement' (*Vergleich*, also known as *Rezess* and *Abschied*),[23] which
in today's language means compromise. This was a compromise not
only between the different estates but also between each of the proprietors of privilege within the estate groupings. People should read
the records of any of these assemblies and ask themselves whether a
modern state could be governed in such forms. Yet these forms
(however fluid they may have been on points of detail) are precisely
the most fundamental elements of that type of formation, and it
begins to change as soon as the ultima ratio of the *voting slip* (the
most important, although not the only feature of the modern
parliament) begins to find its way into the proceedings of such forma-

---

[23] *Rezess, Vergleich, Abschied* are technical terms for different legal forms of recess (or
ordinance), settlement and treaty. The *Landtagsabschied*, for example, was a summary
of the legislation enacted during a legislative period and read out by the monarch at
the closing ceremony of the Diet.

tions. Not until this happens does the modern, rational form of determining the will of the state (*Willensbildung*) come into being. Even in today's constitutional state there are crucial points (such as determining the budget) where state action still rests, legally and politically, on compromise. But this is not *legally* the case with elections, nor with the transactions of a parliamentary body, nor can it be the case without destroying their foundations. Only when compromise was the *legal* basis of political action did a structure of estates based on occupation inherently have a proper place. But there is no place for it where the voting slip rules – in parliamentary elections.

Furthermore, compromise is still, as it always was, the dominant form in which conflicts of *economic* interest are settled, particularly those between employers and workers. Inevitably, it is bound to be the only way of settling things conclusively in this area, and this very fact is one of the *essential* characteristics of all truly living bodies representing vested economic interests. Naturally, compromise also prevails in parliamentary politics, in inter-party relations, in the form of electoral compromise or compromises on legislative proposals. As we shall see, this latter possibility of compromise is one of the chief merits of the parliamentary system. *But*, it must be stressed, there is *always* the ultima ratio of the *voting slip* in the background. This means that, when compromises are reached, it is under pressure from the fact that, if no compromise is achieved, the subsequent election or ballot may well produce a result which is more or less equally undesirable for *all* concerned. There is no getting away from the fact that the real and approximate *counting* of votes is an integral and essential element both of modern electoral contests and the conduct of business in parliament. Our romantics, for all their horror of 'numbers', will not change this fact. Let them stay away from politics if 'counting' seems to them too prosaic a device. It is simply an extraordinary impertinence, however, to single out *equal* suffrage for slander as the 'democracy of numbers', as opposed to other elections such as those based on 'occupational groups'. For what is the role of numbers in these elections? In all of these projects any talk of an 'organically' meaningful structure based on occupation or other kinds of social grouping is mere window dressing. Anyone interested in reality, as opposed to mere rhetoric, should ignore such talk and should examine each of these proposals to see how the *number* of mandates and votes is to be *distributed* amongst these artfully contrived groups. Since the voting slip remains the ultima ratio in these elections too, only one thing matters in all these schemes, namely the fact that they are all purely and simply *electoral arithmetic*. The Royal Prussian Statistical Office is particularly well versed in this science. For the last thirty years every 'project for electoral reform' with which it has had to deal has been based on calculations of the number of votes which stood to be gained by the Conservatives, the Centre Party or the National Liberals if one particular mode of voting or another were adopted. To see in such conjuring with numbers something loftier than the 'democracy of numbers' is something we shall gladly leave to the phrase-mongers and littérateurs.

In purely political terms it is no mere coincidence that equal 'numbers suffrage' is on the advance everywhere, for the mechanical nature of *equal* voting rights corresponds to the essential nature of today's state. The modern state is the first to have the concept of the '*citizen of the state*' (*Staatsbürger*). Equal voting rights means in the first instance simply this: at this point of social life the individual, for once, is *not*, as he is everywhere else, considered in terms of the particular professional and family position he occupies, nor in relation to differences of material and social situation, but purely and simply *as a citizen*. This expresses the political unity of the nation (*Staatsvolk*) rather than the dividing lines separating the various spheres of life. It has nothing at all to do with any theory of the natural 'equality' of human beings. On the contrary, its intended meaning and purpose (*Sinn*) is to create a certain counterbalance to the social *inequalities* which are *neither* rooted in natural differences nor created by natural qualities but are produced, rather, by social conditions (which are often severely at variance with nature) and above all, inevitably, by the *purse*. As long as anything resembling the prevailing social order persists – and it has a very stubborn hold on life – the inequality of the outward circumstances of life, particularly of *property*, may be mitigated, as may the relationships of social dependence which it produces, but it can never be eliminated altogether. Thus those who are privileged by it will never even come close to losing all their influence on national politics, which they exert to a far greater degree than their numbers warrant. Equally, the way the modern state and economy are organised ensures that a privileged position is permanently given to *specialised training* and thereby to 'education' (*Bildung*), which is not identical with specialised training but is promoted by it for purely technical, educational reasons, this being one of the most powerful factors in status group (*ständisch*) differentiation in modern society. For this very reason there is good sense in making parliamentary suffrage into something of equivalent weight, so as to counterbalance these other factors by making the ruled in society (who have a numerical advantage) the equals of the privileged strata at least when it comes to electing the body which both exercises *control* and functions as the place where *leaders are selected*.

An authoritative institution (*Instanz*) of this kind becomes even more indispensable if we assume that the wartime economy really is to be succeeded by the *permanent*, extensive 'organisation' of national economic life in interest groups (*Interessenverbänden*) *in which state officials participate*, in other words the regulation of the economy (or of certain of its more important branches) by occupational cooperatives which would be bureaucratically 'supervised' or 'co-administered', or which were otherwise linked to the agencies of the state on a firm and permanent basis. Have any of our childishly enthusiastic littérateurs ever thought what the *political* consequences would be if one did not create a counterweight to such an arrangement by enormously increasing the powers of a parliament *not* organised along occupational lines? They imagine that 'the state' would then be the wise regulator of the economy. The *reverse* would be the case! The bankers and capitalist entrepreneurs they hate so much would then have *unlimited and uncontrolled command over the state*! For *who on earth is the 'state'*, as distinct from this machinery of large and small capitalist *cartels* of every kind into which the economy is to be 'organised', if the formation of the state's own will (*Willensbildung*) is to be placed in the hands of precisely *these* 'co-operative' organisations? Even the participation of the state in the coal syndicate and in mining generally means in practice that the interest of the exchequer does *not* lie in supplying the nation with cheap coal in the best possible way, but in obtaining *high returns* from its mines. It means that private and public pits and private and public bureaucracy have an *identical* interest here, in relation both to the workers and to the consumers of coal. Every further advance in *state-*run cartelisation naturally means purely and simply the further spread of this state of affairs. Perhaps it is inevitable nevertheless – but that is not something I wish to consider here. It is, however, sheer naiveté on the part of our scribbling ideologues to believe that *this* is the way to weaken or eliminate the rule of the 'profit motive' and the interest in producing goods 'for gain' which they so despise, and to replace them with a 'natural', 'communal economic' interest in providing good and as far as possible cheap commodities to the *people* who desire and consume them! What abysmal nonsense! The interest of the capitalist producers and profit-makers represented by these cartels *would itself then rule the state exclusively, unless* that organisation of producers' interests is confronted by a power strong enough to control and steer them as the *needs* of the population require. But an individual's *needs* are *not* determined by his position in the machinery of goods-*production*. The worker has exactly the *same needs* for bread, housing and clothing, regardless of the type of factory he works in. Thus if that method of organising the economy is imminent, it is absolutely imperative, *before* it begins to function – which means immediately – for us to have a parliament elected on the principle that the *needs* of the masses must be represented, and *not* one which represents the way an individual is employed in the production of goods – in other words a parliament of equal suffrage, wholly sovereign in its power, which can take an independent stand in relation to this type of economic organisation. Parliament must be much more sovereign in its powers than hitherto, for in the past its position of power has *not* sufficed to break the power of vested commercial interests nor the inevitable rule of fiscal interests in state-run industries. This is a *negative* reason for equal suffrage.

Considered purely in terms of national politics, however, the positive argument for equal suffrage consists in the fact that it is closely related to the equality of certain *fates* which the modern state as such creates. People are 'equal' before death. They are approximately equal in the most elementary requirements of physical existence. But precisely these most basic needs on the one hand and, on the other, that most solemn and lofty fact of all are encompassed by those equalities which the modern state offers all its citizens in a truly lasting and undoubted way: sheer physical security and the minimum for subsistence, but also the battlefield on which to die. All inequalities of political rights in the past ultimately derived from an economically determined inequality of *military* qualification which one does not find in the bureaucratised state and army. In the face of the levelling, inescapable rule of bureaucracy, which first brought the modern concept of the 'citizen of the state' into being, the ballot slip is the *only* instrument of power which is at all *capable* of giving the people who are subject to bureaucratic rule a minimal right of co-determination in the affairs of the community for which they are obliged to give their lives.

In Germany it is the *Reich* which wages war, but of the individual states it is *Prussia* which, by virtue of its hegemonial position in the Reich, has an absolutely decisive say in the politics of the *Reich* as a whole. The individual citizen therefore expects the *Reich* to guarantee that this hegemonial state will fulfil its obligation to show at least the absolute minimum of political decency towards the soldiers returning from the war. It is in the interest of the *Reich* to ensure that none of these men is disadvantaged in his electoral rights in the decisive individual state *as compared with anyone who stayed at home*; any form of franchise other than equal suffrage would inevitably result in such inequitable treatment. ^A Equal suffrage is a demand of national politics; it is not a party-political demand. We do not know what the mood and political convictions of the returning soldiers will be. Perhaps it will be 'authoritarian'. Strong 'conservative' parties will always exist because there will always be people of conservative inclination. Let them then use their ballot papers to build the state in accordance with their ideals, and those of us who stayed at home will go about our daily work. The only thing I am attacking here is the shameless reluctance of the so-called 'fighters on the home front' to fulfil the elementary obligation of decency towards the returning soldiers. The ineluctable realities of the present will ensure that the antiquated, negative form of democracy, which demanded only freedom *from* the state, will not grow out of all proportion; the best way to ensure this would be for the leaders of the parties in parliament to share power *in* the state and to accept direct, personal responsibility for its exercise. Precisely the experiences of this war (including what is now happening in Russia) have demonstrated a point we have emphasised already, namely that *no* party, whatever its programme, can assume the *effective* direction of the state *without becoming national*. This would happen

---

^A The apparently intended linkage of suffrage to *length of residence*, which would mean that the working class, presently in the third franchise class, would be *deprived* of the franchise (since it is forced to move from place to place frequently), would also *disenfranchise* those sections of the proletariat who are on active service! As a result of the major restructuring of the economy the *majority of all workers* might perhaps have to seek a new place of work at the next election, and thus *lose* the franchise!

in Germany just as surely as it has happened everywhere else. It was *because* socialist parties in other countries were not excluded from the government of the state that they were more 'national' than our Social Democrats (once) were.[24] Whatever the mood of the returning soldiers proves to be, they will at all events bring back with them experiences, impressions and discoveries which are *theirs alone*. What we believe we are entitled to expect of them is at least a relatively higher degree of *objectivity* (*Sachlichkeit*), for the tasks presented by modern warfare are objective in the highest degree. We also expect them to be more immune to the empty rhetoric of mere littérateurs, whatever political party they support. By contrast, the war years have revealed amongst those who stayed *at home*, particularly amongst the littérateurs and the wealthy, such a repulsive lack of objectivity, such a lack of political judgement and so much deliberately cultivated blindness to reality, that the time has come to say to them, 'Your ringing days are over, come down from the belfry'. At the very least, the franchise must be redefined while the war is still in progress. The returning soldiers must not be faced with the need to fight sterile domestic battles for electoral rights before they can acquire the instruments of power which will give them a decisive say in the running of the state they have defended. They must come back to find that purely formal political rights have *already* been so ordered that they can turn their hands immediately to the material reconstruction of the structure of the state. This is the decisive, purely practical argument for equal suffrage in Prussia and for its immediate introduction at this very moment, *before* the war is over.

We have heard all the empty phrases used by vested interests to frighten the philistines, and particularly the littérateurs, on this issue. Above all, the fear that 'democracy' will destroy our allegedly 'distinguished' (*vornehm*) and hence culturally productive 'traditions', as well as the supposedly unfathomable wisdom of the allegedly 'aristocratic' strata who rule the state. Let us go straight to the heart of these arguments, even if they initially lead us away from the question of suffrage as such.

---

[24] After considerable dissension, the German Social Democrats voted unanimously for the credits required to fight the war in 1914, although a minority gave their support only with reluctance. The issue of war credits later split the party in 1916, leading to the creation of the USPD (Independent Socialist Party) in 1917 which was internationalist and opposed to war. The 'patriotism' of Social Democrats was therefore an acute issue at the time Weber was writing this piece.

There is no doubt that a *true aristocracy* can stamp an entire nation with its own ideal of distinguished conduct, for the plebeian strata imitate the 'gesture' of the aristocracy. By combining the advantage of their 'small numbers' with the benefits of a stable tradition and wide social horizons, an aristocracy can achieve very great political successes in the leadership of a state. As far as national politics are concerned, rule by an aristocracy with political traditions has the further advantage over democratic forms of rule that it is less dependent on *emotional* factors. To put it another way, an aristocrat generally has a *cooler head* as a result of his consciously shaped conduct of life and an education directed at maintaining *contenance*.[25] The aristocrat regularly has the gift of *silent action* to a considerably higher degree than the democratic masses on the one hand and the non-parliamentary modern monarch on the other (a fact usually suppressed by sycophants although it is much more damaging in its consequences). *All* non-parliamentary modern monarchs are exposed to the danger of believing that they need to make *speeches* in order, as it were, to advertise their person, in the same way as democratic leaders in a class-state are forced to make speeches in order to recruit support for their party. Any nation can therefore thank heaven if its monarch *lacks* both the gift and the inclination to make personal speeches, for this is wholly unwelcome as far as national politics are concerned. Indeed, one of the strengths of the parliamentary system is the fact that it preserves the monarch from such self-exposure. An old political aristocracy is least likely to succumb to this danger, a merit which it combines with the gift of *cultured tastes*. 'Parvenu' democratic states, such as Italy, usually tend to be just as lacking in good taste as newly founded monarchies. The terrible barbarism of the 'impious' defacement of Rome, inspired as it was by an anti-clerical tendency to expunge 'embarrassing' (which means humiliating) 'memories', elicited from the great Italian poet Carducci the wish to see the Papal State restored for just one month so that it could sweep away the hollow theatricality and tastelessness of 'terza Roma'. Yet compared with Munich or Vienna, or even with other, smaller provincial capitals, Berlin today, now that it has been stripped of its austere simplicity and been given a wretched cathedral, the monstrous monument to Bismarck and other such things, is such an

---

[25] Weber uses the French word; it means 'bearing'.

example of banal monumentalism that one shudders to think what aesthetic judgement posterity will pass on this epoch in German history, and one thinks with shame both of the generation of artists who lent themselves to such a task and of the public who did nothing to oppose it. But at least this disfigurement proves that monarchy *as such* assuredly does not provide the slightest guarantee of artistic culture, indeed it can often represent a threat to it. The Bismarck memorial in Hamburg, on the other hand, the only truly valuable example of monumental art in Germany, will always do honour to the patricians of Hamburg, and can show our myopic littérateurs that 'capitalism' and 'art' do not necessarily live in the state of natural enmity which some attribute to them. The same has been demonstrated on behalf of democracy by trade union buildings in Italy or, generally, by cities like Zurich. A culture of high good taste such as one finds in an old, firmly established and self-assured aristocracy, or in a democracy imitating such traditions, is certainly not a matter of indifference as far as national politics are concerned. The prestige of France throughout the world rests on the store of treasure it has salvaged from its aristocratic past and which, despite the disgraceful decline in official care for the arts, is still being preserved and developed amongst small groups of creative artists and in the aesthetic shaping of the French character. Here democratisation has led, at least in part, to the spread of the old, exclusive culture; in a different way the same holds true for the Italian character, particularly amongst the lower social strata.

Let us consider how this problem affects Germany as a matter of principle, quite independently of the question of suffrage which we are discussing. One has to begin by asking *where the German aristocracy with its 'distinguished' tradition is to be found?* If such a thing existed, there would be something to discuss. Aside from a few *princely* courts (minor ones at that), however, *it simply does not exist.* For what does 'aristocracy' mean, or rather, what conditions must obtain if a social stratum, whether it be essentially feudal ('nobility') or bourgeois ('patricians'), is to function as an aristocracy in the *political* sense of the word and be put to political use? The chief requirement is a life untouched by economic storms. The most elementary precondition of all is that an aristocrat should be able to live *for* the state and should not have to live *from* it. What matters is not merely having the kind of income which makes it not too difficult to forego a ministerial salary. Above all he needs to be 'economically dispensable' (*abkömmlich*), so that he is available for political purposes, both outwardly and, even more importantly, inwardly. This means that work in the service of a commercial *business* must not lay claim to his time and energies, or at least not exhaustively. Of all the ways of earning a living in the private sector which depend on intense, personal, intellectual work, the profession of the *advocate* is the one which most readily allows its practitioner to keep himself available for political purposes (by belonging to a group practice or by engaging people to deputise for him, and because there is no capital at risk). Also, because the advocate not only has an organised *office* at his disposal but also knowledge of the law and experience of the day-to-day requirements of life, his chances of a political career are particularly favourable in all democracies, and it is relatively easy for him to return to running his business if he experiences electoral defeat. People have inveighed a good deal against the importance of advocates in many democracies, and the low social esteem of the lawyer has been particularly responsible for this verdict here, together with the not infrequently justified accusation of 'formalism' in the way they deal with political problems. Yet, if arbitrariness is to be avoided, formalism is an essential part of legal training, including that of a judge or an administrative official. On the other hand, the work of an advocate, in contrast to that of a judge or official involves training in how to 'fight with words'; the great superiority of our enemies in recruiting support for their cause, and generally in using the important weapon of the word, results from the *lack* of training in advocacy (which can take place at a thoroughly distinguished level) that is so characteristic of *any* government run purely by officials, as opposed to the advocate-ministers who are to be found in democracies. Anyone seeking change here must therefore be prepared to accept the *means*, which is to increase the political influence of advocates by improving their political *chances*. Germans generally, and German littérateurs in particular, have no idea of the nature of the truly great vocation of the advocate, since their image of it is shaped by the magistrates' courts or divorce hearings or the minor daily annoyances which take them to an advocate. Anyone familiar with the profession knows that it is the crown not only of *all* legal work, but of all free positions of trust, and that it stands high above most legal work in the degree of intellectual intensity and *responsibility* it entails. Officialdom, of course, *hates* the advocate as a tedious intermediary and troublemaker, but also because the official resents his earning capacity. It is certainly not desirable for parliaments and cabinets to be governed entirely by advocates. But a healthy admixture of distinguished advocacy is something desirable in any modern parliament. Admittedly, today's advocates are no longer an 'aristocracy', not even in England. They form a bourgeois occupational group (*bürgerlichen Erwerbsstand*), but one, it has to be said, which is available for political work.

The modern *entrepreneur*, by contrast, is never an 'aristocrat' in the *political* sense of the word. Unlike the advocate, he is specifically *indispensable* from his place of work, and the larger his business and the greater the demands it makes on him, *the less* is he available for other things. The old merchant patricians in the city republics were a stratum of *occasional* entrepreneurs, but otherwise they were *rentiers* and *this* was the basis of their political usefulness. A modern manufacturer, chained to the unremitting, intense, exhausting work of running his business, is, of all the representatives of the propertied strata, the type who is least able to make himself available for politics. This is the main reason for the fact that the members of this stratum, despite their economic importance and practical intelligence, are of relatively slight importance for political work and self-government. It is not, as the usual stupid moralising of the littérateurs would have it, due to any lack of 'willingness for self-sacrifice' or 'worship of mammon'; it results from the fact that such men are tied inwardly by their duty to the business and outwardly by the demands of the work inherent in running and making profits in a bourgeois-capitalist business. The seasonal character of *agriculture* leaves at least the winter months free for political work. But *all* strata directly involved as entrepreneurs in the struggle of economic interests lack something else, something more important, which one might call inner availability, *distance* from the everyday *conflicts* of interest in the private economic sphere. In contrast to the advocate, the modern entrepreneur, including the farmer, is an *interested party* who is too directly involved in this struggle to be politically useful.

Only the *grand rentier* has ever possessed sufficient distance from the conflict of economic interests. This applies above all to the very large landowner or hereditary lord (*Standesherr*), but also to anyone who owns a large fortune in investments. He alone is sufficiently removed from the daily economic struggle which every entrepreneur constantly has to fight for his existence, his economic power, the survival of his business. The relatively much less embattled existence of the *grand rentier*, his much greater *distance* from the everyday business world (even if large enterprises are among the sources of his unearned income) – these factors free his energies, both inwardly and outwardly, for political interests, whether in the affairs of state or in the political–cultural sphere, for the life of a 'man of the world', for patronage and the acquisition of knowledge of the world in the grand manner. It is not that he lives in some kind of economically 'disinterested' sphere. No such thing exists. But he is not engaged in the daily struggle for the survival of his business, he is not the *organ* of such a business, nor the bearer of plutocratic *class* interests, since he is removed from the immediate *conflict* of interests. *Only* a stratum with *this* kind of structure could lay claim to the title of an 'aristocracy' today, in the sense of having a particular kind of *economic* qualification.

Even in small things the importance of this economic qualification is quite plain. To take an everyday instance, everyone knows what it means for the morale of a corps of officers to have a 'nervous' regimental commander. All other things being equal, such 'nervousness' usually arises from his economic situation, from the lack of a private fortune which means that the commander is faced with a shabby future – and a family accustomed to social pretensions – if he is dismissed. This oppresses and weighs him down in the performance of his duties and makes it infinitely more difficult for him, as compared with a wealthy commander, to stay calm and – a very important practical point – to defend the interests of his subordinates vigorously to his superiors. Every alert officer will have noticed this, and it hardly needs to be illustrated with individual examples. Things are similar in other areas. Many of our officials who have shown most character in the area of social policy – in the factory inspectorate, for example – were wealthy men who, for this very reason, did not need to bend before every breath from vested interests and who were prepared to resign their office if they were expected to do things which were incompatible with their conscience. Considering his fairly limited intellectual gifts, the importance of Paul Singer[26] and his position

---

[26] Paul Singer (1844–1911), industrialist and Social Democrat.

within the Social Democratic party were to a considerable extent a function of his wealth, since this allowed him to live *for* the party in the way he did, rather than having to live *from* it. 'Political character' is simply cheaper for the man of means, and no amount of moralising can change this fact. Nor is it simply a matter of showing character towards one's superiors. The fact that the property-less masses, who must struggle daily for survival, are relatively more susceptible to all *emotional* motives in politics, to passions and momentary impressions of a sensational kind, as compared with the 'cooler head' of the man whose wealth raises him above such worries, makes it a matter of great urgency for democratic parties in particular to have people in secure economic circumstances occupying *leading* positions who can devote themselves to political work purely out of personal conviction, and thus to counterbalance these influences in ways which are not always open to the party *bureaucracy* as such. Admittedly, because the masses cannot intervene *directly* in politics, and because their behaviour is more readily forgotten, their emotional qualities are nothing like as dangerous as those of *monarchs* who can compromise the nation's political position for decades to come by excited and incautious telegrams and speeches. But the masses, too, are with us and, all things being *equal*, it is *cheaper* for a man of property to show 'political character' and cool reflection in his dealings with them too. It is an important question for the future whether men of property, whose wealth gives them independence and who will be with us as long as the system of private property exists, enter the service of politics, and work politically for the *democratic* parties in particular. It is easy for the party official who works hard for his living and is dependent on his salary to feel *ressentiment* towards such people, but this should not prevent the parties from taking to heart the lessons of experience in this regard. On the other hand, the *ressentiment* of party and co-operative (*Genossenschaft*) officialdom is ideally suited as a counterbalance to any danger of the parties coming under 'plutocratic' leadership. The experiences of the Russian democratic parties, including those on the extreme left, in which the daughters of princes fought on the barricades and the wealthiest of patrons produced the funds for the popular movement, show that the economic self-interest of propertied ideologues leaves them *much* more scope for the idealistic pursuit of reliably 'democratic' *convictions* than is the case with a more plebeian (from a social point of view) stratum entangled directly in the conflict of interests. This is because the economic situation of the wealthy does not necessarily dictate the direction of their political activity, whereas it *can* provide support for independent political convictions. In purely material terms, the prosaic share certificate performs this service for the person who owns it just as effectively as the possession of a hereditary lordly estate. Admittedly, an estate of this kind provides much more specific training for political activity (in the kind of large-scale tasks of management with which it confronts the owner and the sounding board of a lordly position) than can be acquired by cutting off share-coupons and a life spent in the purely consumerist household of a *rentier* living off paper investments.

Thus there can be no doubt that a stratum of landed nobility of the kind that existed in England, and similar to that which formed the core of the senatorial nobility in ancient Rome, is a bearer of political tradition, training and moderation, for which there is no substitute as far as national politics are concerned. *But where does it exist* here? How many hereditary lords of this kind exist in Germany, and more particularly in Prussia? Where is their political tradition? Politically they have virtually *no significance*, and *least of all in Prussia*. It is surely clear that it is impossible nowadays to have as an aim of state policy the breeding of such a truly aristocratic stratum of *grands rentiers*. Although it would be possible to use forest land, the only land-title qualified in socio-political terms for fee-entailment, so as to bring into being a number of new, large hereditary lordships, there is no possibility of producing numerically significant results by this means. The deepest inner dishonesty of the entailment bill discussed in Prussia at the beginning of 1917 was that it sought to extend to the *'Mittelstand'* of average estate-owners east of the Elbe an institution of property appropriate to *hereditary lordships*, and thereby to *inflate* to the status of 'aristocrats' people who simply are not aristocrats and who cannot be aristocrats. Anyone who knows the much (and often unjustly) maligned and (equally unjustly) idolised Junker of the eastern provinces is bound to take delight in them on a purely personal level – when out hunting, drinking a drop of something decent, at the card-table, amidst the hospitality of the estate farm – in these areas everything about them is genuine. Everything becomes false only when one stylises as an 'aristocracy' this essentially 'bourgeois', entrepreneurial stratum, *economically dependent* as it is on agricultural entrepreneurialism and the *conflict of interests*, a conflict of social and economic interests every bit as ruthless as that which any factory owner has to engage in. Ten minutes spent in such circles are enough to make one realise that they are *plebeians*, and that their virtues in particular are overwhelmingly plebeian in character. An estate in eastern Germany *'supports no lordly household today'*, as Minister von Miquel once put it quite correctly (but in private!). If one tries to put the stamp of an 'aristocracy', with its feudal gestures and pretensions, onto a social stratum which depends nowadays on plain, bourgeois-capitalist work, the inevitable result will simply be to create *the physiognomy of the parvenu*. The parvenu aspects of the way we conduct ourselves in the world, both politically and in other respects, derive at least in part, although not entirely, from suggesting to sections of society who quite simply lack the qualification to do so that they should play the part of aristocrats.

Nor is *this* stratum *alone* in lacking the necessary qualification. Of course the physiognomy of the Junker is by no means the *only* reason for the absence here of the educational forms which distinguish the man of the world. Rather, the reason for their absence lies with the unmistakably bourgeois character of *all* those social strata which were the specific bearers of the Prussian state system during the years of its impoverished but glorious rise. The old officer families who preserve with honour the tradition of the old Prussian army, despite their own, often extremely exiguous circumstances, and the families of officials who do the same, are – regardless of whether or not they have titles of nobility – a *bourgeois middle class*, both economically and socially and in their mental horizons. Within their circle the social forms of the German officer corps are generally appropriate to the character of that stratum and, in their most important features, closely resemble those of officer corps in democracies (France, Italy). Outside that circle, however, these forms of behaviour immediately become caricatured when non-military circles treat them as a model for emulation, particularly when they enter a *mésalliance* with social forms originating in the undergraduate atmosphere of the *training colleges for officials*, as happens here.

As is generally known, the *student fraternities*[27] are the typical form of social education for the next generation of non-military officials,

---

[27] The term *Couleurwesen* refers to the German institution of (frequently political) student clubs or fraternities, the members of which wore distinctive coloured sashes and

prebendaries and the socially elevated 'free' professions. The 'academic freedom' to duel, to drink and to laze around dates from a time when no other freedoms of any kind existed in Germany, and when only this lettered stratum of prospective office-holders was *privileged* with these very freedoms. Even today it is not possible to eradicate the influence of the conventions originating in that atmosphere on the 'gesture' of the 'man with a degree', a type who has always been important in Germany and whose importance continues to grow. The colours worn by the students would be unlikely to disappear, even if the mortgages on the clubhouses and the need for the 'old boys' to pay the interest on them, were not in any case a sufficient guarantee of their economic immortality. On the contrary, the fraternity system is expanding steadily, for the simple reason that the fraternities' *'old boy network'* is nowadays a specific form of *selecting officials*, and because the status of a reserve officer and the ability to offer 'satisfaction' which this presupposes (something visibly attested by the club ribbon) admit a man into 'society'. Admittedly, the compulsion to drink and the duelling rituals of the colour corps are being modified more and more to meet the needs of the weaker constitutions among the constantly growing numbers of those who aspire to the coloured ribbon for the sake of the connections it bestows; they say there are even teetotallers in some fraternities. What is crucial is the fact that the last few decades have seen the *intellectual incest* of these clubs *increase steadily* – the clubhouses with their own reading rooms, the special club newspapers which 'old boys' keep supplied with an unspeakably subaltern, petit bourgeois kind of well-meaning, 'patriotic' politics, the fact that contact with people of the same age but of different social or intellectual backgrounds is abhorred or at least made very difficult. At the same time, ever wider sections of society are being drawn into the networks of these fraternities. A clerk bent on acquiring the qualities of an officer of the reserve and the opportunity these afford of marrying into 'society' (the boss's daughter above all) attends one of those business schools which recruit a good number of their students precisely because of the activities of the fraternities. Whatever one's verdict on the intrinsic merit of all these student formations – and the criterion of morality

enjoyed certain privileges in law. Their members would acquire 'the ability to give satisfaction', meaning the ability to settle a matter of honour by duelling.

is not that of the politician – they certainly do *not* train the individual to be *a man of the world*; in fact the result produced by their undeniably banal, undergraduate atmosphere and their subaltern social forms is the very opposite. The most mindless English club offers more in this respect, however 'empty' one may find, for example, the sporting activity which is so often the be-all and end-all of their existence. The main reason for this is the fact that English clubs, although often highly selective, are always built on the principle that *all gentlemen are equal*, and not on the principle of *schoolboy subordination* which the bureaucracy prizes so highly in our colour corps as a *training for the discipline* of office, and which the clubs deliberately cultivate in order to ingratiate themselves in higher places.[28] At any rate, the ritualised conventions and undergraduate mentality of so-called 'academic freedom' which those aiming for an official post are obliged to submit to are becoming ever *less* a means of educating the aristocratic man of the world, the *more* they turn into a way of boasting about the wealth of one's *parents*, which inevitably happens wherever circumstances permit. A young person who ends up in this school has to be an unusually independent character and a very free spirit if he does not wish to acquire the disastrous features of a *varnished plebeian* which are so often to be observed even in the products of this system, however able they may be in other respects. For the interests cultivated in these communities are thoroughly *plebeian* and far removed from anything that is in any sense 'aristocratic'. Here again, the decisive point is that undergraduate antics which are essentially *plebeian* in character and harmless enough as a simple outlet for youthful exuberance are claiming to be a means of *aristocratic education* qualifying a man for leadership in the state. The heavy price to be paid for *this* quite incredible contradiction is the *physiognomy of the parvenu* it creates.

Let no one believe that these parvenu features in the face of Germany are quite irrelevant politically. To begin with an example: the practice of making 'moral conquests' of enemies (that is people with opposing interests) is a vain business, rightly scorned by Bismarck, but what about present or future *allies* or *federal partners*? [29] We and

---

[28] Here we have omitted a lengthy but unimportant footnote about drinking habits in student clubs.

[29] Here the term *Bundesgenossen* requires a double translation, since Weber is reminding his readers both that Prussia, however dominant its position, belongs to a federal

our Austrian allies are permanently dependent on one another *politically*. We and they are both aware of this fact. Unless major acts of stupidity are committed there is no danger of a break between us. They acknowledge without reserve or envy the German *achievement* – and would do so even if we were *not* always talking about it here; indeed the less we do so, the easier we make it for them. Yet not everyone here has a proper conception of the Austrians' objective difficulties, which Germany has been spared, and consequently there is insufficient appreciation here of *their* achievement. This is also the place to state plainly what the whole world knows, namely that the one thing neither they nor any other nation with whom we might wish to have friendly relations could tolerate is the kind of parvenu airs and graces which have recently been spreading here in an intolerable way. That sort of thing will be met with silent, polite but firm *rejection* from any nation which, like Austria, has a longstanding tradition of unquestionably good social education. Nobody wants to be governed by ill-bred parvenus. Every step beyond what is absolutely indispensable for foreign policy, in other words everything that 'Central Europe' (in the inner sense of the term)[30] might want (or which might be desirable in any future community of interests with other nations) – however one views the question of *economic rapprochement* – could fail politically for both parties because people are utterly determined *not* to accept the imposition of what has recently been declared, with boastful gesture, to be the 'Prussian spirit', and which is supposedly under threat from 'democracy', according to the frequent declarations of our phrase-mongering littérateurs. As we are all aware, such declamations have accompanied absolutely *every* step towards inner reform here for the last 110 years.[31]

The true 'Prussian spirit' is one of the finest expressions of the German national character (*Deutschtum*). Every line written by

---

Reich, and that Germany as a whole must respect the sensitivities of other countries with which it has alliances and with which it might conceivably enter into a wider confederation in the future.

[30] Here Weber is following the relatively common practice in Germany, particularly before, during and after the First World War, of treating *Mitteleuropa* as a metaphorical/spiritual concept rather than a merely geographical, political or economic one. The metaphorical sense is that Central Europe is both 'central' to an idea of Europe and a 'middle ground' between the extremes of East and West.

[31] The administrative reforms of Freiherr von Stein (1757–1831) had taken place in Prussia 110 years earlier.

Scharnhorst, Gneisenau, Boyen, Moltke[32] breathes this spirit, as do the words and deeds of the great Prussian reforming officials who do not even need to be mentioned by name (a good number of whom, admittedly, originated from outside Prussia). The same is true of Bismarck's eminent intellect, so miserably caricatured by the blinkered, philistine advocates of 'Realpolitik' today. It sometimes seems as if the old Prussian spirit flourishes more strongly today amongst the officials of *other* states in our federation than it does in Berlin, and the misuse of the term by the conservative demagogy we are hearing now is nothing short of impiety towards the great figures of the past.

To repeat the point, an *aristocracy* of adequate breadth and political tradition does not exist in Germany. Its most likely home was in the 'Free Conservative' Party and the Centre Party (although this had ceased to be the case there too), but not in the Conservative Party. Equally important is the fact that no *distinguished German social form* exists. Despite the occasional boasts of our littérateurs, it is quite untrue that 'individualism', in the sense of *freedom* from conventions, exists in Germany, in contrast, so it is alleged, to the conventions governing the 'gentleman' in English-speaking countries or salon life in the Latin countries. Nowhere are more rigid and binding conventions to be found than those of the 'colours student' which, directly or indirectly, rule the lives of as large a fraction of the next generation in Germany's ruling circles as do the conventions of any other country. Except where the conventions of the officer corps hold sway, *these are 'the German form'*! This is because the experiences in the colour-corps subsequently determine to a large extent the forms and conventions of the most influential sections of German society, namely the bureaucracy and all those who wish to be admitted into the 'society' that is dominated by it. However, one cannot call these forms 'distinguished'. What is more important as far as national politics are concerned is the fact that, in contrast to the conventions in England and the Latin countries, these conventions are wholly unsuited to serve as a *model* for the whole nation, right down to its lowest levels, and thus to make its gesture *uniformly* that of a self-assured 'nation of masters' (*Herrenvolk*), entirely confident in its out-

---

[32] These men were all outstanding Prussian generals: G. von Scharnhorst (1755–1813), N. von Gneisenau (1760–1831), H. von Boyen (1771-1843) and H. von Moltke (1800–91).

ward manner, as has happened with the English and Latin conventions. It is a grave error to believe that 'race' is the decisive factor in the striking lack of grace and dignity[33] in the outward bearing of the Germans. Despite the fact that he is of the same race, the public demeanour of a German from Austria (whatever other weaknesses he may have) is not marred by *these* qualities, for it has been thoroughly moulded by a real aristocracy.

The forms governing the behaviour of people in the Latin countries, right down to the lowest strata, are produced by imitating the *'gesture of a cavalier'* as this evolved from the sixteenth century onwards. The conventions of English-speaking countries, which also shape the behaviour of society down to the lowest stratum, derive from the social habits of that section of society which set the tone from the seventeenth century onwards, a stratum which developed in the late Middle Ages from a peculiar mixture of rural and urban bourgeois notables – 'gentlemen' [34] who were the bearers of 'self-government'. The important thing was that in all these cases the decisive features of those conventions and gestures could be imitated readily by all, and were therefore capable of being *democratised*. By contrast, the conventions of prospective German officials with their academic diplomas, and of the strata influenced by them, particularly the habits inculcated by the colour corps, were and are, as we have said, patently *not* suitable for imitation by any circles outside those taking university examinations and certainly not by the broad mass of the public. They were therefore not capable of being 'democratised', despite the fact, or rather precisely *because*, they were in their essence profoundly plebeian and not the manners of the man of the world or aristocrat. The Latin code of honour, like the very different English one, was susceptible of being democratised to a great extent. The specifically German concept of 'being qualified to give satisfaction', on the other hand, cannot be democratised, as will be plain to anyone who thinks about it. Yet it is of very great political importance. What matters from a social and political point of view is not, as so many

[33] Weber's irony borders on the sarcastic as he claims that the Germans, despite the lip-service paid to the 'values of classical Weimar', fail in practice to live up to the ideals (*Anmut*, 'grace' or *Würde*, 'dignity') at the heart of Schiller's project of an aesthetic education for humanity. See Friedrich Schiller, *On the Aesthetic Education of Man*, translated and edited by E. Wilkinson and L A. Willoughby (Oxford, 1967), in which (fifteenth letter) Schiller pleads for a fusion of grace and dignity.
[34] 'Gentlemen' is in English.

believe, the validity of the so-called 'code of honour' in the strict sense within the *officer* corps, where it is quite properly at home. The politically important fact is that a *Prussian* district superintendent (*Landrat*) absolutely must be able to 'give satisfaction' in the sense understood by students if he is to *command the respect* necessary to carry out his function, as must any other administrative official who can easily be discharged or transferred, in contrast to the independent stipendiary judge (*Amtsrichter*), say, who is socially *declassed* in comparison with the *Landrat* precisely because of his independence. The concept of the ability to give satisfaction and all the other conventions and forms which are supported by the structure of the bureaucracy and by the honour of the German student which exercises so much influence on it, *formally* represent *caste conventions* because they are inherently not susceptible of democratisation. In *substance*, however, because they lack any kind of aesthetic dignity or distinction, their character is *plebeian* rather than aristocratic. It is this inner contradiction which makes them such a political liability and an object of scorn.

The Germans are a *plebeian people* – or, if people prefer the term, a bourgeois (*bürgerlich*) people, and this is the only basis on which a specifically 'German form' could grow.

Any democratisation of society resulting from or promoted by a change in our political arrangements, which is the topic under discussion here, would not find pre-existing aristocratic forms and values amongst us Germans (considered from a *social* point of view) which would either have to be destroyed or, conversely, be stripped of their exclusiveness and propagated throughout the nation, as happened to the formal values of the English and Latin aristocracies in the process of just such a social transformation. On the other hand, the formal values of the German university graduate who is entitled to give satisfaction do *not* give inner support even to the members of that social stratum because these values are not sufficiently those of a man of the world. As any test will show, they are not even adequate to disguise a real feeling of insecurity when dealing with foreigners who have been brought up to be men of the world, except possibly in the form of an 'arrogant' manner which generally stems from embarrassment and strikes others as ill-mannered.

Let us leave aside the question of whether *political* democratisation would really result in *social* democratisation. The absence of barriers in America's political 'democracy', for example, has not prevented the gradual growth of an estate of 'aristocrats' alongside the crude plutocracy of property (as people here believe), and the slow, but generally overlooked growth of this 'aristocracy' is just as important for the history of American culture.

At any rate, the development of a truly distinguished 'German form' which would also match the *bourgeois* character of the leading social strata here is still only a possibility for the future. Political and economic developments since 1870 have not so far led to any further development of those specifically bourgeois conventions which first began to take shape in the cities of the Hanseatic League. As the present war is bestowing on Germany so many parvenus whose sons will busy themselves at university acquiring the usual conventions of the colour corps (which make no demands on any tradition of distinction) as an easy training by which to gain access to the ranks of the reserve officers, there is little hope of renewal in the immediate future. One thing at least is certain: if the process of 'democratisation' were to succeed in *doing away with* the social prestige of the university graduate – which is far from certain, for reasons that cannot be gone into here – this would *not* destroy any politically valuable social forms. It *could* then perhaps clear the way for the development of formal values which would be appropriate to our *middle class* social and economic structure and therefore be both 'genuine' and distinguished. Such values are as impossible to invent for oneself as a style, and there is just one, essentially negative and formal observation to be made about all of them, namely that they can only be developed on the basis of inner *distance* and *reserve* in a person's personal bearing. This prerequisite of all personal dignity has often been gravely lacking throughout the whole of German society. The latest breed of littérateurs with their need to prattle about their 'experiences' in word and print, be they erotic, 'religious' or whatever, are the enemies of all dignity. Various 'prophecies' produced under the influence of Nietzsche are based on a misconception, for 'distance' is certainly not to be achieved by standing on the pedestal of some 'aristocratic' contrast between oneself and the 'all too many'[35]; indeed, on the

---

[35] Weber is referring to Nietzsche's concept of 'distance', as found, for example, in *Beyond Good and Evil*, Section 257 and *The Genealogy of Morals*, Section 24. The term 'the many-too-many' occurs, in particular, in 'Of The New Idol' in *Thus Spake Zarathustra*.

contrary, distance is always inauthentic if it needs this inner support nowadays. It may be that the need to maintain one's inner distance within a 'democratic' world will prove to be a valuable test of its genuineness.

All this shows yet again that in this, as in so many other respects, the German Fatherland is, as Alexander Herzen said so beautifully of Russia, *not* the land of its fathers but of its *children* and that this is how things must be.[36] This is particularly true of its *political* problems. These problems cannot be solved by distilling the 'German spirit' from works of the past, however great their value may have been. Let us pay all due respect to the great shades of our intellectual ancestors, and let us make use of their achievements to give formal training to our own minds. But as soon as the vanity of our littérate-urs, simply because it is *their* vocation as writers to interpret the classic authors to the nation, claims that this function entitles them to lay down the future political shape of Germany with a *schoolmaster's pointer*, then *it is high time to throw the old tomes aside.*[37] There is *nothing* to be learnt from them on this question. Among other things, the German classics could teach us that the German people was able to be one of the leading cultural nations (*Kulturvolk*) in the world at a time of material poverty, political impotence and even foreign rule. The ideas of our classic writers originated in an *un*political epoch, even where these ideas concern politics and economics. Inspired by the debates surrounding the French Revolution, these ideas were in part constructed in an atmosphere in which political and economic passions were lacking. The only kind of political passion which inspired them, other than angry rebellion against foreign rule, lay in their ideal enthusiasm for *moral* demands. Anything beyond that remained at the level of philosophical ideas which could stimulate us to adopt a position appropriate to *our* political realities and the demands of *today*, but they cannot serve as signposts to the future.

---

[36] We have found no source for this attribution in the works of Alexander Herzen, although it certainly accords with his sentiments.

[37] It is not entirely clear who are the targets of Weber's attack here, but it could well have been directed against the circle around the poet Stefan George which looked back on the classical past as a model for the future. In particular, the most prominent literary historian of the circle, Friedrich Gundolf, had attracted the attention of intellectual circles with the publication of his biography of Goethe (1916) just one year before Weber wrote this piece.

The modern problems of parliamentary rule and democracy, and indeed the essential nature of our modern state generally, lay wholly outside their field of vision.

To return to equal suffrage: it is alleged that this means the victory of the inarticulate political 'instincts of the masses' (which are supposedly inaccessible to political reflection) over well-considered political conviction, or the victory of the politics of emotion over the politics of reason. To deal with this latter question first: Germany's foreign policy – *this* certainly must be said here – proves that a monarchy ruling with a class-based suffrage (for German policy is and was dictated by the hegemony of *Prussia*) certainly holds the all-comers' record for a policy influenced by the purely personal and emotional moods of the leadership. For proof of this, one only needs to compare the ineffectual, zig-zag course of this kind of noisy politics here in Germany over the last few decades with the calm sense of direction in, say, English foreign policy. As far as the irrational 'instincts of the masses' are concerned, these only dominate politics where a compact mass *as such* exerts *pressure*, namely in large modern cities, particularly where the Latin style of city life prevails. Climatic conditions there, together with coffee-house civilisation, allow the politics of the '*street*', as they have been aptly termed, to subject the country at large to violation from the capital city. The rule of the 'man in the street'[38] in England, on the other hand, is connected with very specific structural peculiarities of the urban 'masses' there (which are entirely absent here), while street politics in the Russian capital are linked to the secret societies there. All of these preconditions are absent in Germany, and the temperate nature of German life makes it quite unlikely that we will follow suit in succumbing to this *occasional* danger – for this is what it is, as compared with the source of influence which has been a *chronic* threat to *our* foreign policy. It is not the workforce tied to their places of work but the *layabouts* and coffee-house intellectuals in Rome and Paris who have manufactured the bellicose politics of the 'street', and who have done so, by the way, entirely in the service of the government and *only* to the extent desired or permitted by the government. What was *lacking* was the counterbalance of the industrial proletariat. The industrial proletariat, when it acts in solidarity, is undoubtedly a mighty force,

---

[38] Weber misquotes the idiom (in English) as 'men of the street'.

among other things in controlling the 'street'. Compared with those wholly irresponsible elements, however, it is a force which is at least *capable* of being ordered and led by its trusted representatives, which is to say by politicians who think rationally. As far as the politics of the state are concerned, the most important thing of all is to increase the power of these leaders – in our case the union leaders – over momentary instincts, and, beyond this, *generally* to increase the importance of *responsible* leaders, indeed of political leadership as such. One of the most powerful arguments *for* the creation of orderly, *responsible* political leadership by *parliamentary* leaders is that such an arrangement weakens, as far as this is possible, the impact of purely emotional influences both from 'above' and 'below'. 'The rule of the street' has *nothing* to do with 'equal suffrage'; Rome and Paris were ruled by the 'street' at a time when Italy had the most plutocratic form of suffrage in the world and when Napoleon III governed in Paris with his sham parliament. On the contrary, *only* the orderly *leadership* of the masses by responsible politicians is at all capable of breaking *unregulated* rule by the street and leadership by chance demagogues.

Only in the leading state in the federation, *Prussia*, is equal suffrage a problem which powerfully affects the political interests of the *Reich*. Thanks to the recently issued interpretation of the Easter Message,[39] the question now seems to have been settled there, at least in principle. In principle, but the route by which we are to arrive at that goal has not been settled. It is quite unlikely that the present class parliament will voluntarily give up its electoral privilege unless driven to do so by political circumstances. Or if it does so, then it will only be in the form of some apparent renunciation, for example, by linking equal suffrage to the existence of an upper house constructed with the aid of electoral arithmetic. The *legal* introduction of equal suffrage in Prussia is, however, a demand of the *Reich* in the interests of national politics, for the Reich must be able to call on its citizens to fight for their own existence and honour again in the future, should this prove

[39] The 'Easter Message' refers to the statement made by the Kaiser on 7 April 1917 in which he promised reform of the Prussian upper house and the introduction of the secret ballot and direct election (but not universal suffrage) as soon as the war ended. This promise of political reform as a reward for the sacrifices of the people came one day after the American declaration of war on Germany and in the wake of the radicalisation of Social Democracy produced by the Russian Revolution. An imperial proclamation in July 1917 'clarified' matters by promising equal suffrage.

necessary. It is not sufficient for this purpose to have supplies of munitions and other materials and the necessary official organs; what is also needed is the nation's *inner readiness* to defend this state as *its* state. We can see from events in the east what happens when this readiness is lacking.[40] One thing is certain: *the nation can never again be mobilised for war as it was on this occasion* if solemn assurances are rendered worthless by some superficially 'clever' piece of deception. That would never be forgotten. This is the *crucial* political reason why the *Reich* must ensure that equal suffrage is implemented everywhere, by coercion if necessary.

Finally, let me deal briefly with the relationship between *parliamentarisation* and *democratisation* as a question of principle. There are quite a number of very honest and indeed fanatical 'democrats' who regard 'parliamentarisation' as a corrupt system for careerists and parasites, leading to the perversion of democracy and to rule by a clique. 'Politics', in their view, may be fairly 'interesting' but in other respects it is a sterile activity for layabouts. The only thing that matters, particularly to the broad masses of the nation, is good 'administration', and this alone will guarantee the 'true' form of democracy which we in Germany, the country of the 'true notion of freedom', already possess in a superior version to that of other countries, or would be better able to create than other countries without any need for parliamentarisation. Naturally, the advocates of a bureaucracy free of all controls delight in playing one type of democracy off against another, claiming that 'true' democracy is only fully achieved where the 'pack' of advocates in parliament is unable to disturb the objective work of officials. This barefaced swindle – or in the case of our littérateurs, this self-deception stemming from a naive belief in empty phrases – has no difficulty in finding supporters in all camps, as does anything that serves the interest of the bureaucracy and the capitalist interests which are in league with it. It is as clear as can be that this is a swindle, and for two reasons. Firstly, *what organ would democracy have with which to control the administration by officials in turn*, if one imagines that parliamentary power did not exist? There is no answer to this. Secondly, *what would it put in place of rule by parliamentary 'cliques'*? Rule by much more hidden and – usually – smaller cliques whose influence would be even more inescapable. The system of

---

[40] Here the 'east' means, of course, Russia, where revolution had just broken out.

so-called direct democracy is technically possible only in a small state (canton). In all mass states democracy leads to bureaucratic administration and, without parliamentarisation, to pure *rule* by officials. Certainly, where the system of 'Caesarism' (in the wider sense of the word) operates, which is to say the direct, popular election of the head of state or a city, as in the United States and in some of its large cities, democracy can exist *without* a parliamentary system – which does not mean *entirely* without parliamentary power (this is not the place to go into the political and administrative strengths and weaknesses of that arrangement). But the full power of parliament is indispensable wherever *hereditary* organs of state – monarchs – are the (formal) heads of officialdom. Inevitably, the modern monarch is always just as much of an *amateur* as any member of parliament, and therefore quite incapable of controlling an administration. But there is this difference: a member of parliament can learn to weigh the *power of words* in party *conflict*, whereas the monarch is required to remain *outside* this struggle; furthermore, provided it has the right to hold *enquiries*, parliament is in a position to acquire the relevant facts on a subject (by cross-examining experts and witnesses under oath) and thus to control the actions of officials. How is this to be effected by the monarch or by a democracy without a parliament?

Quite generally, any nation which is under the impression that there is *nothing more* to the leadership of the state than 'administration', and that 'politics' is an occasional activity for amateurs or a side-line for officials, must be prepared to *abandon* all thoughts of participating in world politics and must accommodate itself in future to the role of a small state, like a Swiss canton or Denmark or Holland or Baden or Württemberg, all of them well enough administered polities. Otherwise it is bound to repeat our experience with the 'true freedom' preached in certain quarters, which is to say, it must face the consequences of an uncontrolled body of officials attempting to conduct high *politics*. Enthusiasm for 'democracy without parliamentary rule' was nourished during the war, of course, by the fact that – as in any serious war – in all countries without exception, in England, France, Russia and Germany, a political–military *dictatorship* of the most comprehensive kind actually replaced the normal form of government, whether this was called a 'monarchy' or a 'parliamentary republic' and this will undoubtedly cast its shadow far into peacetime. This type of rule operates everywhere with a specific kind of mass demagogy and shuts down all normal [41] valves and controls, including control by parliament. These and other specific products of the war blind the eyes of amateur littérateurs whose minds are bent on the rapid and 'up-to-the-minute' production of books. Yet just as the war economy cannot serve as a model for a normal peacetime economy, these wartime political arrangements cannot be the pattern for a peacetime political structure.

What, we ask, is to replace the political functions of a parliament? Should referenda, say, cater for legislation? Firstly, there is no country in the world where the referendum has been introduced to carry out the most important task performed by regular parliamentary work, namely the *budget*. It is plain that this would simply be impossible. It is easy to predict what would be the fate of virtually any *taxation bill* if it were to be decided by popular referendum. In a mass state a referendum would mean a powerful mechanical brake on all progress, if applied to any at all complicated *laws* and ways of ordering the substance of the nation's culture (*Kultur*); at least this must be so in any geographically large state (the case of a canton is different). The simple, purely technical reason for this is that it *rules out party compromise*. The only questions which can be resolved by referendum in a politically and technically satisfying manner are those which can be answered by a simple 'yes' or 'no'. Otherwise the *variety* of conflicting objections to a proposal would prevent *anything at all* being achieved; and in a socially and geographically highly differentiated mass state there are bound to be incomparably more such objections than in one of the states of America or a Swiss canton. *This* is the specific function performed by parliament: to make it possible to achieve the 'best' solution (relatively speaking) by a process of negotiation and compromise. The price to be paid for this function is the same sacrifice as that made by the voter in a parliamentary election when he has to vote for the party which is *relatively* the most acceptable to him. Nothing else can replace this purely technical superiority of parliamentary legislation – which is not to say that there are no cases where the referendum might be a suitable corrective instrument. As far as the popular election of officials is concerned – unless it is restricted to the election of the *leader*, that is 'Caesarism' – it has to

---

[41] Here the second printing has 'normal' where the first printing of the brochure (1917) had *erworben* ('inherited', 'acquired').

be said that it not only destroys the hierarchical discipline of office in any mass state, but also fosters corruption (to judge by the American experience) by eliminating the *responsibility* for appointment. In a monarchic state every attack on parliamentary rule in the name of 'democracy' means that, thanks to resentment and blindness, the interests of pure bureaucratic rule are being promoted, and in particular the interest of the bureaucracy in remaining free of control.

'Democratisation' in the sense that the structure of social estates is being levelled by the *state run by officials*, is a fact. There are only two choices: either the mass of citizens is left without freedom or rights in a bureaucratic, 'authoritarian state' which has only the appearance of parliamentary rule, and in which the citizens are 'administered' like a herd of cattle; or the citizens are integrated into the state by making them its *co-rulers*. A *nation of masters (Herrenvolk)*[42] – and only such a nation can and may engage in 'world politics' – has *no* choice in this matter. Democratisation can certainly be obstructed – for the moment – because powerful interests, prejudices and cowardice are allied in opposing it. But it would soon emerge that the price to be paid for this would be the entire future of Germany. All the energies of the masses would then be engaged in a struggle *against* a state in which they are mere objects and in which they have no share. Certain circles may have an interest in the inevitable political consequences. The Fatherland certainly does not.

---

[42] Weber's use of the term *Herrenvolk* ought not to be confused with the National Socialists' later misappropriation of Nietzschean vocabulary. Weber's usage does not have imperialist implications but rather conceives of a nation in which each individual is master of his own life and responsible for his own political fate.

Parliament and Government in Germany under a New Political Order

Towards a political critique of officialdom and the party system

Preface

This political treatise is a reworked and extended version of articles which appeared in the *Frankfurter Zeitung* in the summer of 1917.[1] It has nothing new to say to the constitutional expert, nor does it take cover behind the authority of a science, for the ultimate positions adopted by the will cannot be decided by scientific means. Anyone for whom the historical tasks of the German nation do not take *precedence*, as a matter of principle, over all questions of the *form* the state should assume, or anyone with a fundamentally different perception of these tasks, will not be open to the arguments advanced here. For in this respect they proceed from certain assumptions, on the basis of which they attack those people who still consider that this is an appropriate juncture to discredit the popularly elected parliament (*Volksvertretung*) in particular, while favouring other political powers. Unfortunately, this has been going on for the past forty years, including the war years, especially in fairly wide academic and academically educated circles of littérateurs, very often in the most arrogant and intemperate manner, with dismissive animosity and without the least sign of any goodwill even to try to understand the vital conditions

---

[1] *Parlament und Regierung im neugeordneten Deutschland. Zur politischen Kritik des Beamtentums und Parteiwesens* (Munich and Leipzig, 1918). This essay is based on five articles first published in the *Frankfurter Zeitung* between April and June 1917. These were highly controversial, particularly because of the criticisms of the monarch's interventions in politics. The 'usual technical difficulties of printing' which Weber offers as an explanation for their delayed publication as a brochure is a euphemism for difficulties with the censor.

required by parliaments if they are to be effective. The political achievements of German parliaments have certainly not been beyond criticism. But if the Reichstag is to be criticised, so should other organs of the state which these littérateurs have always been careful to spare, indeed have often flattered and courted. If these amateur critics seek cheap sport in tilting at parliament, it is high time to submit their own political insight to unsparing scrutiny. It would of course be a pleasure to debate in a sober and objective manner (*sachlich*) with objective and chivalrous (*vornehm*) opponents – and no doubt such opponents do exist. But it would conflict with German honesty to show respect to groups of people from whose ranks many others, including the present author, have been slandered time and again as 'demagogues' or as 'un-German' or as 'foreign agents'. The undoubted ingenuousness of most of the littérateurs involved was perhaps the most shameful aspect of their excesses.

It has been said that this is not the time to stir up problems of domestic politics, since there are other things we should be doing. 'We'? – who is that? Presumably those who stayed at home. And what ought such people to be doing? Abusing the enemy? That does not win wars. The fighting men out in the field are not doing so, and this wave of abuse, which grows in intensity the further its authors are from the trenches, is hardly worthy of a proud nation. Or are speeches and resolutions called for about all the territories 'we' must first annex before 'we' can conclude peace? One fundamental thing needs to be said on this point: if the army fighting Germany's battles were to take the view that, 'What *we* have won with our blood must remain German', then 'we' who stayed at home would still have the right to say, 'Have a care, that might perhaps be politically imprudent'. But if they stuck to that position nevertheless, 'we' would have to remain silent. Yet it seems to me absolutely intolerable, purely from a human point of view, as well as being utterly damaging to morale, that 'we' who stayed at home have no qualms about poisoning the soldiers' joy in their achievements by proclaiming (as has happened time and again), 'If you fail to achieve one or other of the war-aims devised by us, *you will have shed your blood in vain*'. Instead it would be better simply to keep repeating that Germany is fighting for its very life against an army in which there are negroes, Ghurkas and all manner of barbarians who have come from their hiding places all over the world and who are now gathered at the borders of Germany, ready to lay waste to our country. That is the truth which everyone understands, and to say this would have kept us united. Instead the littérateurs have taken it upon themselves to fabricate all sorts of 'ideas' for which, in their opinion, the men at the front are giving their blood and their lives. I do not believe that this vain activity has lightened the heavy burden of duty for any of our soldiers. The damage it has done to objective political discussion is grave.

It seems to me that the prime task for *us* at home is to ensure that the soldiers come back to find that it has *already been made possible* for them to elect their own representatives at the ballot box and through them to build anew the Germany whose existence they have preserved. This means that we must clear away the obstacles which our present arrangements put in their path, so that, on their return, they do not have to begin by fighting sterile battles against those obstacles instead of getting down to the task of reconstruction. No sophistry in the world can argue away the fact that the only means of achieving this are suffrage and parliamentary power. It is dishonest and impertinent for some people to have complained, in all seriousness, that a reform is being carried out 'without consulting the soldiers' which, for the first time ever, will give them even the *possibility* of decisive co-determination.

It is also said that any criticism of our political arrangements simply puts weapons into the hands of our enemies. For twenty years we were gagged with this argument, until it was too late. What, at this stage, do we still have to lose abroad by making such criticisms? Our enemies would have cause for celebration if the old, grave defects continued to exist. At this precise moment, when the Great War has reached the stage where diplomacy is making its voice heard again, it is high time to do everything we can to prevent the old errors being committed all over again. Unfortunately there is little sign that this will be the case. Our enemies know, or they will learn, that German democracy will not conclude peace on bad terms – unless it wants to throw away its own future.

If there is anyone whose deepest conviction places *every* form of authoritarian rule exercised for its own sake above *all* the political interests of the nation, let him confess his beliefs openly. He cannot be proved wrong. But let no one offer us instead some vain nonsense about the antithesis between the 'Western European' and the 'German' idea of the state. On the simple, technical questions of how the will of the state is determined, which are the questions dealt with here, a mass-state has only a restricted, not an infinite, number of possible forms to choose from. For an *objective* (*sachlich*) politician, the question of which of these forms is the most efficacious for his state at any given time is a question of fact, to be answered in the light of the political tasks facing the nation. Only someone with a regrettable lack of faith in the independence and strength of the German people (*Deutschtum*)[2] could believe that the essential character of the nation would be called into question if we were to share effective institutions for running the state with other nations. Quite apart from which, it is neither the case that parliamentary rule is alien to German history, nor that any of the systems opposed to parliamentary rule is uniquely peculiar to Germany. Compelling objective circumstances will ensure that a German state under parliamentary rule will look *different* from any other state. Yet it would be the politics of the littérateurs rather than objective politics to turn this into an object of national *vanity*. At present we do not know *whether* a truly viable new parliamentary order will come about in Germany. It could be sabotaged by the right, or thrown away by the left. Yes, the latter, too, is possible. It goes without saying that the vital interests of the nation take precedence even over democracy or parliamentary rule. But if parliament were to fail and, as a result, the old system were to return, the consequences would be far-reaching indeed. Even then one could quite properly bless Fate for the fact that one is a German. But we should have to abandon finally all great hopes for Germany's future, *regardless* of the kind of peace that awaits us.

The present author, who voted for the Conservatives almost thirty years ago and later for the Democrats, who once wrote an occasional column for the *Kreuzzeitung*[3] and now writes for liberal papers,[4] is not an active politician, nor will he ever be one. It should however be said, by way of precaution, that he enjoys no connections of any kind to any German statesmen. He has every reason to believe that

---

[2] *Deutschtum* is both a collective noun and one which sums up the qualities of 'German-ness'.

[3] The *Kreuzzeitung* was the name commonly given to *Die Neue Preußische (Kreuz-) Zeitung*, an ultra-conservative newspaper.

[4] The liberal newspapers and journals Weber has in mind are the *Frankfurter Zeitung*, the *Münchener Neueste Nachrichten* and *Die Hilfe*.

no party, including those on the left, will want to identify themselves with what he has to say, particularly not with those things which matter most to him personally (section IV below), these being things about which there is *no* dispute at all amongst the political parties. He has arrived at his chosen political standpoint because the experiences of recent decades convinced him some time ago that the kind of political machinery and the method of determining the will of the state which we have employed hitherto are bound to condemn *any* German policy to failure, whatever its goals. He believes that exactly the same thing will go on being repeated in the future if our political arrangements remain the same, and he considers it unlikely that under those circumstances army leaders will arise time and time again who will be able to hack a way out of the political catastrophe by military means and at the cost of unimaginable sacrifices of the nation's blood.

Technical changes in the running of the state do not in themselves make a nation vigorous (*tüchtig*),[5] nor happy, nor valuable. They can only clear away mechanical obstacles in its path and are therefore merely means to an end. Some may regret that so much importance *can* attach to the sober issues of civil (*bürgerlich*) life which are to be discussed here under a deliberately self-denying ordinance, without any reference to the great, *substantive* questions of culture (*Kultur*) confronting us. But this is simply how things are. On a large scale it is the lesson taught by the politics of the last few decades. On a smaller scale, an official of rare abilities and human qualities very recently failed utterly to give political leadership to the Reich,[6] something which I regard as a kind of practical proof of the account advanced in a series of articles published shortly before those events. Anyone who remains unconvinced after these experiences will not be convinced by any kind of evidence. In considering technical questions of government, the politician thinks in terms of the next few generations. This small piece of occasional writing, too, aims purely and simply to 'serve the present moment'.

[5] *Tüchtig* is a recurrent term of evaluation for Weber. He uses it both in the Darwinian sense of 'fitness' for life (*lebenstüchtig*), and to refer to the cardinal, German-bourgeois virtues of 'efficiency' and 'ability'.
[6] This is a reference to G. Michaelis (1857–1936), Reichskanzler from 14 July to 1 November 1917.

The long delay in following up the suggestion of like-minded friends that these thoughts should be published in the present form was caused firstly by other claims on my time and, since November, by the usual technical difficulties of printing.

1 Bismarck's legacy

The state of our parliamentary life today is a legacy of *Prince Bismarck's long years of rule* in Germany and of that inner attitude which the nation has adopted to him since his last ten years as chancellor of the Reich. This attitude has no equal in the stance adopted by any other great nation towards a statesman of such stature. Nowhere else in the world has even the most unbounded admiration for the personality of a politician led a proud nation to sacrifice its own, objective convictions so unreservedly. On the other hand, objective opposition to a statesman of such enormous dimensions has very rarely given rise elsewhere to such a measure of hatred as was once felt by the extreme left and the Centre Party towards Bismarck. How did this come about?

As so often happens, the after-effects of the mighty events of 1866 and 1870 were first felt by the generation for whom the victorious wars were the indelible experiences of their youth but who did not have their own clear view of the profound domestic political tensions and problems which had accompanied those wars. It was in the minds of these people that Bismarck first became a legend. That generation of political littérateurs who entered public life from about 1878[7] onwards fell into two camps of unequal size in their attitudes towards him. The larger group was filled with adulation, not for the grandeur of his subtle, sovereign mind, but exclusively for the element of violence and cunning in his statesmanship, the real or apparent brutality in his methods, while the other camp reacted to this with feeble *ressentiment*.[8] If this second variant disappeared rapidly after his death,

---

[7] Weber is specific about the year 1878 presumably for several reasons: it was the year of the Congress of Berlin, of the introduction of Bismarck's anti-socialist legislation and of a general shift away from the more liberal policies pursued in the first years of the new Reich.

[8] Cf. Nietzsche, *On the Genealogy of Morals* (1887). Weber described the essay, with its discussion of 'ressentiment', as 'brilliant', *From Max Weber*, ed. H. H. Gerth and C. W. Mills (London 1948), p. 270.

it was only then that the other attitude began to issue in a full-blown literary cult. For a long time now it has stamped the historical legend not only of conservative politicians but also of genuinely enthusiastic littérateurs and finally of all those intellectual plebeians who think they can legitimate themselves as spirit of his spirit through the outward imitation of his gestures. It is well attested that Bismarck himself had nothing but the deepest scorn for this last stratum, which is not without political influence here, although he was of course quite prepared, on occasion, to make political use of those of them who were among his courtiers, just as he used others, such as Herr Busch.[9] 'Content: empty phrases. Form: puerile', was his comment in the margin of a 'Pan-German' (in today's terms) memorandum he had once requested as an experiment from a man who at least differed fundamentally from today's representatives of this line of thought in that he could point to national achievements of his own, done not with his mouth but in the form of bold action. What Bismarck thought of his conservative peers is recorded in his memoirs.

He had some cause to look down on them. For what did he experience when he had to relinquish office in 1890? To be fair, it was too much to expect expressions of sympathy from the Centre Party, to whose 'coat-tails' he had tied the assassination attempt by Kullmann,[10] or from the Social Democrats whom he had harried with the expulsion paragraph in his anti-Socialist legislation, or from the 'Freisinnigen' (Independent Liberals)[11] whom he had branded 'enemies of the Reich'. But what of the others who had applauded these actions so loudly? Prussian ministerial posts and the offices of the Reich were filled by *conservative* creatures who owed their political existence entirely to Bismarck. What did they do? They sat just where they were. 'A new superior' – that was the end of the matter, as far as they were concerned. *Conservative* politicians occupied the praesidial chair in the parliaments of the Reich and of Prussia. What was their parting cry to the creator of the Reich as he left office? They passed over the incident in silence. Which of the great parties in his following even so much as demanded to know the reasons for his

---

[9] M. Busch (1821–99), journalist and war reporter.
[10] E. Kullmann, an apprentice cooper and a Catholic, attempted to assassinate Bismarck in July 1874. Bismarck attempted to link him with the Catholic Centre Party.
[11] The 'Deutsch-Freisinnige Partei' (1884–93), a left-liberal party which strongly advocated free trade and opposed the *Septennat* in 1887.

dismissal? None of them even lifted a finger. They simply turned towards the new sun. The event is unparalleled in the annals of a proud people. But what heightens the disparagement it deserves is the enthusiasm for Bismarck to which these same parties subsequently laid claim as their inheritance. At *no time* in the last fifty years have the Prussian Conservatives shown any political *character* in the service of great political or ideal goals – as the Stahls[12] and Gerlachs[13] once did and as did the old Christian-Social politicians in their own way. If you examine what happened, you will find that *only* when there was any threat to their financial interests or their monopoly of the prebends of office and the patronage of office or (which was the same thing) to their electoral privileges, did their local electoral machine begin to operate ruthlessly, and then it did so even *against* the king. Then (as now) the whole, sad apparatus of 'Christian', 'Monarchist' and 'National' phrase-mongering usually went into action – exactly the kind of behaviour which these same gentlemen denounce as 'cant' in the rhetorical store of English politicians. Only when their own *material* interests (on tariff policy above all) were at stake some years after Bismarck's dismissal, did they think of hitching their waggon to Bismarck, since when they have boasted, in all seriousness, of being the guardians of his traditions. There are strong reasons for assuming that in those days Bismarck always regarded such activities with contempt. Remarks made in private prove it. Who can blame him? But any feelings of shame one may feel about that caricature of a politically mature people which the nation presented in 1890 must not be allowed to obscure one thing: when his supporters showed such an utterly squalid lack of dignity, Bismarck was reaping a tragic harvest which *he himself had sown*. For he had sought and deliberately brought about just such political nullity in parliament and amongst the party politicians.

Never has a statesman who was not put at the helm by the trust of a parliament had as his partner a political party so easy to deal with and yet so full of political talents as Bismarck enjoyed between 1867 and 1878. One may reject the political views of the National

---

[12] F. J. Stahl (1802–61), political theorist and conservative politician, proponent of the idea of an absolute and paternalistic monarchy for Prussia.

[13] E. L. von Gerlach (1795–1877), political theorist and one of the founders of the Prussian Conservative Party. He argued for the revival of a corporatively (*ständisch*) organised state.

Liberal leadership at that time. Of course one must not measure them by the standard of Bismarck himself in the area of high politics or in terms of sovereign intellectual energy, for even the best of them seem only mediocre in comparison; after all, this is even more true of all other domestic politicians and most foreign ones too. If one is lucky, a genius appears just once every few hundred years. But we might thank fate if the politicians into whose hands it had placed the present and future leadership of the country proved to be as able on average as those in the National Liberal party in those days. It is indeed a most impertinent distortion of the truth for political littérateurs here nevertheless to try to persuade the nation that 'Parliament in Germany has failed so far to produce great political talents'. It is deplorable that the subaltern fashion among today's littérateurs should deny that representatives of parliamentarism like Bennigsen, Stauffenberg, Völk, or of democracy, like the Prussian patriot Waldeck, possessed the quality demanded of representatives of '*the German spirit*', for that spirit was at least as alive in the Paulskirche[14] as it is amongst the bureaucracy, and more so than in the inkwells of these gentlemen. The great merit of those politicians from the heyday of the Reichstag was, firstly, the fact that they knew their own limitations and past errors and acknowledged Bismarck's vast intellectual superiority. Nowhere did he have more passionate and quite personal admirers than in their ranks, and in particular amongst those who subsequently seceded from the party. One thing above all attests to their personal distinction, namely their complete lack of feelings of *ressentiment* about his superior stature. Everyone who knew these men would completely absolve all the significant figures amongst them of any such thing. Anyone familiar with the events would have to regard it as bordering on paranoia if Bismarck seriously entertained the idea that *these* particular politicians had ever considered 'overthrowing' him. I have heard their leaders say on numerous occasions that 'Caesarism', the governmental form of genius, would be the accepted political arrangement in Germany if there were the slightest chance of some new Bismarck always emerging to fill the highest position. That was their sincerely held conviction. It is true that they had crossed swords fiercely with him in the past. For this

---

[14] The German Constituent National Assembly of 1848 met in St Paul's Church ('die Paulskirche'), Frankfurt.

very reason they were also aware of *his limitations* and were certainly not inclined to make any unmanly *sacrificium intellectus*, although they were always prepared, even to the point of self-abnegation, to go a long way to meet him in order to avoid a break with him – much further, indeed, than was permissible in view of the mood of the voters, who then threatened to withdraw their support. The National Liberal politicians avoided a fight for formal parliamentary rights with the creator of the Reich, not only because they foresaw that, in party political terms, any such contest would only help the *Centre Party* to gain power, but also because they knew that it would paralyse Bismarck's own policies as well as the substantive (*sachlich*) work of parliament for a long time to come: 'Nothing is successful any more' was the well-known watchword of the eighties. Their innermost intention, often expressed in their own circles, was to steer safely through the period when this grandiose personality ruled the Reich those institutions which would ensure continuity of Reich policy once the time had come to adjust once more to politicians of normal stature. Admittedly, these institutions included, in their view, a *parliament* which would have a positive share in decision-making and therefore be capable of attracting great political talents – and strong parties.

They were perfectly aware that the achievement of this goal absolutely *did not depend on them alone*. On the occasion of the great change of direction in 1878, I very often heard people from their ranks say, 'No great political skill is needed to destroy a party in such an utterly precarious position as ours or to make its continued existence impossible. If this happens, however, it will not be possible to create another great party which collaborates in a purely objective way. Instead it will be necessary to have recourse to the politics of interest groups and the system of petty patronage, and it will be necessary nevertheless to accept the most severe political upheavals into the bargain.' As I have said, one may judge particular positions taken by the party as one will. After all, it was ultimately on their initiative that the office of the Reichskanzler received its constitutional definition (Bennigsen's motion), that civil law was unified (motion by Lasker), that the Reichsbank was created (motion by Bamberger), indeed that the majority of the great institutions of the Reich still in effective operation today were introduced. With the benefit of hindsight it is easy to criticise their tactics, but these constantly had to take account of the party's difficult position in relation to Bismarck. In part the decline of the party's position can be blamed on the natural difficulties of a party which was so purely political in its orientation and yet burdened with antiquated economic dogmas when faced with problems of the economy and social policy, although the position of the conservative parties on all these issues was certainly no better. The opposition between Bismarck's aims and the constitution they wanted to see after 1866 did not arise, as some would have it, from their 'shortsightedness', but from their *unitarist* ideals (in the manner of Treitschke)[15] at that time (which we have abandoned in the meantime, partly for reasons of foreign policy). Subsequent developments have proved the fundamental political premises of their conduct to have been *entirely correct*.

They were unable to achieve their chosen political objective and fell apart, not ultimately for reasons of substance, but because Bismarck was unable to tolerate *any* kind of at all independent power alongside himself, that is to say one that acted on its own responsibility. *Neither* within the ministries – entry to the ministries was offered to individual parliamentary politicians, but they all had to learn that Bismarck had already shrewdly arranged for the new colleague to be brought down at any time, if necessary, by discrediting him on purely personal grounds; this and only this was ultimately the reason why Bennigsen declined to join him. *Nor* in parliament, where Bismarck's whole policy was aimed at preventing the consolidation of any strong and yet independent constitutional party. Apart from his quite deliberate and skilful exploitation of the conflicts of interest on tariff policy, the *army estimates* and the *anti-Socialist legislation* provided him with the main means of achieving this aim.[16]

As far as I am aware, at that time the inner standpoint of National Liberal politicians towards *military questions* was as follows. The peacetime strength of the army, which they were inclined to keep as large as need be, had, for this very reason, to be treated as a purely *technical (sachlich)* question, thus burying the old divisions from the

---

[15] H. von Treitschke (1834–96), historian, politician and political thinker. Proponent of a united Germany as a *Machtstaat* under Prussian leadership.

[16] Bismarck countered the opposition to renewal of the army estimates (the *Septennat*) in 1886 with the dissolution of the Reichstag. In 1878 two attempts to assassinate the Emperor provided a pretext to dissolve the Reichstag and, subsequently, to enact the (anti-) Socialist Law which denied the rights of assembly and of publication to socialist organisations.

time of the Prussian Constitutional Conflict,[17] and sealing off at least this source of demagogic unrest for the good of the Reich. The only means of achieving this was for the size of the army simply to be stated in the annual *budgetary legislation*. None of the leaders ever doubted that the requisite enlargement of the army would proceed in this way without domestic or foreign excitement or upheaval. Above all they believed that this purely *factual* way of dealing with the question would enable the army administration to gain acceptance for much higher demands and in a less conspicuous way than would be the case if this technical question were to become mixed up with the domestic political power interests of the government offices in relation to parliament, which would mean that military questions would be blown up every seven years into a catastrophic political sensation threatening the foundations of the Reich and would lead to a furious electoral campaign fought on the slogan, 'The Kaiser's army or Parliament's army?' A *profoundly dishonest* slogan, since an annual budget would have made the army not a whit more of a parliamentary army than if the budget were agreed every seven years – especially as the seven-yearly budget (*Septennat*) remained a fiction in any case. The Reichstag was dissolved in 1887 solely on the issue of whether the requisite peacetime size of the army, which had been accepted by *all* bourgeois parties, should be approved for three or seven years, and on the alleged grounds that approval for just three years represented an 'attack on the prerogatives of the crown'. In 1890, just three years later, however, a new bill on the peacetime size of the army was indeed introduced, something about which Windthorst did not fail to taunt his opponents scornfully and with every justification. In this way the old, buried dispute about the army in Prussia was carried over into Reich politics, so that the military question became linked to party political interests. It must be recognised, however, that *this is precisely* what Bismarck wanted. He saw that demagogic slogan as a means to make the Kaiser, who had lived through the period of constitutional conflict in Prussia, suspect that the Reichstag and the Liberal parties were 'hostile to the army', while at the same time using the *Septennat* to discredit the National Liberals in the eyes of their own voters for having betrayed budgetary rights.

---

[17] A reference to the conflict that took place between the Prussian Diet and King Wilhelm from 1861 until 1865 concerning the question of army reform and its funding.

It was the same with the *anti-Socialist legislation*. The party was prepared to go a long way to meet Bismarck, and even the Progressives were inclined to approve regulations which made what they called 'class-agitation' punishable in common law as a *general* and permanent arrangement. What Bismarck was seeking, however, was the *Emergency Law as such*. Dissolving the Reichstag amidst the excitement generated by the second assassination attempt, without even attempting to reach an agreement with parliament, was for Bismarck merely a demagogic means of splitting the only powerful party at the time.

He succeeded. *And what was the result?* Instead of the need to take account of a *parliamentary* party which, for all its criticisms, had close inner ties to him and which, from the outset, had co-operated in the foundation of the Reich, Bismarck had substituted permanent dependence on the *Centre Party*, a party supported by *extra*-parliamentary instruments of power which he had no means of attacking, a party with a deadly hatred of him which – despite everything – lasted until his death.[18] When he later gave his famous speech about the passing of the 'springtime of the peoples',[19] Windthorst retorted scornfully, but justifiably, that Bismarck himself had destroyed the great party which had supported him in times past. He had rejected the National Liberals' demand that the right of the Reichstag to approve government expenditure should be safeguarded in a particular way, on the grounds that this legitimated 'parliamentary rule' – yet now he had to grant exactly the same thing to the Centre Party, and in the most pernicious form possible – in the 'perquisites paragraph' of the so-called Franckenstein clausula, to which Prussia added the even more pernicious 'lex Huene', which was subsequently removed only with great difficulty.[20] Apart from this, he had to accept the severe defeat of state authority in the *Kulturkampf*, while vainly (and dishonestly) trying to disown responsibility for the quite inappro-

[18] The hatred to which Weber refers was the consequence of Bismarck's campaign against Catholics (the *Kulturkampf*).
[19] Bismarck's speech to the Reichstag, 13 March 1885.
[20] The 'Franckenstein clause' refers to the proposal made by Deputy Franckenstein of the Zentrum in 1878 that revenues raised by the Reich from customs duties and tobacco duty should be distributed to the federal states in proportion to the size of their populations. The *lex Huene* refers to the bill introduced by the Prussian Deputy Huene in 1885 requiring a large proportion of the additional finances from increased duties on cattle and grain to be distributed to local associations.

priate methods used in that struggle, and at the same time supplying the Social Democrats with the most brilliant electoral slogan imaginable in the shape of the 'Emergency Legislation' (*Ausnahmegesetz*). In Bismarck's hands the social welfare legislation of the Reich, too, became mere demagogy, and bad demagogy at that, no matter how valuable one may consider it to be in purely objective terms. Industrial protection legislation, the most indispensable means of maintaining the physical strength of the nation, he rejected as an intrusion into the rights of masters (using arguments of incredible triviality at times). He adopted the same stance when he used the police and the anti-Socialist legislation to smash the unions, the only institutions which could possibly represent workers' interests in an objective manner, thus driving their members into the most extreme, purely party-political radicalism. On the other hand, taking his lead from certain American models, he thought he could generate 'loyalty to the state' (*Staatsgesinnung*) and 'gratitude' by granting state *pensions* or pensions enforced by the state. A grave political error this, for every policy that has ever gambled on gratitude has failed. The saying, 'They have their reward'[21] also applies to the blessedness of political work. We were given pensions for the sick, the injured, the war-disabled and the old. That was certainly admirable. But we were *not* given the guarantees which are necessary above all else to *maintain* physical and mental strength and to make it possible for the *strong* and *healthy* to *represent their interests* in an objective and confident way, the interests, in other words, of precisely those people who mattered most in purely political terms. As in the *Kulturkampf*, he had simply ridden roughshod over all the decisive psychological preconditions. Particularly in his treatment of the unions he overlooked the one thing which some politicians have still not grasped today, namely that a state that seeks to base the spirit of a mass army on *honour and comradeship* must never forget that in everyday life, in the workers' economic struggles, the sense of honour and comradeship produces the only decisive moral forces for the education of the masses, and that these forces must therefore be given free rein. From a *purely political* point of view, *this and this alone* is what 'social democracy' means in an age which will inevitably remain capitalist for a long time to come. We are still suffering the consequences of this policy today. All in all, it

---

[21] Weber is quoting Matthew 6, 5.

was Bismarck himself who had created an atmosphere and situation which meant that if he stayed in office in 1890 the only possible alternatives were a coup d'etat or unconditional surrender to the will of Windthorst.[22] It was not by chance that the nation received the news of his resignation with complete indifference.

In contrast to the usual undifferentiated, uncritical and above all unmanly hymns of praise to the policies of Bismarck, it seemed high time to remind people of this aspect of the matter for a change. For a large (and certainly the most influential) part of the popular literature on Bismarck is written for the Christmas table of the philistine who prefers the wholly unpolitical brand of hero-worship which has become the normal thing here. It says what these sentimental readers want to hear and thinks it serves its hero well by concealing his limitations and slandering his opponents. This is not the way to educate a nation to think for itself politically. Bismarck remains a giant in stature even when we seek to understand objectively others whose view of things differed from his, and even if we acknowledge candidly the consequences of his profound misanthropy and of the fact that, from 1875[23] onwards, his rule led the nation to lose the habit of sharing responsibility, through its elected representatives, for its own political fate, which is the only way a nation can possibly be trained in the exercise of political judgement.

What interests us here is the question of the *political legacy* bequeathed by Bismarck as a result of all these things. He left behind a nation *entirely lacking in any kind of political education*, far below the level it had already attained twenty years previously. And above all a nation *entirely without any political will*, accustomed to assume that the great statesman at the head of the nation would take care of political matters for them. Furthermore, as a result of his misuse of monarchic sentiment as a cover for his own power interests in the struggle between the political parties, he left behind a nation accustomed to *submit passively* and fatalistically to whatever was decided on its behalf, under the label of 'monarchic government', without criticising the political qualifications of those who filled the chair left

---

[22] L. Windthorst (1812–91), leader of the Centre Party and opponent of Bismarck during the *Kulturkampf*.

[23] In Winckelmann's edition (p. 319) 1875 has been changed (probably correctly) to 1878, the year when Bismarck made the momentous change of direction to which Weber refers at the beginning of this section and in his letters.

empty by Bismarck and who seized the reins of government with such an astonishing lack of self-doubt. It was in this area that the most severe damage by far was done. *In no sense* did the great statesman leave behind a political tradition. He did not recruit, nor could he even tolerate, men with an independent cast of mind, to say nothing of men of character. It was the nation's misfortune that, in addition to his furious suspicion of anyone who could possibly be thought of as his successor, he had a son whose truly modest qualities of statesmanship he overestimated to an astonishing degree. At the same time his enormous prestige had the purely negative consequence of leaving *parliament utterly without power*. It is well known that, after leaving office, he accused himself of having made a mistake in this respect, and was then made to suffer the consequences as part of his own fate. The powerlessness of parliament also meant that its intellectual level was very low. Admittedly, the naively moralising legend of our littérateurs would have us believe that cause and effect were in fact the other way round, namely that parliament deserved to remain powerless because of the low quality of parliamentary life. The true state of affairs, self-evident on any sober reflection, is indicated by some very simple facts and considerations. Whether a parliament is of high or low intellectual quality depends on *whether great problems* are not only *discussed* but are *conclusively decided* there. In other words, it depends on *whether anything happens in parliament* and on *how much depends on what happens there*, or whether it is merely the reluctantly tolerated rubber-stamping machine for a ruling bureaucracy.

II Rule by officials and political leadership

In a modern state real *rule*, which becomes effective in everyday life neither through parliamentary speeches nor through the pronouncements of monarchs but through the day-to-day *management of the administration*, necessarily and inevitably lies in the hands of *officialdom*, both military and civilian. The modern high-ranking officer even conducts battles from his 'office'. Just as so-called progress towards capitalism has been the unequivocal criterion of economic modernisation since the Middle Ages, so the equally unequivocal criterion for the modernisation of the state has been progress towards a bureaucratic officialdom based on recruitment, salary, pension, promotion, professional training, firmly established areas of responsibility, the keeping of files, hierarchical structures of superiority and subordination. This applies as much to the monarchic as to the democratic state, and at any rate wherever the state is a great mass-state rather than some small canton where responsibility for government is taken by turns. Both the absolutist state and democracy dispense with government by notables, whether feudal or patrimonial or patrician or other types which operate on an honorary or hereditary basis, replacing them with paid officials. Paid officials decide on all our daily needs and complaints. In this decisive respect there is no difference between the civilian administrative official and the military bearer of rule, the officer. The modern mass army, too, is a *bureaucratic* army, with the officer being a special category of official in contrast to the knight, *condottiere*, tribal chief or Homeric hero. The effectiveness of the army as a fighting force rests on the disciplined performance of duty. The onward march of bureaucracy is also taking place, with only minor modifications, in municipal administrations. This is the more the case, the larger the community is, or the more inevitably it is being divested of its organic, local rootedness by the creation of single-purpose associations (*Zweckverbände*) of a technical or economic nature. In the church the most fundamentally important outcome of 1870 was not the much discussed dogma of papal infallibility but the universal episcopate. This created bureaucratic 'rule by chaplains' and, in contrast to the Middle Ages, made the bishop and priest into simple officials of the central power of the Curia. The large private firms we have today have undergone the same development, and the larger they are the more this has occurred. In statistical terms, the numbers of office workers in private firms are growing faster than manual workers, and it is quite ridiculous for our littérateurs to imagine that there is the slightest difference between the mental work done in the office of a private firm and that performed in an office of the state.

Fundamentally they are both exactly the same kind of thing. Looked at from a social-scientific point of view, the modern state is an 'organisation' (*Betrieb*) in exactly the same way as a factory; indeed this is its specific historical characteristic. In both cases the relations of rule within the organisation are subject to the same conditions. The relative independence of the craftsman or the home-worker, the freehold farmer, the *commendatar*, the knight and the vassal, rested in each case on the fact that they themselves owned the tools, provisions, finances or weapons which they used to perform their economic, political or military functions, and lived off them while they were carrying out those functions. Conversely, the hierarchical dependency of the worker, clerk, technical employee, the assistant in an academic institution *and also* of the official and soldier of the state rests in every case on the fact that the tools, provisions and finances which are indispensable both for the performance of his work and for his economic existence are concentrated in the hands of an entrepreneur in the one case, and in those of a political master in the other. The majority of the Russian soldiers, for example, did not *want* to fight a war any longer. But they were obliged to do so, because the provisions they lived on and the material means of conducting the war were under the control of men who used these things to force the soldiers into the trenches, in exactly the same way as the capitalist who owns the means of conducting economic activity forces workers into factories and down the mines. Whether an organisation is a modern state apparatus engaging in power politics or cultural politics (*Kulturpolitik*) or pursuing military aims, or a private capitalist business, the same, decisive economic basis is *common* to both, namely the 'separation' of the worker from the material means of conducting the activity of the organisation – the means of production in the economy, the means of war in the army, or the means of research in a university institution or laboratory, and the financial means in all of them. In both cases control of these means is in the hands of that power which the *bureaucratic apparatus obeys* directly (judges, officials, officers, foremen, clerks, N.C.O.s) or to which it makes itself available when summoned to do so. This apparatus is the common feature shared by all these formations, its existence and function being inseparably linked, both as cause and effect, with the 'concentration of the material means of operation'. Or rather this apparatus is the form taken by that very process of concentration. Today increasing 'socialisation' inevitably means increasing bureaucratisation.

Historically, too, 'progress' towards the bureaucratic state which adjudicates in accordance with rationally established law and administers according to rationally devised regulations stands in the closest relation to the development of modern capitalism. The main inner foundation of the modern capitalist business is *calculation*. In order to exist, it requires a system of justice and administration which, in principle at any rate, function in a *rationally calculable* manner according to stable, general norms, just as one calculates the predictable performance of a *machine*. By contrast, it finds quite uncongenial what is popularly called 'cadi justice',[24] where judgements are made on each *individual* case according to the judge's sense of fairness, or according to other irrational means of adjudication and principles which existed everywhere in the past and still exist in the Orient today. Equally uncongenial to capitalism is the patriarchal form of administration based on arbitrary decision and grace, but otherwise operating according to binding, holy but irrational tradition, such as one finds in the theocratic or patrimonial associations of rule (*Herrschaftsverbände*) in Asia and in our own past. The fact that this form of 'cadi justice' and the type of administration that corresponds to it are very often *venal*, precisely because of their irrational character, allowed a certain form of capitalism to come into existence (and often to flourish luxuriantly thanks to these qualities), that of the trader and government contractor and all varieties of the *pre*-rational capitalism that has been in existence for four thousand years, specifically the adventurer and robber capitalism which was tied to politics, war, administration as such. *Nowhere* in such irrationally constructed polities, however, did or could there emerge the *specific* feature of *modern* capitalism that distinguishes it from those ancient forms of capitalist acquisition, namely the strictly rational *organisation of work* on the basis of *rational technology*. These modern types of business, with their fixed capital and precise calculations, are far too easily damaged by irrationalities of justice or administration for them to have emerged under such circumstances. They could only emerge where law was practised in one of two ways. *Either*, as in England, the practical shaping of law was in fact in the hands of advocates who, in the service of their clientele (men with capitalist interests), devised the appropriate forms for conducting business, and from whose ranks there emerged judges who were bound strictly by 'precedent', and thus to *calculable* schemata. *Or where*, as in the bureaucratic state with its rational laws, the judge is a kind of legal para-

---

[24] Weber contrasts 'cadi justice' with common law and Roman law in *Economy and Society* (where the word is spelt 'Khadi'); see pp. 976–8 in particular. In Weber's terminology the term refers to a form of dispensing justice which rests neither on a formal legal code, nor on prophetic revelation, nor on precedent but upon informal judgements made on the basis of particular ethical values. A 'cadi' is an Islamic judge.

graph-machine into which one throws the documents on a case together with the costs and fees so that it will then spit out a judgement along with some more or less valid reasons for it; here again, the system works in a more or less *calculable* way.[A]

Finally, the same progress towards bureaucratisation as is taking place in economic life and in state administration is now also to be found in the *parties*.

The existence of parties is acknowledged by no constitution and by no law (at least here in Germany), although they are nowadays by far the most important bearers of the political will of those who are ruled by the bureaucracy, the 'citizens of the state' (*Staatsbürger*). However many devices they employ to bind their clientele permanently to them, parties are essentially voluntarily created organisations directed at free *recruitment* which is necessarily continuous, in contrast to all corporations which are firmly delimited by law or by contract. Nowadays their goal is always the canvassing of votes for elections to political positions or to an electoral corporation. Fund-raising is the responsibility of a permanent core of people with a vested interest in the party who are grouped together under the direction of a leader or a group of notables; the structure of this core varies greatly in its stability and often has a fully developed bureaucracy nowadays; finances are raised with the help of party patrons or persons with economic interests or with interests in the patronage of office, or through membership subscriptions; usually a variety of such sources is involved. This core decides on the current programme,

---

[A] The characteristically amateurish notion of the littérateurs that 'Roman law' promoted the development of capitalism belongs in the nursery. Every student is obliged to know that all the characteristic legal institutions of modern capitalism were completely unknown under Roman law and are medieval in origin, to a considerable degree even specifically Germanic, and that Roman law has never gained a foothold in England, the motherland of modern capitalism. These institutions include shares, bonds, the modern law on the use of land as a security, bills of exchange and all forms of commercial documents up to and including the capitalist forms of association in industry, mining and trade. Here in Germany the advent of Roman law was facilitated by the absence of the great national guilds of advocates which resisted Roman law in England and further by the *bureaucratisation* of the administration of justice and state administration. Modern early capitalism did not *come into being* in countries which were models of bureaucracy (which in turn emerged there from pure state rationalism). Modern high capitalism was also not restricted to these countries, initially was not even predominantly at home there, but in places where the judges began as advocates. Nowadays, however, bureaucracy and capitalism have met and belong together intimately.

the strategy and the candidates. Even in a mass party with a very democratic form of organisation (the consequence of which is always the development of a staff of salaried officials) the mass of voters at least, and to a considerable extent the ordinary 'membership' too, is *not* (or only formally) involved in deciding on programmes and candidates. The electors only participate in the sense that both programmes and candidates are adapted to, and chosen in accordance with, the chances of winning their votes.

One may complain moralistically about the existence of parties, about the way they canvass support and conduct their campaigns and the fact that minorities inevitably have the power to determine programmes and lists of candidates, but it is not possible to eliminate the existence of parties, and the kind of structure they have and the way they proceed can only be eliminated to a very limited extent at most. The law may regulate (as has repeatedly happened in America) the way in which the active core of the party is formed (by laying down conditions such as those governing the formation of trades unions) and it can regulate the 'rules of combat' on the electoral battlefield. But it is not possible to eliminate party conflict as such without thereby destroying the existence of an active popular assembly (*Volksvertretung*). The muddled notion that this nevertheless can and should be done is a constant preoccupation of our littérateurs. Consciously or unconsciously, this idea is one of the presuppositions underlying the many suggestions for the creation of electoral corporations based on 'occupational estates' (*berufsständisch*), whereby the corporatively constituted bodies representing occupations would also function as electoral bodies for parliament; these are to exist alongside or instead of parliaments formed on the basis of general (equal or graduated) 'civil suffrage'. In itself this is simply unthinkable at a time when formal membership of a particular occupation or profession (which electoral law would require to be linked to external criteria) tells us virtually nothing about the social and economic function of the person concerned, since every technical innovation and every shift and re-formation of economic life changes the function and thereby also the meaning of these formally constant occupational positions as well as the numerical relationship between them. But of course such an arrangement is also not the way to achieve the desired end. If all voters were to be represented in occupationally based corporations on the model, say, of today's chambers of trade or agriculture, and if these bodies in turn were to elect the parliament, the consequences would of course be as follows: (1) On the one hand the bodies representing *interests* and based on free recruitment would exist *alongside* these legally linked professional organisations, in the same way as the Farmers' Union exists alongside the agricultural chambers, or as the various free organisations of entrepreneurs exist alongside the chambers of trade. On the other hand, far from disappearing, the *political* parties based on free recruitment would of course adapt the direction and manner of their recruitment to the new situation. This would certainly not be advantageous, as elections in those occupational corporations would continue to be influenced by those who provide electoral finances, while the exploitation of capitalist relations of dependency would continue to exist and be at least as resistant to scrutiny as before. (2) The second self-evident consequence would be that, as soon as the composition of the occupational corporations began to influence parliamentary elections, and hence the patronage of office, the solution of the *substantive* tasks facing these bodies would be sucked into the turmoil of party-political power struggles, so that they would be filled, not by technically competent experts but by party representatives. (3) On the other hand, it would mean that parliament would be a marketplace for compromises between purely *material* interests, without any overriding concern for the politics of the *state*. In these circumstances there would be greater temptations and scope for the bureaucracy to maintain its own power, and above all to render any control of the administration illusory, by playing off conflicts of material interest against one another and by intensifying the system of patronage and 'gratuities' for delivery. The decisive events and compromises between interested parties would now take place behind the closed doors of their unofficial concerns where they would be even less subject to control. Instead of the political *leader*, it would be the cunning *businessman* whose interests would be served quite directly by parliament, while a so-called 'popular assembly' of this kind would be the most unsuitable place imaginable for the solution of political questions in the light of political considerations. To the initiated all this is perfectly obvious, as is the fact that no such arrangement can be a means of reducing the influence of capital on parties and parliament or of getting rid of the party machinery or cleaning it up. The result would be the very opposite. The fact that parties are formations resting on free recruitment is an obstacle to their regulation. Failure to understand this fact underlies the ideas of littérateurs who would like there to be only organisations created by state regulation, not the 'voluntary' formations which have grown up on the battlefield of today's social order.

In modern states in particular, political parties can be based on two distinct, fundamental inner principles. They are either – as in America since the disappearance of the great conflicts on the interpretation of the Constitution – essentially organisations for the *patronage of office*. Their aim is then simply to get their leader elected to the top position so that he can then distribute the offices of state to his following, the party's electioneering and organisational apparatus. Lacking any specific convictions, they compete with one another by including in their programmes the demands which they think will attract most support from the voters. In the United States parties are so strongly of this kind because *no* parliamentary system exists there; rather, the President of the Union, who is elected by popular vote, with the assistance of the elected Senators of the states, has in his hands the patronage of an enormous number of federal offices which are to be allocated. Despite the resultant corruption, this system was popular because it prevented the emergence of a bureaucratic *caste*. It was technically possible because – and for as long as – the limitless abundance of economic opportunities could support even the most amateurish management of politics. The growing need to replace the party protégé and occasional official lacking any professional training by a technically trained official who performs his duties as a life-long career, is increasingly taking prebends away from the American parties and inescapably creating a bureaucracy along European lines there too.

Alternatively, parties can be mainly parties of a particular *Weltanschauung*, in which case their aim is to achieve victory for *substantive* political ideals. In Germany, the Centre Party in the 1870s and the Social Democratic Party before it became thoroughly bureaucratised are fairly pure examples of this type of party. It is normal, however, for parties to be a mixture of both types. They have concrete political goals, handed down by tradition which, because of their respect for tradition, are only capable of slow modification. Besides this, however, they strive for the *patronage of office*. Either their primary aim is to fill the leading offices, those of a *political* character, with their own leaders. If the leaders achieve this goal in the electoral contest, it enables them and those with an interest in the running of the party's affairs to provide their protégés with a place in secure state positions as long as the party remains in political power. This is normally the case in parliamentary states and this is therefore the path taken by the ideological parties of *Weltanschauung* there too. In non-parliamentary states patronage of the *leading* offices is not in the gift of the parties. Alternatively, the most influential of them are usually in a position at least to force the ruling bureaucracy to grant *non*-political state positions to their protégés *as well as* to those in line for such office thanks to their connections with officials. In other words they can exercise *minor* patronage.

In their internal structure all parties have gone over to the bureaucratic form of organisation in the course of the last few decades as the techniques of electoral struggle have become increasingly rationalised. The individual parties have reached different stages of development on the road to this goal but the general direction is absolutely clear, at least in mass-states. Joseph Chamberlain's 'caucus' in England, the development of the revealingly named party 'machine' in America and the growing importance of party officials everywhere (including Germany, where this is happening most rapidly in the Social Democratic Party, which is to say, quite naturally, precisely in the most democratic party); all these are comparable stages in this process. In the Centre Party the duties of the party bureaucracy are performed by the church apparatus or 'chaplainocracy', while in the Conservative party in Prussia since Puttkamer's [25] ministry they are performed, covertly or openly, by the county and local governmental apparatus of the state. The power of the parties rests in the first instance on the organisational quality of these bureaucracies. The difficulties of amalgamating parties also stem more from the mutual hostilities between the bureaucratic apparatuses of the parties than from differences in their programmes. The subsequent disintegration of the 'Deutsch-Freisinnigen' party was prefigured in the fact that Eugen Richter [26] and Heinrich Rickert [27] each retained his own apparatus of agents.

---

[25] R. von Puttkamer (1828–1900), Conservative politician and Minister of the Interior for Prussia under Bismarck.

[26] Eugen Richter (1838–1906), leader of the Progressives, later of the 'Deutsch-Freisinnigen'.

[27] Heinrich Rickert (1833–1902), also a member of the 'Deutsch-Freisinnigen'.

Of course, in certain respects a state bureaucracy looks very different from a party bureaucracy, and within the state bureaucracy the civil section looks different from the military one, and all of them are different from the bureaucracy of a local community, a church, a bank, a cartel, an occupational cooperative, a factory, a lobby (Employers' Federation, Farmers' Union). In each of these cases the degree to which honorary officials or interested parties are actively involved varies greatly. The party 'boss' and the board of directors in a limited company are not 'officials'. Under the multiple forms of so-called 'self-government' all kinds of notables or elected representatives of the ruled or of interested parties who are forced to bear a burden of taxation are subordinated to or placed alongside or in charge of the officials, either as a body or individually, with powers of co-determination, or in a supervisory or advisory, or occasionally in an executive capacity. It is particularly common for such people to be in charge of local government. But these phenomena, although of undoubted practical importance, are not our concern here.[B] The only thing that matters here is the fact that in the administration of *mass* associations the permanently appointed officials with *specialist training* always form the core of the apparatus, and its 'discipline' is an absolute prerequisite of success. This is increasingly the case, the larger the association becomes, the more complicated its tasks are, and – above *all* – the more its existence is determined by power (whether in the shape of power struggles in the market place, on the electoral battlefield or on the military battlefield). The same is true of the parties. In party politics the situation is doomed to disappear whereby, as in France (where the whole parliamentary *misère* stems from the *absence* of bureaucratised parties), and partly here too, parties still cling to the system of administration by local notables which once dominated all kinds of association in the Middle Ages and is still predominant in small and medium-sized municipalities today. Nowadays the parties consider using such 'respected citizens', 'leading scholars' and whatever else they are called as an advertising device, and only as such, but not as bearers of decisive, everyday work. Their

---

[B] This means that numerous institutions are excluded from consideration here, of which we in Germany have every reason to be proud, and which can indeed be described as *exemplary*, at least in individual cases. But it is an enormous error on the part of the littérateurs to imagine that the *politics* of a major state are basically no different from the *self-government* of any middle-sized town. Politics is *struggle*.

role is exactly the same as the names of the notables who decorate the boards of directors of limited companies, or the princes of the church at Catholic assemblies, the genuine and spurious aristocrats at the meetings of the Farmers' Union or the distinguished historians, biologists and other such (usually quite unpolitical) experts who are cited in the propaganda of the pan-German interest groups seeking electoral privileges and war-profits. In all organisations the real work is done to an increasing extent by the paid employees and agents of all kinds. Everything else is, or is becoming increasingly, mere window-dressing and cloth-finishing. It was the Italians, followed by the English, who developed the modern capitalist form of economic organisation. Similarly it was first Byzantium, followed by the Italians, then the territorial states during the age of Absolutism, French revolutionary centralism and finally, outdoing them all, the *Germans* who developed to a virtuoso degree the rational, *bureaucratic* organisation of all human associations of rule, on the basis of expertise and the division of labour, whether in factory, army or state. So far they have only been partially outdone by other nations, particularly the Americans, in the techniques of party organisation. But the present World War means above all the victory of this form of life throughout the whole world. It was under way in any case. Universities, technical and commercial colleges, trades schools, military academies, specialist schools of all imaginable kinds (including schools of journalism!) – the specialist examination is the precondition of all rewarding and above all 'secure' private and public appointments, the examination diploma the basis of all claims to social standing (marriage and social intercourse with the circles that consider themselves as belonging to 'society'), the secure, pensionable salary 'appropriate to one's status' and, if possible, increments and promotion according to seniority – it is well known that this was the real 'demand of the day', which rested on the one hand on the universities' interest in increasing student numbers and, on the other, on the hunger of students for prebends, both within the state and outside it. What concerns us here are its consequences for *political* life. For in truth this sober fact of universal bureaucratisation also lies behind the so-called 'German ideas of 1914',[28] behind what the littérateurs euphemistically term

---

[28] 'The German Ideas of 1914' refers to plans for a future form of state-managed economy based on the desire for a 'rebirth of the spirit of national unity'. These ideas gained considerable popularity and were supported by, among others, Plenge,

the 'socialism of the future', behind the slogans of 'organisation', of the 'cooperative economy' and indeed behind all current phrases of this kind. Even when their aim is the very opposite, the result of all these things is the same: the creation of bureaucracy. Bureaucracy is certainly far from being the only modern form of organisation, just as the factory is far from being the only form in which manufacture can be conducted. But these are the two forms which have put their stamp on the present age and the foreseeable future. The future belongs to bureaucratisation and it was (and is) self-evident that the littérateurs would yet again fulfil their vocation to act as an outburst of applause for whatever powers are currently in the ascendant, just as they once did during the age of 'Manchesterism'[29] – and with the same ingenuousness on both occasions.

Bureaucracy is, however, distinguished from other historical bearers of the modern, rational way of ordering life by the fact of its far greater *inescapability*. History records no instance of it having disappeared again once it had achieved complete and sole dominance – in China, Egypt, or in a less consistent form in the later Roman Empire and Byzantium, except when the whole culture supporting it also disappeared completely. Relatively speaking, however, these were still highly irrational forms of bureaucracy; they were 'patrimonial bureaucracies'.[30] Compared with all these older forms, modern bureaucracy is distinguished by a characteristic which makes its inescapability much more absolute than theirs, namely *rational, technical specialisation and training*. The ancient Chinese mandarin was no specialist official; on the contrary, he was a 'gentleman' with a literary–humanist education. The Egyptian, later Roman and Byzantine official was essentially much more of a bureaucrat in our sense of the word. But the tasks of state for which he had responsibility were infinitely more simple and modest than modern ones, his conduct always being bound in part by tradition, and being in part patriarchal, and thus irrational, in its orientation. He was a pure empiricist, just like the practitioner of a trade in the past. As befits the rational

Rathenau, Troeltsch, Sombart and Alfred Weber. The term was introduced by J. Plenge, *Der Krieg und die Volkswirtschaft* (Münster, 1915) and R. Kjellen, *Die Ideen von 1914. Eine weltgeschichtliche Perspektive* (Leipzig, 1915).

[29] 'Manchesterism' refers to the doctrines of free trade and laissez-faire.

[30] Patrimonialism is discussed by Weber in *Economy and Society*. See, especially, ch. 12 and 13.

technique of modern life, the modern official is always and increasingly a person with professional training and a specialisation. All bureaucracies throughout the world follow this path. The fact that they had not reached the end of this road before the war gave us our superiority over others. Although, for example, the older American official (a creation of party patronage) was a 'connoisseur' of the electoral arena and the practices appropriate to it, he was in no sense an expert with specialist training. It is on this fact, and not on democracy as such (as our littérateurs would have the public believe), that the corruption over there rested, for this is as alien to the university-trained, professional official in the 'civil service' which is only just emerging there as it is to the modern English bureaucracy that is now increasingly taking the place of 'self-government' by notables ('gentlemen').[31] But wherever the trained, specialist, modern official has once begun to rule, his power is absolutely unbreakable, because the entire organisation of providing even the most basic needs in life then depends on his performance of his duties. In theory one could probably conceive of the progressive elimination of private capitalism – although this is certainly not the trivial matter some littérateurs, who are unfamiliar with it, imagine it to be, and it will quite certainly not be a consequence of this war. But assuming this were to be achieved at some point, what would it mean in practice? Would it perhaps mean that the steel housing (*Gehäuse*) of modern industrial work would break open? No! It would mean rather that the *management* of businesses taken into state ownership or into some form of 'communal economy' would also become bureaucratised. Is there any appreciable *difference* between the lives of the workers and clerks in the Prussian state-run mines and railways and those of people working in large private capitalist enterprises? They are *less free*, because there is *no hope* of winning any battle against the state bureaucracy and because no help can be summoned from any authority with an interest in *opposing* that bureaucracy and its power, whereas this is possible in relation to private capitalism. *That* would be the entire difference. If private capitalism were eliminated, state bureaucracy would rule *alone*. Private and public bureaucracies would then be merged into a single hierarchy, whereas they now operate alongside and, at least potentially, against one another, thus keeping one

[31] 'Civil service', 'self-government' and 'gentlemen' are in English.

another in check. The situation would resemble that of ancient Egypt, but in an incomparably more rational and hence more inescapable form.

A lifeless machine is *congealed spirit.*[32] It is *only* this fact that gives the machine the power to force men to serve it and thus to rule and determine their daily working lives, as in fact happens in factories. This same *congealed spirit* is, however, also embodied in that *living machine* which is represented by bureaucratic organisation with its specialisation of trained, technical work, its delimitation of areas of responsibility, its regulations and its graduated hierarchy of relations of obedience. Combined with the dead machine, it is in the process of manufacturing the housing of that future serfdom to which, perhaps, men may have to submit powerlessly, just like the slaves in the ancient state of Egypt, *if they consider that the ultimate and only value by which the conduct of their affairs is to be decided is good administration and provision for their needs by officials (that is 'good' in the purely technical sense of rational administration).* Bureaucracy achieves this, after all, incomparably better than any other structure of rule. This housing, so praised by our naive littérateurs, will be augmented by shackles chaining each individual to his firm (the beginnings of this are to be found in so-called 'welfare arrangements'), to his class (by an increasingly rigid structure of ownership) and perhaps at some time in the future to his occupation (by state provision for needs on a 'liturgical' principle,[33] whereby associations structured along occupational lines carry a burden of state responsibilities). This housing would become even more indestructible if, in the social area, as in those states in the past where enforced labour existed, an organisation of the ruled based on their social and occupational status were to be attached (which in truth means subordinated) to the bureaucracy. An 'organic', that is an Oriental–Egyptian social structure would begin

---

[32] The very odd-sounding term used by Weber is 'geronnener Geist'. It may be an allusion to Marx or G. Simmel (1859–1918, philosopher, sociologist and friend of Weber), who both use similar language. Marx, for example, refers to 'bloße Gerinnung von Arbeitszeit' in *Das Kapital*, vol. I. pp. 178–9. Simmel uses similar terms in, for example, his essay 'Der Begriff und die Tragödie der Kultur', in *Philosophische Kultur* (Leipzig, 1911).

[33] Weber links the liturgical principle and the *Liturgiestaat* with patrimonialism. Under such arrangements social groups, such as guilds, were made responsible by the state for ensuring that their members delivered the contributions, whether in kind or in labour, prescribed by the state. See Weber's discussion in *Economy and Society*, pp. 1022–5 and in his *General Economic History*, especially pp. 110–11, 156–7 and 248.

to emerge, but, in contrast to that ancient form, one which would be as strictly rational as a machine. Who would deny that some such *possibility* lies in the womb of the future? Such things have often been said, and a confused, shadowy notion of these possibilities drifts through the products of our littérateurs. Assuming that precisely this possibility were to be an inescapable fate, who could help smiling at the anxiety of our littérateurs lest future social and political developments might bestow on us *too much* 'individualism' or 'democracy' or the like, or that 'true freedom' would not emerge until the present 'anarchy' in our economic production and the 'party machinations' in our parliaments had been *eliminated* in favour of 'social order' and an 'organic structure' – which means in favour of the pacifism of social impotence under the wing of the one quite definitely *inescapable* power, that of the bureaucracy in the state and the economy.

In view of the fundamental fact that the advance of bureaucratis-ation is unstoppable, there is only one possible set of questions to be asked about future forms of political organisation: (1) How is it *at all possible* to salvage any remnants of 'individual' freedom of movement *in any sense*, given this all-powerful trend towards bureaucratisation? It is, after all, a piece of crude self-deception to think that even the most conservative amongst us could carry on living at all today with-out these achievements from the age of the 'Rights of Man'. How-ever, let us put this question to one side for now, for there is another which is directly relevant to our present concerns: (2) In view of the growing indispensability and hence increasing power of state offi-cialdom, which is our concern here, how can there be any guarantee that forces exist which can impose limits on the enormous, crushing power of this constantly growing stratum of society and control it effectively? How is democracy even in this restricted sense to be *at all possible*? Yet this too is not the only question of concern to us here, for there is (3) a third question, the most important of all, which arises from any consideration of what is *not* performed by bureaucracy as such. It is clear that its effectiveness has strict internal limits, both in the management of public, political affairs and in the private economic sphere. The *leading* spirit, the 'entrepreneur' in the one case, the 'politician' in the other, is something different from an 'official'. Not necessarily in form, but certainly in substance. The entrepreneur, too, sits in an 'office'. An army commander does the same. The army commander is an officer and thus formally no different from all other officers. If the general manager of a large enterprise is the hired official of a limited company, his legal position is also no different in principle from that of other officials. In the sphere of the state the same applies to the leading politician. The leading minister is *formally* an official with a pensionable salary. The fact that, according to all known constitutions, he can be dismissed at any time and can demand to be discharged distinguishes his position outwardly from that of many, but not all other officials. Yet much more striking is the fact that, unlike other officials, he and he *alone* is not required to demonstrate any kind of *qualification based on training*. This fact indicates that the meaning and purpose (*Sinn*) of his position differs from that of other officials in the same way as the position of the entrepreneur and managing director in a private firm is a special one. Or to be more accurate, he is *meant* to be something different. And this is how it is in fact. If a man in a *leading* position performs his leadership function in the *spirit* of an 'official', even a most able one, if he is a man accustomed to performing his work dutifully and honourably in accordance with regulations and orders, then he is useless, whether he is at the head of a private firm or a state. Unfortunately, we in Germany have seen the proof of this in our own political life.

Only in part does the difference lie in the kind of achievement expected of this type of person. Like 'leaders', 'officials' too are expected to make independent decisions and show organisational ability and initiative, not only in countless individual cases but also on larger issues. It is typical of littérateurs and of a country lacking any insight into the conduct of its own affairs or into the achievements of its officials, even to *imagine* that the work of an official amounts to no more than the subaltern performance of routine duties, while the leader alone is expected to carry out the 'interesting' tasks which make special intellectual demands. This is not so. The difference lies, rather, in the kind of *responsibility* borne by each of them, and this is largely what determines the demands made on their particular abilities. An official who receives an order which, in his view, is wrong can – and should – raise objections. If his superior then insists on the instruction it is not merely the duty of the official, it is also a point of *honour* for him to carry out that instruction as if it corresponded to his own innermost conviction, thereby demonstrating that his sense of duty to his office overrides his individual wilfulness. It is irrelevant whether his superior is a 'public authority' or a 'corporation' or an 'assembly' from which he has an imperative mandate. This is what is demanded by the spirit of *office*. A political *leader* who behaved like this would deserve our *contempt*. He will often be obliged to make compromises, which means sacrificing something of lesser importance to something of greater importance. If, however, he is incapable of saying to his master, whether this be a monarch or the *demos*, 'Either you give me this instruction *or I resign*', he is not a leader but merely what Bismarck called a miserable 'clinger' to office. The official should stand 'above the parties', which in truth means that he must remain outside the *struggle* for power of his own. The struggle for personal power and the acceptance of full *personal responsibility for one's cause (Sache)* which is the consequence of such power – this is the very element in which the politician and the entrepreneur live and breathe.

Ever since Bismarck's resignation, Germany has been governed by men who were 'officials' (in mentality) because Bismarck had excluded all other political minds beside his own. Germany continued to have the best military and civilian bureaucracy in the world, as far as its integrity, education, conscientiousness and intelligence were concerned. Germany's achievements out on the battlefield, and at home too, broadly speaking, have demonstrated what can be achieved with these means. But what of the leadership of German *politics* in recent decades? The kindest thing that has been said about it was that, 'the victories of the German armies have made up for the defeats of German politics'. But at the cost of what sacrifices? It is better to pass over this in silence and to ask instead what the reasons were for these failures.

People *abroad* imagine that German 'autocracy' is to blame. At *home* the childish speculations of our littérateurs have led many to the opposite view, namely that a conspiracy of international 'democracy' against Germany has supposedly brought about the unnatural coalition of the world against us. Abroad they use the hypocritical slogan, 'Free the Germans from autocracy!' At home those with vested interests in the status quo – we shall get to know them better – speak with equal hypocrisy of the need to preserve the 'German spirit' from the stain of 'democracy', or they look for other scapegoats.

For example, it has become customary to heap blame on German diplomacy – wrongly, one suspects. On average it was probably just as good as that of other countries. A confusion has taken place here. What we lacked was *leadership* of the state by a *politician*, which does not mean a political genius (they can only be expected every few centuries), nor even an important political talent, but simply by anyone who was a politician *at all*.

Simply to say this is to have embarked already on a discussion of the only two powers – the *monarch* and *parliament* – capable of playing a controlling and directing role in the life of a modern constitutional state alongside the all-enmeshing bureaucracy. Let us begin by considering the first of these.

The position of the German dynasties will still be intact at the end of the war, unless very great acts of folly are committed and nothing has been learnt from past failings. Long before fourth August 1914 anyone who had the opportunity to hold a long and detailed discussion with German Social Democrats would eventually hear them concede that a constitutional monarchy was 'actually' the form of state best suited to the particular international situation of Germany. I am not talking here about 'revisionists', nor about parliamentary deputies of the party, nor trade unionists, but about party *officials*, some of whom had very radical views. Indeed one only needs to glance briefly at Russia to see that the transition to a *parliamentary* monarchy sought by liberal politicians there would have preserved the dynasty on the one hand, while getting rid of naked bureaucratic rule on the other. The result would have contributed as much to the strengthening of Russia as the present 'republic' of littérateurs,[34] for all the subjective idealism of its leaders, has contributed to the weakening of the country.[C] As the English are very well aware, the whole strength of the British parliamentary system is connected with the fact that the highest formal position in the state has been filled

[34] The 'Literaten-Republik' referred to here is the Kerensky government in Russia in 1917.
[C] As Russians have told me that Mr Kerensky has quoted this sentence from the *Frankfurter Zeitung* at public meetings in order to demonstrate the need for an offensive as a proof of 'strength', let me expressly state the following for the benefit of this gravedigger of young Russian freedom: One can start an offensive if one has at one's disposal the material instruments of war, for example, artillery to pin down the infantry ahead of one in the trenches, and transport and provisions to make the soldiers confined to the trenches aware that their food depends on one. The 'weakness' of the so-called social-revolutionary government of Mr Kerensky lay in its lack of *credit-worthiness*, as has been demonstrated elsewhere, and in the need for it to deny its own idealism in order to obtain credit to support its own rule *within the country* by making a pact with the bourgeois–imperialist entente, and thereby allowing hundreds of thou-

once and for all. This is not the place to discuss how the mere existence of a monarch can perform this function, nor whether this function could only be performed, inevitably and in every country, by a monarch. For Germany at any rate this is simply the situation as we find it. We can have no appetite for a return to the age of wars of succession and counter-revolutions; our very existence is under too great an international threat for that.

Under the conditions of the modern state, however, no monarch anywhere has ever been, nor can he be, a counterweight to and a means of controlling the all-embracing power of *specialised officialdom*. He cannot control the administration, for this is an administration with training and special expertise, and a modern monarch is *never* an expert, except in the military sphere at best. What concerns us here, however, is the fact that, above all, the monarch as such is never a *politician* trained in the machinations of party struggle or in diplomacy. Not just his entire education, but his very position in the state simply militates against this. He did not win his crown through party struggle, and the fight for power in the state is not his natural element, as it always is for a politician. He does not learn about the conditions of struggle directly and personally by climbing down into the arena; rather he is removed from the ruthlessness of the struggle by his privileged position. *Born* politicians do exist, but they are rare creatures. The monarch who is *not* a born politician becomes a great danger to his own interests and to those of the state if he attempts, as the Tsar did, to exercise 'personal government', or to exert influence in the world by employing the means of the politician, that is 'demagogy' in the broadest sense of the term, in order to propagate his own ideas or his own personality through the written or spoken word. He is then not only gambling with his own crown – that would be his own private affair – but with the existence of his state. Inevitably this is a temptation or even a necessity for the modern monarch, when he faces *no one else* in the state other than the *officials*, which is to say when parliament is powerless, as it was in Germany for decades. Even in purely technical terms this has severe disadvantages. If he does not have a powerful parliament at his side, today's monarch

sands of its own countrymen to bleed to death as the mercenaries of *foreign interests*, as has happened up to now. Unfortunately, I believe that I have been proved correct with this and other assumptions I made about Russia's attitude elsewhere. (I shall leave the passage unrevised even now, although it was written many months ago.)

is dependent on the reports of *other officials* when he wants to scrutinise the officials' performance of their duties. Then everything goes round in circles. The constant warfare between the different departments, which was typical of Russia, for example, and is still prevalent here even now, is the natural consequence of this kind of ostensibly 'monarchic' government in which there is no leading *politician*. For these struggles amongst the satraps are mostly not primarily concerned just with conflicts on matters of substance but also with personal antagonisms; inter-departmental struggles are used by their chiefs as means to compete for ministerial posts wherever such posts are regarded simply as *prebends for officials*. Under these circumstances court intrigues rather than objective reasons or qualities of political leadership are what decide who is to occupy the leading positions. Everyone knows that parliamentary states are full of *personal* power struggles. The error is to believe that things are somehow different in monarchies. In monarchies there is a further evil. The monarch believes he is governing personally, whereas in truth officialdom enjoys the privilege of exercising power without *control* or *responsibility*, thanks to the cover he provides. The monarch is flattered and is shown the *romantic semblance* of power because he is able to change the *person* occupying the post of leading minister at will. The truth is that monarchs like Edward VII and Leopold II, although certainly not ideal characters, held *far* more *real* power in their hands, although, and indeed *because*, they governed in strictly parliamentary form, never bringing themselves to public attention, or at least only doing so in these forms. Modern littérateurs only reveal their own ignorance when they describe such monarchs as 'shadow kings', and their stupidity when they accept the moral gossip of philistines as the criterion for their political judgements of them. World history will judge differently, even if their work ultimately fails, as so many other great political projects have failed. One of these monarchs assembled a worldwide coalition, although he had to change even his court officials as changing party constellations dictated, the other a giant colonial empire (compared with our fragments of colonies!) although he only ruled over a minor state. Anyone, whether he be a monarch or a minister, who wants to give political *leadership* must know how to play the modern instruments of power. The parliamentary system only excludes the politically *untalented* monarch, and it does so for the sake of the country's power! Is the state which has succeeded in annexing to its own, numerically small population the best parts of every continent in the world a 'nightwatchman state'? This cliché, so redolent of the *ressentiment* of those who are 'loyal subjects' (*Untertanen*)[35] by nature, is just the sort of philistine nonsense talked by our littérateurs.

Let us now turn to parliament.

First and foremost, modern parliaments are assemblies representing the people who are *ruled* by the means of bureaucracy. It is, after all, a condition of the duration of any rule, even the best organised, that it should enjoy a certain measure of inner assent from at least those sections of the ruled who carry weight in society. Today parliaments are the means whereby this minimum of assent is made manifest. For certain acts, the public powers are obliged to use the form of an agreement in law after prior consultation with parliament; the most important of these is the budget. Today, and ever since the time when the prerogatives of the estates were first created, the right to control the budget, the power to determine the manner in which the state procures its finances, has been parliament's decisive instrument of power. Admittedly, so long as parliament's only means of lending weight to the population's complaints about the administration is to deny the government finances, to refuse its assent to legislative proposals and to put forward motions of its own which lack binding force, parliament is excluded from participating positively in political leadership. It can and will then engage only in 'negative politics', confronting the leaders of the administration like some hostile power, and hence being fobbed off by them with the irreducible minimum of information and being regarded as a mere hindrance, an assembly of impotent grumblers and know-alls. On the other hand, the bureaucracy in turn tends to be regarded by parliament and the voters as a caste of careerists and bailiffs ranged against the people who are the object of its tiresome and largely superfluous arts. The situation is different in countries where parliament has established the principle that the leaders of the administration must either be drawn directly from its own ranks (a *'parliamentary system'* in the true sense), or that such leaders require the expressly stated confidence of a majority in parliament if they are to remain in office, or that they

---

[35] The German word *Untertan* carries a much stronger sense of subservience than does the English 'subject'.

must at least yield to an expression of no confidence (*parliamentary selection* of the leaders). For this reason they must give an account of themselves, exhaustively and subject to verification by parliament or its committees (*parliamentary accountability* of the leaders), and they must lead the administration in accordance with guidelines approved by parliament (*parliamentary control of the administration*). In this case, the leaders of the decisive parties in parliament at any given moment necessarily share positive responsibility for the power of the state. Then parliament is a positive political factor alongside the monarch, whose role in helping to shape policy is not based on the formal *prerogatives of the crown* (or at least not mainly or exclusively on such rights), but on his influence, which will be very great in any case but will vary according to his political astuteness and his determination to reach his goals. Rightly or wrongly, this is what is called a popular democracy (*Volksstaat*), whereas a parliament of the ruled confronting a ruling body of officials with negative politics is a variety of 'authoritarian state' (*Obrigkeitsstaat*). What interests us here is the *practical* significance of the position of parliament.

Whether one loves or hates the whole parliamentary business, it is *not* to be got rid of. It can only be made politically *powerless*, as Bismarck made the Reichstag powerless. Apart from the fact that it generally results in 'negative politics', the powerlessness of parliament has the following consequences. It goes without saying that every parliamentary struggle is a fight not only about objective antagonisms but also for personal power. In circumstances where parliament's position of power means that the monarch normally charges the trusted spokesman of a decisive majority with political leadership, the power struggle between the parties is directed towards the attainment of this highest *political* position. The people who then conduct this fight, and thus have the chance of reaching the highest political positions, are those with a strong instinct for political power and the most fully developed qualities of political leadership. The continued existence of the party in the country, and all the countless ideal and in part very material interests which are bound up with it, make it imperative that a personality endowed with *leadership* qualities should attain the highest position. Then and only then is there an incentive for political temperaments and political talents to submit to selection on this competitive basis.

Things are quite different if, under the label of 'monarchic government', the highest positions in the state are targets of *promotion for officials* or are filled on the basis of chance acquaintances at court, and a powerless parliament has to acquiesce in this method of composing the government. Even then, of course, the ambition for personal power still operates in parliamentary conflict, alongside the objective antagonisms, but it takes quite different, subaltern forms and directions, as it has done in Germany since 1890. Apart from representing the local private economic interests of influential voters, the only point around which everything then turns is *minor*, subaltern *patronage*. The conflict between Reichskanzler von Bülow[36] and the Centre Party, for example, did not arise from differences of opinion on issues of substance; rather it was essentially an attempt by the chancellor of the day to free himself from the Centre Party's patronage of office, which even today still puts its stamp very firmly on the staffing of certain Reich agencies. Nor is the Centre Party alone in having such influence. The Conservative parties have the monopoly of office in Prussia and try to intimidate the monarch with the spectre of 'revolution' as soon as these prebendary interests are threatened. The parties thereby permanently excluded from the offices of state seek compensation in local administration or in the administration of insurance schemes, pursuing policies in parliament which are hostile to the state or alienated from it, just as the Social Democrats did at an earlier period. Things are bound to be thus, for by its nature *every* party strives for *power*, which is to say, to share in the *administration*, and hence to influence appointments to official posts. The ruling strata have just as much influence on such appointments here as they do anywhere else. It is simply that they do not have to take *responsibility* for what they do because patronage and position-hunting go on behind the scenes here and extend to the lower positions which are not *responsible* for personal details. Here, however, officialdom benefits from the arrangement by being free to operate *without* personal *control*, in return for which it pays gratuities to the parties which count in the form of the patronage of *minor* prebends. This is the natural

---

[36] Prince Bernhard von Bülow (1849–1929), diplomat and statesman, Reichskanzler 1900–9. A leading proponent of an expansionist German *Weltpolitik*, which led him to replace the slogan of *Sammlungspolitik* first with the call to oppose the *Zentrum* and then with a block uniting *Zentrum* and Conservatives and isolating the Liberals.

consequence of the fact that the party (or coalition of parties) currently controlling the majority in parliament for or against the government is *not*, as such, officially charged with filling the *highest*, responsible, political post.

On the other hand this system makes it possible for people with the qualities of a useful official but *without the least talent for statesmanship* to maintain themselves in leading political positions for a time, until some intrigue causes them to disappear from the scene and to be replaced by another personality of the same type. Thus, party political patronage of office exists here as it does in every country, but it exists in a dishonestly covert form, and above all it always operates in favour of particular party opinions which are held to be 'acceptable at court'. This onesidedness is far from being the worst feature in the situation as we have it. In purely political terms it would be tolerable, provided it at least created an opportunity for men with the political qualifications to be *leaders* of the nation to arise from the ranks of the parties 'acceptable at court' and to fill the crucial positions. But this is not the case. That is only possible under a parliamentary system, or at least under circumstances where parliamentary patronage of the leading offices exists. We shall start by considering a purely *formal* obstacle to this which is created by the present constitution of the Reich.

The last sentence of Article 9 of the Reich Constitution states: 'No person can be a member of the *Bundesrat* and of the *Reichstag* simultaneously.' Thus, whereas countries with parliamentary government consider it absolutely indispensable for the leading statesmen to be members of parliament, this is legally impossible in Germany. Although the Reichskanzler, or a minister from an individual state empowered to be a member of the Bundesrat, or a state secretary of the Reich, may belong to the parliament of an individual state (such as the Prussian Diet), and thus influence or even lead a party there, he cannot do the same in the Reichstag. This stipulation was simply a mechanical imitation of the English exclusion of peers from the House of Commons (and probably mediated via the Prussian constitution). Thus it is based on thoughtlessness. This rule must *be rescinded*. Its disappearance would not in itself mean the introduction of the parliamentary system or of parliamentary patronage of office in Germany; it would simply make it *possible* for a politically able member of parliament also to hold a position of political leadership in the Reich at the same time. There is no apparent reason why a parliamentary deputy who shows that he is suited to a leading position in the Reich should be required to uproot himself politically before he may take up such an office.

If Bennigsen[37] had joined the government, and therefore left the Reichstag, Bismarck would have turned an important political *leader* into an administrative *official* with no parliamentary roots. The leadership of Bennigsen's party would then have fallen into the hands of the left wing, or the party would have fallen apart – which may have been Bismarck's aim. In exactly the same way, the fact that the deputy Schiffer has now joined the government has deprived him of his influence on the party, thereby handing it over to the wing of heavy industry. In this way the parties are 'beheaded', while the government gains not useful politicians, but officials in specialised areas who lack both the kind of expert knowledge acquired by a professional official during his career and the influence of a member of parliament. It also means that we are using pretty well the most miserable form of 'gratuities system' that can possibly be employed in relation to any parliament. Parliament as a stepping-off board for talented careerists with ambitions to become state secretaries: this characteristic bureaucrat's view is defended by political and legally trained littérateurs who consider this to be a specifically 'German' solution to the problem of parliamentarism in Germany! These are the very same circles who pour scorn on the chase after official positions which is supposedly only found in 'western Europe' and specifically in 'democratic' states. They will never understand that what parliamentary leaders seek is not an official post with its salary and rank but *power* and the political *responsibility* it entails, nor that such leaders can only have these things if they retain their political roots in the parliamentary party supporting them. Nor do they understand that it is one thing to make parliament into a place for the selection of leaders and quite another to use parliament to select people striving after careers as officials. For decades these same circles have been scornful of the fact that parliaments and parties in Germany have always viewed the government as a kind of natural enemy. But it does not disturb them in the least that, because of the barrier aimed exclusively against the Reichstag by Article 9, Sentence 2 of the Constitution, the Bundesrat and the

---

[37] R. Bennigsen (1824–1902), leading National Liberal politician.

Reichstag are treated by the law as mutually hostile powers, so that they can only communicate from the table of the Bundesrat or from the rostrum. It should be left to the conscience of a statesman, of the government which empowers him and of the voters who elected him, to consider whether he is capable of carrying out his office while also holding a mandate, leading a party or being active within one, and whether the instructions which he follows when voting in the Bundesrat are compatible with the personal convictions which he argues for in the Reichstag.[D] The *leading* politician, above all the one who bears responsibility for instructing the 'presidial vote' in the Reich, the Reichskanzler and Prussian foreign minister, in other words, must have the *possibility* of leading the Bundesrat from the chair, subject to the control of representatives of the other states, and at the same time of influencing the Reichstag as a voting and speaking member of a party. Admittedly, it is considered 'dignified' (*vornehm*) today for a statesman to keep his distance from the parties. Count Posadowsky even believed he owed it to his *previous* office to refrain from attaching himself to any party – in other words to misuse the Reichstag by appearing there as an academic performer without influence. Without influence – for how is business conducted in parliament?

Speeches given by a member of parliament are no longer statements of his personal convictions, far less are they attempts to persuade an opponent to change his mind. Rather they are official declarations by the party which are being addressed to the country at large 'through the window'. Once the representatives of all the parties have had their turn of speaking once or twice, the debate in the

---

[D] It is amusing when an anonymous contributor to the *Kreuzzeitung* (of all places) deduces, by a piece of legal formalism, the impossibility of combining these two functions from the fact that deputies have to vote in accordance with their own free convictions, whereas the members of the Bundesrat vote in accordance with instructions. The *Kreuzzeitung* is not disturbed by the fact that numerous district superintendents (*Landräte*) sit in the Prussian Diet who, since the days of Puttkamer, are required to 'represent the policies of the government'! Nor even by the fact that the Bundesrat includes secretaries of state of the Reich who, in their capacity as deputies to the Prussian Diet, ought to criticise, in accordance with their own free convictions, the instructions given to them, in their capacity as members of the Bundesrat, by a government *which is not answerable* to this Diet. If a statesmen at the head of a party is unable, as a member of the Bundesrat, to ensure that he receives instructions which correspond to his own convictions, *he simply must go*. Admittedly, this ought to apply even now to *every* 'statesman'! See below.

Reichstag is closed. The speeches are presented to a party meeting in advance, or at least it is agreed at such meetings what all the essential points will be. Equally, it is decided in advance who is to speak for the party. The parties have their experts on every question, just as the bureaucracy has its officials with particular responsibilities. Admittedly, alongside their worker bees, they also have their drones, show-piece orators who are only to be used with caution for the purposes of public display. Although there are exceptions, the principle generally holds true that influence is exercised by the person who does the work. But this work is carried out behind the scenes, at the meetings of commissions and parliamentary parties, and in the private offices of those members who are really doing the hard work. Eugen Richter, for example, although decidedly unpopular within his own party, had an unassailable position of power thanks to his extraordinary industry, and in particular thanks to his unequalled knowledge of the budget. He was probably the last deputy who could work out where the Minister for War had spent every penny, down to the last canteen; despite their annoyance, gentlemen in this section of the administration often told me how much they admired his ability. In the present Centre Party the position of Herr Matthias Erzberger[38] similarly rests on his bee-like *industry*, which accounts for the otherwise puzzling influence of a politician with such limited political gifts.

No matter how industrious a person may be, however, this fact does not in itself qualify him to give leadership and direction to a state or a party, two things which are *by no means* as unlike one another as our romantic littérateurs believe. As far as I am aware, there were personalities *fully* equipped with all the qualities needed for leadership in *all* the parties in Germany, without exception. Von Bennigsen, von Miquel, von Stauffenberg, Völk and others amongst the National Liberals, in the Centre Party von Mallinckrodt and Windthorst, the Conservatives von Bethusy-Huc, von Minnegerode, von Manteuffel, the Progressive von Saucken-Tarputschen and the Social Democrat von Vollmar – all these men were natural leaders with political qualifications. They all disappeared from view or left parliament, as von Bennigsen did in the eighties, because there was

---

[38] M. Erzberger (1875–1921), Centre Party politician and journalist with a reputation for opportunism.

no chance of them achieving the leadership of the affairs of state in their capacity *as* party leaders. When parliamentarians like von Miquel[39] and Möller[40] became ministers, they had first to abandon their political convictions in order to be fitted into ministries run purely by officials.[E] Yet *born, natural leaders are still to be found in Germany today*; indeed they are numerous. Where are they, then? In the light of what has been said already, the question is easily answered. To take just one example, in which the political and socio-political views of the person concerned are as diametrically opposed to my own as they can be: does anyone believe that the present leader of the Krupp works, formerly a politician from the Eastern Territories and official of the state, was simply destined to direct the greatest industrial enterprise in Germany, *rather* than head one of the most influential ministries or a powerful party in parliament? Why, then, is he doing what he does, and why (as I assume is the case) would he not be prepared to take on those other roles under existing conditions? In order to earn more money? I suspect, rather, that, given the political structure of the state here, which means quite simply, given the *impotence* of parliament and the concomitant, purely *official* character of ministerial posts, the reason is very simply that a man with a strong instinct for power and all the qualities that go with it would have to be a fool to let himself be drawn into the pitiful business of *ressentiment* amongst colleagues and onto the thin ice of intrigues at court, when there is a field of activity waiting to welcome his abilities and desires – the one which is offered by giant enterprises, cartels, banks and large trading concerns. Men of that type prefer to finance pan-German newspapers and to allow the littérateurs to churn out their nonsense in them. All the men of this nation with any talent for leadership have been diverted down this path, into the service of private capitalist interests, as a consequence of *negative selection*, which is what our so-called 'monarchic government' boils down to, once one has stripped away all hypocritical verbiage. *Only* in this sphere does something resembling a selection process for leadership

---

[E] Minister Möller once declared that he was in the *unpleasant* situation that his personal standpoint was so well known from the speeches he had made in earlier years.

[39] J. von Miquel (1829–1901), one of the founders of the National Liberal Party. He advocated and, in 1897, first defined the idea of *Sammlungspolitik*.

[40] T. Möller (1840–1925), National Liberal politician and industrialist. Prussian Minister of Trade 1901–5.

qualities take place nowadays. Why in this sphere? Simply because comfort and cosiness, which in this case means the *empty phrases of the littérateurs*, necessarily come to an abrupt end as soon as economic interests worth hundreds and thousands of millions of marks and tens or hundreds of thousands of jobs are at stake. Why do such selection processes *not* apply to the leadership of the state? Because one of the most damaging legacies of Bismarck's rule has been that he believed it served his own ends to cloak his Caesarist regime with the *legitimacy of the monarch*. His successors imitated his practice faithfully, but they were simple officials and not Caesars. The politically uneducated nation accepted Bismarck's rhetoric at face value, while the littérateurs applauded in their customary manner. This is natural enough, for these people examine future officials, feel themselves to be officials and fathers of officials, and their *ressentiment* is directed against anyone who strives for and achieves power by any route other than via the legitimation bestowed by examination diplomas. Under Bismarck the nation lost the habit of concerning itself directly with public affairs, particularly with foreign policy, and allowed itself to be talked into accepting as 'monarchic government' something which in truth merely meant the complete absence of control over pure rule by officials, something which, *left to its own devices*, has never yet given birth to qualities of political leadership or allowed them to flourish anywhere in the world. It is not that there might *not also* have been people with leadership qualities amongst our officials – *I am very far from claiming that*. Yet not only do the conventions and inner peculiarities of the official hierarchy create quite unusual obstacles to the rise of such men in particular, and not only is the essential position of the modern administrative official, taken as a whole, highly unfavourable to the development of *political* independence (which must be distinguished clearly from the inner independence of his purely *personal* character). Rather, the essence of all politics, as we shall emphasise repeatedly, is *conflict, the recruitment of allies and a voluntary following*. The career of an official in an authoritarian state (*Obrigkeitsstaat*) simply offers no opportunities to practise this difficult art. As is widely known, the school in which Bismarck learnt his politics was the Frankfurt Federal Diet. In the army, training is directed towards warfare and it can give rise to military leaders. But the given palaestra[41] for the modern politician

[41] A 'palaestra' is a wrestling school or gymnasium.

is parliamentary conflict and the fight for the party in the country, and there is nothing of equal value which can replace such struggle – least of all competition for promotion. Naturally this training in political fighting can only take place in a parliament and for a party, where the leader achieves *power* in the state.

What sort of attraction can a party possibly hold for men with qualities of *leadership*, when the best it can offer is the opportunity to change a few elements in the budget so as to suit the interests of its voters or to provide a few small benefices for the protégés of the leading lights in the party? What opportunity does it offer them to develop such qualities? Down to the smallest procedural details and conventions in both the Reichstag and the parties, our parliament today is completely directed towards merely negative politics. I know of several cases of young talents with leadership qualities within the parties simply being held down by old, long-serving, powerful figures at local and party level, as indeed happens in all guilds. It goes without saying that this will happen in a power*less* parliament restricted to negative politics, for in such a place only the instincts of the guild prevail. A party could *never* permit itself such an attitude if the aim of its existence were to share *power and responsibility in the state*, for this would mean that every party member throughout the country would know that the survival of the party and all the interests tying him to it depended on the party *subordinating* itself to whichever of its people possessed leadership qualities. For it is not the many-headed assembly of parliament as such that can 'govern' and 'make' policy. There is no question of this anywhere in the world, not even in England. The entire broad mass of the deputies functions *only* as a following for the 'leader'[42] or the small group of leaders who form the cabinet, and they obey them blindly *as long* as the leaders are successful. *That is how things should be.* The 'principle of the small number' (that is the superior political manoeuvrability of *small* leading groups) always rules political action. This element of 'Caesarism' is ineradicable (in *mass states*).

But it is also this element alone which guarantees that *responsibility* towards the public rests with particular individuals, whereas it would be completely dissipated within a many-headed governing assembly. This is particularly evident in true democracy. Experience shows that

---

[42] 'Leader' is in English.

officials called to office by popular election prove their worth under two sets of circumstances. Firstly, in local cantonal associations where, given a stable population, everyone knows each other personally, so that proven ability within the immediate community can determine the vote. Secondly, but with considerable reservations, in the election of the *highest* political representative of a nation in a *mass state*. Suitable political leaders normally do achieve supreme power in this way, although seldom the most outstanding leader. For the great mass of middle-ranking official positions, however, particularly those which demand specialist training, the plebiscitary system usually fails utterly and for understandable reasons. In America the judges nominated by the President towered above popularly elected judges both in integrity and ability. The reason for this lay in the fact that the leader nominating these men was held *responsible* for the quality of the officials, and the ruling party would later be made to take the consequences if gross errors were made. The operation of equal suffrage in large municipalities has always meant that the mayor was a trusted agent (*Vertrauensmann*) of the citizens, elected by plebiscite and largely given the freedom to appoint his own administrative apparatus. Equally, parliamentary government in England tends to produce such Caesarist traits. In relation to the parliament from which he emerged, the position of the leading statesman there is becoming ever more dominant.

Of course, like any other human organisation, the selection of leading politicians through party recruitment is not free from defects which have been discussed *ad nauseam* by German littérateurs in recent decades. It goes without saying that parliamentary rule, too, demands, and must demand, that the individual submits to leaders whom he can often accept only as the 'lesser evil'. However, the authoritarian state firstly gives the individual *no* choice *at all*, and secondly puts *officials* rather than *leaders* in charge of him. Surely that is a difference which is of some importance. What is more, there are good reasons for the fact that 'plutocracy', albeit in different forms, is flourishing as much in Germany as anywhere else, and that those large capitalist powers whom the littérateurs, in their ignorance, paint in the blackest colours, men who certainly have a better understanding of where their own interests lie than do academics in their studies (particularly the most ruthless of them: the leaders of heavy industry), stand here *to a man* on the side of the *bureaucratic* authoritarian state and in *opposition* to democracy and parliamentarism. It is simply that these reasons are not perceived by literary philistines. Instead, the most narrow-minded kind of moralising underscores the self-evident fact that the will to *power*[43] is one of the driving motives of parliamentary leaders, and that the selfish desire for office motivates their following. As if those aiming at bureaucratic office were not driven in exactly the same way by ambition and the hunger for a decent salary, but were inspired by pure selflessness. As far as the role played by 'demagogy' in the attainment of power is concerned, the events surrounding the current demagogic discussions in the press concerning the appointment to the post of German foreign minister, discussions which are being *promoted by certain official sources*, make it perfectly clear to anyone that it is precisely a supposedly monarchic government which is urging men who are ambitious for office or engaged in inter-departmental conflict to have recourse to the most damaging kind of press agitation.[44] Things could not possibly be worse than this in a parliamentary state with strong parties.

The motives of individual behaviour within parties are certainly just as far from being purely idealistic as are the usual philistine interests in promotion and prebends amongst competitors in an official hierarchy. In the *majority* of cases individual interests are at stake in both areas – and this will remain the case under the vaunted 'comradeship of solidarity' in the future state envisaged by the littérateurs. The only thing that matters is that these universally human, often all-too-human, interests do not at least have the effect of actually *preventing* the *selection* of men with talents for leadership. This is *only* possible within a party if its leaders have the prospect of *power* and *responsibility* in the state as the reward for success. Only then is it *possible*. But this alone certainly does not guarantee that this will be the result.

Only a *working*, as opposed to a merely talking parliament can be the soil in which not merely demagogic, but genuinely *political* qualities of leadership can grow and work their way up through a process

---

[43] Here again, Weber uses Nietzschean terminology. A (controversial) volume with this title (*The Will to Power*), based on notes written by Nietzsche between 1883 and 1888, was assembled by Elisabeth Förster-Nietzsche and published in 1901.

[44] Weber is referring to the 'Kühlmannkrise' of January 1918 when the conflict between Richard von Kühlmann, the Foreign Secretary, who favoured a negotiated peace, and the Supreme Command, who would accept nothing less than victory and a policy of annexation, came to a head.

of selection. A working parliament is one which *continuously shares in the work of government and the control of the administration*. This did not exist here before the war. After the war is over, however, parliament *must* be transformed into a working parliament. Otherwise we shall be left with the same old malaise. This is a topic to which we must now turn.

III Public scrutiny of the administration and the selection of political leaders

The whole structure of the German parliament today is tailored to a merely *negative type of politics*: criticism, complaint, consultation, the amendment and dispatch of bills presented by the government. All parliamentary conventions correspond to this. Unfortunately, the absence of public interest in the topic means that, apart from good legal works on procedure, there is a complete lack of any political analysis of how the life of the Reichstag really proceeds, of the kind that exists for other parliaments outside Germany. Yet, let anyone try to discuss with a member of parliament any kind of desirable internal organisation of the Reichstag and of the way it conducts its business, and he will immediately run up against all manner of conventions and considerations which are merely tailored to the comfort, vanities, needs and prejudices of worn-out parliamentary notables, and which put obstacles in the way of parliament's capacity for any political action. Even the simple task of controlling the officials' conduct of the administration effectively and continuously is thereby impeded. Is such control (*Kontrolle*) really superfluous?

Officialdom has passed every test brilliantly wherever it was required to demonstrate its sense of duty, its objectivity and its ability to master organisational problems in relation to strictly circumscribed, official tasks of a *specialised* nature. Anyone who comes from a family of officials, as I do, will be the last to permit any stain on his shield. But what concerns us here are *political* achievements rather than those of 'service', and the facts themselves proclaim loudly something which no lover of truth can conceal, namely that rule by officials has *failed utterly* whenever it dealt with *political* questions. This has not happened by chance. Indeed, to put it the other way round, it would be quite astonishing if abilities which are inwardly so disparate were to coincide within one and the same political formation. As we have said, *it is not the task of an official* to join in political conflict on the basis of his own convictions, and thus, in this sense of the word, 'engage in politics', which always means fighting. On the contrary, he takes pride in preserving his impartiality, overcoming his own inclinations and opinions, so as to execute in a conscientious and meaningful way what is required of him by the general definition of his duties or by some particular instruction, even – and particularly – when they do *not* coincide with his own political views. Conversely, the *leadership* which assigns tasks to the officials must of course constantly solve political problems, both of power-politics and of cultural politics (*Kulturpolitik*). Keeping *this* under control is the first and fundamental task of parliament. Not only the tasks assigned to the highest central authorities, but each individual question, no matter how technical, at the lower levels of authority *can* become politically important, so that political considerations then determine the way it is resolved. It is *politicians* who must provide a counterbalance to the rule of officialdom. The power interests of those occupying the *leading positions* in a system ruled purely by officials are opposed to this, and they will always follow their inclination to enjoy as much uncontrolled freedom as possible, and above all to maintain a monopoly over ministerial posts for the promotion of officials.

Effective *control* of officialdom is only possible under certain preconditions.

Apart from the division of labour which belongs inherently to the technique of administration, the position of power of all officials rests on *knowledge*. This knowledge is of a two-fold kind. Firstly 'technical', *specialist knowledge* in the widest sense of the word, acquired through specialist training. It is a private matter and purely coincidental if this kind of knowledge also has its exponents in parliament, or if members of parliament can obtain information privately from specialists in individual cases. For the purposes of controlling the administration, this will never take the place of systematic *cross-examination* (under oath) by *experts* before a parliamentary commission with powers to summon the relevant departmental officials. This kind of cross-examination is the only way of guaranteeing the control and comprehensiveness of the questioning. The Reichstag *lacks* the right to do this. Constitutionally, it is *condemned to amateurish stupidity*.

Yet expert knowledge is not the only foundation of the power of officials. In addition there is the official information (*Dienstwissen*) to which only an official has access via the means of the official apparatus, the knowledge of the concrete facts which are decisive for his conduct. Only someone who can procure this knowledge of the facts, independently of the good will of the official, can control the administration effectively in individual cases. Depending on circumstances, this may require access to files, on-the-spot inspection, and again, in extreme cases, the *cross-examination* under oath of those involved as witnesses before a parliamentary commission. The Reichstag also *lacks* this right. It is deliberately prevented from obtaining the requisite knowledge to control the administration, and is thus *condemned*, not just to amateurism, but also to *ignorance*.

There are absolutely *no objective* (*sachlichen*) reasons for this. It is due entirely to the fact that officialdom's most important *instrument of power* is the transformation of official information into *secret information* by means of the infamous concept of 'official secrecy', which ultimately is merely a device to *protect* the administration *from control*. Whereas the lower ranks of the official hierarchy are controlled and criticised by their superiors, all control, whether it is technical or in any sense political, breaks down here in relation to those in the highest positions, precisely those who deal with 'politics'. Both in content and in form, the manner in which administrative chiefs answer enquiries and criticisms from members of parliament is not infrequently an insult to a people with a sense of its own dignity, and this is only possible because parliament, without the so-called '*right of enquiry*' (*Enqueterecht*), is denied the means of acquiring the knowledge of the facts and of technical and specialist considerations which alone would make it possible for parliament to participate in and influence the direction taken by the administration on a continuous basis. Change must take place here first of all. It is not that the commissions of the Reichstag should in future immerse themselves in vast studies and publish fat volumes of findings; its burden of work will in any case ensure that this does not happen. Rather the right of enquiry is an indispensable aid to be used *on occasion*. Apart from this, it is to be used as a rod of chastisement, the mere existence of which forces the administrative chiefs to give an account of themselves in a way that obviates the need to use it. The finest achievements of the English parliament have come from using the right of enquiry in this way. The integrity of English officials and the high level of political education among the English public rest essentially on this practice (among other things), and it has often been stressed that the best criterion of political maturity is to be found in the way in which the proceedings of these committees are followed by the English press and public alike. Political maturity is not expressed in votes of no confidence, denunciations of ministers and similar spectacles of *unorganised* parliamentary rule in France and Italy, but rather in the fact that a nation is well informed about how its officials are *conducting their affairs*, so that it constantly controls and influences their work. The committees of a powerful parliament are the only possible places from which that educative influence can be exerted. In the end, officialdom as such can only gain from such an arrangement. It is rare, particularly in nations educated in parliamentary matters, for the relation of the public to officialdom to be so uninformed and unsympathetic as is the case in Germany. And no wonder. The *problems* with which officials have to wrestle in their work never become clearly visible here. Their achievements can never be understood and appreciated, one cannot go beyond the sterile complaints about the 'Blessed Saint Bureaucracy' in order to replace them with positive criticism so long as the present state of *uncontrolled* rule by officials continues. Nor would the power of officialdom, in its proper place, be weakened thereby. The 'permanent undersecretary' (*Geheimrat*) with his specialist training always has an advantage over his minister (in many cases, even over a minister who has risen from the ranks of specialist officialdom) when it comes to conducting departmental business; this applies to England just as much as it does here (but no more so). This is how things *ought* to be, for under modern conditions specialist training is the indispensable prerequisite of any understanding of the technical means needed to attain political goals. Setting political goals, however, is not a matter of expertise, and *policy* should not be determined by the specialist official purely in this capacity.

The outwardly quite modest change which would be produced here in Germany by having parliamentary committees which cooperated with the administration and used the right of enquiry to ensure continuous control of the officials, is the fundamental precondition of all further reforms aimed at enhancing the positive role of parliament as an organ of state. More particularly, it is also an indispensable prerequisite if parliament is to become the place where political leaders are selected. The fashionable chatter amongst littérateurs here likes to discredit parliaments as mere 'talking shops'. In a similar vein, but much more wittily, Carlyle had thundered against the English parliament just three generations ago,[45] yet it increasingly became the decisive bearer of England's power in the world. Nowadays the physical instrument of leadership (both in the political and the military spheres) is no longer a blow from a sword but quite prosaic sound waves and drops of ink – written and spoken *words*. What matters is simply that these words – whether in the form of orders or an electioneering speech, diplomatic notes or official declarations in one's own parliament – should be shaped by intellect and knowledge, by strength of will and well-considered experience. In any parliament which is only allowed to criticise without being able to obtain knowledge of the facts, and where its leaders are never put in the position of having to demonstrate what they themselves can achieve politically, words are spoken either on the basis of uninformed demagogy or of routine impotence (or both of these things together). It is part of the store of political immaturity accumulated here by a quite unpolitical age for German philistines to regard political structures like the English parliament with eyes blinded by our own current circumstances, imagining he can look down on them smugly from the heights of his own political impotence – without even considering that this body is, after all, the place where political leaders were selected who had the ability needed to bring a quarter of mankind under the rule of a tiny, politically astute minority and, even more importantly, to submit to this rule on a largely *voluntary* basis. Where can the much vaunted German authoritarian state point to similar achievements? The political training for such achievements is, of course, not to be gained in the set-piece speeches delivered in plenary sessions of parliament. It can only be acquired through unremitting, strenuous *work within* a parliamentary career. None of the significant English parliamentary leaders has risen to power without being trained in committee work, and without having moved through a whole series of administrative departments and being introduced to the work done there. *Only* this school of intensive work with the realities of administration which a politician goes through in the committees of a powerful *working* parliament, and in which he has to prove his worth, turns such an assembly into a place for the selection

---

[45] Weber is probably referring to Thomas Carlyle's *Past and Present* (1843).

of politicians who work objectively (as opposed to mere demagogues). No one could honestly deny that the English parliament is the best example we have ever seen of this process. Only this kind of cooperation between specialist officials and professional politicians can guarantee continuous control of the administration and thereby the political education and training of both the leaders and the led. An effective system of *parliamentary supervision and control* which forces the administration to work *publicly* must be demanded as a prerequisite of the political education of the nation and of any fruitful parliamentary work. We, too, have already started down this path.

The war emergency, which swept away so much conservative cant, also brought into being the '*Main Committee of the Reichstag*', an entity which is at least a start in the direction of developing a working parliament, although its method of operation and the way its work is made public are still highly imperfect from both a technical and a political point of view.

Its shortcomings for political purposes were inherent in the quite misconceived and unorganised *form* of publicity given to the discussion of highly political problems here. This was due simply to the fact that the discussions were held in and before much too large a forum, so that they necessarily became emotional. It was a scandal and a threat to national security for 'confidential' diplomatic problems or those of a technical military nature (the submarine question!) to be known to hundreds of people, as a result of which they were leaked to others or found their way into the press, partly in distorted form or in the form of sensational hints. *Current* discussions of foreign policy and the war are properly subjects for the attention of a small circle of trusted party representatives in the first instance. As policy is always made by a small number of people in any case, the parties should not be organised like guilds when it comes to the highest political questions but rather along the lines of 'followings'. Their trusted *political* spokesmen (*Vertrauensmänner*) must therefore be 'leaders', which means that they must have unrestricted authority to take important decisions, or at least be able to obtain such authority in the space of a few hours from committees capable of being summoned at any time. The 'Seven Man Committee' of the Reichstag, which was assembled for one particular purpose, is ostensibly a step in this direction. Yet the vanity of the heads of the administration was pandered to by designating this institution as 'provisional' only, and by attempting in the first instance to treat the members of parliament as if they were *not* 'party representatives'. As this would have deprived the arrangement of its political significance, it is fortunate that this gambit failed. Yet, appropriate as it may have been in itself for these seven party representatives to sit around a table to discuss matters with government commissars, the most suitable form of augmentation would have been for the seats of the seven delegates of the Bundesrat to be filled by three or four representatives of the largest middle-sized states, and the rest by the four or five most powerful administrative chiefs of the army and the home civil service or their representatives. At any rate, only a small committee bound by the rule of confidentiality can *prepare* truly *political* decisions in a highly charged situation. For the duration of the war it was perhaps appropriate to create this committee which brought together representatives of *all* the major parties and representatives of the government. In peacetime, too, it could perhaps be useful to consult party representatives on a similar basis when discussing our position on particular matters of high policy, especially issues of foreign policy. In other respects, however, this system is of limited importance, being neither a substitute for a genuine transfer of the business of government to parliament nor a means of creating a unified governmental will. If a majority of the parties is to support it, such a unified will could only be created through *free*, inter-party conferences involving only the parties capable of forming a *majority* and the leaders of the government. A committee in which a representative of the Independent Socialists can sit beside a representative of the Conservatives is inherently incapable of acting as a substitute for that method of determining the nation's political will. Such a thing would be politically inconceivable. Such formations achieve nothing as far as giving a unified direction to *policy* is concerned.

On the other hand, following the establishment of the *Main Committee*, mixed special committees could be developed and become a suitable device for normal, peacetime *control of the administration*, provided that there was provision for good, continuous reporting to the public and a suitable procedural framework was created to ensure uniformity, despite the specialisation of the topics dealt with in the sub-committees, to which representatives of the Bundesrat and of departments would be invited. The possible political effect of such an extension of committee work will depend entirely on the future position of parliament in the Reich and thereby also on the way its parties are structured. If everything remains as before, in particular if the mechanical constraint contained in Article 9 of the Reich Constitution continues in existence, and if parliament generally continues to be restricted to 'negative politics', then the parties will presumably bind their representatives on the committees to petty, imperative mandates, and in any case will not delegate any powers of *leadership* to them. In other respects each will go its own way, striving merely to negotiate small, special advantages for its protégés, and the whole arrangement will become a useless and time-wasting obstacle to administration, not an instrument of political education and fruitful cooperation on substantive issues. At the outside, the positive result of this could be something similar to what happens in some Swiss cantons, where the parties exercise proportional patronage; this would mean the peaceful distribution among the individual parties of fractions of influence on the administration, and, to the extent that this happens, a reduction in the intensity of party conflict. (Although it is far from certain that even this negative result can be achieved in a mass state which has tasks of high policy to perform. As far as I am aware, the Swiss differ in their views as to the positive practical effects of the arrangement. These too must naturally be assessed quite differently in a large state.) Yet, no matter how uncertain those idyllic prospects may be, they will certainly delight anyone who regards the elimination of party-political conflict as the highest good, while officialdom for its part will hope to profit from it by making its own position of power more secure through the continuation of the system of minor gratuities. If one then added to this some kind of proportional allocation of the prebends of office to the various parties which were 'acceptable at court', the likely outcome would be yet more 'happy faces all around'. Clearly, however, it is quite unlikely that any such peaceful distribution of prebends could really be achieved in the area of *internal administration* (district superintendents, government presidents, provincial presidents) in Prussia in the face of the Conservative Party's monopoly of office there. In any case, in purely political terms the result would merely mean that opportunities were opened up for party *officials*, but not for party *leaders*, to gain *prebends*, but *not* political *power* and responsibility – certainly not a suitable means of raising the political level of parliament. The larger questions of whether this would make control of the administration more effective, and whether the population would be made more mature in its judgement of the administration's performance, must remain completely open.

The *indispensable* guarantee of any effective discussion of even the simplest technical administrative questions, even in such a bureaucratic committee, is the right of that committee to obtain at short notice, by its own enquiries, such technical and official information as it may require. This demand does not in itself mean that any decision has been taken on the question of 'parliamentary government'; it simply sustains a prerequisite of its being established in a form appropriate to its aims; the only obstacles to it are the quite non-objective concerns of officials with their own prestige, or, to put it more plainly, their own *vanity* and their wish to remain *free of control*.

Teachers of constitutional law usually raise just one substantive and weighty objection to the right of enquiry, which is that the Reichstag is entirely autonomous in determining procedure, so that the majority at any given time could decide unilaterally not to hold an enquiry, or to construct one in such a way that it did not arrive at conclusions unwelcome to that majority. Undoubtedly, procedural autonomy (Article 27 of the Reich Constitution), which (indirectly) was copied uncritically from English theory is not suitable for *this* right. Rather, the guarantee of reliability must be created by *statutory* norms. In particular, it is *essential* that this right be created as the *right of the minority* (so that an enquiry could be demanded by, say, one hundred members of parliament), and, naturally, with the right of the minority to be represented, to ask questions, to submit a minority report. This is necessary to provide the *counterbalance of publicity* to the possibility of parliamentary affairs being run wholly *in the interest of the majority* at some time in the future and the well-known dangers of such a thing; this counterbalance is lacking in other states, and has only been guaranteed in England up till now by the parties' courtesy to one another. Yet guarantees in other directions are also needed. As long as competing industries exist, especially competition between different countries, it will be essential to protect at least their technical operational secrets adequately against tendentious publication, and, even more importantly, secrets of a military–technical nature. Finally, this must also apply to *foreign policy* deliberations which are still in the balance. At this stage these matters absolutely must be dealt with in a small committee protected by a guarantee of confidentiality. Of course, it is a mistake (one which is particularly mocked by the facts at the moment) made by certain littérateurs, particularly Russian ones, to believe that the conduct of foreign policy, let us say on the objective conclusion of peace between warring nations, could be achieved by them outdoing one another in the public proclamation of general 'principles' rather than by objective negotiation of the best available compromise between the conflicts of interest which in fact exist between states and nations, and which underlie these alleged 'principles'. At any rate, quite different means from the amateurish notions of littérateurs are required to eradicate *our* past mistakes in this area. The view, widespread in democratic circles, that *conducting things in public*, particularly diplomacy, is a panacea and, above all, one which will always operate in favour of peace, can be misleading when expressed in such general terms. It has some justification for final *statements* of a standpoint which has been considered carefully in advance. As long as states are in competition with one another, there is as little justification for publicising the deliberations *themselves* as there is in the case of competing industries. In direct contrast to questions of domestic administration, making things public at this stage can seriously *interfere* with the *objectivity* and unprejudiced character of current deliberations, thus actually endangering or preventing peace. The experiences of this war have made this utterly plain. However, foreign policy is a topic to be dealt with separately.

Permit me at this juncture, however, simply to indicate how the lack of parliamentary leadership manifests itself today in situations of domestic 'crisis'. The fate of Erzberger's initiative in July of this year and the course which the two later crises took is instructive.[46] In all three cases the consequences of a situation became apparent in which, firstly, government and parliament confront one another as two separate organs, whereby parliament is *only* an assembly representing the ruled and thus in the habit of practising 'negative politics' (in the sense outlined above); secondly, where the parties are guild-like formations, since political leaders find no vocation within parliament and therefore no place in the parties; and thirdly and finally, where the official leaders of the state, the leading officials, are neither

[46] The 'July crisis' of 1917 was initiated by Erzberger when he made it clear before the Main Committee of the Reichstag that the policy of unrestricted submarine warfare had been a failure and that Germany must sue for peace.

the leaders of parliamentary parties to which they belong, nor in *continuous* contact with the party leaders, discussing current issues with them in advance; instead, they stand outside the parties, or, as the conventional rhetoric of prestige has it, 'above the parties', so that they are unable to lead them. The system fell apart immediately whenever a strong majority in the Reichstag insisted on a positive decision from the government of the Reich. The representatives of the government had to let go of the reins in consternation, as they had no foothold in the party organisations. The politically leaderless *Reichstag* itself presented an image of complete anarchy because the (so-called) party leaders had never had a place at the table of government, and did not come into consideration as possible future leaders of the government. The parties found themselves faced with a task which had never entered their field of vision before, a task they were not equipped to perform, neither in terms of their organisation nor of their personnel: the task of forming a government from their own ranks. Naturally, they showed themselves quite incapable of doing this; they neither attempted to do so nor were they able even to attempt to do so. From the far right to the far left no party contained a politician who would have been acknowledged as leader, while officialdom itself was just as incapable of producing such a man.

For the last forty years all parties have worked on the assumption that the task of the Reichstag is merely to practise 'negative politics'. It became frighteningly obvious that the effect of Bismarck's legacy was the 'will to powerlessness', to which the parties had been condemned by his actions. But the parties did not even participate in deciding who the new leaders of the nation should be. The ruling officials' need for prestige (or, more plainly, their *vanity*) would not tolerate even this, and not even at this critical juncture, although the most elementary prudence would have demanded it. The bureaucracy could have confronted the parties with the captious question of who *they* would put forward as candidates for the leading positions in the Reich, or at least the more practical question of how they would respond to the personalities of the individuals who could be considered as possible political leaders of the Reich. Instead, however, the bureaucracy stubbornly insisted on its prestige, arguing that this was a matter which was no concern of parliament. Forces outside parliament then stepped in and appointed the new government, which did not then approach the parties with a definite, objective proposal and the categorical demand that the parties should respond to it with a 'yes' or 'no'. The new Reichskanzler, it will be recalled, was forced to make a series of statements on the crucial issue, each of them different, and to accept supervision by the Seven Man Committee for an act of foreign policy – all this because he did not possess the *confidence* of parliament. Of course, our chattering littérateurs regarded this sorry spectacle, which could only damage the standing of the country, as confirmation of their smug conviction that parliamentary rule was 'impossible' in Germany. Parliament, it was said, had 'failed'. In truth something else had failed – the attempt to have parliament led by a body of officials which stood in no relationship to it, the very same system which for decades, to the applause of the littérateurs, had rendered parliament incapable of positive political action and had served officialdom's interest in remaining free of control. The situation would be completely different if the practice of government placed responsibility fully, or at least mainly, on the shoulders of the party leaders, thereby offering natural political leaders the chance of playing their part in directing the fate of the nation. Then the parties could not have allowed themselves the kind of petty-bourgeois, guild-like organisation we now have in the Reichstag. They would have been absolutely compelled to *subordinate themselves* to leaders and not, as happened in the Centre Party, to men of an industrious, official nature whose nerve failed them at the very point when they should have developed qualities of leadership. In any such crisis, however, the leaders in turn would have been compelled to form a coalition and to present the monarch with a positive programme and the names of specific individuals with gifts of leadership. Under the existing system the only possible consequence was that of purely negative politics.

The new leader of the Reich, whose appointment was decided outside parliament, found himself faced with a muddle which immediately created the same situation all over again. Taking some very able members of parliament into offices in the government simply meant, as Article 9 of the Reich constitution provides, that they lost their influence in their party, leaving it headless or disoriented. Exactly the same thing happened during the crises of August and October.[47] The complete failure of the government resulted yet again

---

[47] Pope Benedict XV issued his peace note to the belligerent states on 1 August 1917. This called on them to begin peace negotiations. The failure of this peace initiative

from the fact that the statesmen stubbornly stuck to the principle of *avoiding* both *continuous* consultation with the party leaders and any preparatory discussions of the problems to be dealt with at the forthcoming conference, at least with representatives of those parties whom they wished and hoped to win over to their side. The mere fact that the new Reichskanzler, who was appointed in November, made contact with the majority parties in the Reichstag, at their request, *before* taking up office, together with the fact that the purely political ministries were filled from now on with trained parliamentarians, sufficed to make at least the machinery of domestic politics function tolerably well, although the continued existence of Article 9, Sentence 2 continued to exert its pernicious influence even then. The January crisis[48] also made it plain to even the weakest eyes that domestic political crises here do not have their source in *parliament*, but in two sets of circumstances. Firstly, in the abandonment of the political principle, always strictly adhered to by Bismarck, that the commander of the army conducts war in the light of *military* considerations, whereas the politician concludes peace in the light of *political* considerations (of which purely technical, strategic questions are *one*, but only one, element). Secondly, but most importantly, in the circumstance that some subaltern courtiers considered it useful and compatible with an ostensibly 'monarchic' government to leak internal discussions of high policy *to the press* – and did so for reasons of *party-political* interest.

Conditions here are a clear lesson that pure rule by officials, for the sake of this characteristic, does not necessarily mean the *absence* of *party* rule. It is impossible for a district superintendent to be anything but *Conservative* in Prussia, and Germany's spurious parliamentary system, with all its consequences, rests on the axiom adopted since 1878 by those with vested party interests (after the eleven most fruitful years of parliamentary work in Germany had been interrupted), namely that every government and its representatives

heightened the political crisis in Germany, and in October 1917 Hertling succeeded Michaelis as chancellor.

[48] This is a reference to the peace negotiations between Russia and Germany taking place at Brest–Litovsk during January 1918. Weber and much of German public opinion was inclined to place the blame for the breakdown of the negotiations upon the intervention of the German Supreme Command. Subsequent historical investigations have shown that there was less disagreement between the government and the Supreme Command than Weber believed.

must necessarily and by the nature of things be 'conservative', allowing for some concessions to the patronage of the Prussian bourgeoisie and the Centre Party. This, and nothing else, is what is meant here by the 'non-partisan' character of rule by officials. The lesson the war has taught all other countries, namely that *all* parties become 'national' when they share responsibility for *power* in the state, has changed nothing here. The party interests of conservative officials who hold power, and of the interest groups attached to it, exercise exclusive control over leadership. The inevitable fruits of this 'cant' are evident, and they will emerge after the war too. It will not be parliament alone which has to pay for this but the supreme power of the state as such.

The one and only question one can properly ask about the future ordering of the state in Germany is, '*How is parliament to be made capable of assuming power?*' Anything else is a side issue.

One has to be clear about the fact that one thing above all is needed in order to achieve this goal, namely the development of a suitable body of *professional members of parliament*, in addition, that is, to the outwardly modest but practically important extensions of parliamentary powers discussed above, the removal of the mechanical obstacle created by Article 9, and major changes in procedure and current conventions.

The professional member of parliament is a man who exercises his mandate in the Reichstag, not as an occasional and subsidiary duty, but as the main content of his life's work, equipped with his own office and staff and with every means of information. One may love or hate this figure, but he is indispensable in purely technical terms and is therefore *already with us* today. It is, however, particularly characteristic of the most influential examples of this type of person that they mostly work behind the scenes and have only a fairly subaltern status, as befits the subaltern status of parliament and the subaltern prospects of a parliamentary career. The professional politician can be a man who merely lives *from* politics and its machinations, its influence and opportunities. Or he can be a man who lives *for* politics. Only in the latter case can he become a politician of great stature. Naturally, this is easier for him, the more he has a fortune which gives him independence and makes him 'available' (*abkömmlich*), not tied to a business (as entrepreneurs are) but a person with an unearned income. Of the social groups who are tied to their businesses, the only ones who are 'available' and therefore suited to becoming professional politicians, are the advocates. While it would certainly not be desirable for rule to be exercised purely by advocates, it is foolish to deprecate, as our littérateurs so often do, the qualification of advocates for political leadership. In an age where *lawyers rule*, the great *advocate* is the only lawyer who, in contrast to the official, is trained to *fight* and to *represent a case* effectively by fighting, and one would wish to see *far more* skills in (well-mannered, objective) advocacy in evidence in our public pronouncements. But *only* if parliament holds out the prospect of positions of leadership with the responsibility of leadership will advocates of any stature, or indeed any independent personalities at all, want to live for politics. Otherwise only salaried party officials and representatives of vested interests will want to do so.

The *ressentiment* which men who are party officials by nature feel towards towards genuine political leadership is a powerful element in the attitude of some parties to the question of parliamentarisation, which also means the parliamentary selection of leaders. Of course, their *ressentiment* harmonises perfectly with the like-minded interests of the bureaucracy. For the professional parliamentarian as such is instinctively felt as a thorn in the flesh by the heads of bureaucratic administrations. He offends them simply by being someone who exercises uncomfortable control over their work, and as someone laying claim at least to a certain share of power. He offends them even more strongly when he appears in the guise of a potential contender and competitor for *leading* positions (whereas the representatives of vested interests offer *no* such threat). This is the reason for the fight to keep parliament in ignorance. Only qualified, professional parliamentarians who have been through the school of intensive committee work in a *working* parliament can give rise to responsible leaders, as opposed to mere demagogues and amateurs. The whole internal structure of parliament must be such as to produce such leaders and enhance their effectiveness, as has long been the case with the structure of the English parliament and its parties. Admittedly, the conventions of the English parliament cannot simply be transplanted to Germany. But the structural principle surely can be. The mass of detailed changes in procedure and conventions which would be needed are not matters to be considered here; they will emerge of their own accord as soon as the parties are *compelled* to engage in responsible rather than merely 'negative' politics. However, we do have to consider briefly a genuinely serious obstacle which the peculiar structure of the German *party system* puts in the path of parliamentarisation, something which is often discussed, but usually in a distorted way.

There is no doubt that the simplest basis on which to introduce parliamentary government is a two-party system of the kind which existed until recently in England (albeit with some very noticeable infringements of the principle already). But it is certainly not an indispensable means of achieving that end, and the trend everywhere (including England) is moving in the direction of forcing parties to form coalitions. There is another, much more important difficulty: parliamentary government is only possible when the largest parties are at all *prepared*, on principle, to assume the responsible leadership of the affairs of state. This has certainly not been the case here up till now. Above all, the largest party, the Social Democratic Party, was inhibited, not only by its pseudo-revolutionary conventions (against 'attendance at Court') which were a legacy of the years of persecution, but also by certain evolutionary theories, from being prepared to enter a coalition government on any conditions (or to take over the government when, as happened in one small state, it temporarily had an absolute majority).[49] Of much more importance than these theoretical anxieties, however, was then, and continues to be, its fear of losing its roots and becoming discredited in the eyes of its own class, given the fact that all governments are tied to the fundamental conditions underpinning a society and economy which will remain capitalist for the foreseeable future. This situation caused the Social Democratic leaders to lock the party into a kind of political ghetto existence for decades in order to avoid being soiled by any contact with the workings of a bourgeois state apparatus. Despite everything, this is still the case even today. Syndicalism, the heroic, unpolitical and anti-political ethic of fraternity, is undergoing a period of growth, and its leaders are fighting shy of any breach in class solidarity which would later weaken the workers' effectiveness in the economic struggle, especially as they have no guarantee that the traditional attitude of the bureaucracy will not be revived again after the war. It is a fundamental question for Germany's future what attitude the

---

[49] This was the situation in Gotha between 1900 and 1912.

party will take in the future, whether its will to power in the state gains the upper hand, or whether the unpolitical ethic of class fraternity and syndicalism, which will surely spring up in strengthened form everywhere after the war, wins the day. For rather different reasons, the attitude to parliamentarism of the second largest party in Germany, the Centre Party, has also been sceptical. There is a certain inner affinity between its own authoritarian convictions and the authoritarian state which serves the interests of the bureaucracy. But something else is more important. As a born minority party, the Centre feared that it would also be driven into the minority in parliament under a system of parliamentary government, and that this would threaten its position of power and its role in representing those interests which, in practice, it serves today. Its position of power rests in the first instance on extra-parliamentary means, on the fact that the clergy also rules the political attitudes of the faithful. Within parliament, however, the *material* interests of its supporters were served by exploiting the opportunities offered by the practice of 'negative politics'. After achieving all the essential political goals of the church, at any rate all those which could be sustained in the long term in Germany, the Centre increasingly changed in practice from being an ideological party of a particular *Weltanschauung* into an *organisation for providing assured patronage to Catholic candidates for office* and to other Catholic vested interests who have felt themselves disadvantaged since the period of the *Kulturkampf* (whether they had good cause for these feelings is irrelevant here). A good deal of its power today rests on this foundation. The very nature of its position in parliament, where it tips the scales in one direction or the other, enables it to promote the private interests of its protégés. Officialdom acquiesced in this patronage and yet did not 'lose face', because the patronage remained unofficial. Those party members with an interest in patronage now fear not only that parliamentarisation and democratisation will threaten their chances in periods when the Centre belongs to the minority, but something else besides. Under the present system the Centre Party was *spared* having to take any *responsibility*, whereas it could not have avoided it if its leaders had belonged formally to the government. This responsibility would not always have been comfortable. For while the Centre Party still has a number of very able minds amongst its politicians, the officials it patronises include not only useful people but people so obviously untalented that a party participating responsibly in government would be unlikely to have entrusted them with official posts. Such personalities can *only* make careers under a system of *ir*responsible patronage. As an official governing party the Centre would have to present more gifted candidates.

Because it is irresponsible, *unofficial* patronage is the most pernicious form of parliamentary patronage of all, since it favours mediocrity, and this type of patronage is a consequence of the conservative *rule by officials* which owes its continued existence to this system of gratuities. Admittedly, it is not surprising that those sections of today's National Liberal Party which are conservative, or specifically represent big business, feel quite comfortable under the prevailing conditions. Here the patronage of office is not decided by politicians and parties who could be made *accountable* to the public, but by all kinds of private connections, beginning with the very important connections made in *student fraternities* and including both the coarser and finer forms of capitalist recommendation. Big business, suspected by our littérateurs, in their weak-minded ignorance, of being in league with the heresy of parliamentarism, stands *to a man* on the side of preserving the uncontrolled rule of officials. And it knows full well why it does so.

This is the state of affairs which our phrase-mongering littérateurs have been in the habit of defending stubbornly while raging against the idea that the patronage of office should be an open responsibility of the parties, something which they abhor as 'corrupt' and 'un-German'. In truth it is assuredly not the 'German spirit' that is committed to the fight against parliamentary control of patronage but a strong material interest in official prebends, allied to the capitalist exploitation of 'connections' . There can be no doubt at all that only the pressure of absolutely compelling political circumstances could ever produce any change here. Parliamentarisation will certainly not come 'of its own accord'. Indeed there is nothing more certain than that the most powerful forces imaginable are working against change. Admittedly, in all the above-named parties there are ideologues and purely objective politicians as well as those subaltern types interested in patronage and simple parliamentary time-servers. Under the system as it stands, however, it is the latter who are absolutely dominant. If these prebends and gratuities were extended to other parties, this state of affairs would only become more general.

The beneficiaries of existing conditions, and the littérateurs who naively place themselves at the service of their slogans, usually conclude an argument by asserting triumphantly that Germany's character as a *federal state* is a sufficiently compelling, purely formal reason for excluding parliamentarism. Let us first consider the *legal* sense of the question on the basis of the written constitution currently in force. If one does so, it becomes quite incredible that anyone should dare to make such an assertion. According to the Constitution (Article 18), the Kaiser *alone* has the right to appoint and dismiss the Reichskanzler and all the officials of the Reich, without any interference from the Bundesrat. Within the framework of the laws of the Reich they owe obedience to him and to no other. As long as this holds true, the federalist objection is contrary to the Constitution. According to the Constitution, no one can prevent the Kaiser using his right to appoint one or other of the leaders of the parliamentary majority to direct the policy of the Reich and to appoint them as plenipotentiaries to the Bundesrat, or, equally, to dismiss them on the grounds of a vote by a clear and firm majority of the Reichstag, or at least, in the first instance, to consult the parties and to give full weight to their views before making the appointment. *No* majority in the Bundesrat has the right to depose the Reichskanzler or even to require him to answer politically for his actions, whereas he is bound by the Constitution to account for himself before the Reichstag (according to the undisputed interpretation of Article 17, sentence 2). The recent suggestion that the Reichskanzler should be declared to be accountable not only to the *Reichstag* but also to the *Bundesrat* would be just as much of an innovation as the proposal made in these pages for the rescission of Article 9, sentence 2, although it is certainly one which deserves to have its political usefulness examined and discussed further. Later we shall have to confront the fact that the real problems, not only of parliamentarisation but of the Reich Constitution generally lie not so much with the constitutional rights of the other federal states but with their relations to the hegemonial state of *Prussia*. First we need to illustrate how the system of government we have had up till now has functioned in the important area of *foreign policy*. For it is precisely here that the *inner* limitations of what can be achieved by the rule of officials become manifest, as well as the terrible price we have had to pay for allowing ourselves to be ruled in this way.

IV Rule by officials in foreign policy

The administration of *domestic* affairs is dominated here in Germany by the specifically bureaucratic concept of 'official secrecy'. In astonishing contrast to this practice, a whole series of the most diverse *foreign* policy actions have taken place in the most dramatic way in public. And indeed amidst publicity of a very special kind.

For more than a decade, from the Krüger telegram[50] to the Moroccan Crisis,[51] we saw how the political leadership in Germany partly tolerated and partly even collaborated in the publication of *purely personal pronouncements by the monarch* on questions of foreign policy through some dedicated court officials or telegraph agencies. The events concerned were of the greatest importance for the shaping of our policy in the world and particularly for the emergence of the worldwide coalition against us. It has to be said at the very outset that the point at issue here is *not* the correctness of the position taken, nor whether the substance of the monarch's statements was justified. I am concerned only with the behaviour of the *officials*. Convinced as I am of the value of monarchic institutions, I would as much spurn any covert polemic against the monarch as I do the pseudo-monarchic flattery or the sentimental, loyal-subject talk of interested parties and philistines. Admittedly, any monarch who steps onto the public stage with quite personal and in part extraordinarily pointed utterances must be prepared to hear equally sharp public criticism, should it be called for. We are faced with the fact that this method of presenting ourselves in public by the *publication* of statements by the monarch was in fact repeatedly *tolerated* in Germany. If this method was a grave political error – a point to which we shall return – then tolerating its repetition, despite all that has happened (to the extent that the mon-

---

[50] The telegram from Wilhelm II in January 1896 to President Paul Krüger of the Transvaal, congratulating him on the failure of the 'Jameson raid' to overthrow his government, caused a deterioration in Anglo-German relations.

[51] In 1905 the Kaiser interrupted a cruise to make a landing at Tangier where he promised to support the independence of the Sultan against French expansion. In 1911 a German gunboat was sent to Agadir in protest against further French expansion. Both actions resulted in a diplomatic fiasco for Germany.

arch was materially responsible) proves that it is necessary for him to be advised *exclusively* and decisively by the leading politicians, and that all other instances, whether at court or in the military or elsewhere, must be excluded from any possible interference in politically important questions. If 'real guarantees' that this would be the case were not to be forthcoming, then certainly it would be one's unquestionable political duty to subject the monarch to quite unsparing criticism, including criticism of his person. This kind of public discussion of the monarch would quite certainly not be politically desirable. It is certainly not old hat; it is, rather, the product of ancient political wisdom and experience to ensure that the monarch is not dragged into the public gaze in a demagogic manner, as has happened here on several occasions, by imposing strict forms and conditions on his appearance in public and thereby making it possible, as a matter of principle, to keep his person out of the public discussion of party conflict. This very fact makes it possible for him to intervene personally and with an authority that is all the more unquestionable at times of national upheaval, when such action is really necessary. Thus, what is involved here is not a discussion of any mistakes the monarch might have made, but something else entirely, namely the fact that the responsible *leaders* of the Reich, despite the monarch's own reservations in at least one case, both used his *public* appearance or the *publication* of his views as a diplomatic device, and, without immediately resigning their office, tolerated the fact that statements by the monarch were issued to the public over their heads by non-responsible sources. There is no question that the monarch has the right to make clear his position on any political matter. But whether his views and the manner of their expression (both in content and in form) should be presented to the *public*, and the likely effects of doing so – these are matters which absolutely must be considered and decided only by trained and responsible leading *politicians*. The leading statesman must therefore be *asked for his advice in advance* of every *publication* (indeed, before the *transmission* of any utterance by the monarch on high policy which could lead to its *publication*, and *this advice must be followed for as long he remains in office. He and his colleagues are in dereliction of their duty if they stay in post, should this fail to happen on even a single occasion.* If the leading statesmen of the Reich do not draw this conclusion, all talk about the nation 'not wanting a shadow monarch' and the like is merely a pretext for the desire to stay in office. Essentially, this question has nothing to do with 'parliamentary rule' as such but simply with obligations of *political honour*. Yet there have been repeated failures in precisely this area in Germany, and they have been of the most serious kind. That these errors were committed was entirely a result of the false political structure of government here, which appoints people with the minds of officials to positions which should be filled by men with their own sense of political responsibility. The whole question of parliamentarisation here is so highly charged politically because in present circumstances there is no other technical means available with which one could simultaneously create both change and *guarantees* of change. Just in case the point at issue gets shifted somewhere else, let me state quite explicitly: not only was the personal stand taken by the monarch quite understandable from a subjective point of view in almost every case, it was also politically correct – as far as one could see at the time – in at least some of these cases. In a number of cases it was also not unlikely that the *diplomatic* transmission of his forceful personal views (in a suitable form) to the relevant governments could have had a useful political effect. What was politically irresponsible was the *publication* of these views, for which the German political leaders who tolerated or initiated the publication were responsible. It seems to have been forgotten here that it makes an enormous difference whether a leading *politician* (Minister President or even President of the Republic) delivers a declaration in public – in parliament, say – however forcefully it is expressed, or whether he publishes a personal utterance by the *monarch* and then 'covers' it by a gesture that is both theatrical and cheap. The truth is that a public statement by the monarch is protected from the fiercest criticism *within the country*, where it therefore also covers the *statesman* who misuses it against unconstrained criticism of his own conduct. *Abroad*, however, no one pays any heed to this convention, and criticism is levelled directly at the *monarch*. A politician can and should resign if a changed situation demands that a different position be taken. The monarch, by contrast, must remain. But so also do his words. Once he has committed himself personally in *public*, any attempt to take back his words, as required by the changed situation, will be in vain. Passions and the *sense of honour* have been aroused; it becomes a point of honour for the nation to stand firm behind its monarch, and amateurish littérateurs like the 'pan-Germanists' and their *publishers* do good business.

Both at home and abroad people cling *permanently* to the words once they have been uttered, and the situation becomes intractable. In fact this pattern has been followed in *all* of these cases. Let us go through a number of them quite objectively, in order to see where the political error lies.

First, the *Krüger telegram*. The outrage at the Jameson raid was justified and shared throughout the world (and by many people in England too, it will be recalled). Strong diplomatic representations in London (which included reference to the monarch's anger) could very well have led, under these circumstances, to declarations by the English cabinet at the time which perhaps would not have been so easy to brush aside later. In addition, we might perhaps have come closer to the possibility of reaching a general understanding on the interests of both parties in Africa; this would have been entirely acceptable to Cecil Rhodes, for example, and it was an absolute necessity if we wanted a free hand in other directions (in the Orient) and to keep Italy in the alliance. When *published*, however, the telegram had of course the effect of a *slap in the face*, which precluded any objective discussion on both sides. Now a point of honour was at stake and interests of Realpolitik were excluded. Consequently, later initiatives to reach agreement on Africa (before, during and after the Boer War) could not command the inner assent of *either* of the two nations, since their sense of honour had become involved in mutual hostility, although both parties could have stood to gain objectively by an agreement. The result was to cast Germany in the role of the dupe after the war. In 1895, however, we would simply *not* have had sufficient instruments of power at our disposal to back any protest effectively. It is best to make no criticism of the end of the affair – the failure to receive the President when he fled the country – for the main issue, the abandonment of the Boers, despite the intervention of the monarch, was inevitable. As is well known, General Botha declared in the South African parliament in 1914, 'It was the conduct of the Germans which cost us our independence.'

The behaviour of Japan in 1914 and of China in 1917 produced astonishment in Germany.[52] Japan's decision is usually explained solely in terms of the well-known Port Arthur intervention in 1895,[53]

---

[52] Japan and China declared war on Germany in 1914 and 1917 respectively.

[53] Here Weber's text gives the incorrect date of 1897.

that of China solely in terms of American pressure; in both cases opportunist motives are also cited. Although there may be much truth in this, there was an additional factor of some importance. Does anyone here really believe that any educated Chinese or Japanese would have forgotten that it was the monarch in Germany who *publicly*, in word and image, warned about the 'Yellow Peril' and called for the 'preservation of our most sacred values'?[54] Racial problems are among the most difficult questions in international affairs, because they are complicated by the conflicts of interest amongst the white peoples. It is laudable that the monarch was seeking to form a view on the question. But what goal, in particular what *German* political goal, of whatever kind, was served by *publishing* the position he took at the time in this manner? Could it be reconciled in any way with German interests in the Far East? What instruments of power were there to back the publication of the Kaiser's views? Whose interests was it bound to serve in practice? What political goals were served by publishing the speeches on China at the time when Graf Waldersee was being dispatched? Which objectives were served by publishing the Kaiser's speeches on the navy, however appropriate they might have been for delivery before a group of officers? Germany's policy towards China produced a yield that was embarrassingly and, it must be added, by no means coincidentally disproportionate to his words, so that these then did much damage to our prestige. Let us simply pass over the unedifying episode of the way the 'mission of atonement' was handled and the discussion, again in *public*, which surrounded it. It is impossible to imagine what goal of *German* Realpolitik Prince Bülow thought could be served by condoning this piece of romanticism which offended the Chinese sense of honour to no purpose at all. If he was clever enough to see how politically worthless and harmful all these events would be, but was obliged to take account of conditions which led to the toleration of these events, it was imperative for him to *resign*, both in the interests of the nation and those of the monarch in particular.

Others have already expressed grave doubts as to whether, in view of the political situation in relation to Russia, the *publication* of the

---

[54] Wilhelm II had spoken of the 'Yellow Peril' in a speech in 1905 when referring to the Japanese defeat of Russia at Mukden. In 1895 he had commissioned an infamous painting from the court painter Knackfuß, to which he gave the title 'Wahret eure heiligsten Güter!', depicting the threat to Germany from other, less 'civilised' peoples.

Kaiser's speech in Damascus was constructive. The peoples and politicians involved were already aware of our sympathies for Islamic culture and of our political interest in the integrity of Turkey without any such attention-catching action. In any case, regardless of the political constellation at the time, it would have been better for us to avoid the false impression created by this *public* pronouncement. Here again, it was easy to see whose designs were bound to be served by all this.

If there is some room for doubt in this last instance, the facts are quite clear in the case of the (yet again) *public* speech in Tangiers at the beginning of the Morocco Crisis. Germany's position as such met with full approval, even from neutral parties. Yet again, the great error was to involve the person of the monarch *publicly*. Although it is not yet known what offers were made by France after the fall of Delcassé, it was at least clear that one either had to be fully prepared to *go to war* for the sake of Morocco's independence, or the matter had to be settled for good in a manner which took account of the interests and the *sense of honour* of both sides, in exchange for French compensation. That could possibly have had far-reaching consequences for relations with France. Why did it not happen? The *honour* of the nation, it was said, had become involved through the *monarch's words* in support of the Sultan of Morocco whom we could not now 'leave in the lurch'. Yet there was no intention of going to war. The result was the defeat of Algeciras, then the 'Panther' episode and finally the abandonment of Morocco, but at the same time, under the pressure of the endless nervous tension, a welling-up of the desire for war in France. A further consequence was to promote England's policy of encirclement. In addition to this, the impression was created yet again – despite the Kaiser's words – that Germany *pulls back*. It resulted in all this, *without* Germany gaining *any* adequate political compensation.

The aims of German policy, including overseas policy in particular, were *exceedingly* modest in comparison with the acquisitions of other nations, and the actual results were downright meagre. At the same time, it created areas of friction and made more noise than that of any other country. Again and again it was the *publication* of statements by the monarch which created these politically quite useless and damaging sensations. Nor were our relations with neutral or unfriendly powers the only ones to be damaged by this method.

After the Algeciras Conference the monarch felt the need to express his thanks to Count Golukhovski.[55] Instead of the means usually employed for such purposes, the famous telegram was *published*. The immediate, and for us embarrassing, downfall of the addressee showed too late that no government will allow its leading statesmen to be given good marks *in public*, even by its closest allies.

Domestic politics, too, have been affected by exactly the same mistakes.

Or was the 'prison speech',[56] delivered in a fit of bad temper, really suited to the *public* domain, where it immediately had the effect of seeming to be a political programme? What is one to make of the fact that, simply because mention had been made of 'imprisonment' as a punishment for strikes, the bureaucracy then had to set about drafting an appropriate paragraph for the anti-strike bill? It took first the momentous events of 1914 and then the present announcement of equal suffrage to eradicate the effects which this utterly pointless publication quite naturally had on the attitude of honourable workers. Was this in the interest of the dynasty? What other politically defensible objective was the publication intended to achieve?

Yet it was our intention to consider only foreign policy at this point, and this naturally prompts the question: when those remarks were being published, where were all those parties in the Reichstag who could have had a crucial influence on the attitude of the government, and who then reproached Chancellor Bethmann Hollweg with the 'failures' of this policy which, allegedly, 'had made enemies of the whole world', or who accused him of 'taking cover behind the monarch'? What did they do in each of these cases? *They exploited the criticism of the extreme left by seizing the opportunity to denounce the 'anti-monarchical' principles of the left*! It cannot be emphasised too strongly that they did not raise objections in *public* until it was too late. Even then they *only* did so to the extent that their own selfish interests were not affected. I do not want to rake over the details of the well-known events of 1908, but I would remind you of one thing: the Conservative Party, in contrast to the undoubtedly impressive address of their spokesmen to the monarch, later left Prince Bülow completely

---

[55] G . A. Golukhovski (1849–1921), Austro-Hungarian Foreign Minister 1895–1906.
[56] In a speech in 1898 Wilhelm II announced, without first informing his ministers, that a new law for the protection of labour would include prison terms for those who encouraged strikes or prevented workers from attending their place of work.

in the lurch and, as usual, dug out their pseudo-monarchism once again when their own *material* interests were at stake.[57] (Incidentally, the monarch was probably quite astonished when this chancellor, of all men, who on at least one occasion had advised him directly to make a very demonstrative public appearance, despite his own reservations, suddenly turned against him under pressure from an excited public!) But above all, where were our littérateurs in all these cases? *They applauded publicly* or chattered – as the press of the right-wing parties still does – about how Germans simply have no liking for monarchy on the English model. They blamed the failures on 'diplomacy', pandering to the most pitiful instincts of the philistines, but without asking even once how diplomacy was supposed to operate at all under such conditions! *In private*, admittedly – but that would be a long and dishonourable story for the agitators who are now publicly denouncing the majority which favours a '*hunger peace*'.

Above all, however, it was the conduct of our leading statesmen in all these cases which was irresponsible and without parallel in the politics of any great state. A *public* initiative from this quarter was only admissible if the intention was to go to war and *indeed to do so immediately*. But we did not truly intend an armed intervention, neither on the side of the Boers, nor against the Mongols, nor on behalf of the Sultan of Morocco, and in the first two cases we had neither the vocation nor the means of power to do so. Yet the leading politicians permitted the monarch's personal and *public* involvement to destroy the possibility of any substantive understanding with England on mutual interests in Southern Africa, or with France on interests in North Africa, because our position now seemed to have been fixed as if it were a point of *honour* – which then had to be abandoned in the end. The inevitable consequences were embarrassing diplomatic defeats which still burn in the soul of every German even today, and grave, permanent damage to our interests. Above all, we gave the highly dangerous impression that Germany, after using the strongest public gestures, tended to *pull back* after all; this belief, which doubtless contributed to the conduct of English policy at the end of July

1914, stems from those events. To a great extent these quite incredible errors also led to the formation of the unnatural world coalition against us. Not only that, they are still having an effect. The swindle being perpetrated in the outside world by all the chatter about German 'autocracy' is indeed just that – a swindle. Yet the fact that such a swindle is possible is by no means unimportant politically. Who enabled our enemies to perpetrate this swindle so successfully, although they do not believe it any more than they believe any other fairy stories about Germany? Who heaped the enormous, and politically far from negligible, hatred of the whole world on the head of *this* particular monarch, whose conduct notoriously tipped the scales in favour of preserving the peace on numerous occasions, even at moments when, in terms of Realpolitik, war might perhaps have suited our purposes better? Who made it possible for the masses abroad to believe, in all seriousness, that Germany longs to be 'liberated' and that, if they persevere with the war for long enough, this suppressed mood will eventually come to the surface? Who made the unheard-of nonsense of the present situation possible? As long as there is any possibility of a return to that situation, the nation must not be allowed to forget that all this was done by the *rule of conservative officialdom*. At decisive moments, this form of rule put people with *the minds of officials* into leading positions which ought to have been filled by *politicians*, in other words by men who had learned, through political struggle, to weigh the potential significance of *public statements* and who, above all, would have had the *leading politician's* sense of responsibility, rather than the official's feeling that his duty lies in subordination, something which is quite proper in its place but which was very damaging here.

The gulf separating these two types of mind can be seen most clearly here. The *official* has to *sacrifice* his own convictions to his *duty of obedience*. The leading *politician* must publicly *refuse* to accept responsibility for political actions if they conflict with his own convictions; his duty is to sacrifice his office to his convictions. Yet this has never happened here.

All we have said so far still does not make plain the worst aspect of our situation. It is reliably known that almost all those men who have had the leadership of our politics in their hands during this fateful decade, have *refused*, in private, not just occasionally but repeatedly, to accept material responsibility for the crucial publication which they had 'covered' formally. If one then asked in astonishment, why on earth the statesman concerned *remained at his post*, when he so plainly lacked the means of power to prevent a publication which he was sure was inadvisable, the answer one received was usually, 'Someone else would have been prepared to do it.' That is probably true, and that is the crucial point of weakness – and the cause of all other problems – in the *system as such*, which is what concerns us here. Would *someone else have been prepared to do it* if the political leader had been obliged to *bear responsibility as the spokesman of a powerful parliament?*

This crucial point makes clear what it means to have a parliament to which the officials are *effectively* responsible. Quite simply, *there is no other power which can substitute for it. Or if there is another, which is it?* Anyone here who still feels justified in disparaging 'parliamentarism' is obliged to answer this question. On this same point, it is utterly clear that the sense of responsibility of an official on the one hand and of a politician on the other is appropriate to their respective situations – but *there and there alone.* For the officials and diplomats concerned were not untrained or lacking in ability, indeed some of them were outstanding, but they lacked what is called 'character' in the purely political sense of the word, which has nothing to do with private morality. Nor was it by chance that they lacked it; it was the result, rather, of the *structure of the state*, which simply has *no use* for such a thing as political character. What can one say about these conditions which are to be found in no other great state – about the fact that civilian cabinets or court servants or telegraph agencies or whoever can take it on themselves to make *public* such events which are of the greatest importance for international politics, and thereby play havoc with our politics, causing them to become bogged down for decades; about the fact that the leading *politician* resigns himself to such incidents with a shrug of the shoulders and some, as he imagines, noble gestures; about the fact that this should happen in a state where, at the same time, '*official secrecy*' on matters of *domestic* politics is regarded as the jewel in the crown of an official's obligations because it suits the power interests of the administrative chiefs? It is as plain as can be that this apparent contradiction can be explained purely and simply in terms of the officials' vested interest in holding office *without responsibility*. What can one say about a system which left politicians in post who, contrary to their own convictions, tolerated grave errors? Finally, what is one to say about the fact that, despite all these things which are obvious to everyone, there are still littérateurs who have the impertinence to claim that a state structure which has *functioned like this* on the politically decisive point has 'stood the test brilliantly'? As we have said, the achievements of our officers and officials have stood the test more than brilliantly where what mattered was the quality of their *service*. When occupying positions which ought to have been filled by *politicians*, however, rule by officials has not only failed for decades, it has shielded itself by *burdening the person of the monarch* with the *odium* of its own conduct. Because it lacked all sense of political direction, this helped to bring about the world constellation against us which, without the brilliant achievements of our army, could have cost the monarch his crown and Germany its entire political future. *Any* state structure which prevents such things happening must serve the interests of the nation and the monarch better than the present state of things. *This must cease, whatever the cost.* There is absolutely no doubt (and it can easily be proved) that the political parties in Germany *do not disagree* about the seriousness of the damage that has been done. It is simply that politicians on the right have been too lacking in political character on the one hand, and have been too self-interested on the other, to defend an opinion *in public* which they had always expressed in the strongest terms in private, and above all to draw the *substantive conclusions* from that view. For there can be no progress here without '*real guarantees*'. The *utter incorrigibility* of those court circles who were responsible for these publications has taught us that. The creation of such guarantees is of far greater political importance than all other political problems, of whatever kind, including parliamentarisation and democratisation. The former is for us the indispensable *means* of creating such real guarantees, for there can be no doubt that *only* parliamentary power and the effective accountability of leading politicians to parliament can provide a guarantee that such things will not happen.

After decades of routine ineffectuality, the creation of a truly effective parliamentary leadership will take years at least. What can be done *in the meantime*, until this reform has been carried out or has had time to bear fruit?

One thing is of course self-evident: everywhere, including and especially in 'democracies', the most responsible decisions on *foreign* policy are made by a *small* group of people. America and Russia are the two best examples at the present moment. No ideology purveyed by littérateurs will change this fact. Every attempt to change it reduces the burden of responsibility, whereas what matters is to increase that burden. There will therefore be no change in the prerogatives of the Kaiser, as defined in Article 11 of the Reich constitution, which are to be exercised under the *effective* responsibility of the Reichskanzler. *Legal measures must be taken immediately* to end the dangerous *public* abuse to which irresponsible and anonymous vested interests at court and in the press have subjected purely personal remarks by the monarch which affect the foreign relations of the Reich. There should be a special law threatening severe punishment for anyone who dares to publish such statements in future or to spread them abroad without all guarantees having been given *in advance*. In cases where the abuse is deliberate the punishment should involve the loss of that person's honour. Of course, this means that the leading politician must have accepted *in advance* his constitutional responsibility specifically for *publication. Everything depends on this.* It is mere empty rhetoric for the leading politician to declare retrospectively, in answer to complaints in parliament, that he 'assumes personal responsibility for the publication'. Even then, the monarch's statement cannot be subjected to *unconstrained* criticism without endangering his political position. Above all, however, that kind of cliché is not only meaningless, it is simply *untrue* in political terms if the leading politician has not been consulted *in advance* and has approved the publication, as required by the constitution. If that has not happened, the phrase merely means that, *despite the publication, he feels no inclination to be pensioned off yet*; in other words he is 'clinging' to his office. In order to exert the necessary pressure on the Reichskanzler to proceed with the greatest caution, the possibility must be created of calling him to account, preferably before a committee of parliament, using the otherwise hardly practicable procedure of 'impeachment'. This would lead to his being removed and permanently debarred from office if he has approved or condoned any such *publication*. Quite apart from this, anyone guilty of unauthorised publication must be punished.

The approval of *every* such publication by the Reichskanzler should be given only after thorough consultation with experienced politicians. It would therefore be advisable to stipulate that a suitable *consultative* body should be given the opportunity beforehand to express its views on the expediency of *publication* (this being the only point at issue here). If it is not to be a purely parliamentary committee, perhaps some other body is available to which it could be attached.

The *'Foreign Affairs Committee of the Bundesrat'*, which the constitution requires to be composed of delegates from the medium-sized states, has so far been a bad joke in the Reich constitution, a purely decorative institution, without formal powers and without actual influence. Not only does the Reichskanzler not have a statutory *obligation* to give a real account of himself before this committee, this duty is in fact precluded by Article 11. Formally, he may restrict himself to receiving passively the observations of the committee. He is being courteous if he presents it with a formal 'exposé' of the kind customarily presented to the public in parliament. Evidently this is usually how things went, although it would have been perfectly possible to discuss the merits of any proposal in this more intimate circle. During the war the practical significance of the committee appears to have increased slightly, at least for a time; this too is probably no accident. It could quite well be assigned an advisory function before the publication of important *foreign policy* statements by the monarch. Certainly, it would be even better if it could be developed into an *Imperial Crown Council* which could conduct its business, in consultation with the responsible heads of department and elder statesmen, *before* particularly important decisions on imperial policy, preferably in the presence of the monarch. The Prussian Crown Council quite often does this at present (there being no collegial body of the Reich), even on questions which are not internal to Prussia but affect issues of crucial political concern to the Reich (and hence also to the non-Prussian states in the federation). Formally, the committee's activity can only be *advisory*, for there must be no weakening of the constitutional responsibility of the Reichskanzler, nor of the constitutional position of the monarch in representing the Reich externally. Any such thought would, of course, immediately be discredited by any attempt to exploit it (as the bureaucracy is rather inclined to do), in order to exclude or weaken the influence of parliament. But at least the 'responsibility' of the Reichskanzler towards the Bundesrat could be laid down expressly in statute on precisely this point – the duty *to answer for his actions*. The problem would lie, however, in the relation of this advisory body to the special committees of parliament, particularly when and if there were any question of including members of parliament in the committee. We shall return to this point later.

Regardless of whether and how this suggestion is realised, the kind of incidents and conditions we have described must *never again* be tolerated. It must therefore be made clear that the profoundly dishonest, *pseudo-monarchical* legend to which the Conservatives appealed was fabricated by that party on the basis of Bismarck's demagogy. Purely *domestic* party-political interests were concealed behind this legend, just as they are concealed behind the '*fronde*' now, in wartime.[58] The objectives served by this legend, a creation of vested interests, were to keep the official posts, from district superintendent up to minister, in the gift of the Conservative Party; to maintain the official apparatus of the state as an electoral apparatus of the Conservative Party; and to preserve the electoral privileges in Prussia which were necessary to maintain this arrangement (an aim also served by discrediting and weakening the Reichstag, which is, after all, the best parliament Germany has ever had). If today, now that the political results are there for all to see, we demand that the power and scope for action of parliament be increased as a place where the administration is controlled and where, at some time in the future, political leaders are to be selected, we know in advance which hollow phrase will be used by those with vested interests in *uncontrolled* rule by officials: 'The monarchy is in danger.' It would be a poor look-out for the monarchy if these self-interested flatterers alone were to have the ear of the princes permanently, as has been the case until now. It is a matter for the dynasties themselves, and not for us, to deal with attempts to intimidate them with fears of 'democracy'.

V The introduction of parliamentary government and democratisation

Here we shall be concerned not with the problem of social democratisation, but only with the issue of democratic, which is to say equal, *suffrage* in its relation to parliamentarism. Nor shall I be discussing the question of whether it *was* politically advisable for the German Reich, as a state, to yield to fierce pressure from Bismarck

---

[58] The 'fronde' referred to here was the campaign organised from the right in early 1917 to bring down Reichskanzler Bethmann Hollweg.

to introduce this form of suffrage. Here this state of affairs is simply and unreservedly accepted as a given fact which could not be undone without terrible upheavals; the only question posed here concerns the relation between parliamentarisation and democratic suffrage.

It is certainly not necessary for a reciprocal relationship to exist between parliamentary government and democratisation; indeed they are often at odds with one another. In recent times not a few people have even believed that they are necessarily at odds with one another. It is claimed that real parliamentarism is only possible under a two-party system, and this in turn only where the parties are ruled internally by aristocratic notables. Even after the Reform Bill and right into the war, England's venerable parliamentary system, in accordance with its origin in the social estates, was indeed not truly 'democratic', even in its suffrage arrangements, in the sense in which the term is understood on the continent. The domestic census, and the fact that multiple voting rights actually existed, were so important that, were they to be transferred to conditions here, probably only half the present number of Social Democrats and significantly fewer Centre Party deputies would now be sitting in the Reichstag. (Admittedly, the role of the Irish in the English parliament does not apply to our situation.) Until Chamberlain introduced the caucus system both parties were completely ruled by clubs of notables. If the demand for universal, single-vote suffrage (first raised by the Levellers in Cromwell's camp) and even for women's suffrage (limited at first) is now truly going to be realised, the character of the English parliament is certainly bound to change a great deal. The two-party system, already breached by the Irish, will collapse further with the growth of support for the Socialists and the bureaucratisation of the parties. The well-known Spanish two-party system, which rests on the firm convention amongst party notables that elections will be settled in such a way that power will alternate periodically between those seeking office on both sides, seems now to be succumbing to the first moves towards serious elections. But will such changes eliminate parliamentarism? The existence and the formal position of power of parliaments is not threatened by electoral democracy as such. That is shown by France and other states with equal suffrage where the ministries are filled from the parliaments in every case and rest on the parliamentary majorities. Admittedly, the spirit of the French parliament is very different from that of the English parliament. However, France is simply not the best country in which to study the *typical* consequences of democracy for parliamentarism. The markedly petit-bourgeois character of its stable population, and above all the numbers of people with a small unearned income, creates the conditions for a specific kind of rule by party notables and a particular kind of influence from high finance which could not exist under the conditions of a predominantly industrial state. Admittedly, the French party structure is just as unthinkable in this kind of industrialised state as is England's historical two-party system.

In industrial states a two-party system is impossible simply because of the division of the modern economic strata into bourgeoisie and proletariat, and because of the significance of socialism as a gospel for the masses. That creates what one might call a barrier of 'creed', particularly here in Germany. Further, the fact that Catholicism has become organised as a minority protest party, as a result of the relations between the religious confessions in Germany, is hardly likely to be eliminated, even if the Centre Party owes its current number of deputies entirely to present constituency boundaries. At least four, indeed probably five major parties will exist permanently alongside one another, coalition governments will remain a necessity, and the power of the crown, if it operates astutely, will always remain significant.

The rule of notables in the parties is untenable everywhere, except in isolated agrarian areas with large patriarchal estates, for the reason that, thanks to modern mass propaganda, electoral success depends on a rationalised party organisation – on party officials, party discipline, the party exchequer, the party press and party advertising. The parties are becoming ever more tightly organised. They are making efforts to persuade even young people to commit themselves to their following. The apparatus of the church automatically takes care of this for the Centre Party; in the case of the Conservatives it is done by the social milieu. Other parties have their special youth organisations, the 'Young National Liberals', for example, and the youth events organised by the Social Democrats. Equally, the parties harness all economic interests to their service. They organise cooperatives, consumer organisations, trades unions, and push their representatives as officials into the party posts created thereby. They create their own schools of public speaking and other institutions for the training of agitators, editors and clerks, sometimes with funds running into millions. An entire party literature comes into being, fed from the same capital sources (donated by vested interests) which buy up newspapers, found advertising agencies and other such things. The budgets of the parties grow, for the costs of elections rise, as does the number of paid employees needed to carry out electioneering. A large, fiercely contested constituency is not to be won without spending at least 20,000 marks. (At present the war profits of vested interests are being invested to a very large extent in all kinds of so-called 'patriotic' party newspapers and in preparations for the first elections after the war.) The party apparatus is growing in importance and the significance of notables is declining correspondingly.

The situation is still in flux. If we take a cross-section through the apparatuses of the bourgeois (*bürgerlich*) parties, which are more or less tightly organised at present, something like the following picture emerges. The active local organisation is usually run by notables on an honorary basis, officials being employed only in large cities. In medium-sized towns the party offices are those of lawyers or the editorial offices of newspapers. Secretaries with fixed salaries who travel about the country are only found in larger electoral districts. The nomination of candidates and the formulation of electoral slogans is done by local and regional organisations cooperating with one another in a great variety of ways. The role played by the regional organisation is determined particularly by the demands of electoral pacts and agreements about second ballots. The local leaders surround themselves with the permanent members of the local party organisations, whom they recruit to varying degrees of intensity. Public meetings are the main means of recruitment. The active involvement of members is slight. Often they do no more than pay their dues, take the party paper, attend with, at best, tolerable regularity the meetings addressed by party speakers, and do a moderate share of whatever jobs need to be done at election time. In return they participate, at least formally, in resolutions on the election of the local committee and spokesmen (*Vertrauensmänner*), and directly or indirectly, depending on the size of the place, on the election of delegates to party conferences. All persons to be elected are, however, usually designated by that core of permanent leaders and officials, and are usually drawn from that group, augmented by some useful or deserving notables with a well-known name or personal influence in society or some special readiness to make material sacrifices. The activity of that second class of party members is thus restricted to attendance and voting at these elections (held at fairly long intervals) and to debates leading to resolutions, the outcome of which is always largely prepared in advance by the leaders. A complete change of personnel, of local leaders and officials, is rare and almost always the result of an internal revolt which usually has personal motives. The ordinary voter, courted by the parties but not a member of their organisation, has no active role at all, and notice is only taken of his person during elections or in public advertisements formulated for his benefit at other times. The organisation of the Social Democratic Party has often been described; its forms are democratic but it is centralised and more tightly organised, embracing a much larger proportion of the electors who might possibly vote for it. The organisation of parties on the right was looser, tied more to local circles of notables, although it now receives support from a very disciplined mass organisation in the shape of the Farmers' Union (*Bund der Landwirte*). Formally, centralism and authoritarian leadership are most fully developed in the Centre Party, although the power of the clergy has its limits in all matters other than church politics, as has become evident in a number of instances.

The stage of development reached so far has at any rate caused the old state of affairs to disappear for good, whereby elections took place on the basis of ideas or slogans which were formulated in advance by ideologues and propagated and discussed in the press and free assemblies; the candidates were proposed by ad hoc committees; those elected then grouped themselves together in parties; these parliamentary groupings with fluid membership were now the leaders of the like-minded voters scattered throughout the country, and in particular they formulated the slogans for the next election. Although the speed at which it is happening varies, the party *official* is coming to the fore everywhere as the driving force behind party tactics, and, along with him, fund-raising. Apart from regular taxes, which, relatively speaking, are of most importance in class-based mass organisations like the Social Democratic Party, of course, financial worries repeatedly lead to the renewed involvement of that group of wealthy party patrons who once were all-powerful. Such patronage has never been completely absent even from the Social Democratic Party. In the Centre Party at present it is possible for an individual Maecenas, such as Herr A. Thyssen, to lay claim to a social role equivalent at least to that of an archbishop. Patronage is moderately important as a source of finance in the parties of the bourgeois left, but of considerably greater importance on the right. By the nature of things, its role is greatest, however, among parties of the bourgeois centre such as the National Liberals and the old Free Conservatives. The currently modest strength of these middle-of-the-road parties is therefore one of the best approximate guides to the intrinsic importance of money as such, which is to say money donated by individual interested parties, in circumstances where elections are based on equal suffrage. In the case of these parties, too, there is no question that the money, which is of course particularly indispensable to them, is the only thing determining the numbers of votes they receive. Rather, these parties live from a peculiar mixed marriage between financial powers and that broad section of littérateurs, particularly teachers both within and outside the universities, who are emotionally attached to memories of the Bismarck era. Because they subscribe to newspapers, a disproportionate (in relation to the numbers of voters) section of the bourgeois press directs its activities at them, and the attitude of these newspapers is imitated, in watered-down form, by the wholly unprincipled advertising press because this line is acceptable to official and business circles.

Although the inner structure of the German parties varies in accordance with these factors, bureaucratisation and the rational management of finances are concomitants of democratisation here as they are everywhere else. As a result, far more continuous and sustained work is now put into canvassing votes than ever happened in the old parties run by notables. The number of electioneering speeches a candidate must make today, preferably in each small town in his constituency, the number of visits and reports he has to make, the demand for party correspondence and clichés for the party press and for advertisements of every kind is increasing constantly. The weapons, too, are becoming ever sharper and more unsparing. This has been much regretted and it has been blamed on the parties, as if it were something peculiar to them. Yet it is not only the party apparatuses, but also and equally the government apparatus holding power in its hands which participates in this intense struggle. The Bismarckian press, financed by the so-called 'Guelph Fund',[59]

---

[59] From 1868–9 Bismarck used the appropriated fortune of the Hanoverian royal family to influence and manipulate various newspapers. This was known as the 'Guelph Fund'.

undoubtedly took the lead, particularly from 1878 onwards, in its tone and the unscrupulousness of its means. Attempts are still being made to create a local press wholly dependent on the ruling official apparatus. The existence and quality of these weapons thus has nothing to do with the degree of *parliamentarisation*. Nor have they anything to do with the gradation of suffrage.[F] Rather, they are purely a consequence of *mass* elections as such, regardless of whether the elected bodies are the place where politically responsible leaders are selected or whether they are only able to engage in the negative politics of interest groups and 'gratuities', as happens here in Germany. In the latter case party conflict tends to assume particularly subaltern forms, precisely because the interests underlying it are purely material and personal. One can and should use severe penal sanctions to prevent political fighting from being turned into an attack on the personal honour and particularly the private life of an opponent, and to combat the irresponsible spread of sensational, false allegations. But so long as elected bodies exist which take decisions affecting material interests, it is not possible to change the manner and character of struggle as such. This certainly cannot be achieved by reducing the importance and quality of parliament. One simply has to accept unreservedly that this is how things are. Turning up one's nose in moralising or aesthetic distaste is an utterly sterile approach to the question of the future shape of domestic politics. The political question is simply this: what consequences does this progressive democratisation of the means of political struggle and its organisational forms have for the way the business of politics is conducted, both within parliament and outside it? For the developments just described go hand in hand with the shape of parliamentary work discussed earlier.

Yet both things cry out for a characteristic figure, the *professional politician*, which is to say a man who, at least ideally and in most cases materially, makes the business of politics within a party into the content of his existence. Whether one loves or hates this figure,

---

[F] Towards the end of 1917, the *Frankfurter Zeitung* and a Reichstag deputy were accused in those sections of the press which are in the pay of heavy industry of having been bribed with English money. Equally, my name and that of a (National Liberal) colleague were linked with bribes from Lloyd George. Such claims *were believed in the circles of littérateurs*. This fact alone suffices for a verdict on the political 'maturity' of this stratum. The activities of these sycophants, however, shows that *without* parliamentarism and *without* democracy the existence and nature of demagogy here in Germany is entirely comparable with the state of things in France.

he is, in his present shape, the inevitable product of the rationalisation and specialisation of party political work in the context of mass elections. Here again, this is the case *regardless* of the degree of political influence and responsibility placed in the hands of the parties by the process of parliamentarisation.

There are two kinds of professional politician. There are those who live materially *'from'* the party and the business of politics – the large and small political 'entrepreneurs' or bosses in America, and, under the conditions prevailing here, the political 'workers', the paid party *officials*. Or there are those whose financial circumstances put them in a position to live *'for'* politics and whose beliefs impel them to do so, people who thus find the ideal content of their lives in politics, people like Paul Singer in the Social Democratic party, a man who was simultaneously a wealthy party patron in the grand manner. Let me make it clear that I have no intention here of denying that there is 'idealism' among party officials. On the left at any rate, the party officials in particular have supplied us with numerous impeccable political characters, and it would be hard to find their equals in other sections of society. Thus, although idealism is *far* from being a function of a person's financial situation, living 'for' politics is certainly cheaper for the friend of the party who is also well-off. Precisely this group of people who are equally independent of those above and those below them represent a highly desirable element in party life, and I hope it will not disappear completely, especially from the radical parties, in the future. Admittedly, the actual running of the party's business can no longer be carried out by this element alone, and the bulk of work outside parliament will always fall to the party officials. Simply because of the demands made on them by day-to-day party business, however, these officials are by no means always the obvious candidates for parliament itself. Only in the Social Democratic Party does this apply to any great extent, whereas in most bourgeois parties the party secretary who is tied to his office is by no means always the most suitable candidate. It would be an unwelcome development if the party bureaucracy *alone* were predominant within parliament, but it is useful, and urgently desirable, to have this element represented there. They are not predominant, however, even within the most strongly bureaucratised party, the Social Democrats. Besides, the danger that real, natural leaders might be ousted by the rule of the 'official mentality' is most unlikely to be posed by party officials as a group. A greater source of this danger is the need to take account of modern pressure groups when canvassing votes. The danger lies in the fact that employees of these organisations can be infiltrated into the parties' lists of candidates; in other words, this is a danger which would grow considerably if proportional voting were introduced in the form of voting for general lists. A parliament composed entirely of such paid officials would be politically sterile. Nevertheless, the employees of organisations such as the parties themselves or the trades unions, have a fundamentally different outlook from that of a state clerk sitting peacefully in his office, for their minds have been trained in the *struggle* with the public. Among the radical parties, and particularly the Social Democrats, the danger would therefore be relatively slight, because the ferocity of the struggle militates against any tendency for them to ossify into a stratum of party prebendaries, although this is not unusual even amongst them (although there, too, only a small proportion of the actual leaders were party *officials*).

The nature of the demands made nowadays on the conduct of politics means that *one* profession is particularly important in the recruitment of members of parliament in all democratised parliaments and parties, namely the profession of *advocate*. Apart from knowledge of the law as such, and in addition to the even more important training in *fighting* which the profession of advocacy entails (in contrast to the official posts occupied by salaried lawyers), one purely material factor is crucially important, namely the fact that the advocate has his own *office premises*, something which today's professional politician absolutely must have. Whereas the work entailed in running a business means that every other kind of free entrepreneur is specifically 'not available' to meet the rising demands of regular political work – indeed he would have to give up his profession in order to become a professional politician – the advocate finds it relatively easy to switch between his legal work and professional political activity, both technically and with regard to the inner requirements. It is simply to play into the hands of the much (and generally quite unjustly) criticised 'rule by advocates' in parliamentary democracies for members of parliament to be faced with the poor working accommodation, means of information and office staff which are still to be found in German parliaments today. Yet this is not the place to discuss these technical aspects of the working of parliament. What interests us, rather, is the direction in which the *leadership* of the parties is developing under the pressures of democratisation and the growing importance of professional politicians, party officials and the officials of pressure groups, and the effect all this has on parliamentary life.

The popular view amongst our littérateurs has a ready answer to the question of the effects of 'democratisation'; in their view, the *demagogue* rises to the top of the heap, and the successful demagogue is the one who is the most unscrupulous in his choice of the means to woo the masses. It would simply be pointless self-deception to idealise the realities of life. What people say about the growing importance of demagogues in the bad sense of the word has often been accurate enough, and in the *proper* sense of the word this view is wholly correct. In its bad sense, this view fits democracy about as accurately as the remark once made by a well-known general to a monarch who ruled personally captures the effect of monarchic rule: 'Your majesty will soon find yourself surrounded only by rabble.' Any sober consideration of democratic selection will always involve *comparisons* with other human organisations and their system of selection. One just needs to look into the personal details of bureaucratic organisations, including even the best officer corps, to recognise that it is the *exception* rather than the rule for subordinates to acknowledge inwardly that their superior officer deserves his position (especially where he has been promoted rapidly). Even if we disregard all small-minded gossip, the great majority of serious-minded people within the organisation are deeply sceptical of the wisdom of those who make appointments to such positions, the motives guiding their choice and the means by which particularly fortunate appointees come by their posts. Yet this mostly silent criticism goes on out of sight of the public which remains unaware of it. Wherever we look, countless experiences tell us that the qualities guaranteeing promotion are most certainly the degree of a person's *compliance* in relation to the apparatus, and the degree to which a subordinate makes life 'comfortable' for his superior. Generally speaking, born leaders are certainly not selected in this way. In academic appointments the same scepticism is to be found amongst those in the know, although public scrutiny could have an impact here, since the achievements of candidates are in the public domain, something which does not generally apply to the appointment of officials. By contrast, the *politician* who achieves public power, and especially the party leader, is exposed to the glare of criticism from enemies and rivals in the press, and he can be sure that the motives and means underlying his rise will be ruthlessly exposed in the fight against him, Thus one could say from sober observation that by and large selection amongst the party demagogues is certainly not based on any less useful criteria than those employed behind the closed doors of the bureaucracy. To prove the opposite, one must turn to politically young countries like the United States. The assertion would simply not hold true of the Germanic states in Europe. But if a completely unsuitable Chief of General Staff at the beginning of the World War is not to count as an argument against the value of selection by the monarchy, then mistakes by democracies in selecting their leaders cannot count as arguments against their method.

However, I shall not pursue these politically sterile comparisons and recriminations any further here. What is crucially important is the fact that the only persons with the training needed for political leadership are those who have been selected in political *struggle*, because all politics is essentially struggle. On average, this is achieved more effectively by the much reviled 'craft of demagogy' than by sitting in an office surrounded by files, which admittedly is far superior as a training for objective *administration*, although there have certainly been striking examples of mismatch. It does happen that men with mere technical skill as speakers but lacking intellect and political character attain great political power. Yet even August Bebel,[60] for example, cannot be properly characterised in these terms. He was certainly no great intellect, but he did have character. He won the unqualified trust of the masses because of his period of martyrdom and because, coincidentally, he was one of the first, but also because of quality of character – and this could not be challenged by comrades in the party who were of far greater intellectual weight. Eugen Richter, Lieber, Erzberger were all men of similar quality. They were successful 'demagogues' – in contrast to much stronger intellects and temperaments who, despite the greatest success with the masses as orators, did not win *party* power. That is *no* coincidence; rather it is the result, not of democratisation, but of the enforced restriction to

---

[60] A. Bebel (1840–1913), one of the founders and leader of the Social Democratic Workers' Party.

'negative politics'. Democratisation and demagogy belong together. However – I repeat – this is the case, *quite irrespective* of the type of constitution a state has, provided only that the masses can no longer be treated purely as passive objects of administration but are in some way active in throwing the weight of their own opinion into the balance. In their own way, modern monarchies, too, have gone down the road of demagogy. They employ speeches, telegrams, all kinds of emotive devices in order to enhance their prestige, and it cannot be claimed that this kind of political propaganda has proved to be any less of a danger to *national* politics than the most passionate electioneering demagogy imaginable. Quite the opposite, in fact. During the war we have even witnessed demagogy from an admiral, a new phenomenon here. The satrap conflicts between the previous Reichskanzler and Admiral von Tirpitz were carried into the public arena by Tirpitz's supporters in a campaign of wild agitation (which was tolerated by the admiral himself, as was rightly emphasised in the Reichstag). People with vested interests in domestic politics then joined in, thereby turning a question of diplomacy and military technology, which could only be decided by the most highly informed experts, into an object of unparalleled demagogy amongst the masses who, in *this* case, were in fact incapable of judging the issue. At any rate, it cannot be claimed that 'demagogy' is peculiar to the politically democratic form of state. The distasteful conflicts between satraps and intrigues between candidates for ministries in January 1918 were also conducted in the press and at public gatherings. This demagogy was *not* without influence. In Germany we have *demagogy and the influence of the rabble without democracy*, or rather, *because we lack an orderly democracy*.

The topic to be discussed here, however, is the actual importance of demagogy for the structure of the leading political positions, in other words the question of how democracy and parliamentarism relate to one another as a result of it.

Active democratisation of the masses means that the political leader is no longer declared a candidate because a circle of notables has recognised his proven ability, and then becomes leader because he comes to the fore in parliament, but rather because he uses the means of *mass* demagogy to gain the confidence of the masses and their belief in his person, and thereby gains power. Essentially this means that the selection of the leader has shifted in the direction of *Caesar-*

ism. Indeed every democracy has this tendency. After all, the specifically Caesarist instrument is the plebiscite. This is not the usual
'casting of votes' or 'election', rather it is a confession of 'belief' in
the vocation for leadership of the person who has laid claim to this
acclamation. Either the leader arises by the military route – like the
military dictator, Napoleon I, who then has his position confirmed
by plebiscite. Or he rises via the civil route, as a non-military politician (like Napoleon III) whose claim on the leadership is confirmed
by plebiscite and then accepted by the military. Both routes to the
selection of a leader are as much in tension with the parliamentary
principle as (of course) they are with the legitimism of hereditary
monarchy. Every kind of direct *election by the people* of the bearer of
supreme power, and beyond this every kind of position of political
power which in fact rests on the trust of the masses rather than on
that of parliaments – including the position of power of a war-time
popular hero like Hindenburg – lies on the road towards these 'pure'
forms of Caesarist acclamation. In particular, of course, the position
of power of the president of the United States of America which is
legitimated by (formally) 'democratic' nomination and election; the
president's superiority in relation to parliament rests on this very fact.
The hopes which a Caesarist figure like Bismarck pinned on equal
suffrage, as well as the manner of his anti-parliamentary demagogy,
pointed in the same direction, the only difference being that their
formulation and phraseology were adapted to the de facto legitimist
conditions of his ministerial position. The reaction of monarchic hereditary legitimism to these Caesarist forces was apparent in the
manner of Bismarck's departure from office. Every parliamentary
democracy, too, assiduously seeks for its part to exclude the plebiscitary methods of leadership election because they threaten the power
of parliament. A specific example of this is the constitution currently
in force in France and French electoral law (the renewed abolition
of list-voting on account of the danger from Boulangism). Admittedly,
France paid a price for this, in that the supreme powers lack authority
with the masses, something that is typical of the country and contrasts
so characteristically with the American president's position of power.
On the other hand, in democratised hereditary monarchies the Caesarist – plebiscitary element is always greatly tempered, although it is
not absent. The position of the present English prime minister certainly does not rest de facto on the confidence of parliament and its

parties but on the trust of the masses in the country and the army in the field. Parliament submits to this situation with great inner reluctance. Thus there exists an opposition between the plebiscitary and the parliamentary selection of leaders. But this does not mean that the *existence* of parliament is worthless. For, in relation to the (de facto) Caesarist representative of the masses, the existence of parliament guarantees the following things:(1) the *stability* and (2) *controlled nature* of his position of power;(3) the preservation of civil *legal safeguards* against him; (4) an ordered form of *proving*, through parliamentary work, the political abilities of the politicians who seek the trust of the masses; (5) a peaceful way of *eliminating* the Caesarist dictator when he has *lost* the trust of the masses. But the major decisions in politics, particularly in democracies, are made by *individuals*, and this inevitable circumstance means that mass democracy, ever since Pericles, has always had to pay for its positive successes with major concessions to the Caesarist principle of leadership selection. In the great American municipalities, for example, corruption was only tamed by plebiscitary city dictators to whom the trust of the masses granted the right to assemble their own administrative committees. Wherever mass democratic parties have been faced with major tasks they have been obliged to submit more or less unconditionally to leaders who had the trust of the masses.

The importance attaching to *parliament* in a mass democracy as a result of this very circumstance has already been explained and exemplified in the case of England. As well as sincere 'socialists', however, there are sincere 'democrats' who so hate the machinations of parliament that they proclaim their allegiance to 'socialism without parliament' or to 'democracy without parliament'. Of course, very powerful emotional aversions cannot be 'refuted'. But one has to be clear what they would mean today if taken to their practical conclusions, particularly under the conditions of our monarchic state order. What would a democracy without any kind of parliamentary system mean within a constitution such as this, where officials have authoritarian power? Any merely *passive democratisation* of this kind would be the purest form of *uncontrolled bureaucratic rule*, with which we are very familiar here, and it would call itself a 'monarchic regiment'. Or, if it were linked to the organisation of the economy which these 'socialists' hope to see, it would be the modern rational equivalent of the ancient 'liturgical state'. Interest groups legitimated and (allegedly) controlled by the state bureaucracy would actively carry out the duties of self-government in the syndicates and passively bear the burdens imposed by the state. The officials would then be controlled by these syndicalised vested interests intent on *commerce* and *profit*, not by the monarch (who would be incapable of doing so), nor by the unrepresented citizens of the state.

Let us examine this prospect for the future a little more closely. If it were put into practice for the entire foreseeable future, even with extensive 'nationalisation', it would not mean the elimination of the private entrepreneur. Rather, it would mean an organisation of large and small capitalists, small producers without property and wage labourers, with the opportunity for each category to *pursue gain*, this being regulated in some way and – most importantly of all! – monopolistically *guaranteed*. That would be 'socialism' roughly in the sense that the state in the 'New Kingdom' of Ancient Egypt was socialist. It would only be 'democracy' if care were taken to ensure that the will of the *masses* was decisive for the way this syndicalised economy was managed. It is not evident how this could be achieved without a representative body to safeguard the power of the masses and continuously control the syndicates – in other words without a democratic parliament which would intervene in this administration both on matters of substance and of personnel. *Without* a body representing the people, of the kind that exists today, one would expect the future policies of a syndicalised economy to develop in the direction of *assured nourishment*, in other words towards a static economy and the elimination of the interest in economic rationalisation. Wherever people with little or no capital have once become organised in monopolies, their interest in *guaranteeing* their nourishment for the future has been paramount. Anyone who feels so inclined may regard this as a 'democratic' or 'socialist' ideal for the future. But it takes the shallow amateurism of our littérateurs persistently to confuse this kind of cartelisation of the interests in profits and wages with the ideal which is advocated so often these days, namely that the production of goods should be directed in future to the satisfaction of *needs* rather than the interest in *profit*. The way to realise this latter ideal would quite clearly not be to start from the syndicalisation and monopolisation of the interests in *production*, but the complete opposite, namely to begin by organising the interests of *consumers*. The organisation of the future should then not be based on the model of state-organised, obligatory cartels, compulsory guilds and compulsory unions, but would have to be a kind of vast, state-organised, obligatory *consumers' cooperative*. This would in turn have to manage production in accordance with demand, just as individual consumer associations are already trying to do (by producing for themselves). How 'democratic' interests – those of the mass of the consumers – are to be safeguarded under such circumstances other than through a parliament with decisive and continuous control over the production of goods is again not apparent.

But enough of these speculations about the future. The complete elimination of parliaments has never actually been a serious demand of any democrat, no matter how hostile he might be towards them in their present form. Everyone probably wants to see them continue to exist as an authority which can compel *openness of administration*, the fixing of the *budget* and finally the discussion and passing of *legislation*, functions for which they are indeed irreplaceable in any democracy. The opponents of parliaments who are sincere democrats and not, as is generally the case, dishonestly covering up *bureaucratic* power interests, essentially want to see two things:(1) that the decisive role in creating laws should be played not by decisions of parliament but by compulsory referenda; and (2) that the parliamentary *system* should not continue to exist, which is to say that parliaments should not be the places where leading politicians are selected, and that the confidence (or lack of it) of parliaments should not decide whether or not such leading politicians remain in office. As is well known, this is the law as it stands in American democracy, where it follows partly from the popular election of the head of state and other officials, and partly from the so-called principle of the 'separation of powers'. The lessons to be learnt from American democracy, however, are clear enough, namely that, compared with the parliamentary system, their method of eliminating parliamentarism also fails to offer even the slightest guarantee that administration will be more objective and less corrupt; in fact the very opposite is the case. It is true that the election of the head of state by the people has generally proved to be no bad thing. At any rate, in the last few decades the number of truly unsuitable presidents has at least not been greater than the number of unsuitable monarchs in hereditary monarchies. On the other hand, Americans themselves are only satisfied to a very limited extent with the principle of the popular election of officials. If the principle is generalised, it not only eliminates the distinctive technical feature of the bureaucratic machinery, namely the discipline of office, but it also fails to guarantee the quality of the officials, particularly when applied on a mass scale in a large modern state. In contrast to the parliamentary system, it places the selection of candidates for office in the hands of invisible cliques who, compared with a parliamentary party and its leader, are, to a great extent, not responsible to the public; these cliques then present the candidates to voters who lack expert training; this is a most unsuitable method of appointing administrative officials who need to have expert, technical qualifications. It is well known that the officials with specialist training who are *nominated* by the head of state are incomparably better, both technically and with regard to their incorruptibility, particularly for the most modern requirements of administration, but also for the office of judge. The selection of *specialist* officials and the selection of *political leaders* are simply *two* quite different things. On the other hand, mistrust of the impotent *and, for that very reason*, corrupt parliaments in individual states in America has led to the extension of direct *legislation* by the people.

Both as an electoral and a legislative instrument, the *popular referendum* has inner limits which follow from its technical peculiarity. The only answers it gives are 'Yes' or 'No'. In none of the mass states has it been assigned the most important function of parliament, namely the determination of the budget. In a large mass state it would also be a most worrying obstacle to the creation of any laws which rested on a compromise between conflicting interests. The most conflicting reasons can give rise to a 'no' if there is no means of settling conflicts of interest through a process of negotiation. The referendum knows nothing of compromise, and yet it is inevitable that the majority of laws must be based on compromise in a mass state with an internal structure characterised by powerful regional, social, religious and other oppositions. It is not clear how any taxation laws could be accepted by referendum in a mass state with powerful class antagonisms, other than perhaps progressive confiscations of income and wealth and 'nationalisations'. Now this particular consequence might perhaps not seem a frightening prospect to a socialist. Yet there is no known case of a state apparatus, under pressure from a referendum, *effectively* implementing such taxes on wealth which are nominally very high, in part even confiscatory – not in America and not even under the very favourable conditions of the Swiss cantons where, thanks to ancient tradition, the population is politically educated and thinks in terms of the objective issues. Plebiscitary principles also weaken the role of the party leaders and the responsibility of officials, A disavowal of the leading officials by a referendum rejecting their proposals does *not* result in their resignation, as a vote of no confidence does in parliamentary states, nor can it have this result. This is because it is not apparent from a negative vote what the reasons for it were, and because there is no obligation on the masses who have voted negatively to replace the disavowed officials with their own responsible leaders, in the way that the vote of a majority in parliament against the government does.

The more the management of the economy by officials of the state were to grow, the more one would notice the fatal lack of an independent organ of control which would demand, as parliaments do, that the all-powerful officials give a public account of themselves, and one with the power to call them to account. In a mass state the specific instrument of purely plebiscitary democracy, namely direct popular elections and referenda, and above all the referendum on removal from office, are completely unsuited to the task of selecting *specialist* officials or of criticising their performance. Although the money of vested interests plays no small part in the parties' conduct of parliamentary elections, the power of money and the leverage of the demagogic apparatuses supported by it would assume colossal dimensions in any mass state ruled exclusively by popular elections and popular referenda.

Obligatory popular elections and referenda are, it is true, the diametrical opposite of the often regretted fact that the only political contribution made by the citizen in a parliamentary state consists in placing a voting slip (pre-printed and provided for him by the party organisations) into a ballot box every few years. The question has been asked whether this is a means of political education. Undoubtedly, it can *only* be educative under the conditions of open administration and control of the administration discussed above, since these things accustom the citizens to keeping a watchful eye on the way their affairs are administered. But the obligatory referendum can summon the citizen to the ballot box dozens of times in just a few months to decide on laws. The obligatory popular election requires him to vote on long lists of candidates for office who are completely unknown to him personally, and about whose *expert* quali-fication he can make no judgement. Now the lack of expert qualifica-tion is not in itself an argument against the democratic selection of officials (the monarch, too, has no such qualification). One certainly does not have to be a cobbler oneself in order to know whether a shoe made by the cobbler pinches. Yet the danger is too great that the popular election of officials will suffer, not only from a waning of interest, but also because the voter is deluded as to the true identity of the person guilty of maladministration. In the parliamentary system, by contrast, the voter directs his criticism at the leaders of the *party* responsible for appointing the officials. When it comes to creating any kind of technically complicated laws, the referendum is too prone to leaving the result in the hands of astute but hidden vested interests. In this respect conditions in European countries with a fully developed expert body of officials are fundamentally different from those in America, where the referendum is regarded as the only corrective to the corruption of the inevitably subaltern legislatures there.

All of this, however, is no argument against the use of the referen-dum as the *ultima ratio* in appropriate cases, despite the fact that conditions in mass states differ from those in Switzerland. But it does not make powerful parliaments superfluous in large states. Even in electoral democracies parliament is indispensable as an organ for controlling officialdom and ensuring public scrutiny of the adminis-tration, as a means of excluding unsuitable leading officials, as a place where the budget is determined, and as a means of achieving compromises between the parties. Most of all, it is indispensable in hereditary monarchies, since the hereditary monarch can neither work with purely elected officials nor, if he nominates the officials, can he himself take sides without compromising his specific function in domestic politics, which is to facilitate a conflict-free solution when the political mood or distribution of power is ambiguous. Apart from 'Caesarist' leaders, however, the power of parliament is indispensable in hereditary monarchies simply because of the fact that there can be long periods in which widely accepted, trusted representatives of the masses are *absent*. The problem of *succession* has always been the Achilles heel of all purely Caesarist rule. A Caesarist leader can rise, be excluded and fall without the danger of a domestic catastrophe occurring, provided rule is effectively shared by powerful representative bodies which can preserve political continuity and ensure that the constitutional guarantees of civil order remain uninterruptedly in force.

In reality, the point which ultimately offends the democrats who are hostile to parliament is plain enough: it is the largely *voluntary* character of the conduct of politics by parties and thereby also of the power of the parties in parliament. As we have seen, this system is indeed divided between 'active' and 'passive' participants in political life. The business of politics is carried out by *interested parties*. (By 'interested parties' I do *not* mean those vested material interests which influence politics in varying degrees, whatever form the state takes, but rather those people with political interests who strive for political power and responsibility in order to realise particular political ideas.) Yet precisely this conduct of politics by interested parties is the heart of the matter. For it is not the politically passive 'mass' which gives birth to the leader; rather the political leader recruits his following and wins over the mass by 'demagogy'. That is the case in even the most democratic form of state, which is why the very opposite question arises, namely: do parties in a fully developed, mass democracy allow natural leaders to rise to power? Are parties at all capable of accepting new ideas? After all, they succumb to bureaucratisation in much the same way as the state apparatus. Today the creation of completely new parties with all the necessary apparatus of organisation and press undertakings demands such an expenditure of effort and money, and is rendered so difficult by the established power of the existing press, that it cannot be contemplated in practice.[G] Yet the existing parties are stereotyped. Their official posts 'feed' their proprietors. To a great extent, their store of ideas is already largely fixed in propaganda writings and in the party press. The material interests of the publishers and authors concerned put obstacles in the path of any devaluation of these writings by new thinking. Above all, the professional politician who has to live from the party does not want to see his 'ideal' property of thoughts and slogans – his intellectual tools – devalued. This is why new ideas are only absorbed relatively quickly by parties in circumstances where completely unprincipled parties based purely on the patronage of office, like those in

---

[G] Only the plutocracy of war profits has succeeded in doing so under the very special conditions of war.

America, will fit new 'planks' into their 'platform' for every new election if they believe that these will attract more votes. The rise of new leaders seems even more difficult. One sees at the head of our parties the same leaders who have been there for a long time, mostly very respectable people but not outstanding either in intellect or in the strength of their political temperament. We have already mentioned the *ressentiment* of the 'guild' towards new men; this is simply in the nature of things. Here again the situation is partly different in parties like the American ones. The holders of power *within* the parties, the 'bosses' remain virtually stable. They seek power, not honour or responsibility, and it is precisely to preserve their own position of power that they do not expose themselves to the reverses of standing as candidates, since this would lead to public discussion of their political practices, so that they personally could compromise the chances of the party. Not infrequently, therefore, they present 'new men' as candidates, even if they are sometimes reluctant to do so. They do so gladly when these men are 'reliable' in their sense of the word; they will do so reluctantly, but out of necessity, when their 'newness' in some way, by some specific act of notoriety, is so attractive to the public that their nomination seems essential to achieve electoral victory.

This situation, created by the conditions of the referendum, cannot be transferred to Germany, nor would we consider it desirable. Equally untransferable are the conditions in Italy and France where, as a consequence of their party structures, a fairly limited number of political individuals (augmented from time to time by newcomers) who are considered worthy of ministerial posts do the rounds through the leading positions in ever-changing combination. The situation in England is very different again. There it is evident that sufficient numbers of natural leaders and men with the temperament for politics emerge and rise from within a parliamentary career (which cannot be described in any detail here), and also from within the parties, which are strictly organised thanks to the caucus system. On the one hand, a parliamentary career opens up rich opportunities to satisfy political ambition and the will to power and responsibility, while on the other hand the parties are forced by the 'Caesarist' features of mass democracy to submit to the leadership of men with genuinely political temperaments and gifts as soon as such men show themselves capable of winning the trust of the masses. Again and again one can see that the chance of natural leaders reaching the top is in fact a function of the chances their party has of gaining *power*. At any rate, neither the Caesarist character and mass demagogy, nor the bureaucratisation and stereotyping of the parties are in themselves a rigid barrier to the rise of leaders. Tightly organised parties in particular, if they really want to attain power in the state, must *subordinate* themselves to the trusted representatives of the masses *if* these men are natural leaders, whereas the loose following of the French parliament is known to be the true home of pure parliamentary intrigue. The firm organisation of the parties and above all the fact that the leader of the masses is compelled to train and prove himself in parliamentary committee work, where participation is governed by firm conventions, provides on the other hand a powerful guarantee that these Caesarist representatives of the masses will submit to the established legal forms of political life, and that they are not selected on a purely emotional basis, simply because of 'demagogic' qualities in the bad sense of the word. Especially under the conditions in which leaders are selected today, a strong parliament and responsible parliamentary parties, in their function as places where mass leaders are selected and have to prove themselves as statesmen, are fundamental requirements of stable politics.

The *danger* which mass democracy presents to national politics consists principally in the possibility that *emotional* elements will become predominant in politics. The 'mass' as such (no matter which social strata it happens to be composed of) 'thinks only as far as the day after tomorrow'. As we know from experience, the mass is always exposed to momentary, purely emotional and irrational influences. (This, incidentally, is something it shares with a modern monarchy practising 'personal government', which exhibits exactly the same features.) When responsible decisions are being taken, a cool and clear head – and it is a fact that successful politics, particularly successful democratic politics, are conducted with the head – is all the more in command, (1) the smaller the number of those who participate in the deliberations, and (2) the more unambiguously responsibilities are understood by each of the participants and by those whom they lead. The superiority of the American Senate over the House of Representatives, for example, is very much a function of its smaller membership; the finest political achievements of the English parliament are the products of unambiguous responsibility. Where this breaks down, party rule fails to perform adequately, as indeed does any other form of rule. The national–political efficacy of the arrangement whereby parties are run by *firmly* organised political interest groups rests on the same foundations. By contrast, as far as national politics are concerned, the *un*organised mass, the democracy of the street, is wholly irrational. It is at its most powerful in countries with a parliament that is either powerless or politically discredited, and that means above all where *rationally organised parties* are absent. In addition to the absence here of the coffee-house civilisation of Latin countries and our greater evenness of temperament, organisations like the trades unions, but also the Social Democratic Party, create a very important counterbalance to the rule of the street which is so typical of purely plebiscitary nations and so prone to momentary and irrational influences. From the cholera epidemic in Hamburg onwards[61] it has been necessary to turn to these organisations repeatedly whenever the apparatus of the state has proved to be inadequate. *That* must not be forgotten when this period of *emergency* is finally over.

Of course, the difficult years immediately after the war will put all the elements of mass discipline to the test in this country too. The trade unions above all will undoubtedly face difficulties as never before. The rising generation of adolescents who are earning wartime wages up to ten times greater than those in peacetime, and enjoying a period of temporary freedom from constraint such as they will never experience again, is being educated to forget all feelings of solidarity and usefulness and adaptation to orderly economic struggle. A 'syndicalism of immaturity' will flare up when these young people are faced with the realities of normal peacetime order. No doubt we shall have our full measure of this kind of purely emotional 'radicalism'. It is entirely possible that attempts at a syndicalist putsch will take place in the largest centres of population; it is equally likely that the difficult economic situation will result in an initially powerful upsurge of the kind of political mood to be found in the group around Liebknecht.[62] The question is whether the masses *remain* in an attitude of predictable, sterile negation of the state. *That* is a question of *nerves*. Initially everything depends on whether the proud boast that,

[61] The Hamburg cholera epidemic of 1892.

[62] A reference to the 'International Group' of the socialist left opposed to the war. It was formed in January 1916 and led by Karl Liebknecht and Rosa Luxemburg.

'The appeal *to fear* will find no echo in German hearts'[63] *also holds true for those who sit on German thrones*. It also depends on whether such explosions unleash yet again the familiar and usual *fear* of the propertied classes; in other words, it depends on whether the emotional effect of undirected mass fury produces the equally emotional and equally undirected cowardice of the bourgeoisie, as those with an interest in uncontrolled rule by officials hope it will.

Unless it wants to risk the kind of consequences affecting Russia at the moment, every government, even the most democratic and socialist, would be bound to institute summary jurisdiction against putsches, sabotage and other politically sterile outbursts of this kind, which occur in every country, although less frequently here than elsewhere. There is no more to be said on this point. *But* the proud traditions of politically mature nations unaffected by *cowardice* have proved their worth at all times and in all places, in that these people have kept a cool head and their nerve. Admittedly, they have suppressed violence with violence, but then they have sought to dispel the tensions expressed in the outbreak in a purely objective way; above all, they have restored the *guarantees of civil liberty* immediately, and have refused to allow such events to deflect them from their normal way of reaching political decisions. Here in Germany we may certainly expect that those with an interest in the old order and in the uncontrolled rule of officialdom will exploit any outbreak of syndicalist putschism, no matter how insignificant, to put pressure on the (unfortunately still far too weak) 'nerves' of the philistines. One of the most humiliating experiences of the period when Michaelis was in power was the way it *speculated on the cowardice* of the middle classes, which emerged in the attempt to exploit the behaviour of a few dozen pacifist fanatics for party political purposes in a purely sensationalist manner, with no regard to the effects on our enemies or our allies. This kind of speculation will recur after the war on a larger scale. Depending on how it reacts, it will then become clear whether the German nation has reached political maturity. One would be bound to despair of our political future if such attempts were successful. Unfortunately, we know from many experiences that this is undoubtedly possible.

---

[63] Weber is quoting from a speech made by Bismarck to the *Zollparlament* (the Customs Union Parliament) in 1868.

It is a now an irreversible *fact* that party organisation here, both on the left and on the right, has become democratised – for the current, unscrupulous demagogy of the 'Pan-German' and 'Father-land' parties is without parallel, even by French standards. However, the democratisation of suffrage here, and particularly in the hege-monial state of Prussia, is a compelling and urgent political necessity which cannot be postponed. Quite apart from anything else, the fol-lowing considerations are crucial as far national politics are con-cerned: (1) that the only possible *outcome* of conflicts about suffrage nowadays must be equality of voting rights, and that these terribly embittering, sterile conflicts should be eliminated from political life *before* the soldiers return from the war to rebuild the state; (2) that it is politically impossible to give the returning soldiers less advantageous voting rights than people who have maintained or improved their social position, their wealth or their clientele during the war years, while the fighting men shed their blood defending them. Of course, it is certainly 'possible' to obstruct even this political necessity in practice. But we would pay a terrible price for doing so. *Never again* would the nation stand together against any external threat as it did in August 1914. We would be condemned to remain a small, conser-vative, inland nation, perhaps well enough administered in a technical sense, but with no prospect of counting for anything in world polit-ics – and, what is more, without any *inner claim* to do so.

VI Federalism and the introduction of parliamentary government

The suggestion has been made on an earlier occasion[64] that, for the good of the Reich, the question of suffrage in individual states should be regulated in such a way as to entitle *everyone who fought in the war* to the *best* class or type of suffrage in all federal states where different classes of suffrage exist. Formally, this meant only a temporary change in the constitution of the Reich and thus left the federalist principle intact. The proposal could be formulated in such a way that any appeal to the Prussian Diet would be unnecessary. Resistance to this solution was to be expected.

---

[64] A reference to Weber's article 'Ein Wahlrechtsnotgesetz des Reichs. Das Recht der heimkehrenden Krieger' ('An emergency suffrage law for the Reich. The right of the returning soldiers'), published in the *Frankfurter Zeitung* on 28 March 1917.

However, I was astonished to read the assertion in some Berlin newspapers that the *question of the Prussian franchise* was a purely domestic matter for Prussia, and that for any other member of the Reich to concern himself with the question was 'interference' or even the attempt to 'mediatise' Prussia.[65] We shall completely disregard the fact that the German Reichstag, which would have to decide on this law, is one in which the overwhelming majority of members are *Prussian* deputies, although admittedly not deputies of the Prussian plutocracy. To illuminate the worth of such turns of phrase as that just cited, one only needs to be clear about the position of the *Prussian Diet* within the *German Reich*. Admittedly, it is hidden behind a thick veil of constitutional formulae. As we know, the Kaiser and king of Prussia exercises the rights to which he is entitled in the Reich partly as Kaiser under the responsibility of the Reichskanzler, and partly as king of Prussia by instructing the Prussian delegates to the Bundesrat under the responsibility of the Prussian ministry. Formally the Reichskanzler is responsible only to the Reichstag, while the Prussian ministers are formally responsible only to the Prussian Diet. So far everything seems to be in order and in harmony with the legal position of other states in the Federation. As Prussia has at its disposal not quite half as many votes in the Bundesrat as its size would entitle it to, we appear to be looking at an example of extraordinary self-denial. Only when one looks more closely does it become apparent that the Prussian Diet and certain purely Prussian authorities occupy a special position which is in principle entirely divergent, privileged and exceptional in relation to *all* the other parliaments and authorities of individual states.

As well as having the right to the 'Presidency of the Federation', Prussia enjoys a special position in the Reich, firstly by virtue of the constitutional requirement (Article 5, para. 2, Article 37) that the votes of Prussia alone in the Bundesrat suffice to veto any change of legislation, not only on the army and navy, but also on all tariffs and the consumer taxes under Article 35, and thus also on *trade policy*

---

[65] In the Holy Roman Empire to 'mediatise' a state was to limit its sovereignty by transferring some powers to another, more powerful state, so that its status in the Empire became 'mediate' rather than 'immediate' (*reichsunmittelbar*). This is another instance of Weber's habit of carrying over medieval terminology into the discussion of contemporary problems. In this case, however, the claim of the '*Second* German Empire' to be the successor of the Holy Roman Empire may explain the continued use of the terminology.

and all administrative measures by the Reich relating to it. Prussia has the right to veto them even if *all* the other governments in the Federation *and* the entire Reichstag decide unanimously in favour of the change. As regards finances, this Prussian privilege did *not* exist in the North German Federation; rather it is an innovation of the Versailles Treaty which was first agreed with *Baden*. The Prussian government is formally responsible only to the Prussian Diet for its instructions to the mandates in the Bundesrat which are equipped with these privileged powers. As the well-known taxation motion put forward by the Prussian Conservatives shows, the Prussian Diet has no scruples about making use of these powers.

Furthermore, Prussia has the right to a casting vote. There are sixty-one votes in the Bundesrat. The votes of Alsace – Lorraine, however, are cast on the instructions of the governor, whom the Kaiser and king of Prussia appoints and dismisses as he sees fit. One of the dwarf states (Waldeck) is already administered and represented by Prussia for financial reasons. Thus, all three kingdoms, all six grand duchies, all three Hansa cities and the largest duchy (Brunswick) are together unable to achieve a majority, if Prussia, in addition to the votes of Alsace – Lorraine, has just the remaining votes of the dwarf states on its side. If the Conservative proposal to cover the deficit of the Reich in future by levies on the states of the federation were to be accepted, *all* smaller and medium-sized states would be obliged in practice to follow Waldeck's example in future. In addition to this, the Prussian Minister of Railways has at his disposal instruments of power to make these governments bend to his will. Wherever it is not a matter of purely dynastic questions or strictly particularist interests, in all positive questions of Reich politics, there-fore, Prussia has and always has had a firm majority because the dwarf states are, in a sense, bearers of the Prussian mandate and will become so even more in future for financial reasons. Thus, it is *not* responsible to the *German Reichstag*, but rather to the *Prussian Diet* which, according to the constitution, always determines the attitude of the casting vote held by the presidency of the Bundesrat, and thereby also determines the policy of the Reich.

Nor does the matter end there. As everyone knows, the constitu-tional position is that we do not have a unitary army but an army composed of contingents of troops under the supreme command of the Kaiser. This arrangement has, however, been changed by the military conventions agreed between the king of Prussia and those responsible for supplying the contingents in the smaller states of the Federation who, in most cases, have transferred to him virtually the whole of their military sovereignty. The agreement with Baden, for example, transformed the army of '*Baden*' into the XIV Corps of the Royal *Prussian* Army. A Prussian district commander is to be found in every larger town in Baden, while Karlsruhe is the seat of a Prussian General Command. A Prussian supervisor of military administration, Prussian provisioning offices, Prussian administrations dealing with garrisons, hospitals and other areas of expenditure are in charge of all economic acquisitions, and the tradesmen and businessmen of Baden have had a taste of their power during the war. The sons of Baden are led into war by officers with a Prussian commission proposed by the Prussian military cabinet without any involvement of a Badensian authority, with even the monarch of Baden being excluded. The Prussian Minister for War is also Baden's Minister for War. The situation is similar in the other states of the Federation, excepting only some of the largest ones.

For dispensations made on the basis of these conventions there is, formally, *no* responsibility to parliament *at all*, unless budgetary rights are affected, in which case the Reichskanzler must at least be one of the countersignatories. Otherwise they are signed by the Minister of War and published in the Prussian Army's bulletin of regulations. The Minister of War, however, is neither under the command of the Reichskanzler nor (formally) responsible to the Reichstag, since he is a *Prussian* official. In Prussia, however, there is also no substantive object for which he could be required to answer, nor any means of doing so effectively, since the Reichstag, not the Prussian Diet, is the place where decisions are taken on the military budget.

Even this astonishing state of affairs does not exhaust the privileges of Prussia. The Reichskanzler, who is responsible to the Reichstag, only formally directs the Bundesrat in this capacity. He only has a vote there by virtue of his status as the plenipotentiary of *Prussia* (as must be the case in accordance with Article 15, taken in conjunction with Article 11). As such, however, he is strictly bound in formal terms by the instructions of the Prussian government and consequently *not* responsible to the Reichstag for the way he votes. Rather, responsibility for his vote is borne by the *Prussian* government in relation to the *Prussian* Diet which therefore has the decisive say in every serious political action of the Reich as soon as it decides to exercise its power. Inevitably, the Reichskanzler must simultaneously be the Prussian Minister for Foreign Affairs. It is not inevitable that he should also be the Minister President of Prussia, and indeed this has not always been the case. Yet if he is not, he is politically power-less in the Bundesrat as a mere bearer of the Prussian mandate and *subordinate* to the Prussian ministry. If he *is* Prussian Minister President, however, he must pay heed to the views of his Prussian colleagues even as Reichskanzler, and above all to the attitude of the *Prussian Diet.*

Only in his capacity as a 'minister of the Reich' is the Reichskanzler accountable to the Reichstag for the decisions 'of the Kaiser' as such, and hence for expressions of his will, whether made by virtue of the constitution or particular laws which require his countersignature. As far as Reich legislation is concerned, the Kaiser is in principle only the organ of publication for the Bundesrat and has no right of veto of his own. However, numerous laws prescribe that particular ordinances are to be made 'by the Kaiser with the agreement of the Bundesrat'. In other cases they declare the Kaiser alone to be the decisive authority, under the responsibility of the Reichskanzler. For-eign policy is one of the matters of high policy which the constitution puts in this category. International treaties, declarations of war and the conclusion of peace can only be achieved with the involvement of the will of the Kaiser whose decision is also independent of the Bundesrat (Article 11). The dissolution of the Reichstag is a matter of high domestic policy which, according to the constitution, requires such a decision by the Kaiser (Article 24). Leaving aside the fact that declarations of war, most treaties and dissolutions of the Reichstag require the agreement of the Bundesrat (and hence of Prussia), most decisions on high policy in Germany are almost always subject to the peculiar circumstance that the Reich possesses no institution for advance consultation comparable to the Prussian Crown Council. As the Bundesrat is a piece of voting machinery, how is any weight to be given to the 'advice' of the statesmen from Schwarzburg-Rudolstadt? Since the composition of the Crown Council is a *Prussian* matter, the fact that the Reichskanzler is required to answer to the Reichstag after the event, particularly in the absence of any legal device for making this responsibility effective, cannot change the often crucial influence on the course of politics exerted by this purely Prussian institution. There is no provision for collegial discussion amongst the chiefs of the Reich offices. The offices of the Reich are mutually independent departments, and relations between them take the form of a chronic struggle between the 'departmental' overlords. Future historians will probably find in the archives numerous excellent memoranda from all the offices of the Reich on every question that has arisen during the war (Belgium, Poland), each of them contradicting the others. Only in part are there objective causes for these antagonisms, for what underlies them are personal struggles between the heads of the administration. When things begin to happen politically, however, all such memoranda usually become just so much waste paper; according to public statements, the manner in which policy on Poland was inaugurated in November 1916 was decided by the Army High Command, but the influence of the Prussian Diet and its ministers undoubtedly shared responsibility for the way the policy was then prosecuted.

There is no need to go on adding to this list. I have completely disregarded here the far-reaching, *purely* personal powers of the Kaiser as such, although of course the way in which the composition of the Prussian government takes account of the Prussian Diet has repercussions for all these decisions too. Now if the Prussian Diet is composed on the basis of a different franchise from that of the Reichstag, the government in Berlin is required to open a *double account*; while giving out the slogan of 'unhindered progress for the man of ability' in the Reichstag,[66] it proposes in the Diet that the creation of fee-entailed property should be made easier in order to ennoble war profits. The odium of having to speak with a forked tongue like this, however, undoubtedly falls on the *Crown*. The fateful half-heartedness of many of the steps undertaken by the Reich government largely stems from the same source. Quite apart from this, however, the following things are clear from all we have said: (1) purely *Prussian* authorities intervene constantly, not only in vital concerns of the Reich, but also in those of other states of the federation and their citizens; (2) quite apart from its factual hegemony, the Prussian government, formally responsible to the *Prussian* Diet alone,

---

[66] Reichskanzler Bethmann Hollweg had claimed in the Reichstag on September 1916 that the motto of German life must now be 'freie Bahn für alle Tüchtigen'. Nevertheless he permitted the reintroduction of the bill to create new fee-entailed properties which would benefit only those with already established fortunes.

is so privileged legally that the relation of the Prussian Diet to the Reich is completely *unlike* that of any other Diet to the Reich, and is subject to *no kind* of political compensation, except in cases where individual states in the Federation, Bavaria in particular, have protected themselves against it purely negatively through special 'reserve rights'. As far as the *political* facts are concerned, then, it is entirely apt to describe states which find themselves in such a situation, particularly Baden, as states which have been *mediatised* by Prussia and its organs, particularly by its Diet. In stating this fact openly, I am not putting any kind of 'anti-Prussian' point on things. The author of these lines has not himself given up his Prussian citizenship. The Versailles Treaty and the Military Convention with Prussia were concluded by a Baden statesman whom I admire greatly. I would be glad to say nothing about the deleterious effects which have resulted from the Military Convention in the past. Nobody wants to revoke it because it serves the *objective* purpose of unifying the defence forces of the Reich. Our politics are guided by *objective* considerations, not those of vanity. But if a small clique of those who enjoy Prussian electoral privileges assert that the nature of the Prussian suffrage 'is no concern of ours', the challenge is so impertinent that the answer has to be spelled out very clearly. Nobody wishes to lay a finger on Prussia's hegemony within the Reich, but if we are to put up with this state of affairs any longer, we demand that the voice of Prussia in the Bundesrat, which is crucial in all questions of Reich policy, should be responsible to a parliament of the Prussian *people* and not to some privileged caste, however it might be composed. We refuse absolutely to be the vassals of Prussia's privileged castes.

The arrangements of the Prussian Diet for dealing with *internal* Prussian affairs are of course entirely a question for Prussia, one which has to do with the composition of the *House of Lords* there. However, because the material power of Prussia far exceeds its formal position in the Reich, and because this is itself so privileged, since it is decisive for absolutely all questions of high policy, it is a vital question for the Reich, affecting all of us just as much as anyone voting for the Prussian Diet, how the Prussian upper chamber is composed, since it has in its hands the *right to determine the budget*, and therefore exerts a crucial influence on high policy decisions in Prussia which affect the *direction of the Reich*. If the present situation continues, with one horse in front of the cart and another behind, where a parliament of Prussian *privilege* thwarts the Reichstag and can undertake to overthrow the Reichskanzler, it will inevitably be the *Crown* which has to bear the costs in terms of public opinion. Let that be considered well.

Of course, one must be clear about the fact that the relations between Prussia and the Reich, and the need to strike a balance between them through compromise, represent an enduring problem which will continue to exist even after the hoped-for change in the Prussian franchise, since this will only remove the conflict between their internal structures. So long as Germany retains its present shape, the German Bundesrat can never be constructed like, say, the United States Senate, the members of which are elected representatives of the people in individual states and therefore vote according to their convictions and those of their party. The delegates to the Bundesrat, by contrast, are empowered by their governments who give them instructions which have the binding power of 'imperative mandates'. This would remain the case even if the governments issuing those instructions were completely parliamentarised and effectively controlled by democratic parliaments. Then we would have the problem of the relationship between the parliamentarisation of the individual states (particularly Prussia) and the parliamentarisation of the Reich government. To clarify the problem, it is necessary to fill out the picture drawn above of the relations between Prussia and the Reich, since the formal legal position, as described so far, is not an exhaustive account of the political facts.

If the policies of the Reich are determined by Prussia to a far greater degree than is apparent from the constitution of the Reich, then, equally and conversely, the attitude of the Prussian government is determined by the situation in the Reich. For decades the Conservative Party has been all-powerful in Prussia because the franchise favours the plutocracy. It was quite out of the question for an administrative official to have different political views from those which the Conservative Party regarded as harmless at least. The mass of all officials absolutely had to be Conservative, otherwise they would have made no progress, even socially. Apart from a few colourless 'token liberals', ministers, too, had to try to put their past behind them as soon as they entered their ministry. What the rhetoric of our littérateurs likes to conceal is the fact that Prussia was dominated by *party rule* as pronounced as any in any parliamentary country in the world.

Whenever the social or material power interests of the circles behind the ruling party were at stake, even the Crown was completely power-less and incapable of insisting on its wishes if these ran counter to those which carried real weight.[H]

The bourgeois plutocrats' fear of the 'democracy' which they believed to be embodied both in the Reich franchise and in the Reichstag supported these party interests in Prussia. Admittedly, there is also a majority against the left in the Reichstag if one counts the larger part of the Centre and the right wing of the National Liberals as belonging to the right. But at least the majority does not actually belong to the Conservative Party, and in practice a majority has been formed on the left on a number of important issues. If, however, the majority in the Prussian Diet had determined unam-biguously the decisions of the presidial vote in the Bundesrat and the Reichskanzler (who is always also a Prussian minister, indeed usually Minister President) in the conduct of the policies of the Reich – and this would not be precluded by the wording of the constitution – the Reich would be governed purely by the Conservative Party. Yet the majority in the Diet cannot do this *because it rests on a plutocratic suffrage.* This circumstance, which weakened the Prussian Diet in relation to the democratically elected Reichstag, gave the latter the upper hand in questions of Reich policy and gave at least limited effectiveness to the 'responsibility' of the Reichskanzler to the Reichstag.

The right of the Reichstag to approve the budget forces the Reichskanzler, not only as a minister of the Reich but also as the holder of the presidial vote in the Bundesrat and representative of the hegemonial state, to answer to the Reichstag for the conduct of Reich policy as it is influenced by Prussia, which means in practice

---

[H] Although it is quite laughable, Miquel's income tax is cited as proof that the Prussian state is not plutocratic in character. Yet it came about merely as a classic expression of the predominance of large landowners *within* this plutocracy. Its introduction was paid for by abandoning a secure and important state tax which fell on landownership, namely the land tax, in the form of the so-called 'transfer'. The introduction of income tax meant a huge relative reduction in taxation for landowners with mortgages and an increased burden on movable property. For the rural vested interests it con-tained no threat at all under circumstances where the assessment of large landowners lay in the hands of authorities who were wholly dependent on them politically and economically. It was Miquel's great skill to have harnessed these agrarian interests to a technically excellent tax. All reforms have failed which did not yield gratuities of this kind for those with vested interests in the ruling party.

having to face up to questioning. The same applies to the Ministers of War, and for the same reason: the military budget is a matter for the Reich. It applies above all to the Prussian Minister of War who actually appears in the Reichstag as an organ of the Reich. Admittedly, the only instrument of power the Reichstag possesses in order to lend weight to its position, is its right to approve the budget. The direct exploitation of this right so as to remove a Reichskanzler or Minister of War in an opposing party has not been customary in Germany (outside Bavaria) since the period of constitutional conflict in Prussia and would provoke 'patriotic' outrage, particularly among the littérateurs. Yet the mere possibility of obstructing the political work of a political leader who was strongly of an opposing party is sufficient to make it impossible for a chancellor or Minister of War to remain in office *in the long run* if he is strongly opposed by a majority in the Reichstag which sticks to its convictions and is not to be removed by the calling of fresh elections. It would however be completely impossible for the Reichstag to cooperate with the Reichskanzler as bearer of the presidial vote [in the Bundesrat – Eds.], if in fact the rule of the Conservative Party in Prussia were applied to the leadership of politics in the Reich with the kind of ruthlessness that is usual within Prussia itself. For the same reason, even if a Prussian Minister President holding the office of Reichskanzler were to identify himself too completely and too openly with the Conservative Party in his Prussian policies, it would be difficult for him to sustain his position. It has always been essential for Prussia to take account of the composition of the Reichstag in its direction of the politics of the Reich and even in the way it conducts Prussian politics.

The politics of the Reich can enjoy a certain degree of independence from Prussia for another reason, namely the fact that the Reich has at its disposal an independent official apparatus. The offices of the Reich are not filled simply by taking over Prussian officials. Admittedly, the peculiar weakness of the Reich bureaucracy rests on the fact that the majority of the central authorities in the Reich, particularly the one with the greatest political importance so far, the Reich Office of the Interior, does not have its own complete staff of officials equipped with powers of compulsion, as does the Ministry of the Interior in any individual state. The Reich bureaucracy found support for its independence from Prussia in the Reichstag. In party terms it consequently felt the effects of the difference between the composition of the Reichstag and that of the Prussian Diet: the patronage of the Centre Party played a not inconsiderable role in its own composition. Yet I do not wish to go into the entire problem of the administrative apparatus of the Reich here, but merely to say something about the way it reaches a decision on laws and general administrative regulations for which the Bundesrat is responsible.

As a rule, bills for the Bundesrat are drafted in the offices of the Reich. The votes of Prussia are then canvassed in negotiations with the Prussian ministries. After achieving an agreement (not always easily), either through compromise or by accommodating the wishes of Prussia, it is usual to hold discussions with Bavaria on the finished draft. As a rule, all other states in the Federation are confronted with the bill in the Bundesrat as a *fait accompli*. In order to win the votes of Prussia more easily, some of the most important secretaries of state in the Reich have regularly held simultaneous appointments as Prussian ministers without portfolio. Where decisions of high policy were so important as to require a vote of the Prussian Ministry of State, this could also have an impact on the *domestic political* situation in Prussia. According to press reports which, as far as I know, have never been contradicted, the order from the royal cabinet promising equal suffrage was accepted by a majority of just one vote, and even this was only achieved because, in addition to the Reichkanzler, two Reich secretaries of state voted for it in their capacity as Prussian ministers, positions which they held as adjuncts of their office. On the other hand, it has been a firmly established rule so far that all secretaries of state are Prussian plenipotentiaries to the Bundesrat. The same also applies to the Prussian Ministers of State, including above all the Minister of War who functions politically as an organ of the Reich, but legally as a Prussian official, and who, if he were not delegated to the Bundesrat, would be quite unable to represent his department in the Reichstag in his own right as an administrative chief. When answering to the Reichstag, the Minister of War naturally only goes as far as is made inescapably necessary by the political situation. In order to ensure that he remains largely free of control, he has at his disposal the concept, undefined in its scope, of the Kaiser's 'power of command'; this is a prerogative which parliament may not violate and behind which everything can be hidden that is to be withheld from parliamentary scrutiny.

The outcome of all this is that the internal politics of Prussia remain free of influence from the Reich, except when considerations of high policy simply make such influence imperative. As part of Prussian hegemonial policy within the Reich, the bureaucratic direction of the Reich, which is influenced by the Reichstag, and the government of Prussia, which is influenced by the Diet, influence one another reciprocally, both in terms of personnel and on substantive issues. Depending on whether the balance is tipped one way or another, either by the agencies controlled by the Reich leadership (which are subject to pressure from the Reichstag), or by the leadership of Prussia (which is subject to pressure from the Prussian Diet), the attitude of the hegemonial state towards Reich policy is determined by organs of the Reich, or, conversely, the Reich is led by 'Greater Prussia'. The inner structure of the Reich and its individual states, however, ensures that the latter tendency – the Great Prussian character of the leadership of the Reich – generally predominates. What are the interests pushing in this direction?

Apart from the Hanseatic cities, the individual states are monarchies with a bureaucracy growing steadily in significance and training. Before the foundation of the Reich, many of them had gone fairly far down the road towards having a parliamentary government and administration, and with entirely satisfactory results. At any rate, in view of conditions at the time, it is quite ridiculous for our littérateurs to claim that the parliamentary system of government is a foreign import in Germany and that it has not yet 'proved its worth' here. The foundation of the Reich changed that. The princely courts and the administrations in the individual states were tempted to regard the Reich above all as an *insurance institute* protecting their own position, to regard their thrones as prebends guaranteed by the Reich and to view their relationship with Prussia as a way of maintaining uncontrolled bureaucratic rule in all the other states. Although Bismarck occasionally held the Reichstag in reserve as a means of bringing pressure on recalcitrant individual governments, he exploited this tendency amongst the courts and administrative officials in the individual states, so as to seem to be their protector. The consequences of this tradition can still be felt today, for what was hidden, and is still hidden, behind the slogan 'protection of federalism' in Germany was and is an insurance policy for the prebends of the dynasties and the bureaucracy which in practice issues in a guarantee that the bureaucracy will remain largely free of control. Which also, and above all, means that the adminstration of the *individual* states remains free of control. Very soon after the foundation of the Reich the bureaucracy of the individual states proceeded to eliminate as far as possible the scrutiny of their work by the parliaments of the individual states, so that they could instead govern 'by virtue of princely prerogative'; convincing evidence of this can easily be found by examining their internal political development since the seventies. Thereby they succeeded in causing the importance and hence the intellectual quality of most parliaments in the individual states to fall, much as happened in the Reichstag. That system of mutual insurance explains, however, the behaviour of the bureaucracy in the individual states in relation to the situation in Prussia, and conversely that of Prussia towards the situation in the individual states. In the individual states a gradual democratisation of suffrage has begun during the last twenty years. At the same time, however, the uncontrolled position of the bureaucracy remained inviolate. It found inner support in the political conditions in Prussia and in Prussia's influence in the Reich. Above all, the bureaucracy of the individual states could only look on the disappearance of the Three-Class Suffrage in Prussia with the most intense disquiet. After all, it seemed good that there was a large conservative truncheon in readiness in Berlin in case any threats to their own freedom from control were to come from the individual state parliaments; thereby they could be assured that nothing serious could befall the power position of the bureaucracy as such. At the same time, the Prussian bureaucracy which supported the Conservative Party and those with vested interests in the Prussian system of electoral privilege were content to let the bureaucracies in the individual states 'play at democracy' a little, provided not only that no one in the Reich was allowed to attempt to violate the incredible internal political structure of Prussia, but provided also that the bureaucracy in the individual states (with the exception of the Bavarian government at most) renounced any effective share of power in the Reich, thereby essentially leaving the Reich to be governed in the interests of Greater Prussia. This arrangement determined the whole way in which the business of the Bundesrat was conducted, and this tacit compromise must always be borne in mind if one wants to understand what 'federalism' has meant here until now and the interests underlying the concept.

As a result of all this, the Bundesrat, the body in which both the princely courts and ministries were represented, has led a comfortable and harmonious 'still life' on the whole.[67] As the minutes are kept secret, it is not possible to criticise the character of its deliberations. Since, according to the constitution, only the imperative instructions counted, the personal positions taken by its members were always bound to be non-decisive and subject to the views of their own government – which is to say, without weight. The Bundesrat was therefore never a place for statesmen to be effective or to become trained (in marked contrast to the Frankfurt Parliament). There have certainly been occasions when governments gave their plenipotentiaries the freedom to vote as they saw fit on an issue. Some did so – as, for example, when there was a dispute about the Lippe succession – simply to be rid of the odium of making their views known on an embarrassing question. On genuinely political issues Prussia kept an iron grip on its supremacy, as guaranteed by the votes of the dwarf states. On other important matters voting was essentially formal (although the possibility of taking a vote was exploited by Bismarck as an *ultima ratio* against the governments), for the situation had been settled in advance through negotiation and compromise with the courts and ministries, particularly those of Bavaria. Bismarck had built domestic politics, as well as foreign politics, around these means of diplomacy and cabinet politics. In principle, this remained the case subsequently, although the method changed, and not always to the delight of the individual states. If the Bundesrat nevertheless occasionally went off on its own track, Bismarck knew how to bring it back to heel. The offer of his resignation (on some formally insignificant pretext) was a means he could rely on: the Bundesrat would then withdraw its resolution. Occasionally he simply passed over resolutions of the Bundesrat in silence and proceeded with the agenda, without anyone from the Bundesrat daring to appeal to the constitution of the Reich. There has been no word of serious conflicts since his day. By the nature of things, any difficulties which existed were expressed less through open conflict than by the fact that there was no movement on certain problems.

One has to be clear about the fact that this 'still life' will come to an end in the future. Just as the meetings of monarchs and the

---

[67] The 'still life' is a deliberate pun (not of Weber's invention) which likens the inactive state of German political life to this type of painting.

means of cabinet politics which Bismarck employed, particularly in Petersburg and Vienna, have diminished in importance, the same will happen in domestic politics. There will be no more of the easy-going ways of the old regime as soon as we are confronted by the questions of financial and economic policy which peace will bring. In future, all the individual state diets, with Prussia in the lead, will increasingly assert their formal right to influence voting in the Bundesrat and to work towards exercising the right to present bills to the Bundesrat. In this way the Prussian Diet could seize the initiative and dominate Reich politics thanks to its economic power over the North German dwarf states, a power which will grow in future. Its restraint up till now has simply been a product of its weakness which resulted in turn from the antagonism between Prussia's Three Class Suffrage and the democratically elected Reichstag. Presumably this will disappear when the Prussian franchise is democratised, and the great weight of Prussia will make itself felt much more keenly. Assuredly, the bureaucracy of all the individual states will feel united in opposition to this, as to every other consequence of parliamentarisation. The united bureaucracy of the Reich, Prussia and the individual states is certainly a power which, with the princely courts behind it, can obstruct the development towards parliamentarisation. But let us be clear about one thing: if this happened it would block the path that could lead to the peaceful development of domestic politics and towards the political education and cooperation of the nation in support of the external power position of the Reich. Anyone who wants to avoid that must begin by asking the question: *how is the parliamentarisation of Germany to be combined with healthy, which is to say, active federalism?*

The principle seems clear: (1) first and foremost, the stream of parliamentarisation must be directed into the channels of the Reich; (2) the legitimate influence of the federal states other than Prussia on the politics of the Reich must be strengthened. How is this to be achieved? Here again we come up against the mechanical barrier of Article 9 (last sentence) of the Reich Constitution which we have discussed above and which formally stands in the way of the first of these postulates, and as a matter of fact generally stands in the way of the second of them, as will become apparent. In practice, this requirement means the following: the plenipotentiaries sent to the Bundesrat by the individual states, including the Reichskanzler and the secretaries of state, can be members of the parliaments of individual states, particularly the Prussian Diet. Further, according to firmly established rule, the Reichskanzler *must*, and the secretaries of state *should*, be Prussian delegates to the Bundesrat, and are thus in any case influenced by the Prussian Diet. Conversely, the governments are forbidden to nominate any member of the Reichstag who retains his mandate as a member of parliament to the positions of Reichskanzler or plenipotentiary to the Bundesrat. The Reichskanzler and the secretaries of state, who belong to the Bundesrat, are thereby excluded from the Reichstag.

The disappearance of this regulation is a precondition, not actually of parliamentarisation as such, but of healthy parliamentarisation in the Reich. One could either suspend the regulation only for the Reichskanzler and the secretaries of state (or at least for the politically most important secretaries of state, above all the Secretaries of the Interior and the Imperial Treasury) – which would actually be the most efficacious method. This would make it possible for party leaders as such to assume the responsible leadership of Reich politics and at the same time – the important thing here – would place the burden of responsibility on their *party* in the Reichstag, since they would retain their position and influence within their parties. Clearly, this is the only way to put an end to the merely 'negative' politics of the parties in the Reichstag. Or, for the sake of the 'parity' of the federal states, the regulation could be revoked entirely, so that not only Prussian plenipotentiaries but also those of other federal states could be drawn from the Reichstag and yet remain members of it. This is the suggestion which has been accepted by the Constitutional Committee of the Reichstag. It has been the target of lively attacks.

Of these attacks, the formal objection raised by the Conservatives does not deserve serious consideration, namely that members of the Reichstag who are also plenipotentiaries to the Bundesrat would experience 'conflicts of conscience', since they vote in the Reichstag out of personal conviction, whereas they have to vote in the Bundesrat in accordance with their instructions. At best this argument could apply to the district superintendents in the Prussian Chamber of Deputies whose duty as officials, according to Puttkamer's edict, is 'to represent the policy of the government'. Yet in their case there is little evidence of such 'conflicts of conscience', and the Conservative Party at any rate has remained unperturbed by this possibility. But above all, Prussian ministers and secretaries of state in the Reich who were also Prussian plenipotentiaries to the Bundesrat have sat in the *Prussian Chamber of Deputies* and can still do so today. As deputies, they have not only the right but also the duty to *criticise*, in the light of their own convictions, *the instructions given to them by their own government* as plenipotentaries to the Bundesrat. The Conservative Party, too, did not regard these 'conflicts of conscience' as tragic. Indeed the only purpose of this naively moralistic phrase is to dupe the philistines. For the truth of the matter is that a politician who receives an instruction as a plenipotentiary to the Bundesrat which his convictions do not allow him to support *must resign his office*. He is commanded to do so by his *honour* and by his *political responsibility*, which differs from that of an official. Otherwise he is a man who '*clings*' to office. Indeed one of the political aims in revoking this regulation would be to din this into the leading officials and above all the Reichskanzler. This is precisely why the bureaucracy abhors its abolition.

Much bigger guns than this have been rolled out, however. In the *Bayerische Staatszeitung* parliamentarisation was attacked as 'centralism', while sections of the Bavarian press and, in its wake, conservative littérateurs quite seriously conjured up the possibility that, 'Bavaria should turn its back on the Reich.' In the first place the threat is foolish, for there is no viable way out of the Customs Union for Bavaria, and it is imprudent to remind the real centralists of this fact which, if things became serious, would *immediately* (in Bavaria itself) allow them to dictate the game.

In terms of the future, too, it is very short-sighted to fight for Article 9, sentence 2. Centralism will be promoted by the continued existence of that regulation more than anything else, and in a much more worrying form than the spread of parliamentarism from the Reich. Let us be clear about the situation. According to the final article of the Reich Constitution, absolutely no changes can be made to the reserve rights and the constitutional singular rights (*Singularrechte*) of the federal states without their own consent. All their other constitutional competences, including the present extent of their internal autonomy, cannot be changed as long as fourteen votes – those are the votes of the three kingdoms or two kingdoms and two grand duchies – unite in opposing the change, which will always be the case if there is any threat to impose change by *force majeure.* They are thus assured of adequate freedom *from* the Reich. What they lack is adequate influence *in* the Reich, on the leadership of Reich politics. Precisely this influence will become important in the future, for without it the Reich can, of course, strangle them through its financial and economic policies, no matter how fully their rights are preserved. This influence in the Reich, however, will quite certainly not be diminished if, thanks to the abolition of the prohibitory regulation of Article 9, sentence 2, the federal states are permitted to nominate influential Reichstag deputies to the position of plenipotentiaries to the Bundesrat! Bavaria's influence in the Reich would certainly not have been reduced if, say, Freiherr von Franckenstein in his time had simultaneously retained his position in the party in the Reichstag and been a Bavarian delegate to the Bundesrat in place of an official. The literary opponents of the clause's abolition conjure up the spectre of Prussia being defeated in the Bundesrat by a majority of the minor states – say by Lippe, Reuß and other such members buying the leaders of large parties in the Reichstag as plenipotentiaries to the Bundesrat – a prospect to which they add (in the same breath) the ridiculous warning that the federal states outside Prussia could be subject to centralist *force majeure.* I shall say a word about this nonsense later. First we must establish what genuine worries are concealed behind these patently empty phrases. Firstly and above all, there is the bureaucracy's fear for its *monopoly of office.* 'If members of parliament are made ministers, ambitious officials would in future seek a career in large-scale industry' – this assertion was made quite openly in the Bavarian Diet. Yet even now Article 9 is not an obstacle to the nomination of members of *individual state* parliaments as plenipotentiaries to the Bundesrat without the loss of their mandate in parliament. Equally, it does not prohibit the attainment of the posts of minister or secretary of state (including membership of the Bundesrat) as the culmination of a parliamentary career. This has happened time and again, both in the past and very recently. It simply meant that the member of parliament concerned then had to leave the Reichstag immediately. Precisely this notion that membership of the Reichstag could be a 'career', a path to the attainment of offices, that the offices would be thrown open to 'able' and 'ambitious' members of parliament, is something which those littérateurs who oppose the removal of this prohibition find highly desirable! They consider that it would be possible to work much 'better' with a Reichstag that offered these opportunities to its members. Everything would indeed be in perfect order, if the solution to the problem of parliamentarism in Germany were simply a matter of *filling parliament with careerists and office-seekers*. The small gratuities of patronage we have at present would then be joined by big ones! But that is at best a bureaucrat's ideal, and not even a gratifying one. This system has already been operated here, and we know both from earlier and more recent experiences that we have made no progress with it. The political aim of parliamentarisation is, after all, to turn parliament into a place where *leaders* are selected. Yet a political leader does not strive for an official position and the pensionable salary accompanying it, nor to exercise the competence of that office without control as far as this is possible. Rather he seeks political power, and that means politically *responsible power*, and he finds support in the trust and following of a *party* in which he must therefore want to remain when he becomes a minister, so that he may retain his influence on the party. This last point is at least as important as anything else. The removal of the mechanical barrier of Article 9, sentence 2 aims, therefore, not only to make legitimate party influence on the business of government possible (in place of the present, equally great, but irresponsible and hence illegitimate influence), but also, conversely and to at least the same degree, to facilitate the legitimate influence of the government on parliament (instead of the present illegitimate influence exerted through petty patronage). The *fight against reform*, however, is entirely conditioned by the desire to reduce the political standing of the Reichstag to a minimum and to serve the interests of the bureaucracy in maintaining its prestige. Seen from this point of view, the barrier between Bundesrat and Reichstag must be preserved, of course, because the stereotyped, arrogant expression, 'The federated governments will never etc.' belongs to that store of 'gestures' with which the rule of officialdom feeds its traditional understanding of its role and importance, and which would become redundant if Reichstag and Bundesrat were no longer separated by a barrier.

Let us look more closely at the spectre of introducing parliamentary principles to the Bundesrat, in order to clarify the various possibilities, and thereby to see the *positive* significance of revoking Article 9, sentence 2. In itself its abolition would simply clear away a mechanical obstacle. It would create *possibilities* for development, nothing more.

It would remain open to the individual governments to make no use of the new permission to delegate to the Bundesrat members of the Reichstag who retained their mandate there. They will not use this opportunity unless they see a political advantage in doing so. It is far from desirable to adopt a schematic, once-and-for-all kind of approach. Even if parliamentarisation were implemented to the maximum extent possible, it would not be at all desirable (nor will it happen) for the leading positions to be filled entirely and exclusively by members of parliament, while officials with qualities of leadership are excluded from them.[1] But, it is said, the abolition of Article 9, sentence 2 will in any case unleash efforts to parliamentarise the Bundesrat, and this, so it is believed, will endanger the federalist structure of the Reich. Let us look at the position. Let us assume that the trend towards parliamentarisation were to prove *entirely* victorious at some point, both in the individual states and in the Reich. Let us further assume (although it is quite unlikely) that the process, including all its theoretical consequences, were carried out in such a way that *only* members of parliament were in fact appointed to the leading posts, including the seats in the Bundesrat. What difference would the abolition or retention of Article 9, sentence 2 make to the way political power is distributed?

If this provision were to remain in force the consequence would be that the Reichskanzler could never simultaneously be a member or leader of a party in the Reichstag, and therefore could never have an assured influence within a party. It would further mean that secretaries of state who wanted to secure this influence for themselves and thus sit in the Reichstag, would have to remain outside the Bundesrat. On the other hand, if parliamentarisation were implemented in the individual states, Prussia would delegate the representatives of the ruling parties in Prussia to the Bundesrat, while the other individual states would delegate those of the ruling parties in their states. The Reichskanzler and any secretaries of state sitting in the Bundesrat would then be Prussian party politicians, while the representatives of the other federal states would be party politicians of the parliaments in the individual states. Thus, the parliamentarisation of the Bundesrat would not be prevented in the slightest by Article 9. Inevitably, it

---

[1] Equally. one can only agree with Deputy Stresemann's wish that the *specialist* ministeries in Prussia should *not* be parliamentarised. But up till now what mattered here was precisely not specialist qualifications but an individual's position in the *party*.

would then be steered onto the path leading to a *particularised* Bundesrat. Yet this particularisation would in no way mean a strengthening of the positive influence of the individual states in the Bundesrat, nor would it protect them against being outvoted, for Prussia's position of economic and financial power would condemn the dwarf states, as before, to being Prussian 'lobby fodder'. Only the power of the *Reichstag* could provide a counterweight to a Prussian controlled majority in the Bundesrat. Now the Reichskanzler, as we have said, could not be a member of the Reichstag. In the case of the secretaries of state, however, who are not required by the constitution to sit in the Bundesrat, there would be no obstacle to their membership of the Reichstag, provided only they remain outside the Bundesrat, as Deputy von Payer initially appears to have thought of doing. If Article 9 continued in force this is presumably what would happen, for the Reichstag politicians appointed to the position of secretary of state would not be able to give up their positions within their parties in the Reichstag for the simple reason that they in turn would need to have their parties behind them as a necessary counterweight to the support of the Reichskanzler in parliament and that of the Bundesrat plenipotentiaries in the parliaments of the individual states, above all in the Prussian Diet. Otherwise the same thing would happen to them as happened to the deputies Schiffer and Spahn.[68] Thus the Reichstag would fill the positions of secretary of state still remaining outside the Bundesrat with their own trusted agents who would then act in solidarity *vis-à-vis* the Bundesrat. This would not diminish the pressure of the Reichstag parties on the government of the Reich; that pressure would simply be channelled into a relationship of *mistrust* because of the exclusion of the secretaries of state from the Bundesrat, and it would preclude any legitimate influence on the Reichstag parties being exerted by the members of the government sitting in the Bundesrat. The secretaries of state who, as members of the Reichstag, would not enter the Bundesrat, would legally be subordinate to the Reichskanzler and only be his 'deputies'; politically, however, they would be the representatives of the Reichstag. As a representative of the Prussian Diet, the Reichskanzler would have to take account of them as independent political forces, for

---

[68] These two deputies lost the support of their parties when they became ministers. An example of the operation of Article 9, sentence 2.

better or worse, consulting them and doing deals with them, because otherwise his government would lose the support of the Reichstag parties concerned. The Reich constitution makes no provision for a collegial 'Reich Ministry', just as the official legal language of England does not contain the concept of the 'cabinet'. But the Reich constitution in no way prohibits the Reichskanzler and the secretaries of state from coming together in practice for collegial consultations. A collegial institution of this kind would assuredly develop in fact out of these relationships and would assume the power of government. In any such arrangement the secretaries of state would represent the Reichstag and the Reichskanzler the Prussian Diet, and both would be dependent on compromises. The Bundesrat, however, would be confronted with this collegial institution as a political power outside itself and would be ruled on the one hand by the Prussian majority and on the other be condemned to insignificance. The federalist influence of the *non*-Prussian states would be *eliminated*.

If the prohibition contained in Article 9, sentence 2 were revoked, however, the parliamentarisation of the Bundesrat would presumably take a different course. More or less without exception, the Reichskanzler would be drawn from the Reichstag, as would some of the secretaries of state, and they would all retain their parliamentary mandates. Formally they would belong to the Bundesrat as Prussian delegates, but politically as representatives of the Reichstag. Other secretaries of state, and occasionally perhaps the Reichskanzler, would be members of the Prussian parliament. The other individual states would send representatives of their parliaments to the Bundesrat, but if they had a number of votes at their disposal they would perhaps also send Reichstag deputies; probably they would be most inclined to send those members of their own parliaments who were also members of the Reichstag. One could be sure that the non-Prussian parliaments would be increasingly zealous in seeing to it that representation in the Bundesrat would at least predominantly be in the hands of their own members.[J]

[J] For this very reason there is absolutely no danger that, if parliamentarisation were to be fully implemented and Article 9, sentence 2 abolished, the spectre of Prussia being outvoted by a majority of delegated party leaders from some minor states could become a reality. Just how mindless this objection is, becomes clear when one considers that the dreaded outcome, the establishment of the political parties in the Bundesrat, is already *just as possible* today. Without any objection from the constitution, the government of any individual state today can send any party leader of any individual state it

Thus if Article 9, sentence 2 remains in force we shall have a situation whereby mutually hostile party representatives from the individual parliaments confront one another in the Bundesrat, where they will simultaneously be representing the *particularist* interests of their states. The removal of the barrier of Article 9, by contrast, would make it possible to temper that tendency to particularism through the influence on the Bundesrat of the unity of the Reich. If the Bundesrat is *also* to include representatives of the *Reichstag* parties, instead of members of individual state parliaments alone, the cohesion of these parties across the Reich will make it possible to neutralise these regional differences *within* the fold of the party.

It is at any rate in the interest of individual states and of the Reich if the parliamentarised representatives of the three power groups (Reich Government and Reichstag, Prussian Royal Government and Prussian Diet, the Princes of the Federation and the diets of the smaller states) were to seek a balance of power *within* the Bundesrat as far as possible. This will only be possible if the parliamentarised highest officials of the Reich enter the Bundesrat. The stream of parliamentarisation will then have been channelled into the bed of Reich unity, while at the same time the living influence of the individual states on the course of the Reich's affairs will have been secured. *It is not true* that what is given to the Reich is thereby taken away from the individual states. Rather, what counts is how much weight the individual states are able to exert within the Reich. This weight can only be increased if the process of parliamentarisation is steered properly. In a famous speech Bismarck warned against underestimating the Bundesrat, and he placed great emphasis on the fact that the Saxon envoy there does not carry weight as an individual but as the product and representative 'of all the political forces' in Saxony. Admittedly, if the system is one of rule by officials, the 'forces' mentioned could at best mean the princely court and the bureaucracy. Yet this is precisely where parliamentarisation would create change. If, say, a representative of a strong and foreseeably

pleases to the Bundesrat – Bavaria, for example, could send a member of the Bavarian Centre Party against a Liberal Reichskanzler, or Reuß (younger line) a Social Democrat. The situation is just the same as it was when, under Caprivi, Conservatives held up the threat that Prince Bismarck might have himself delegated to the Bundesrat by Mecklenburg–Strelitz. If, as a result of retaining Article 9, sentence 2, the Bundesrat were to be parliamentarised along 'particularist' lines, something similar would inevitably happen to some extent.

lasting majority in the Bavarian parliament were to issue a statement on some question, it would not be easy simply to move on to next business in a parliamentarised Bundesrat; rather, a settlement would be sought before the appeal to the *ultima ratio* of a vote, because the odium would rebound on any party which proceeded ruthlessly. By the nature of things, this settlement would be prepared within the fold of the large parties which are distributed throughout the Reich. Even in past decades, internal debates within the Centre Party have repeatedly resulted in compromises between Reich interests and those of individual states, while similar things have happened in other parties. Precisely this will be made more difficult if the barrier of Article 9 is preserved, thus directing parliamentarisation into the course of a 'Greater Prussian' development which forces the representatives of the other parliamentary governments to follow a particularist course under the slogan of 'maximum freedom *from* the Reich', that is from Greater Prussia. Let this be considered well.

This whole account of the *possible* future effects of abolishing or leaving in place the barrier of Article 9, sentence 2 deliberately presupposes something that does not yet exist, namely that complete parliamentarisation will in fact come about both in the Reich and in individual states. Yet it is quite uncertain that this assumption will be confirmed by events. The point of making it is, firstly, just to show that, even if a parliamentary system in the shape of responsible *party* government is introduced fully, the federalism of the Reich Constitution will not only have its rights respected but will, indeed, only fully realise those rights if this happens. Now, it is fairly certain that the situation assumed here, namely the complete parliamentarisation of both the Reich itself and of individual states, will certainly not be achieved in a single step. The entire construct is also without immediate relevance, inasmuch as it presupposes an internal restructuring of the parties which, in their present state, would in any case not be 'capable of government' immediately. But one should be clear about one thing: every step on the road to parliamentarisation can *either* lead in the direction of a Greater Prussian solution *or* towards a genuinely federalist solution. As we have seen, the inconspicuous final sentence of Article 9 plays a quite considerable role in this question. That is why one should be clear, even as one takes the first steps, which of the two solutions is promoted thereby.

A further point to consider is this: would the parliamentarisation of the Bundesrat entail the *'mediatisation of Prussia'*, as is maintained by those who oppose Germany's development along liberal lines, an assertion which alternates with the charge that there exists a threat to the federal foundations of the Reich? The days are gone when people talked of 'Prussia's absorption into Germany'. It is certainly correct that the transition to equal suffrage will now only take place, if at all, as a result of strong pressure from the Reich. It is also correct, as I believe and as I have argued here, that, should this pressure prove insufficient, it would be an inevitable political necessity for the Reich to intervene directly, through emergency legislation in the form of a temporary change to the constitution. What is at stake is something quite other than the 'mediatisation of Prussia'. In order to exercise *leadership* within the Reich, the government of Prussia must create for itself a suitably *broad internal base* (in just the same way as any state must adapt its internal structure to the objectives of its foreign policy). The necessity of this *adaptation to the role of leader* is the sense in which Prussian electoral reform is a pre-eminently German and not simply a Prussian question. In every federal state in the world the principle holds true that certain, quite fundamental structural foundations must exist in each of the member states for the sake of the federation. For that reason, these foundations are regarded as a federal matter, notwithstanding the very extensive autonomy and division of competences between federation and individual state. This and *only* this principle of federal politics is being applied here to the hegemonial state of Prussia. Apart from this, Prussia's internal questions are of course the concern of this state alone, and there cannot be, nor has there ever been, any question of 'mediatisation' in the sense that other states of the federation should interfere in internal Prussian affairs. Problems begin to arise from Prussia's relation to the *politics of the Reich*. These problems stem entirely from the fact that Prussia occupies a highly *privileged* position within the Reich, as shown at the beginning of this chapter, and as a recapitulation of the prerogatives described there will make clear. Under certain circumstances this privileged position can give rise to the obligation on Prussia to accept certain *privilegia odiosa*. Thus it has already necessitated the appointment of Reich secretaries of state to the Prussian ministry. The parliamentarised Prussian state of the future may perhaps resist this practice. But the need to strike a balance between hegemonial power and the power of the Reichstag will continue to exist even then. The Reichskanzler will still have to be a Prussian minister in future, and it will then not be possible to determine the instruction of the presidial vote purely in the light of internal party constellations in Prussia without this resulting in grave conflicts with the Reichstag.

The actual political situation today is as follows: the instruction of the presidial vote in the Bundesrat comes under double pressure, from Prussia on the one hand and the Reichstag on the other, while the Reichskanzler is subject to, and in fact seeks to satisfy, demands from both directions that he should be accountable for these instructions (which belong formally only before the forum of the Prussian Diet). Binding constitutional practice at any rate has so defined his 'responsibility' towards the Reichstag as meaning that this has to take place there. The contrary would be quite impossible politically. Things cannot be any different in the future. If a Prussian Diet had ever tried, systematically and *against* the Reichstag, to seize control of the instruction of the presidial vote, then a situation would have arisen which would have obliged the Crown and the Reichskanzler to override the Prussian authorities by interpreting the constitution, expressly or in practice, in accordance with the principle that 'the instruction of the presidial vote takes place under the *sole* responsibility of the Reichskanzler towards the Reichstag'. That would not have been to mediatise Prussia, although it would have been to lower its status; fortunately, no such thing has ever been provoked. In part, however, this was undoubtedly a consequence of that unspoken policy of mutual assurance, and hence also of the Three Class Suffrage and the *absence* of parliamentarisation. How will things be in future if we assume that an increase in the power of parliament in the Reich *and* in Prussia will result from the existence of equal suffrage in both Prussia and the Reich?

In future, particularly if parliamentary government is fully implemented, the course of politics in the Reich will still rest on compromises between the power of the Prussian votes in the Bundesrat, which have parliamentary support, and the power of the government of the Reich, which is supported by the Reichstag. The question is how difficult it would be to achieve this compromise if parliamentarisation were fully implemented. It is clear from the outset that it will be easier to achieve than if the present, class-based Prussian Diet, say, had seized control of the Prussian votes; that would have had virtually unforeseeable consequences, and this would have been even more the case in the future. If equal suffrage is established – in reality and not just in appearance – the composition of the Reichstag and of the Prussian Diet will grow increasingly similar in future, whatever else happens. Admittedly, it is not possible to say what they will look like in detail, but this much seems certain: party conflicts within the Prussian Diet would initially be more acute than in the Reichstag. 'Conservatives' in the Prussian sense of the word hardly exist outside Prussia and Mecklenburg, for outside Prussia there is not the abrupt contrast between large landowners on the one hand and workers and bourgeoisie (*Bürgertum*) on the other. Also absent (not entirely, but virtually so) is Prussian heavy industry and its imprint on the character of the middle-class parties in Prussia. Also absent elsewhere are the accents of heavy industry within the Centre Party, as well as the national conflict with the Poles. Furthermore, outside Prussia the most radical strain of Social Democracy is strongly represented only in Saxony. But precisely this brand of Social Democracy is represented at this very moment in the Prussian Diet. Anti-monarchic currents are present to a much lesser extent in the states of southern Germany. Given equal suffrage, it would very probably be easier to govern with the Reichstag than with the Prussian Diet, much as it is to be hoped and (with some *patience*!) surely to be expected, that the severity of the conflicts will diminish even there once the hated electoral privileges have finally been done away with. However, until that is the case, the Reichstag will probably be superior in purely national-political terms. This will be even more the case if, in order to placate vested interests, they commit the political error of constructing the Prussian House of Lords as a kind of superstructure for those with a vested interest in electoral privilege on top of a chamber elected on the basis of equal suffrage, and the further mistake of giving these two chambers equal status. That would cause acute conflicts to flare up again in the form of tension between the first and second chambers, and it would nourish radicalism. The position of the diet would be weakened more seriously if suffrage were formally equal but in fact so constructed as to disenfranchise parts of the lower stratum (by a long residential qualification). If, on the other hand, equal suffrage were introduced, there would no longer be conflicts within a single party such as exist at present in the relations between the National Liberal Party in the Reichstag and the National Liberal Party in Prussia.

If parliamentary government were fully implemented, the compromise needed on each occasion between the Reich and Prussia would, of course, be prepared inside the great *parties* which were common to both the Reich and Prussia. If the barrier of Article 9, sentence 2 were abolished, these compromises would be concluded formally in the *Bundesrat*. Even if parliamentarisation is fully implemented, two figures who belong both to the Reich and to Prussia will always play a decisive role in such matters: the *Kaiser*, who is simultaneously king of Prussia, and the *Reichskanzler*, who must simultaneously be leader of the Prussian vote-bearers and a member of the Prussian ministry, indeed normally its president.

Unless the internal structure of Germany is completely overthrown and reconstructed along unitary lines – and there is not the slightest prospect of this at present – the dualism between the Reich and Prussia means that the dynasty is just as indispensable to the Reich as it is (for quite different reasons) to the dualistic structure of Austria – Hungary. Even a purely parliamentary Kaiser and king will have enormous real power in his hands as the commander-in-chief of the army (that is of the officer corps), as the holder of the ultimate power of decision on foreign policy, and finally as the internal political authority which arbitrates when the Prussian and Reich authorities fail to reach agreement. This will particularly be the case if he makes it his duty only to play his role in strictly parliamentary forms, in the manner of the lately deceased Habsburg monarch who was the most powerful man in his empire, and if, like the latter, or better still like King Edward VII, he knows how to play the instrument of the modern state mechanism, without always being visible as the actual player. There is no need to elaborate this point any further. On the other hand, it is desirable, and something which we may hope parliamentarisation will bring about, for the purely *military* influences on politics to decrease, both in domestic and foreign affairs. Many of Germany's worst political failures have stemmed from the fact that the military authorities exercise a crucial influence on purely political decisions, although political tactics and strategy require the use of very different means than do military tactics and strategy. In foreign policy one problem in particular, the Polish question, which is of vital importance to us, has been prejudiced^K in the most worrying manner. In domestic politics, the sad goings-on in the Reichstag when Dr Michaelis was Reichskanzler are proof that military authorities are very ill-advised if they allow themselves to be harnessed to party politics and, in doing so, subscribe to the old notion that 'national' and 'the Conservative Party' mean one and the same thing, a notion to which the officer is predisposed by his origins. In the military area, no authority on earth can boast of such unlimited trust from a nation as the leaders of our army can – and with justification. But they should see to it that no one is obliged to say to them later, *'The good you have done with the sword, you have undone with your unnecessary escapades on the black ice of politics'*[69] It is absolutely essential for the military authorities to be *subordinated* to the political leadership in all political matters; of course decisive weight must be given to their expert opinion on the military situation when political decisions are being made, but their opinion must never be the sole, deciding factor. *That* is a principle which Bismarck fought hard and long to uphold.

The *Reichskanzler* will remain the *political* leader of the Reich in future, and he will retain his central position in the whole interplay of political forces. There is also no doubt that, more or less as at present, he will remain a pre-eminent *individual* minister in relation to the secretaries of state, without colleagues of formally equal status. Admittedly, the Minister of War, who even today is not formally subordinated to him, and (in cases where the Reichskanzler does not come from a diplomatic background) the Secretary of State for Foreign Affairs will inevitably retain a large degree of independence.

---

^{K} The error lay entirely with the demand on the part of the military for the creation of a Polish *army* (i.e. officer corps), *before* Poland's stance towards Germany had been fully clarified through firm agreements with a Polish authority which could legitimately represent the country. It was also typical of the military mind to believe that the acceptance of a 'bond of honour' by monarchic proclamation could be the way to achieve this. It was perfectly understandable that the Poles should have reacted to such grave errors in the way they did.

[69] Field Marshal Blücher is reported to have said in 1815, after the Battle of Waterloo, 'May the pens of the diplomats not ruin again what has been achieved with so much effort by the swords of the armies.' In December 1917 Weber used these words in a speech criticising the 'Vaterlandspartei'. However, he was mistakenly reported to have said the opposite: 'that the pen restores what the sword has ruined.' Weber is quoting his own response to this mistaken criticism. See Weber 'Schwert und Parteikampf', *Heidelberger Tageblatt*, 10 December 1917, reprinted in Max Weber, *Gesamtausgabe*, vol. XV pp. 399–400.

But, particularly if parliamentarisation is fully implemented, there will be no place for a truly 'collegial' Reich ministry. At least, not if the barrier of Article 9, sentence 2 disappears. Contrary to the ideas once beloved of liberals, this is something about which one must be clear. After all, it is no coincidence that the trend in all parliamentary states is towards an *increase* in the power of the head of the cabinet. This is patently the case in England and France. In Russia the abolition of autocracy immediately gave rise to the post of the leading prime minister. As we know, in Prussia, too, the Minister President controls all communications made by his colleagues to the king, and this provision, temporarily suspended under Caprivi at the king's request, had to be reinstated again later. In the Reich the special position and pre-eminence of the Reichskanzler results simply from his leadership of the Bundesrat, as prescribed by the constitution, and from his inevitable position in the Prussian ministry, whereas in the case of the secretaries of state such a position is only fortuitous and expedient, but not indispensable. The development of the secretaries of state into politically independent powers *vis-à-vis* the Reichskanzler would be inevitable if parliamentarisation (given the retention of Article 9, sentence 2) went in the direction of particularisation, because they would then become the spokesmen (*Vertrauensmänner*) of the parties in the Reichstag, as opposed to the Reichskanzler and the Bundesrat in their capacity as bearers of the power of the individual parliaments. Even then the compulsion to negotiate would arise, but not necessarily, or even expediently, a 'collegial body' which reached decisions by voting. In any case, the desire for such a thing rests essentially on the present mechanical separation of Bundesrat and parliament and would become insubstantial once this barrier had disappeared. It cannot be denied that the emergence of a voting, collegial, ministerial body outside the Bundesrat would be a suitable means of reducing the importance of the Bundesrat, and that it is therefore preferable from a federalist point of view to parliamentarise the Bundesrat, so that compromises between the various forces on which the Reich rests are actually achieved within its ranks.

It would certainly be desirable if the present procedure before politically important decisions, which leads to a power struggle between departments, were to be replaced by a system of regular, joint, collegial discussion of political questions between the chancellor and all the secretaries of state.[L] The federalist worries mentioned above, however, mean that a formal weakening of the general responsibility of the Reichskanzler, and indeed of his special position, is improbable and hardly likely to prove useful. Particularly from a federalist point of view, it needs to be considered whether a collegial institution ought not to be created in the Reich which could hold *advance discussions* on important decisions of Reich politics, taking advice from representatives of the most important power factors in domestic politics and from the administrative chiefs who are informed about the issues. The public speeches of the party leaders in the Reichstag are official declarations by the party to the country at large, and they only take place once the party has decided on its position. The decisive party discussions and, where necessary, negotiations between the parties take place without consulting the representatives of individual states. Finally, the discussions at plenary sessions of the Bundesrat, a body at which votes are taken, have no binding force and are basically a waste of time. We ought to make it possible for experienced statesmen to express their *personal* views before important decisions are taken, freely, without prejudice to the eventual, conclusive and formal decisions, and unconstrained by considerations of the public effects in the country. We have already encountered this problem repeatedly, and only wish to ask two questions at this point. To which existing or newly emerging organisations could such an institution be attached? Is any one organisation a particular candidate, or should we be considering several competing possibilities?

The war has created the following new consultative bodies: (1) The Main Committee (*Hauptausschuß*), which is the expanded budgetary commission of the Reichstag; (2) the Seven Man Committee, to which the government once made appointments, but to which the parties now send their representatives; (3) the 'inter-party consultations', to which, on the occasion of the recent crises, those parties sent representatives who smoothed the path for the present

---

[L] And, beyond that, to a struggle using press demagogy against one another, such as we witnessed at the beginning of 1916 and again in 1917 and at the beginning of 1918. Events at that time made it clear to everyone that the worst kind of 'demagogy', the mob rule of sycophancy, is to be found where democracy does not even exist, indeed precisely because of the lack of orderly democracy.

government – National Liberals, Centre Party, Independent Liberals and Social Democrats. We have already discussed the first two of these formations. The official Main Committee of the Reichstag with its future sub-committees could be a candidate in peacetime for carrying out the continuous *control of the administration*. As parliamentarisation progressed, inter-party discussions amongst the parties supporting the government at any given moment would undoubtedly develop into the means whereby the government remained in contact with the parties involved. They are necessary as long as Article 9, sentence 2 prevents the party leaders as such from sitting in the government, and would become superfluous as soon as they could do so. Their future importance or otherwise further depends on as yet unforeseeable circumstances. Amongst other things, they were an expression of the fact that outstanding leaders are *not* to be found in the parties at present. We must demand that, when there is a change of Reichskanzler or amongst the secretaries of state in future, all party leaders should be interviewed personally *by the monarch and not simply by the heir to the throne*, and that there should be *no* repetition of the role once played by the chief of the Civil Cabinet.[M] But one cannot predict the extent to which the parliamentary parties will come together for consultations, and such meetings cannot of course assume an 'official' character. That leaves the 'Seven Man Committee', which in fact has become dormant at the moment, and in truth only owes its existence to the circumstance that Reichskanzler Michaelis accepted office *without* the prior agreement of the parties and expressed himself ambiguously, so that the parties demanded a kind of watch-dog body to control his conduct on the question of peace. We have already spoken about the impractical aspects of the shape this committee was given at the time. It would become wholly redundant if the party leaders sat in the Bundesrat. Again and again, the problem points to the conclusion that the *Bundesrat* should be parliamentarised by allowing the leaders of the Reichstag parties currently supporting

---

[M] Admittedly, if this official is accused of systematically 'blocking' free access to the monarch, the ' Stumm era' and the 'prison speech' could teach us *which circles* benefited from this 'free access' and from influencing the monarch without responsibility. *Only* responsible *statesmen* and responsible *party leaders* (*all of them*) should have the monarch's ear.

the government and the leaders of the major individual state parliaments to have a seat on it as plenipotentiaries. The Bundesrat itself must then make it possible for bodies to come into being as adjuncts of one or more of its committees; these will hold advance discussions with the chiefs of the military and the administration on important political questions, just like a state council of the Reich. It would be desirable for this to happen in the form of a crown council, which is to say, in the presence of the Kaiser and of those princes in the Bund at least who have retained sovereignty over their contingent of the army (appointing the officers and having their own Ministry of War). We have already spoken about the minimal competence it must have, namely advance consultation on whether it is opportune to *make public* any statement by the monarch, and in particular all statements affecting foreign policy. There is already constitutional provision for the medium-sized states to be represented in the Foreign Affairs Committee of the Bundesrat; the new forum could, as has been suggested, be linked to the restructuring of this committee. If Article 9, sentence 2 is removed, it would in any case be possible to create this new entity without any constitutional changes. The only legal innovation needed would be the requirement that, under pain of punishment, all publications of that kind are only permissible *after* it has been attested that they have been countersigned, and, further, that the countersignature should only be given in such cases after a hearing of a council of state to be formed from the Bundesrat.

Provided these bodies are properly set up, federalism will be given all it needs through the combination of parliamentarisation with these consultative bodies to be formed from it: instead of mere freedom *from* the Reich it will have assured influence *within* the Reich. Any revival of the old unitarist tendencies would be thoroughly undesirable. We have left Treitschke's ideals far behind us. Unlike him, we regard the continued existence of the individual dynasties not only as useful purely in terms of national politics, but as desirable for general reasons of a cultural – political kind. The promotion of artistic culture in particular in the many historical centres of German cultural life, the existence of which makes Germany different from France, can be achieved much more satisfactorily if, as now, the dynasties whose lives are closely bound up with their provincial capitals continue to maintain a court there, than would be the case if every such town became the seat of a prefect of the central power.[N] Of course, one cannot deny that there is a force operating against this natural contribution to culture in the majority of princely courts in Germany, in the shape of the purely military type of education, a product of the princes' desire to be generals and to occupy the position of a military inspector (an ambition which is quite worthless from the point of view of national politics). Only a minority of them have educated tastes. Although it may be very desirable for future dynastic generations to be informed and educated in military matters, the exclusive weight placed on these things only causes embarrassment when a serious situation arises. When untalented princes are the nominal supreme commanders of their armies (men like Prince Friedrich Carl being rare exceptions in this respect), they waste the time and restrict the freedom of movement of the real commander, and they become dangerous when they take their formal rights seriously. A prince with genuine military interests and talents, on the other hand, should occupy the position appropriate to his age and his true abilities. Let us hope that there is a change in this area in the future, like that introduced in Austria by the late heir to the throne. But it is at least still possible for the princes to make a contribution to our cultural – political life, and in some cases this has become a reality. As parliamentarisation grew in importance, there is no doubt that the interests of the dynasties would be channelled increasingly into this very appropriate course. Given the fragmentation of the party system in Germany, the existence in the individual states of a dynastic head standing above party struggles is valuable for reasons very similar to those underpinning the relation of Prussia to the Reich (although the arguments are even more compelling in this case).

Thus, even someone who valued the German nation and its future far more highly than any question of the form of the state would not wish to challenge the existence of the dynasties, even if the question were to arise. But he would certainly have to insist that the path

---

[N] Science and scholarship, on the other hand, can expect to gain as little from the monarch's intervention as from the involvement of parliament. Whenever monarchs have intervened personally in appointments to academic posts, virtually the only people to benefit have been compliant mediocrities.

towards a reconstructed Germany was not obstructed by sterile and sentimental reminiscences of the governmental practices of the old regime, nor by any theoretical search for a specifically 'German' form of state. There is no doubt that German parliamentarism will look different from that in any other country. But the vanity of littérateurs whose predominant concern is that the German state should not resemble the other parliamentary states in the world (which include those of almost all the Germanic peoples) is inappropriate to the gravity of the tasks we face in the future.[o] These, and these alone, must decide the form of the state. The Fatherland is not a mummy lying in the graves of our ancestors. Rather, it shall and must live as the land of *our descendants*.

The actual form taken by the future parliamentary distribution of power will depend on where political *personalities with the qualities of leadership* emerge and what role they play. It is undoubtedly necessary for us to have patience and to be able to wait until we have got over the inevitable teething troubles. So far, there has simply been no place for natural leaders in our parliaments. The jubilant cry, 'You see, the nation is not ready for it', is a sterile and cheap amusement of academic littérateurs filled with *ressentiment* towards any human beings whom they have not *examined*, and delighting in every false step that has been made, or is yet to be made, by a parliamentary system slowly getting under way again after an interruption of thirty years. We shall see such behaviour repeatedly, and must respond to it as follows: it is *politically dishonest*, either (1) to deny German parliaments the 'right of enquiry', the instrument of power which would permit them to gain knowledge of the facts and gain access to necessary specialist knowledge, and then to complain about the 'amateurism' and bad work done by these very parliaments; or (2) to mutter about the purely 'negative' politics of these parliaments, while at the same time blocking the road which would permit any natural leaders to do positive work and exercise responsible power with the support of a parliamentary following. The littérateurs in Germany today are in truth the last people entitled to make judgements about political 'maturity'. They collaborated in and applauded *almost all the mistakes of German policy before the war and the lack of judgement nourished

---

[o] I have referred to England repeatedly in this essay so as not to make even this concession to mindless hatred of 'the street'.

by irresponsible demagogy during the war. *Where were they, when the grave errors of the old regime were being committed?* – such patently grave errors that, it will be recalled, Prussia's *Conservative* representatives addressed a joint, public request to the monarch, asking him to conduct policy in accordance with the advice of his appointed counsellors. It was already high time *then*; everyone could see what was happening and where the mistakes lay. Everyone was agreed about this, with no differences of opinion between the parties. *So where were they?* A public statement by a few thousand academic teachers would have been quite opportune at that time; it would doubtless have made an impression and it would have accorded with old traditions. Certainly, it is much cheaper for prebendaries of the state to chide the parties in the Reichstag, as happens at present. All these gentlemen remained silent at that time. Let them therefore be so good as to remain silent now: 'Your chiming days are over, so come down from the belfry.' Other sections of society will have to take charge of the political future of Germany. The examination diploma or the title of professor of physics or biology or any other academic subject bestows absolutely no political qualification on its holder, far less is it a guarantee of political character. Where fear about the prestige of their own social stratum (those with a university degree) is involved – and this is what lies behind all the ranting against 'democracy' and 'parliamentary amateurism' – that section of society always was blind, and will always remain blind, following its instincts rather than sober reflection; this is how university men, in the mass, will always behave in Germany.

If the old regime returns after the war – and parliamentarism will not come of its own accord, it requires *good will* on all sides for this to happen – one can bury any expectation that the much criticised bearing of the Germans in the outside world will change. National pride is simply a function of the degree to which the members of a nation, at least potentially, are *actively* involved in shaping the politics of their country.

Germans, when out in the world, deprived of the accustomed carapace (*Gehäuse*) of bureaucratic regimentation, lose all sense of direction and security – a consequence of being accustomed to regard themselves at home merely as the object of the way their lives are ordered rather than as responsible for it themselves. This is the reason for that insecure, self-conscious way of presenting themselves in public which is definitely the source of the Germans' much criticised over-familiarity. Inasmuch as it exists, their political 'immaturity' results from the uncontrolled rule of officialdom, and from the fact that the ruled are accustomed to submit to that rule without themselves sharing responsibility and hence taking an interest in the conditions and procedures of the officials' work. *Only a politically mature people* is a 'nation of masters' (*Herrenvolk*), which means a people controlling the administration of its affairs itself, and, through its elected representatives, sharing decisively in the selection of its political leaders. Our nation threw away that chance by the way it reacted to Bismarck's greatness as a political ruler. Once a parliament has been run down, it cannot be brought to its feet again overnight, not even by some paragraphs in the constitution. There is of course no question that any such paragraph, say one that tied the appointment and dismissal of the Reichskanzler to a vote in parliament, would suddenly conjure up 'leaders' out of thin air, after they had been excluded from parliament for decades as a result of its impotence. But it is quite possible to create the organisational *preconditions* for the emergence of leaders, and indeed everything now depends on this happening.

Only nations of masters are called upon to thrust their hands into the spokes of the world's development. If nations who do not have this quality attempt to do so, then not only will the sure instinct of other nations rebel, but they will also fail inwardly in the attempt. By a 'nation of masters' we do not mean that ugly, parvenu face worn by people whose sense of national dignity allows them and their nation to be told by an English turncoat like Mr Houston Stewart Chamberlain what it means to be a 'German'.[70] Certainly, a nation that *only* produced good officials, admirable office workers, honest merchants, able scholars and technicians and true and faithful servants, and in other respects submitted to *uncontrolled rule by officials* under the banner of pseudo-monarchic slogans – such a people would *not* be a *nation of masters*, and would do better to go about its daily business than to bother its head with the fate of the world. If the old conditions return, *let no one talk to us again* of 'world politics'. Littérateurs who

---

[70] H. S. Chamberlain (1855–1927), English expatriate writer and propagandist of a pan-German nationalism justified on racial grounds. His *Die Grundlagen des 19. Jahrhunderts* ('The Foundations of the 19th Century') (1899) and his other writings were widely discussed in Germany.

have succumbed to *conservative clichés* will wait in vain for Germans to develop a genuine sense of dignity abroad, if at home they remain merely an object for the activity of purely *official* rule (however efficient such administration may be in purely technical terms), and are even content to have well-fed learned prebendaries discuss the question of whether the nation is 'mature' enough for this or that form of government.

The '*will to powerlessness*' in domestic affairs preached by the littérateurs is not compatible with the 'will to power' in the world, of which some have boasted so loudly. The question of whether the nation feels ready to bear the responsibility which a nation of seventy million people has towards its descendants, will be answered by the way we address the question of the internal reconstruction of Germany. If the nation does not dare do the one, it should reject the other, for it leads nowhere politically. In *that* case, this war, which is a fight to enable *our* nation, too, to share responsibility for the future of the world, would indeed have been 'senseless' and mere butchery, and this would be even more true of any future German war. We would have to seek our tasks elsewhere and 're-orient' ourselves in *this* sense.

The typical snobbery of many littérateurs (even of quite intelligent ones) regards these sober problems of parliamentary and party reform as terribly minor – 'ephemeral technicalities' – in comparison with all manner of speculations about the 'ideas of 1914' or about 'true socialism' and such-like littérateur-interests. Well, one 'ephemeral question' which will be settled soon concerns the outcome of this war. Whoever emerges as the victor, the restructuring of the economic order will take its course. For this to happen, neither a German victory is necessary nor a new, liberal political order in the Reich. A national politician will certainly keep an eye on those universal trends which will hold sway in future over the outward order of the lives and fates of the masses. But when, as a politician, he is moved by the political fate of *his* people (towards which those universal trends are completely indifferent), he will think in terms of the next two to three generations, even where the creation of new political formations is concerned, since these are the people who will decide what is to become of *his* nation. If he proceeds differently, he is no politician but one of the littérateurs. In this case, let him concern himself with the eternal truths and stick to his books, but he should not step into the arena where the problems of the present are contested. Here the fight is about whether or not *our* nation has a decisive say within that universal process. The internal structure of the nation, including its political structure, has to be adapted to this task. Our previous structure was not suited to the task, but only to technically good *administration* and outstanding *military* achievements. That these things suffice for a purely *defensive* form of politics, but not for the political challenges presented by the world – *this* is the lesson we have learned from the terrible fate that engulfed us.

Socialism

Gentlemen!

Honoured as I am by this, my first opportunity[1] to address the Officer Corps of the Royal and Imperial Army of Austria,[2] you will understand that the situation is also a somewhat embarrassing one for me, particularly in view of the fact that I have absolutely no knowledge of the conditions under which you operate, of the internal organisational relations in this army which are decisive for any influence the officer corps may exert on the men. It is obvious that an officer of the Reserve or the militia is always an amateur, not only because he lacks preparatory scientific training at a military academy, but also because he is not in constant touch with the whole internal nervous system of the organisation. Nevertheless, having spent various periods of time in the German Army in very different areas of Germany over a number of years, I believe I have had sufficient experience of the relations between officers, N.C.O.s and men at least to be able to recognise that this or that method of exercising influence is *possible*, or that this or that method is difficult or impossible. As far as the Austrian Army is concerned, of course, I have not the slightest idea

---

[1] *Der Sozialismus* was published as a pamphlet in Vienna in 1918. It began life as a lecture given to officers of the Austro-Hungarian army in June 1918, on the invitation of the Austrian 'Feindespropaganda-Abwehrstelle' ('Section for Defence against Enemy Propaganda'). After the Russian Revolution of 1917 there was widespread fear, particularly in Central Europe, of socialist revolutions breaking out in other countries; hence Weber's theme.

[2] Weber repeatedly uses the standard abbreviation 'k. u. k. Armee' for the 'königliche und kaiserliche Armee' of Austria. Here, for the sake of simplicity, 'Austrian Army' will be used throughout.

of what is or is not possible. If I have any impression at all of internal relations in the Austrian Army, it is only that the multi-lingual nature of the empire[3] is simply bound to create enormous practical (*sachlichen*) difficulties. Officers of the Austrian Reserve have tried on several occasions to explain to me how they manage to keep in touch with the men without any real knowledge of their language, such contact being necessary if an officer is to exert any kind of influence beyond what is strictly essential to the execution of duty. I myself can only speak from a German perspective on these matters, so I hope you will allow me to begin with some introductory remarks about the way such influence has been exerted in our army.

These remarks are based on a 'worm's-eye view' of things. That is to say, when travelling in Germany, as I have done frequently at various times, I made a point of always travelling third class whenever the journey was not very long and the work before me not very arduous. Over time I thus met many hundreds of men returning from or travelling to the front, just at the period when what was known as the work of enlightenment[4] by the officers was beginning in Germany. Without seeking some pretext to question the men or prompting them to speak, I came to hear an extraordinary range of opinions on this subject from the men's side. Moreover, these were almost always very reliable men, for whom the officer's authority stood firm as a rock; only rarely were there also some who adopted a rather different attitude inwardly. The result was always the same, namely that one was forced to recognise very quickly the great difficulty of any work of enlightenment. One thing in particular was clear: as soon as the men had any suspicion that *party* politics, of whatever kind, were involved and were to be promoted, directly or indirectly, many of them became suspicious. When they went on leave they were in contact with people from their party, and then it naturally became difficult to maintain any real relationship of trust with them. There was another major difficulty. Although the men acknowledged the military expertise of the officer quite unreservedly (and I have never encountered anything else, although of course in Germany, too, there was cursing on occasion, sometimes about the staff officers, sometimes about other things, but military authority was never fundament-

---

[3] The Austro-Hungarian Empire encompassed many nationalities and, hence, many languages.
[4] Here the term *Aufklärungsarbeit* is a euphemism for political propaganda.

ally called into question), one also encountered a quite different feeling: 'When we are being instructed by the officers about the way we
lead our own, private lives and the wider consequences this has, the
fact remains that the officer corps simply belongs to a different social
estate from us, and, with the best will in the world, it is impossible
for the officer to put himself as completely into our situation when
we are standing behind a machine or the plough, as we ourselves
can.' That was expressed again and again in a number of sometimes
naive remarks, and I had the feeling that enlightenment practised in
the wrong way could perhaps damage the authority of the officer,
even in the military sphere where it remains solid, since the men do
not accept his authority unconditionally in areas where they claim to
be at home. Next, another frequently made mistake, not at present,
but in previous confrontations with socialism. The party-political
opponents of social democracy used to tell the workers that their
trade union and party officials were 'the real people who quite literally
live off the workers' pennies, far more than the entrepreneurs do';[5]
this practice has long since ceased, and for good reason. The reply
of every worker is, of course, 'Certainly these people live off my
pennies. I pay them. For that very reason I regard them as reliable,
they are dependent on me, I know that they must represent my interests. Nobody's going to tell me any different. That's worth the few
pennies I pay.' Quite rightly, people have stopped trying to discredit
in this way the stratum of intellectuals who are now at work everywhere, coining the watchwords, slogans and – yes, you may say it –
empty phrases used by all parties without exception, including, that
is to say, the parties of the left and the Social Democratic Party. In
my opinion, the fact that we now stand on a good footing with the
trade unions in Germany is a welcome development.[6] In other
respects you may take what attitude you will towards the trade unions.
They do foolish things too. It was, however, prudent precisely from
a military point of view, too, to adopt this stance toward the unions,
for they do after all represent something that is also characteristic of
military bodies. One may think what one likes about strikes. They

---

[5] On 16 March 1904 the Conservative Deputy Pauli had accused the Social Democrats
in the Reichstag of filling their own pockets with the 'Arbeitergroschen': 'All you are
concerned with is living off the workers' pennies.'
[6] Weber is referring to an agreement over legislation which led to the formal recognition
of the power of the Trade Unions by the German government at the end of 1916.

are usually a fight for interests, for wages. Yet very often not just for wages, but also for ideal (*ideelle*) things, for honour, as the workers happen to understand it (and each man claims to know for himself what it means). The feeling of honour, of comradeship among work-mates and allies[7] in a factory or in a branch of industry binds them in solidarity, and that is, after all, a feeling upon which the solidarity of military groups rests, although it takes a different direction there. As there is absolutely no way of doing away with strikes completely – the choice is merely between openly recognised and secret associ-ations of this kind – I consider that it is prudent from the military point of view, too, to take this fact as one's starting point. This is simply how things are, and so long as one can get along with the men and they do not endanger *military* interests, one comes to terms with them, as has in fact been done in Germany. Those are my subjective impressions.

Now I should like to turn to the subject upon which you have done me the honour of inviting me to speak. It is the kind of question that ought to be discussed thoroughly for half a year (this being the stretch of time allocated to such topics when one is addressing a trained academic audience). The subject is the position of socialism and the attitude to be taken to it. I would like to begin by drawing your attention to the fact that there are 'socialists' of the most diverse kinds. There are people who call themselves socialists whom no member of a socialist party, whatever its direction, would ever acknowledge as such. All *parties* of a purely socialist character are *democratic* parties nowadays. I should like to begin by discussing this democratic character briefly. What, then, is democracy today? The point is very relevant to our subject, although I can only touch upon it briefly today. Democracy can mean an infinite variety of things. In itself it means simply that no formal inequality of political rights exists between the individual classes of the population. Yet what varied consequences that has! Under the old type of democracy, in the Swiss cantons of Uri, Schwyz, Unterwalden, Appenzell and Glarus, all citizens – in Appenzell there are 12,000 entitled to vote, in the others between 3,000 and 5,000 still assemble, even today, in a large space and, after a discussion has taken place, they vote by a show of hands

---

[7] German has two words for the English 'comrade'. *Genosse* is the term for a worker-comrade (particularly within socialism), *Kamerad* for a soldier-comrade. Weber's phrasing ('Kameradschaft der Genossen') deliberately mingles these two spheres.

on everything from the election of the cantonal president (*Landamman*) to a resolution on a new tax law or upon some administrative matter. However, if you study the lists of the cantonal presidents elected under this kind of old-style Swiss democracy over fifty or sixty years, you will find that they were the same men remarkably often, or at least these offices were in the hands of certain families from time immemorial. In other words, although a democracy existed in law, this democracy was in fact run aristocratically, for the simple reason that not every man who had a business to run could take on an office like that of cantonal president without ruining his business. He had to be economically 'dispensable' (*abkömmlich*), and as a rule only a man of some wealth has the freedom to absent himself from his business in this way. Or one must pay him highly and provide him with a pension. Democracy has only the choice of being run cheaply by the rich who hold honorary office, or of being run expensively by paid professional officials. The latter alternative, the development of professional officialdom, has become the fate of all modern democracies in which honorary office was inadequate to the task, that is, in the great mass states. That is currently the position in America. In theory, the situation there is similar to that in Switzerland. The president of the whole Union and a good proportion of the officials in individual states are elected, if not by state assemblies, then nevertheless by direct or indirect *equal* suffrage. The president nominates the other officials of the Union. It has been found that the officials *nominated* by the elected president are on the whole far superior to those chosen by popular election, as far as the quality of their work and above all their incorruptibility is concerned, because the president and the party supporting him are of course held responsible by the electorate for ensuring that the officials they nominate possess at least in some sense the qualities expected by the voter.

This American democracy – which rests on the principle that every four years, when the president changes, the 300,000 and more officials he has to nominate will change too, and that every four years all the governors of the individual states will change, and with them in turn many thousands of civil servants – this democracy is now nearing its end. It has been administration by amateurs; for these officials appointed by the party were nominated according to the principle that they had rendered services to the party, for which they were rewarded with official posts. Few questions were asked about their technical qualifications. Until recently, examinations and that sort of thing were formally unknown in American democracy. In fact, the opposite point of view was often taken, namely that offices had to be shared around in rotation to some extent, so that at some point everyone had a turn of putting their hands in the pork barrel.

I have talked to American workers about this on several occasions. The genuine American Yankee worker enjoys a high level of wages and education. The pay of an American worker is higher than that of many an untenured professor at American universities. These workers have all the forms of bourgeois society, appearing in their top hats with their wives, who have perhaps somewhat less polish and elegance but otherwise behave just like any other ladies, while the immigrants from Europe flood into the lower strata. Whenever I sat in company with such workers and said to them: 'How can you let yourselves be governed by these people who are put in office without your consent and who naturally make as much money out of their office as possible, since they owe their post to the party and pay so much of their salary back to the party in taxes, and then have to leave office after four years without any pension entitlement; how can you let yourselves be governed by these corrupt people who are notorious for robbing you of hundreds of millions?', I would occasionally receive the characteristic reply which I hope I may repeat, word for word and without adornment: 'That doesn't matter, there's enough money there to be stolen and still enough left over for others to earn something – for us too. We spit on these 'professionals', these officials. We despise them. But if the offices are filled by a trained, qualified class, such as you have in your country, it will be the officials who spit on us.'

That was the decisive point for these people. They feared the emergence of the type of officialdom which already actually exists in Europe, an exclusive estate (*Stand*) of university-educated officials with professional training.

Now the time has, of course, long since past when administration could still be conducted by amateurs, even in America. Specialist officialdom is spreading with enormous speed. Professional examinations have been introduced. Formally, this was at first obligatory only for certain more technical officials, but the practice quickly spread. There are already about 100,000 officials to be nominated by the president who can only be nominated when they have passed the examinations. This means that the first and most important step towards the transformation of the old democracy has already been taken. It also means that universities in America have begun to play an entirely different role and that the spirit of the universities has changed fundamentally too. For, and this is not always known outside America, it was the American universities and the strata educated by them, not the military contractors who exist in every country, who were the originators of the war. When I was over there in 1904 the question American students asked me more than any other was how formal duels are arranged in Germany and how people go about getting their scars.[8] They thought it a chivalrous institution; this was a sport they had to have too. What was serious about all this was the fact that, particularly in my subject, the literature was tailored to such sentiments. It was actually in the best works of the day that I found the following conclusion: 'It is fortunate that the world economy is moving in such a direction that the moment will soon be here when it will be worth while ('a sound business view')[9] to deprive one another of world trade by means of *war*. Then at last we shall see the end of the age in which we Americans have been undignified dollar-earners; then a warlike spirit and chivalry will rule the world once more.' They probably imagined modern war as being like the battle of Fontenoy, when the herald of the French called out to the enemy: 'Gentlemen of England, you shoot first!' They thought of war as a kind of knightly sport which would replace the sordid chase after money with the distinguished (*vornehm*) sensibility of an aristocratic estate. As you see, this caste judges America in just the same way as America, in my experience, is often judged in Germany, and draws its own conclusions. The statesmen who mattered emerged from this caste. This war will result in America's emergence as a state with a large

---

[8] Many student fraternities in Germany used to train their members in sword-fighting. Part of the training was to accept unflinchingly sabre cuts (*Schmisse*) on the face which left behind scars.

[9] 'A sound business view' is in English. In using this phrase, Weber is probably referring to T. Veblen *The Theory of Business Enterprise* (New York, 1904); see, for example, p. 398: 'Such an ideal [i.e. a militant, coercive home administration and something in the way of an imperial court life – Eds. is not simply a moralist's day-dream; it is a sound business proposition, in that it lies on the line of policy along which the business interests are moving in their own behalf.' Weber refers on several occasions to Veblen's book which intended, 'to show in what manner business methods and business principles, in conjunction with mechanical industry, influence the modern cultural situation' p. 21).

army, an officer corps and a bureaucracy. Even at that time I spoke to American officers who had little sympathy for what American democracy expected of them. For instance, I happened to be at the home of a colleague's daughter one day when the maid was away – maids could give two hours' notice over there. At that moment the two sons, who were naval cadets, came in and their mother said, 'You'll have to go out and clear the snow now, otherwise it will cost me a fine of 100 dollars a day.' The sons, who had just been in the company of German naval officers, thought this was not appropriate to their station, whereupon the mother said: 'If you won't do it, then I shall have to.'

In America this war will result in the development of a bureaucracy and thus in promotion opportunities for people with a university education (that is, of course, at the root of it as well); in short, it will result in America becoming 'Europeanised' just as quickly as people say Europe has become Americanised. In large states everywhere modern democracy is becoming a bureaucratised democracy. This is how things have to be, for democracy is replacing the noble, aristocratic or other honorary officials with a body of paid officials. It is the same everywhere, within the parties too. This is inescapable, and it is the first fact which socialism, too, has to reckon with: the necessity for long years of specialist training, for constantly increasing specialisation and for management by specialist officials trained in this way. The modern economy cannot be managed in any other way.

In particular, this inescapable universal bureaucratisation is precisely what lies behind one of the most frequently quoted socialist slogans, the slogan of the 'separation of the worker from the means of work'. What does that mean? The worker, so we are told, is 'separated' from the material means with which he produces, and on this separation rests the wage slavery in which he finds himself. By this is meant the fact that in the Middle Ages the worker owned the technical tools with which he produced, while the modern wage labourer, of course, neither does nor can own his tools, whether the mine or factory in question is run by an entrepreneur or the state. They have in mind, further, the fact that the craftsman himself once bought the raw materials which he processed, whereas that neither is nor can be the case with the paid worker of today, and that accordingly the product in the Middle Ages was, and still is in places where crafts survive, at the disposal of the individual craftsman, who could sell it on the market and derive his own profit from it. In a large concern, by contrast, the product is at the disposal, not of the worker but of the owner of these means of operation (*Betriebsmittel*), who again may be the state or a private entrepreneur. That is true, but the fact is by no means peculiar to the process of economic production. We encounter the same thing within universities, for example. The old-time lecturers and university professors worked with the library and the technical resources which they themselves acquired or had made for themselves, and they (the chemists, for example) produced with these means the things necessary for carrying on the business of science (*den wissenschaftlichen Betrieb*). By contrast, most employees within the modern university organisation, particularly the assistants in large institutes, are now in precisely the same situation as any worker in this respect. They can be given notice at any time. Their rights in the rooms of the institute are no different from those of the worker in the factory. They must conduct themselves, just like the latter, in accordance with the existing rules and regulations. They have no ownership of the materials or apparatus, machines and so on which are used in a department of chemistry or physics, or in a dissecting room or clinic; these, rather, are the property of the state, but they are husbanded by the director of the department who levies charges for their use, while the assistant receives an income which does not fundamentally differ in amount from that of a trained worker. We find just the same situation in the military sphere. The knight of olden days was the owner of his horse and his armour. He had to equip and provision himself. The army constitution of the time was based on the principle of self-equipment. Both in the cities of antiquity and in the knightly armies of the Middle Ages a man had to supply his own armour, lance and horse, and bring provisions. The modern army came into being with the establishment of the princely household, that is, when the soldier and the officer (who is indeed something different from other officials, but who corresponds exactly to the official in this sense) ceased to own the means of conducting war. It is on this, indeed, that the cohesion of the modern army rests. This, too, is why it was for so long impossible for the Russian soldiers to escape from the trenches, because of the existence of this apparatus of the officer corps, the quarter-master general and other officials, and everyone in the army knew that his whole existence, including his food, depended on the functioning of this apparatus. They were all 'separated' from the means of conducting war, just as the worker is from the means of carrying out his work. In a similar position to that of the knight stood the official of the feudal period, that is, a vassal invested with administrative and judicial authority. He bore the expense of administration and jurisdiction out of his own pocket and in return took the fees for these services. He was therefore in possession of the means of administration. The modern state emerges when the prince takes this business into his own household, employs salaried officials and thereby brings about the 'separation' of the officials from the means of conducting their duties. Everywhere we find the same thing: the means of operation within the factory, the state administration, the army and university departments are concentrated by means of a bureaucratically structured human apparatus in the hands of the person who has command over (*beherrscht*) this human apparatus. This is due partly to purely technical considerations, to the nature of modern means of operation – machines, artillery and so on – but partly simply to the greater efficiency of this kind of human cooperation: to the development of 'discipline', the discipline of the army, office, workshop and business. In any event it is a serious mistake to think that this separation of the worker from the means of operation is something peculiar to industry and, moreover, to *private* industry. The basic state of affairs remains the same when a different person becomes lord and master of this apparatus, when, say, a state president or minister controls it instead of a private manufacturer. The 'separation' from the means of operation continues in any case. As long as there are mines, furnaces, railways, factories and machines, they will never be the property of an individual or of several individual workers in the sense in which the materials of a craft in the Middle Ages were the property of one guild-master or of a local trade cooperative or guild. That is out of the question because of the nature of present-day technology.

What, then, is *socialism* in relation to this fact? As I have already mentioned, the word has many meanings. However, what one usually thinks of as the opposite of socialism is a private economic order, that is a state of affairs in which provision for economic need is in the hands of private entrepreneurs and is so arranged that these entrepreneurs procure the material means of operation, officials and labour force by means of contracts of purchase and wage contracts, and then have the goods made and sell them on the market at their own economic risk and in the expectation of personal gain. Socialist theory has applied the label 'anarchy of production' to this private economic order,[10] because it is unconcerned whether the personal interest of the individual entrepreneurs in selling their products (the profit interest) functions in such a way as to guarantee that those who need these goods are indeed provided with them.

Historically, there has been a change in the question of which of a society's needs should be taken care of by business (that is privately) and which should be supplied, not privately, but socialistically, in the widest sense, in other words by planned organisation.

In the Middle Ages, for instance, republics such as Genoa had their great colonial wars in Cyprus conducted by limited share companies, the so-called 'Maone'. They each contributed a share of the money necessary, hired mercenaries as appropriate, conquered the country, received the protection of the republic and, of course, exploited the country, as plantation land or as a source of taxation, for their own purposes. The East India Company conquered India for England in like manner and exploited the country for itself. The *condottiere* of the late Renaissance period in Italy belonged in the same category. Like Wallenstein, the last of the type, the *condottiere* recruited his army in his own name and out of his own means; a proportion of the army's spoils went into his pocket, and of course he would stipulate that a certain sum be paid to him by the prince or king or emperor as a reward for his efforts and to cover his costs. In a somewhat less autonomous fashion the eighteenth-century colonel was still an entrepreneur who had to recruit and clothe his own soldiers. Sometimes, admittedly, he was partially dependent on the prince's stores, but he always managed his affairs largely at his own risk and for his own profit. The conduct of warfare on a private economic basis was, therefore, considered quite normal, although this would seem monstrous to us today.

On the other hand, no medieval town or guild would ever have thought it conceivable that supplying the town with corn or supplying the guild with the imported raw materials indispensable to the work of the master craftsmen, could simply be left to free trade. On the contrary, beginning in antiquity (on a large scale in Rome) and throughout the Middle Ages, this was the responsibility of the town

---

[10] See 'On the Situation of Constitutional Democracy in Russia', note 64 (p. 71 above).

and not of free trade, which only supplemented what the town did. Then things were roughly as they are now during a wartime economy, when cooperation takes place between large branches of the economy, what is now generally called 'joint state management of the economy' (*Durchstaatlichung*).[11]

What characterises our current situation is firstly the fact that the private sector of the economy, in conjunction with private bureaucratic organisation and hence with the separation of the worker from the means of operation (*Betriebsmitteln*), dominates an area that has never exhibited these two characteristics together on such a scale at any time in history, namely the area of *industrial* production. Secondly there is the fact that this process coincides with the introduction of mechanical production within the factory, and thus with a local concentration of labour on one and the same premises, with the fact that the worker is tied to the machine, and with common working *discipline* throughout the machine-shop or pit. Above all else, it is this discipline which gives our present-day way of 'separating' the worker from the means of work (*Arbeitsmittel*) its specific quality.

It was life lived under these conditions, this factory *discipline*, that gave birth to modern socialism. Socialism of the most diverse kinds has existed everywhere, at every period and in every country in the world. The unique character of modern socialism could grow only on this soil.

This subjection to working discipline is felt so acutely by the production worker because, in contrast to, say, a slave plantation or enforced labour on a manorial farm (*Fronhof*),[12] a modern production plant functions on the basis of an extraordinarily severe process of *selection* (*Auslese*). A modern manufacturer does not employ just any worker, just because he might work for a low wage. Rather he installs the man at the machine on piece-wages and says: 'All right, now work, I shall see how much you earn.' If the man does not prove himself capable of earning a certain minimum wage he is told: 'we are sorry, but you are not suited to this occupation, we cannot use you.' He is expelled because the machine is not working to capacity

---

[11] *Durchstaatlichung*: the idea of progressive and extensive state control and direction of the economy, but taking a corporatist rather than a socialist form.

[12] Weber mentions the manorial estate (*Fronhof*), on which serfs were obliged to labour for their feudal lord, during a discussion of various types of work discipline in *Economy and Society*, pp. 1155–6.

unless the man operating it knows how to utilise it fully. It is the same, or similar, everywhere. In contrast to the use of slave labour in antiquity, where the lord was tied to whatever slaves he had (if one of them died, it was a capital loss for him), every modern industrial firm rests on the principle of selection. On the other hand this selection is driven to an extreme of intensity by competition between entrepreneurs, which ties the individual entrepreneur to certain maximum wages; the inevitability (*Zwangsläufigkeit*) of the workers' earnings corresponds to the inevitability of discipline.

If the worker goes to the entrepreneur today and says, 'We cannot live on these wages and you could pay us more', in nine out of ten cases – I mean in peacetime and in those branches of industry where there is really fierce competition – the employer is in a position to show the workers from his books that this is impossible: 'My competitor pays wages of such and such; if I pay each of you even only so much more, all the profit I could pay to the shareholders disappears from my books. I could not carry on the business, for I would get no credit from the bank.' Thereby he is very often just telling the naked truth. Finally, there is the additional point that under the pressure of competition profitability depends on the elimination of human labour as far as possible by new, labour-saving machines, and especially the highest-paid type of workers who cost the business most. Hence skilled workers must be replaced by unskilled workers or workers trained directly at the machine. This is inevitable and it happens all the time.

All this is what socialism understands as 'the rule (*Herrschaft*) of things over men', by which they mean the rule of the means over the end (the satisfaction of needs). It recognises that, whereas in the past there were individuals who could be held responsible for the fate of the client, bondsman or slave, this is impossible today. Therefore it directs its criticism not at individuals but at the order of production as such. Any scientifically trained socialist will absolutely refuse to hold an individual entrepreneur responsible for the fate which befalls the worker. He will say that the fault lies with the system, with the compulsions inherent in the situation into which all parties, entrepreneurs and workers alike, are pitched.

To put it positively, what would socialism then be, in contrast to this system? In the broadest sense of the term, it would be what is also frequently described as a 'communal economy'

(*Gemeinwirtschaft*).[13] This means, first of all, an economy from which profit is absent – that state of affairs, in other words, whereby private businessmen direct production on their own account and at their own risk. Instead, the economy would be in the hands of the officials of an association of the people (*Volksverband*) which would take over the running of the business according to principles which we shall discuss presently. Secondly, the so-called anarchy of production would therefore be absent, that is competition among entrepreneurs. At present many people, especially in Germany, are saying that, as a result of the war, we are already actually in the midst of the evolution of such a 'communal economy'. In view of this, let me point out briefly that the organised economy of any given people can be based on two essentially different principles, as far as the method of organisation is concerned. Firstly, what is nowadays called 'joint state management', with which all those gentlemen who work in the war industries are doubtless familiar. It rests on the collaboration of all the entrepreneurs in a particular branch of industry with state officials, be they civilian or military. In this way supplies of raw materials, procurement of credit, prices, and customers can be regulated largely according to a plan; the state can share in the profits and in the decision-making of these cartels. Now some think that the entrepreneur is then under the supervision of these officials, and that production is controlled by the state. They claim that this means we already have 'true', 'genuine' socialism, or are moving in that direction. In Germany, however, there is widespread scepticism about this theory. I shall leave on one side the question of how things work in wartime. However, anyone who can count knows that the economy could not be carried on in peacetime as it is now if we are not to go to our ruin, and that in peacetime this kind of state control, that is the compulsory cartelisation of the entrepreneurs in each branch of industry and the participation of the state in these cartels with a share in the profits in exchange for the concession of extensive rights of control, would in fact not mean the control of industry by the state but the control of the state by industry. What is more, this would take a most unpleasant form. Within the cartels the representatives

---

[13] This concept of a 'national communal economy' (*Gemeinwirtschaft*) is another formulation of the idea of the corporatist state. W. Rathenau and W. von Moellendorff were leading exponents of this programme. Von Moellendorff was the author of *Deutsche Gemeinwirtschaft* (Berlin, 1916).

of the state would sit at the same table as the factory owners (*Fabrikherren*) who would be far superior to them in knowledge of their industry, in commercial training, and in the degree of their self-interest. In parliament, however, would sit the representatives of the workers, and they would demand that those state representatives must ensure high wages on the one hand and low prices on the other; for, they would say, they would have the power to do so. On the other hand, in order not to ruin its finances, the state, which would be sharing in the profit and loss of such a syndicate, would naturally have an interest in high prices and low wages. Finally, the private members of the syndicates would expect the state to guarantee the profitability of their concerns. In the eyes of the workers, therefore, such a state would appear to be a class state in the truest sense of the word, and I doubt whether that is politically desirable. I have even greater doubts about whether it would be prudent to represent this state of affairs now to the workers as genuinely 'true' socialism, although there may seem to be an obvious temptation to do so. For the workers would very soon discover that the fate of a worker who works in a mine does not change in the slightest if the pit is a private or a state concern. The life of a worker in the coal-mines of the Saar is just the same as in a private pit: if the pit is badly run, showing little profit, then things are bad for the men too. The difference, however, is that it is impossible to strike against the state, so that the dependence of the worker is quite substantially increased under this kind of state socialism. That is one of the reasons why social democracy is generally opposed to this 'joint state management' of the economy, this form of socialism. It is a community of cartelisation. As before, what matters is profit – the question of how much is earned by the individual industrialists who have joined forces in the cartel, of which the state exchequer is now one, continues to determine the lines along which the economy is run. The embarrassing thing would be that, whereas the political and private-economic bureaucracies (of syndicates, banks, and giant concerns) exist alongside one another at present, as separate entities, so that economic power can still be curbed by political power, the two bureaucracies would then be a single body with identical interests and could no longer be supervised or controlled. In any event, profit would not be done away with as the lode-star of production. Yet the state as such would then have to take its share of the workers' hatred, which is directed at the entrepreneurs at present.

The outright antithesis of this, in the last-named respect, could only be represented by something like a consumer organisation, which would ask: which *needs* are to be satisfied within the area of this state economy? You are probably aware that numerous consumer associations, notably in Belgium, have gone over to setting up their own factories. If one imagined this principle being extended and put in the hands of a state organisation, it would be a totally and fundamentally different kind of socialism – a socialism of the consumers. To date no one has the slightest notion of where its leaders are to come from, and it is quite obscure where the interested parties might be found who would bring it into being. Experience has shown that consumers as such are only capable of organisation to a very limited extent. People with a specific commercial interest can be brought together very easily when they are shown that by doing so they achieve a profit or their profitability will be guaranteed; this is what makes it possible to create a 'socialism of entrepreneurs' of the kind represented by 'joint state management'. On the other hand it is extraordinarily difficult to unite people who have nothing in common except their desire to buy things, or to provide for themselves, because the whole situation of the purchaser is a barrier to socialisation; even the present starvation, in Germany at least, has not been able to persuade the housewives from the mass of the population (or has only done so with great difficulty) to accept war canteen meals, which everyone found excellently prepared and palatable, instead of their own amateurish individual cooking, although the canteen meals were far cheaper.

Having made these preliminary observations, I come finally to the kind of socialism to which the socialist mass parties as they are today, that is the social-democratic parties, are wedded in their programmes. The document which lays the foundation of this form of socialism is the Communist Manifesto, written in 1847 and published and distributed in January 1848 by Karl Marx and Friedrich Engels. Of its kind this document, however strongly we may reject its crucial theses (at least *I* do), is a scholarly achievement of the highest order. One cannot deny this, nor may one do so, because nobody would believe one's denial and because it is impossible to deny it with a clear conscience. Even the theses in it which we nowadays reject contain an inspired error which has had very far-reaching and perhaps not always pleasant political consequences, but which has had very fruitful effects on scholarship, more so than many a work of uninspired correctness. One thing must be said at the outset about the *Communist Manifesto*: it refrains, in intention if not always in its execution, from moralising. It simply does not occur to the authors of the *Communist Manifesto*, at least according to their own contention (in reality they were men of very strong feelings who by no means always remained true to this claim), to rant about the baseness and wickedness of the world. Nor do they think it is their task to say, 'This or that is arranged in a particular way in the world and it should be arranged differently, namely in such and such a way.' Rather the *Communist Manifesto* is a prophetic document; it *prophesies* the demise of the private economic, or, as it is usually called, capitalist organisation of society, and the replacement of this society, as a transitional stage in the first instance, by a dictatorship of the proletariat. However, beyond this transitional stage lies the true, ultimate hope: the proletariat *cannot* free itself from servitude without putting an end to *all* rule by man over man. That is the real prophecy, the core of the manifesto, without which it would never have been written and without which it would never have achieved its great historical effect. How is this prophecy to be fulfilled? That is stated in one of the cardinal points of the manifesto: the proletariat, the mass of the workers, will first, through their leaders, seize political power for themselves. However, this is a transitional stage which will lead to an 'association of individuals', as it is called there. This, then, is the last stage of historical development.

The *Communist Manifesto* is silent about what this association will look like, as are all the manifestos of all socialist parties. We are informed that this is something one cannot know. It is only possible to say that our present society is doomed, that it will fall by a law of nature, and that it will be replaced in the first instance by the dictatorship of the proletariat. But of what comes after that, nothing can yet be foretold, except that there will be no rule by man over man.

What reasons are advanced for the claim that the demise of the present form of society is made inevitable by a law of nature? For it takes place strictly according to the law of nature: that was the second central tenet of this solemn prophecy which won for it the jubilant faith of the masses. At one point Engels uses the following image: just as the planet earth will eventually plunge into the sun, so this capitalist society is doomed to destruction.[14] What reasons are advanced for this?

The first is as follows: a social class like the bourgeoisie – by which is always meant, in the first instance, the entrepreneurs and all those who directly or indirectly have a community of interest with them – such a ruling class can only maintain its rule if it can guarantee at least bare subsistence to the subjugated class, the wage-earners. That, say the authors, was the case with slavery, it was so under the system of enforced labour on the manorial farm, and so on. Here the people were assured of at least bare subsistence, therefore the rule of the ruling classes could be maintained. The modern bourgeoisie cannot do this, however. It is unable to do so, because competition between entrepreneurs compels them to undercut one other progressively and, thanks to the creation of new machines, repeatedly to throw workers breadless on the streets. They must have at their disposal a broad stratum of the unemployed, the so-called 'industrial reserve army', from which they can at any time select any number of suitable workers for their factories, and it is precisely this stratum that is being created by increasing mechanical automation. The result is, however, or so the *Communist Manifesto* still believed, that an ever-increasing class of the permanently unemployed, of 'paupers'[15] appears, and under-cuts the minimum subsistence level, so that the proletarian stratum does not even get its bare means of livelihood guaranteed by this social order. Where this is the case, society becomes untenable, and at some point it collapses as the result of a revolution.

This so-called theory of immiseration, in *this* form, has nowadays been abandoned as incorrect, explicitly and without exception by all sections of Social Democracy. In the jubilee edition of the *Communist Manifesto* it was expressly conceded by its editor, Karl Kautsky, that developments had taken another path and not this one. The thesis is upheld in a different, re-interpreted form which, incidentally, is also not undisputed, but which at any rate has shed its former, pathos-laden character. Be that as it may, on what basis could a

---

[14] Weber is referring to Engels, *Socialism: Utopian and Scientific*, in K. Marx and F. Engels, *Selected Works* (Moscow, 1962), p. 143.

[15] Weber uses the English word.

revolution have any chance of *succeeding?* Might it not be doomed to fail over and over again?

This brings us to the second argument: competition between entrepreneurs means victory for the man who is stronger by virtue of his capital and his business abilities, but above all his capital. This means an ever-diminishing number of entrepreneurs, since the weaker ones are eliminated. The smaller this number of entrepreneurs becomes, the greater, in relative and absolute terms, become the numbers of the proletariat. At some point, however, the number of entrepreneurs will have contracted so far that it will be impossible for them to maintain their rule, and then it will be possible, perhaps quite peaceably and politely – let us say, in return for a life-annuity – to expropriate these 'expropriators', for they will see that the ground has become so hot under their feet, and that they are now so few in number, that they cannot maintain their rule.

This thesis, albeit in modified form, is still upheld today. However, it has become clear that, nowadays at least, it is not *generally* correct in any form. In the first place, it is not valid for agriculture where, on the contrary, there has been a greater increase in the numbers of farmers in very many cases. Furthermore, it has proved to be not so much incorrect, as different in its consequences from what was expected, as far as large sections of industry are concerned, where it has become clear that a simple contraction in the number of entrepreneurs is not the whole process. The elimination of those with a weak capital base takes the form of their subjugation by finance capital, by organisations of cartels or trusts. As a side-effect of these very complex processes, however, a rapid rise in the number of clerks, in the *bureaucracy* of the private sector, takes place – its growth rate being statistically much greater than that of the workers – and it is far from clear that the interests of these bureaucrats point in the direction of a proletarian dictatorship. Then there is the creation of highly diverse and very complicated types of interest-participation, which means that one cannot maintain at present that there is a decline in the power and number of those with direct and indirect vested interests in the bourgeois order. For the time being, at any rate, it is not the case that one could give a definite assurance that in the future only half a dozen, a few hundred or a few thousand capitalist magnates will confront, in isolation. millions upon millions of proletarians.

The third argument, finally, was the calculation of the effects of crises. Because entrepreneurs compete with one another (and then there follows an important but very involved discussion in the classic socialist texts, which I must spare you), it is inevitable that periods of overproduction will constantly recur, alternating with bankruptcies, collapses and so-called 'depressions'. Marx only hinted at this in the *Communist Manifesto*, but it later became a minutely elaborated theory – these periods follow one another at fixed intervals, with the regularity of a law. In fact, such crises have recurred with approximate regularity for nearly a century. As even the leading scholars in our subject are not yet completely agreed as to the reasons for this, it would be quite out of the question to discuss it here at the moment.

Classic socialism, then, built its hopes on these crises. It hoped above all that, by a law of nature, they would increase in intensity and destructive power, producing a frightening mood of revolution, that they would accumulate and multiply and at some point create such an atmosphere that the preservation of this economic order would no longer be attempted even in non-proletarian circles.

Essentially this hope has been abandoned today. For although the danger of a crisis has certainly not disappeared, its relative importance has decreased now that entrepreneurs have moved from ruthless competition to the creation of cartels, in other words since they began to eliminate competition to a large extent by the regulation of prices and turnover, and, furthermore, now that the great banks, including, for example, the German Reichsbank, have taken steps to ensure, by the regulation of credit supply, that periods of over-speculation also occur to a much lesser extent than before. Thus, while we cannot say that it 'has proved to be unfounded', this third hope of the *Communist Manifesto* and its successors has at least undergone a major shift in its presuppositions.

Thus the hopes, full of high pathos, which the *Communist Manifesto* once placed in the collapse of bourgeois society have been replaced by very much more sober expectations. These include, firstly, the theory that socialism will come about of its own accord, by evolution, because economic production is becoming increasingly 'socialised'. What this means is that share companies with salaried managers are taking the place of individual entrepreneurs, and that businesses belonging to the state, municipalities and single-purpose associations are being set up which are no longer to be based, as before, on the risk and profit of a single (or indeed any) private entrepreneur. This is accurate, though it must be added that a share company very often conceals one or several financial magnates who control the general meeting; every shareholder knows that shortly before the annual general meeting he will receive a communication from his bank asking him to make over his vote to them, if he does not wish to go and vote himself, which is pointless for him in the face of a capital of millions of crowns. Above all, however, this kind of socialisation means on the one hand an increase of *officialdom*, of specialist, commercially or technically trained clerks, and on the other, an increase in the numbers of *rentiers*, a stratum of people who just draw dividends and interest, without doing mental work for it, as the entrepreneur does, but who are committed to the capitalist system through their interests in all their sources of income. It is in publicly owned concerns and those of single-purpose associations, however, that the *official*, not the worker, rules completely and exclusively; here it is more difficult for the worker to achieve anything by strike action than it is against private entrepreneurs. It is the dictatorship of the official, not that of the worker, which, for the present at any rate, is on the advance.

Secondly, there is the hope that the machine, as it causes the old class of specialists, the skilled craftsman and those highly skilled workers who filled the old English Trade Unions,[16] to be replaced by unskilled workers and thus makes anyone capable of working at any machine, will bring about such unity in the working class that the old division into different occupations will cease, the consciousness of this unity will become overwhelming and will benefit the struggle against the propertied class. The answer to this is not entirely uniform. It is correct that the machine tries to replace to a very great extent the highly paid and skilled workers, for every industry naturally seeks to introduce precisely those machines which will replace the workers who are hardest to come by. The fastest growing stratum in industry today is that of the so-called 'semi-skilled' workers, that is not the skilled workers who, under the old scheme, followed a particular course of instruction, but those who are put directly at the machine and trained on the spot. Even so, many of them are still

---

[16] Weber uses the English term: 'die alten englischen Gewerkschaften, die Trade Unions'.

specialists to a considerable extent. It takes several years, for example, for a weaver trained like this to reach the highest degree of skill, that is to make the fullest use of the machine for the entrepreneur and earn the highest wage for himself. Certainly, the typical normal training period for other categories of workers is substantially less than for that cited here. Nevertheless, while this increase in semi-skilled workers means a noticeable decline in occupational specialisation, it does not mean its elimination. On the other side, professional specialisation and the need for specialist education are growing at all levels in production *above* that of the workers, down to the chargehand and the overseer, while the relative number of persons belonging to this stratum is growing at the same time. Admittedly, they too are 'wage slaves', but they are mostly not on piece-wages or weekly wages, but on a fixed salary. Above all, the worker naturally hates the foreman, who is perpetually breathing down his neck, far more than the factory owner, and the factory owner in turn more than the shareholder, although the shareholder is the one who really draws his income *without* working, while the industrialist has to do very arduous mental work, and the foreman stands much closer still to the worker. The same thing happens in the army: in general it is the corporal who attracts the strongest antipathy or at least is likely to do so, as far as I have been able to observe. In any case, the development of the entire stratification is far from being unequivocally proletarian.

Finally, there is the argument based on the increasing standardisation or uniformity of production. Everything everywhere seems to be striving – and war in particular promotes this tendency to a high degree – towards increasing uniformity and interchangeability of products, and more and more extensive schematisation of businesses. Only in the highest circle of entrepreneurs, they say, does the old, free, pioneer spirit of the bourgeois entrepreneurs of the past still rule, and even here it is in steady decline. Consequently, so the argument runs, it is becoming ever more possible to manage this new production even if one does not have the specific entrepreneurial qualities which bourgeois society insists are indispensable for business. This supposedly holds true of cartels and trusts in particular, which have installed a huge staff of officials in place of individual entrepreneurs. This again is very true, but again only with the same reservation, namely that this standardisation too enhances the importance of one social stratum, that of the officials, who have to be *edu-*

cated in a quite definite way, and who therefore (it must be added) have the character of a definite *estate*. It is no coincidence that we see commercial high schools, trade and technical colleges springing up like mushrooms everywhere. At least in Germany, this is due in part to the desire to join a student 'colours' fraternity at these colleges, to get scars on one's face, to become capable of 'giving satisfaction' in a duel and therefore of being an officer in the Reserve, and later on in the office to have a better chance of the hand of the boss's daughter – in other words, the desire to be assimilated into the strata of so-called 'society'. Nothing is further from the minds of this class than solidarity with the proletariat; indeed, their aim is, rather, to differentiate themselves increasingly from the proletariat. In varying degrees, but noticeably, the same is true of many sub-strata among these office workers. They all strive at least for similar qualities of this *estate*, be it for themselves or for their children. One cannot say that an *unambiguous* trend towards proletarianisation exists today.

Be that as it may, these arguments show at any rate that the old revolutionary hope of catastrophe, which lent the *Communist Manifesto* its emotive power, has given way to an evolutionary view which sees the old economy with its masses of competing enterprises gradually growing into a regulated economy, whether this regulation is to be carried out by officials of the state or by cartels with the participation of officials. This, rather than the fusion of individual firms under the pressure of competition and crises, now emerges as the preliminary to a truly socialist society in which men will no longer rule over men. This evolutionary mood, which expects the socialist society of the future to develop out of this slow transformation, had in fact already replaced the old catastrophe theory in the minds of the trade unions and many socialist intellectuals before the war. This led people to draw the familiar conclusions. So-called 'revisionism' came into being. Some of its own leaders were at least partially aware that it was a grave step to deprive the masses of their faith in the sudden dawning of a blissful future, a faith which had been given to them by a gospel which proclaimed, like the Christians of old: 'Salvation may come this very night.' A creed such as the *Communist Manifesto* and the later catastrophe theory can be dethroned, but then it is almost impossible to replace it with another. Meanwhile, developments have long since overtaken this debate in the struggle with the old orthodoxy, which arose out of scruples about the orthodox faith. The struggle became mixed up with the question of whether, and how far, Social Democracy, as a party, should engage in 'practical politics' in the sense of entering coalitions with bourgeois parties, participating in politically responsible leadership by taking over ministerial posts, and thereby endeavouring to improve the present lot of the workers; or whether that would be 'class treachery' and political heresy, as the confirmed politician of catastrophe would naturally be bound to regard it. Meanwhile, however, other questions of principle have arisen, and on them opinions are divided. Let us suppose that by a process of gradual evolution, entailing general cartelisation, standardisation and bureaucratisation, the economy were to develop in such a way that it would be technically possible at some point to introduce a form of regulation to replace today's private, entrepreneurial economic system, and hence private ownership of the means of production, thus completely eliminating the entrepreneur. *Who* would then take over and command this new economy? On this point the *Communist Manifesto* remained resolutely silent, or rather it expressed itself very ambiguously.

What is that 'association', of which the Manifesto speaks, to look like? What, in particular, can socialism show by way of germ cells of such organisations, in case the opportunity should in fact ever come its way of seizing power and exercising it as it pleases? In the German Reich, and probably everywhere, socialism has two categories of organisation. Firstly, the political party of Social Democracy with its members of parliament, the editors, party officials and shop stewards it employs, and the local and central associations, by whom these people are elected or employed. Secondly, the trade unions. Each of these two organisations can assume *both* a revolutionary and an evolutionary character. On the question of which character they have, and which it is intended and desired that they should have in the future, opinions diverge.

If we take the hope of revolution as our starting point, there are two mutually opposed views. The first was that of normal Marxism, based on the old tradition of the *Communist Manifesto*. It pinned all its expectations on the *political* dictatorship of the proletariat and considered it necessary to regard the political *party* organisation, inevitably tailored to the *election* campaign, as the vehicle of this dictatorship. The party, or a political dictator with its support, was to seize political power and this was to lead to the new organisation of society.

This revolutionary tendency turned against two sets of opponents. Firstly, those trade unions which were nothing more than trade unions in the old English sense, which is to say, with absolutely no interest in these plans for the future because they seemed a long way off, and chiefly intent on fighting for the working conditions which would make life possible for them and their children: high wages, short working hours, industrial protection and so on. Radical political Marxism turned against this kind of trade unionism on the one hand. On the other it opposed what has been called 'Millerandism' since Millerand became a minister in France, the exclusively parliamentary form taken by socialism's policy of compromise. That, the revolutionaries say, is a policy which leads to the leaders being much more interested in their ministerial portfolios and to the lower-level leaders being more interested in getting an official position than in revolution; this, they allege, kills the revolutionary spirit. The 'radical', 'orthodox' line, in the old sense, has been joined by a new one in the course of the last few decades which is usually termed 'syndicalism', from *syndicat*, the French term for the trade union. Just as the old radicalism wants the aim of the political party organisation to be given a revolutionary interpretation, so syndicalism wants a revolutionary interpretation of the trade unions. It starts from the assumption that it will not be political dicatorship, not the political leaders, and not the officials who are appointed by these political leaders, but the trade unions and their federation who, when the great moment has come, will take the control of the economy into their own hands via so-called *action directe*. Syndicalism derives from a somewhat stricter understanding of the *class* character of the movement. The working class is to be the bearer of the final liberation. All those politicians who loaf about the capital cities and are only interested in how this or that ministry is doing or what chance this or that parliamentary constellation has, are people with vested political interests, not class comrades. Behind their interests in their constituency there are always the interests of editors and private officials who wish to profit from the number of votes gained. Syndicalism rejects all these interests which are bound up with the modern parliamentary electoral system. Only the real working class, which is organised in the trade unions, can create the new society. Away with the professional politicians who live for, which in truth means *from* politics, and not for the creation of a new economic society. The typical instruments of the syndicalists are the general strike and terror. They hope that the general strike (through the sudden paralysis of all production) will impel those involved, in particular the entrepreneurs, to renounce their management of the factories and place it in the hands of committees to be formed by the trade unions. Terror, which some proclaim openly, some secretly, and some reject – opinions diverge here – is what this organisation is to strike into the ranks of the decisive ruling strata in order to paralyse them politically as well. This syndicalism is, of course, the form of socialism which really is a quite ruthless opponent of any kind of army organisation, since every kind of army organisation creates interested parties, right down to the N.C.O., even to the ordinary soldier who, temporarily at least, is dependent for his food on the functioning of the military and state machine, is therefore partially interested in the actual failure of the general strike, and is an obstacle to it at the least. Its opponents are, firstly, all political socialist parties which are active in parliament. At most parliament could be used by the syndicalists as a rostrum from which to proclaim constantly, under the protection of parliamentary immunity, that the general strike will and must come, and thereby whip up the revolutionary passions of the masses. Even this distracts syndicalism from its real task, however, and is therefore suspect; however, to practise parliamentary politics seriously is not merely nonsense but, from this point of view, simply objectionable. Among their opponents are, of course, all evolutionists of every kind. These may be trade unionists who just want to fight to improve working conditions; on the contrary, the syndicalists must argue, the poorer the wages, the longer the working hours, the worse the conditions in general, the greater is the chance of a general strike. Or they may be the party-political type of evolutionists, who say the state today is growing into socialism because of increasing democratisation (for which the syndicalists have the greatest abhorrence – they prefer tsarism). In the view of the syndicalists this is of course gross self-deception, to say the least. Now the critical question is this: where do the syndicalists hope to find people to take charge of production? For it would of course be a grave error to think that a trade unionist, however highly trained, even if he has been at his job for years and knows the *working* conditions perfectly, therefore understands the *running* (*Betrieb*) of the factory as such, since the management of all modern factories is based entirely on calculation, knowledge of the products, knowledge of demand and technical schooling – all things which need increasingly to be practised by specialists, and which the trade unionists, the real workers, have absolutely no opportunity to learn about. Therefore, whether they like it or not, they too will have to rely on *non*-workers, on ideologues from the intellectual strata. Indeed it is remarkable that – in flat contradiction of the dictum that salvation can only come from the real workers uniting in the trade union federation and not from politicians or any outsiders – within the syndicalist movement, which had its main centres in France and Italy before the war, there are vast numbers of intellectuals with a university education. What are they looking for in syndicalism? It is the *romanticism* of the general strike and the *romanticism* of the hope of revolution as such which enchants (*bezaubert*)[17] these intellectuals. If one looks at them, one can see that they are romantics, emotionally unfit for everyday life or averse to it and its demands, and who therefore hunger and thirst after the great revolutionary miracle – and the opportunity of feeling that even they will be in power one day. Of course, there are men of organisational gifts amongst them. The question is whether the workers would submit to their dictatorship. Certainly, in wartime, with the incredible upheavals it brings in its wake, and because of the fate the workers endure, especially under the effects of hunger, even the mass of the workers may be seized by syndicalist ideas and, if they have weapons to hand, they may seize power under the leadership of such intellectuals, if the political and military collapse of a state affords them the opportunity to do so. However, I cannot see people with the skills to manage production in peacetime either amongst the trade union members themselves or among the syndicalist intellectuals. The great experiment now is: Russia. The difficulty is that today we cannot look over the border to find out how the management of production is being carried on in reality. From what one hears, what is happening is the following: the Bolshevik government, which, as we know, consists of intellec-

---

[17] Syndicalism is, for Weber, an example of a way of thinking and feeling which is attractive because it seems to restore to the world the 'enchantment' (*Zauber*) which the advance of rationality is destroying everywhere in a process of 'Entzauberung der Welt'; see, for example, *Max Weber's 'Science as a Vocation'*, ed. P. Lassman and I. Velody (London, 1989), p. 30.

tuals, some of whom studied here in Vienna and in Germany and among whom there are only a few Russians, has now gone over to the re-introduction of piece work in those factories which are working at all – 10 per cent of peacetime production, according to Social Democratic reports – for the reason that output would suffer otherwise. They leave the entrepreneurs at the head of the firms because they alone have the expert knowledge, and pay them very considerable subventions. Furthermore, they have adopted the practice of paying officers' salaries to officers of the old regime, because they need an army and have realised that is impossible without trained officers. Whether these officers, when they once again have the troops under their command, will continue to put up with being led by these intellectuals, seems questionable to me. For the moment, of course, they have been obliged to do so. Finally, by withdrawing the bread card, the Bolsheviks have forced part of the bureaucracy to work for them too. However, in the long term the state machinery and economy cannot be run in this way, and the experiment is as yet not very encouraging.

The astonishing thing is simply that this organisation has functioned at all for as long as it has. It has been able to do so because it is a military dictatorship, not, it is true, of generals, but of corporals, and because the war-weary soldiers returning from the front joined forces with the land-hungry peasants, accustomed to agrarian communism, or the soldiers with their weapons took possession of the villages by force, exacting contributions there and shooting down anyone who came too near them. It is the only large-scale experiment with a 'proletarian dictatorship' to have been undertaken to date, and we can give an assurance, in all honesty, that on the German side the discussions in Brest–Litovsk were conducted in complete good faith, in the hope of achieving real peace with these people. This happened for a variety of reasons: those who had vested interests in bourgeois society were in favour of this approach because they said, 'For Heaven's sake, let us allow them to carry out their experiment. It is bound to fail and then it will serve as a warning.' The rest of us were in favour because we said, 'If this experiment were to succeed and we were to see that culture is possible on this basis, then we would be converted.'

The man who prevented that happening was Herr Trotsky, who was not content to carry out this experiment in his own house and to place his hopes on the fact that, if it succeeded, it would result in unrivalled propaganda for socialism throughout the whole world. With the typical vanity of the Russian littérateur, he wanted more, and he hoped, by means of wars of words and the misuse of such words as 'peace' and 'self-determination', to unleash civil war in Germany. He was, however, so ill-informed as to be ignorant of the fact that at least two-thirds of the German army is recruited from the countryside and a further one-sixth from the petite bourgeoisie, for whom it would be a genuine pleasure to slap down the workers, or anyone else who wanted to start any such revolution. One cannot make peace with people who are fighting for their faith. One can only render them harmless, and that was the meaning of the ultimatum and the enforced peace at Brest. Every socialist must realise this, and I do not know any, of whatever direction, who does not realise it, at least inwardly.

When one gets into discussion with today's socialists and wishes to proceed *in good faith* (which is the only prudent course), there are, in the present situation, two questions to put to them. Firstly: What is their attitude towards evolutionism, that is, to the notion which is a fundamental dogma of what is nowadays regarded as orthodox Marxism, namely that society and its economic system is evolving strictly in accordance with the laws of nature, by stages, as it were, and that therefore a socialist society can never come about anywhere until bourgeois society has reached full maturity? This, even in socialist opinion, is not yet the case anywhere, for there are still small peasants and artisans. What, then, is the attitude of the socialists in question to this basic evolutionary dogma? It will then emerge that, outside Russia 'at least', they *all* base themselves on this assumption, that is all of them, even the most radical of them, expect a *bourgeois* social order, *not* a society led by the proletariat, to come about as the only possible outcome of a revolution, because nowhere is the time yet ripe for the latter. They hope simply that the social order, in some of its features, will be a few steps nearer to that final stage from which, it is hoped, the transition to the socialist order of the future will one day result.

If asked to answer on his conscience, every honest socialist intellectual will have to give this reply. As a result, there is indeed a broad stratum of Social Democrats within Russia, the so-called Mensheviks, who take the point of view that this Bolshevik experiment of grafting a socialist order onto the current state of bourgeois society from above is not only nonsense, it is an offence against Marxist dogma. The terrible mutual hatred of these two factions stems from this dogmatic charge of heresy.

Now if the overwhelming majority of the leaders, at least all the ones I have ever known, take this evolutionary position, one is of course justified in asking the question: 'What, in these circumstances, particularly in wartime, is a revolution actually supposed to achieve, from their own point of view?' It may bring civil war and with it, perhaps, victory for the Entente, but not a socialist society; moreover it can and will bring about, amidst the ruins of the state, a regiment of vested interests from the peasantry and the petite bourgeoisie, that is, the most radical opponents of *any* kind of socialism. Above all, it would bring with it immense destruction of capital and disorganisation, retarding the social development demanded by Marxism, which, after all, presupposes the progressive saturation of the economy with capital. Yet one must remember that the West European *farmer* is a different type from the Russian peasant living in his agrarian communism. There the crucial point is the land question, which is not important at all here. The German farmer, at least, is an individualist nowadays and clings to his inheritance and his soil. He is unlikely to be persuaded otherwise. He is more likely to ally himself with the large landed proprietor than with the radical socialist worker, if he believes there is any threat to these things.

From the point of view of socialist hopes for the future, then, the prospects for a wartime revolution are now the worst imaginable, even if it were to succeed. Under the most favourable circumstances, it could only mean that *political* arrangements would approach the form desired by democracy; this, however, would pull it away from socialism because of the *economically* reactionary consequences it would be bound to have. No fair-minded socialist may deny that either.

The second question is the attitude towards *peace*. We are all aware that radical socialism today has become fused with pacifist leanings in the minds of the masses, with the desire for peace to be concluded as quickly as possible. Now it is quite clear, and every leader of radical, that is truly revolutionary Social Democracy, must, if asked, admit honestly, that for him, the *leader*, peace is *not* his most decisive concern. 'If we have the choice,' he is bound to say, if he is quite candid, 'between another three years' war and then revolution on the one hand, and immediate peace *without* revolution on the other, then of course we are in favour of the three years' war.' Let him settle this with his fanaticism and his conscience. The question is, however, whether the majority of the troops who have to stick it out in the field, including the socialists, hold the same opinion as the leaders who dictate this sort of thing to them. And of course it is only fair and completely in order to compel them to show their colours. It has been clearly admitted that Trotsky did *not* want peace. Nowadays, no socialist I know disputes that any longer. But the same applies to the radical leaders in every country. Given the choice, they too would *not* want peace above all else. If it served the cause of revolution, that is civil war, they would rather choose war. War in the interest of revolution, *although* in their own opinion (I repeat) this revolution *cannot* lead to a socialist society; they hope only that it will lead, at most, to a 'higher' (from a socialist standpoint) stage of development of bourgeois society, one which would be somewhat nearer than that of today (how much, it is impossible to say) to the socialist society that will arrive sometime in the future. Yet, for the reasons outlined above, precisely this hope is extremely dubious.

A debate with convinced socialists and revolutionaries is always an awkward affair. In my experience, one never convinces them. One can only force them into showing their colours to their own supporters on the question of peace on the one hand, and on the question of what revolution is actually supposed to achieve on the other, that is on the question of evolution by stages, which remains a tenet of true Marxism to the present day and has only been rejected in Russia by a local sect there who thought Russia could simply miss out these West European stages of development. This is a thoroughly fair way to proceed, as well as being the only effective or possible one. For it is my opinion that there is no way to eliminate socialist convictions and socialist hopes. Every working class will always return to socialism in some sense or other. The only question is whether this socialism is one that can be tolerated, from the point of view of the interests of the state, and, at present in particular, from the point of view of military interests. No form of rule, not even a proletarian one, like that of the Paris Commune or that of the Bolsheviks at present, has ever got by without martial law when there was a threat to the foundations of its discipline. This much Trotsky conceded with laudable honesty. But the more surely the troops feel that the conduct of the military courts is determined only by the *objective* (*sachlich*) interest in maintaining discipline, (and *not* by the interests of any class or party), so that only what is *objectively* inevitable in war occurs, the more unshaken the foundations of military authority will remain.

The President of the Reich[1]

The first president of the Reich was elected by the National Assembly. *In future the president of the Reich absolutely must be elected directly by the people.* The decisive reasons for this are as follows:

(1) Regardless of whatever name it is given and whatever changes are made to its powers, the Bundesrat will under all circumstances be *carried over into the new constitution of the Reich in one form or another*, for it is utterly Utopian to imagine that the bearers of governmental authority and state power, namely the governments installed by the peoples of the individual free states, will allow themselves to be excluded from the process of shaping the will of the Reich and above all from the administration of the Reich. It is therefore *essential* for us to create a *head of state* resting *unquestionably on the will of the whole people*, without the intervention of intermediaries. Indirect elections have been abolished everywhere; are they then to be preserved here, for the election of the highest office? That would be regarded, quite rightly, as a mockery of the democratic principle in favour of the interest members of parliament have in horse-trading, and it would discredit the unity of the Reich.

(2) Only a president of the Reich who has the votes of millions of people behind him can have the authority to initiate the process

---

[1] 'Der Reichspräsident' was first published in the *Berliner Börsenzeitung*, 25 February 1919, following the election of Friedrich Ebert as German President by the National Assembly, but was then revised by Weber, so that it appeared in its final form in the *Königsberger Hartungsche Zeitung* of 15 March 1919.

of socialisation. Whereas legal paragraphs will do nothing to bring this about, a tightly unified administration will achieve everything. Socialisation means administration, regardless of whether one wants to introduce it merely as an unavoidable financial measure or, as the Social Democrats intend, in order to re-shape the economy.[2] It is not the task of the Reich constitution to lay down the economic order of the future. Its function is to clear a path for every conceivable task with which the administration might be confronted and to make it possible for these tasks, including this one, to be achieved. I hope very much that the Social Democratic Party will not close its mind to these necessities because of a set of misconceived, petit-bourgeois and pseudo-democratic ideas. The Social Democrats should remember that the much discussed 'dictatorship' of the masses demands a 'dictator', a *spokesman elected by the masses themselves*[3] to whom they will subordinate themselves as long as he enjoys their trust. A collective headship of state, in which all the major states in the Federation and each of the major parties would naturally demand to be represented, or a head of state elected by parliament, who would be burdened with the wretched impotence of the French president, could never impose that unity on the administration without which it will be impossible to rebuild our economy on whatever basis is chosen. Let us ensure that the president of the Reich sees the prospect of the gallows as the reward awaiting any attempt to interfere with the laws or to govern autocratically. Let us also debar all members of the dynasties from this office in order to prevent any restoration by means of a plebiscite. But let us put the presidency of the Reich on a firm democratic footing of its own.

[2] Weber is referring to the plans of the Socialisation Commission which sat from November 1918 until March 1919. Among its members were Karl Kautsky, Rudolf Hilferding and Joseph Schumpeter. The plans of the Commission for the nationalisation of heavy industry were distinct from the ideas of economic management represented by Rathenau and von Moellendorf, whose supporters opposed the Commission's work. Apart from the passing of a general Socialisation Law, such plans came to nothing.

[3] Weber's phrasing is rather ambiguous here. He writes of a 'selbstgewählten Vertrauensmann der Massen', which could either mean a 'self-elected spokesman of the masses' or, more plausibly in this context, a 'spokesman chosen by the masses themselves'. This reading is supported by the end of the essay, where it is very unlikely that 'selbstgewählte Führer' can mean anything other than 'leaders elected by the people themselves'.

(3) Only the election of the president of the Reich by the people will provide an opportunity and occasion to *select leaders* and hence also to reorganise the parties along lines which will supersede the completely antiquated system of management by notables that has existed up till now. If this system were to continue in existence, it would mean the end of politically and economically progressive democracy for the foreseeable future. The elections have shown that the old professional politicians have succeeded everywhere, in defiance of the mood of the mass of voters, in excluding the men who enjoy the trust of the masses in favour of political 'shopminders'. As a result, there has been a radical rejection of all politics by precisely the very best minds. Only the popular election of the highest functionary of the Reich can create an outlet here.

(4) The need for this is increased by the *effects of proportional representation*.[4] The next elections will bring to fruition something which was only beginning to become apparent during the last elections: occupational associations (*Berufsverbände*) (houseowners, holders of diplomas, those in salaried occupations, 'leagues' of every kind) will force the parties to put at the top of their lists the paid secretaries of these associations, simply to win votes. In this way parliament will become a body in which those who set the tone will be persons who regard national politics as 'Hecuba'[5] and whose actions are in fact subject to the 'imperative' mandate of vested economic interests, a *parliament of closed, philistine minds*, in no sense capable of serving as a place where political leaders are selected. This must be said openly and quite plainly. Taken together with the circumstance that the resolutions of the Bundesrat are to a considerable extent binding on the Minister President (Reichskanzler), this inevitably puts a limit on the purely political importance of parliament as such, which makes it absolutely essential to have a counterweight resting on the democratic will of the people.

---

[4] The constitution of the Weimar Republic, which came into force on 14 August 1919, specifies a complicated form of proportional representation. Weber is referring to the discussion of the drafts of the constitution which preceded its promulgation.

[5] *Hamlet*, Act 2, Scene 2:
> What's Hecuba to him, or he to Hecuba,
> That he should weep for her?

(5) Particularism cries out for a *bearer of the principle of the unity of the Reich*. We do not know whether the development of purely regional parties will continue to gain ground. There is certainly a mood in favour of it. In the long run this will inevitably have an effect on the formation of majorities and on the composition of the Reich ministries. The electoral movement produced by the appointment of a popularly elected president of the Reich will create a dam to prevent such one-sided tendencies getting out of hand, for it will force the parties to communicate and to have a unified organisation throughout the Reich, just as the popularly elected president of the Reich will himself represent a counterweight to the – unfortunately unavoidable – Bundesrat in the interests of the unity of the Reich, while yet not threatening all the individual states with subjection to *force majeure*.

(6) Previously, when we had an authoritarian state, one had to argue for the power of the majority in parliament to be increased, so as to raise, at long last, the importance and therefore the quality of parliament. The situation today is that all constitutional proposals have succumbed to crude, blind faith in the infallibility and omnipotence of the majority – of the majority in parliament, that is, not of the people. We have gone to the opposite, but equally undemocratic extreme. Let the power of the popularly elected president be subjected to whatever restrictions one will, and let us ensure that he is only permitted to intervene in the machinery of the Reich during temporary, irresoluble crises (by means of a *suspensory veto*[6] and the summoning of ministries headed by officials), and otherwise only by calling a *referendum*. *But let him be given his own ground to stand on by way of a popular election.* Otherwise the whole edifice of the Reich will be in danger of collapsing whenever there is a crisis in parliament, something which will not be unusual when there are at least four to five parties.

(7) Only a *president elected by the people* can have a role that is more than merely tolerated in Berlin *alongside the Prussian head of state*. Almost the entire patronage of office will be in the hands of the governments of the individual states, including those of the

[6] In contrast to an 'absolutes Veto', a 'suspensives Veto' is a limited power which makes it possible to delay the execution of a decision, but which cannot be re-applied if the same decision is presented for a second time in unchanged form.

Prussian head of state, particularly the appointment of all administrative officials who come into contact with the people in their everyday work, probably also at least the lower officer ranks in the army. A president of the Reich who had not been elected by the whole people would therefore play a pitiful role *vis-à-vis* the Prussian head of state, so that the predominance of Prussia in Berlin, and thus in the Reich, would again emerge in a highly dangerous, which is to say particularist, form.

It is quite understandable that members of parliament should be reluctant to practise self-denial by giving up their monopoly in electing the highest organ of the Reich. This must happen, however, and the movement in favour of it will not simply subside. Let democracy not place this weapon of anti-parliamentary agitation in the hands of its enemies. Rather, like those monarchs who acted not only with the greatest dignity but also most prudently when they limited their own power, at the right moment, in favour of parliamentary representative bodies, let parliament, of its own accord, recognise the Magna Charta of democracy, the right to the direct election of the leader. It will have no reason to regret this if ministers continue to be bound strictly by the confidence of parliament. The mighty current of democratic party life developing in relation to these popular elections will also benefit parliament. *Any president of the Reich elected by parliament under particular party constellations and coalitions will be politically dead as soon as there is a shift in that constellation.* A popularly elected president, as the head of the executive, of official patronage, and as the possessor of a delaying veto and the power to dissolve parliament and to consult the people, is the palladium of genuine democracy, which does not mean impotent self-abandonment to cliques but subordination to leaders one has chosen for oneself.

The Profession and Vocation of Politics[1]

The lecture which I am to give at your request will necessarily disappoint you in various ways. You are bound to expect a talk on the profession of politics to take a stand on the topical questions of the day. Yet that will only happen at the end of my lecture in a purely formal way and in response to particular questions concerning the significance of political action within our conduct of life as a whole. What must be completely excluded from today's lecture, on the other hand, are all questions concerning the *brand* of politics one *ought* to practise, which is to say the *content* one ought to give to one's political activity. For this has nothing to do with the general question of what the profession of politics is and what it can mean. Let us get straight down to things.

What do we understand by politics (*Politik*)? The term is an extraordinarily broad one, embracing every kind of independent *leadership* (*leitende*) activity. We talk about the banks' policies on foreign

---

[1] 'Politik als Beruf' appeared as a brochure in the series *Geistige Arbeit als Beruf. Vier Vorträge vor dem Freistudentischen Bund.* ('Intellectual work as a vocation. Four lectures to the Union of Free Students.') (Munich and Leipzig, 1919). Following the editorial change first made by Marianne Weber in the *Gesammelten politischen Schriften* and adopted by the editors of the new *Gesamtausgabe*, the tenth paragraph ('All organised rule . . . means of administration') has been shifted from its clearly erroneous position in the first edition, and certain misprints (e.g. *entlehnte* for *entlohnte*) corrected. Weber's essay is based on a lecture given in Munich in January 1919 but not published until October of that year. Here it appears after the 'President of the Reich' since this article actually appeared in print first; in conception, however, the lecture is clearly the earlier piece. In the title the term *Beruf* has been translated as 'profession and vocation' because the essay deals both with the business and organisation (*Betrieb*) of politics and also with the inner vocation of the dedicated politician.

exchange, the bank-rate policy of the *Reichsbank*, the policy of a union during a strike, one can speak of the educational policy of the community in a town or village, of the policies of the management committee leading a club, and finally we even talk about the policies of an astute wife in her efforts to guide her husband. Naturally, our reflections this evening are not based on a concept as broad as this. Today we shall use the term only to mean the leadership, or the exercise of influence on the leadership, of a *political* association (*Verband*), which today means a *state*.

Yet what is a 'political' association, considered from a sociological point of view? What is a 'state'? This too cannot be defined sociologically in terms of the content of its activities. There is hardly a task which has not been undertaken by some political association at some time or other, but equally there is no task of which it could be said that it is always, far less *exclusively*, the preserve of those associations which are defined as political (in today's language: states) or which were the historical predecessors of the modern state. In the last analysis the modern state can only be defined sociologically in terms of a specific *means* (*Mittel*) which is peculiar to the state, as it is to all other political associations, namely physical violence (*Gewaltsamkeit*). 'Every state is founded on force (*Gewalt*)', as Trotsky once said at Brest–Litovsk. That is indeed correct. If there existed only social formations in which violence was unknown as a means, *then* the concept of the 'state' would have disappeared; *then* that condition would have arisen which one would define, in this particular sense of the word, as 'anarchy'. Violence is, of course, not the normal or sole means used by the state. There is no question of that. But it is the means *specific* to the state. At the present moment[2] the relation between the state and violence is a particularly intimate one. In the past the most diverse kinds of association – beginning with the clan – have regarded physical violence as a quite normal instrument. Nowadays, by contrast, we have to say that a state is that human community which (successfully) lays claim to the *monopoly of legitimate physical*

---

[2] As Weber was speaking, Germany was in the throes of the so-called 'German Revolution' which broke out in November 1918 and had reached a new peak of intensity in January 1919. In Munich, where Weber was addressing these remarks to students, the 'Soviet Republic of Bavaria' had been proclaimed. Intellectuals, such as Kurt Eisner and Ernst Toller, were prominently involved, prompting Weber to return yet again to the recurrent theme of the role played by 'littérateurs' in politics.

violence within a certain territory, this 'territory' being another of the defining characteristics of the state. For the specific feature of the present is that the right to use physical violence is attributed to any and all other associations or individuals only to the extent that the *state* for its part permits this to happen. The state is held to be the sole source of the 'right' to use violence.

In our terms, then, 'politics' would mean striving for a share of power or for influence on the distribution of power, whether it be between states or between the groups of people contained within a single state.

Essentially, this corresponds to ordinary usage. If one says that a question is a 'political' question, or that a minister or official is a 'political' official, or that a decision is determined 'politically', what is meant in each case is that interests in the distribution, preservation or transfer of power play a decisive role in answering that question, determining this decision or defining the sphere of activity of the official in question. Anyone engaged in politics is striving for power, either power as a means to attain other goals (which may be ideal or selfish), or power 'for its own sake', which is to say, in order to enjoy the feeling of prestige given by power.

Just like the political associations which preceded it historically, the state is a relationship of *rule* (*Herrschaft*) by human beings over human beings, and one that rests on the legitimate use of violence (that is, violence that is held to be legitimate). For the state to remain in existence, those who are ruled must *submit* to the authority claimed by whoever rules at any given time. When do people do this, and why? What inner justifications and what external means support this rule?

To begin with the inner justifications: there are in principle three grounds *legitimating* any rule.[3] Firstly, there is the authority of 'the eternal past', of *custom*, hallowed by the fact that it has held sway from time immemorial and by a habitual predisposition to preserve it. This is 'traditional' rule, as exercised by the patriarch and the patrimonial prince of the old type. Then there is the authority of the exceptional, personal *'gift of grace'*, or charisma, the entirely personal devotion to, and personal trust in, revelations, heroism, or other qual-

---

[3] Weber discusses his classification of the forms of legitimate rule in *Economy and Society*; see, ch. 3 in particular.

ities of leadership in an individual. This is 'charismatic' rule, as exercised by the prophet or, in the field of politics, by the chosen war-lord or the plebiscitarian ruler, the great demagogue and leader of a political party. Finally, there is rule by virtue of 'legality', by virtue of belief in the validity of legal *statute* and the appropriate (*sachlich*) juridical 'competence' founded on rationally devised rules. This type of rule rests on a predisposition to fulfil one's statutory obligations obediently. It is rule of the kind exercised by the modern 'servant of the state' and all those bearers of power who resemble him in this respect. It goes without saying that the submission of the ruled is in reality determined to a very great extent not only by motives of fear and hope (fear of revenge from magical powers or from the holder of power, hope of reward in this life or in the hereafter), but also by interests of the most diverse kinds. We shall return to this point shortly. But when one asks what are the reasons 'legitimating' their submission, one does indeed encounter these three 'pure' types. These notions of legitimacy and their inner justification are of very considerable importance for the structure of rule. Admittedly, the pure types are rarely found in reality, but it is not possible today to go into the extremely intricate variants, transitional forms and combinations of these pure types in detail. That is a problem for a 'general science of the state'.[4]

Here we are interested above all in the second of the three types: rule by virtue of devotion to the purely personal 'charisma' of the 'leader' on the part of those who obey him. For this is where the idea of *vocation* (*Beruf*) in its highest form has its roots. Devotion to the charisma of the prophet or the war-lord or the exceptional demagogue in the *ekklesia*[5] or in parliament means that the leader is personally regarded as someone who is inwardly 'called' to the task of leading men, and that the led submit to him, not because of custom or statute, but because they believe in him. Of course, he himself, provided he is something more than an ephemeral, narrow and vain upstart, lives for his cause (*Sache*), 'aspires after his work',[6] whereas

---

[4] Weber was much influenced by the work of his colleague G. Jellinek, particularly by his *Allgemeine Staatslehre* ('General theory or science of the state') (Berlin, 1900).
[5] The 'ekklesia' was the assembly of all free citizens in the city-states of Ancient Greece.
[6] The phrase 'trachtet nach seinem Werke' probably alludes to words spoken by Nietzsche's Zarathustra at the beginning of 'The Honey Offering': 'For long I have not aspired after happiness, I aspire after my work', *Thus spoke Zarathustra*, translated R. J. Hollingdale (Harmondsworth, 1961), p. 251.

the devotion of his adherents, be they disciples or liegemen (*Gefolgschaft*) or his quite personal, partisan supporters, is focused on his person and his qualities. Leadership has emerged throughout the world and in all historical periods, the most important embodiments of it in the past being the magician and prophet on the one hand, and the chosen war-lord, gang-leader or *condottiere* on the other. In the Western world, however, we find something quite specific which concerns us more directly, namely *political* leadership, firstly in the figure of the free 'demagogue', who grew from the soil of the city-state, a unique creation of the West and of Mediterranean culture in particular, and then in the figure of the parliamentary 'party leader' who also sprang from the soil of the constitutional state, another institution indigenous only to the West.

Of course, nowhere is it the case that these politicians by virtue of a 'vocation', in the truest sense of the word, are the only figures who carry weight in the machinery of the political power struggle. Of quite decisive importance is the kind of resources they have at their disposal. How do the powers who rule politically set about the task of asserting themselves as rulers? The question applies to every kind of rule, and thus also to all forms of political rule, to the traditional type as much as to the legal and charismatic types.

All organised rule which demands continuous administration requires on the one hand that human action should rest on a disposition to obey those rulers (*Herren*) who claim to be the bearers of legitimate force, and on the other that, thanks to this obedience, the latter should have at their command the material resources necessary to exercise physical force if circumstances should demand it. In other words, it requires an administrative staff and the material means of administration.

As in any other organisation, the administrative staff, which is the outward organisational form taken by political rule, is of course not bound in obedience to the holder of power solely by that notion of legitimacy which we have just been discussing. It is also bound by two means which appeal to self-interest: material reward and social honour. The fiefs of vassals, the prebends of patrimonial officials, the salary of the modern civil servant, or chivalric honour, the privileges of a particular social estate, the official's honour – these are the rewards, and it is the fear of losing them which forms the ultimate, decisive basis for the solidarity of the administrative staff with the holder of power. The same applies to rule by the charismatic leader, for the military following expects booty and war-honours, while the following of the demagogue expects 'spoils'[7] – the exploitation of the ruled through the monopoly of public offices, profits tied to political power, and prizes to satisfy their vanity.

In exactly the same way as in an economic organisation (*Betrieb*), certain outward, material goods are needed to uphold any rule by force. All forms of state order can be divided into two main categories based on different principles. In the first, the staff of men, be they officials or whatever, on whose obedience the holder of power must be able to rely, *own* the means of administration *in their own right*, whether these consist of money, buildings, war material, carriage parks, horses or whatever. In the other case the administrative staff is 'separated' from the means of administration, in just the same way as the office-worker or proletarian of today is 'separated' from the material means of production within a capitalist enterprise. Thus it is a question of whether the holder of power *controls* the administration *personally* and directly, having the actual administrative work done by personal servants or by paid officials or by personal favourites and confidants, none of whom are proprietors, owners in their own right, of the material means of operation (*Betriebsmittel*) but who work, rather, under the direction of the ruler; or whether the opposite is the case. This difference runs through all the administrative organisations of the past.

We shall apply the term 'association structured by *estates*' (*ständisch gegliedert*) to political associations in which the dependent administrative staff have complete or partial control, in their own right, over the material means of administration. The vassal in a feudal association, for example, paid out of his own purse the costs of administration and jurisdiction in the district for which he held the fief. He also paid for his own equipment and provisioning in war-time; the vassals subject to him did the same in their turn. Naturally this had consequences for the lord's position of power, which rested only on a bond of personal loyalty and on the fact that feudal tenure and the social honour of the vassal derived their 'legitimacy' from the lord.

Yet everywhere, stretching back to the earliest political formations, we also find the lord in direct control of the means of administration.

---

[7] 'Spoils' is in English.

Through people who are personally dependent on the lord – slaves, domestic officials, servants, personal 'favourites' and prebendaries rewarded in money or in kind from his own stores – he seeks to gain direct control of the administration, to pay for the means from his own purse, out of the revenues from his patrimonial estates, and to create an army dependent solely on his person, equipped and provisioned from his granaries, stores and armouries. Whereas the lord in an association of 'estates' rules with the help of an autonomous 'aristocracy', and thus *shares* rule with the aristocracy, here his rule rests either on members of his household or on plebeians, strata of society who lack possessions or social honour of their own and who are entirely chained to him in material terms, having no power of their own to compete with his. All forms of patriarchal and patrimonial rule, sultanic despotism and the bureaucratic state order belong to this type. This is especially true of the bureaucratic state order, that is to say, the order which, in its most rational form, is specifically characteristic of the modern state.

The development of the modern state is set in motion everywhere by a decision of the prince to dispossess the independent, 'private' bearers of administrative power who exist alongside him, that is all those in personal possession of the means of administration and the conduct of war, the organisation of finance and politically deployable goods of all kinds. The whole process is a complete parallel to the development of the capitalist enterprise (*Betrieb*) through the gradual expropriation of independent producers. In the end we see that in the modern state the power to command the entire means of political organisation is in fact concentrated in a single pinnacle of power, so that there is no longer even a single official left who personally owns the money he expends or the buildings, supplies, tools, or machines of war over which he has control. Thus in today's 'state' (and this is fundamental to the concept), the 'separation' of the material means of administration from the administrative staff, the officials and employees of the administration, has been rigorously implemented. At this point the most modern development of all begins, for we are now witnessing the attempt to bring about the expropriation of this expropriator of the means of politics, and hence of political power itself. This much the revolution has achieved, at least to the extent that leaders have taken the place of the legally established authorities and, through usurpation or election, have gained the power of command over the political staff and the material apparatus, deriving their legitimacy – with what justification is irrelevant – from the will of the ruled. It is quite another question whether, on the basis of this at least apparent success, they may justifiably hope to carry out the process of expropriation within capitalist businesses, the management of which, at its innermost core, obeys laws which (despite extensive analogies) are quite different from those obtaining in the sphere of political administration. I shall not take a position on this question today. For the purpose of our deliberations I wish only to establish the purely *conceptual* ground as follows: the modern state is an institutional association of rule (*Herrschaftsverband*) which has successfully established the monopoly of physical violence as a means of rule within a territory, for which purpose it unites in the hands of its leaders the material means of operation, having expropriated all those functionaries of 'estates' who previously had command over these things in their own right, and has put itself, in the person of its highest embodiment, in their place.

Now, in the course of this process of political expropriation, which has taken place in all countries of the world with varying degrees of success, there emerged, in the service of the princes in the first instance, the earliest categories of 'professional politicians' (*Berufspolitiker*) in a *second* sense. These were people who did not want to be lords themselves, as charismatic leaders did; rather, they *entered the service* of political lords. They placed themselves at the disposal of the princes in this political struggle, and made the procurement of the princes' policies into a way of earning their material living on the one hand and, on the other, into an ideal (*ideell*) content for their own lives. Again it is *only* in the West that *this* type of professional politician is also to be found in the service of powers other than the princes alone. In the past they were their most important instrument of power and political expropriation.

Before examining the matter more closely, we need to be absolutely clear about what the existence of such 'professional politicians' entails. One can engage in 'politics' – which means striving to influence the distribution of power between and within political formations – both as an 'occasional' politician and as a full- or part-time professional politician, in exactly the same way as one earns a living in the economic sphere. We are all 'occasional' politicians when we post our ballot slips or express our will in some similar way, such as voicing approval or protest at a 'political' meeting, making a 'political' speech and so on, and for many people this is the entire extent of their involvement in politics. Today the 'part-time' politicians are, for example, all those local political agents (*Vertrauensmänner*) and committee members of party-political associations who, as a rule, only carry out this activity if circumstances require it, and who do not *chiefly* 'live from' this activity, either in a material or in an ideal sense. The same applies to those members of councils of state and similar advisory bodies who only carry out this function when summoned to do so. It is true also of quite broad sections of our members of parliament who only engage in politics during the parliamentary session. In the past such strata were to be found particularly amongst the estates. By 'estates' we mean the owners in their own right of military resources or of important material means of administration or of personal powers of rule and jurisdiction (*Herrengewalten*). Many of these people certainly did not devote their lives completely or predominantly, or indeed more than occasionally, to the service of politics. Rather they used their lordly power for the purpose of extracting rents or even profit, and they only became politically active, in the service of the political association, when this was particularly demanded of them by their lord or the members of their estate. The same applies to some of those assistants whom the prince called on to help him in the struggle to create a political organisation of his own, one that would be exclusively at his disposal. The 'domestic counsellors' (*Räte von Haus aus*)[8] and, going still further back in time, a considerable section of the counsellors who assembled in the *curia* [9] and in the prince's other advisory bodies were of this kind. But such occasional or part-time assistance was of course insufficient to meet the prince's needs. He had to try to create a staff of assistants devoted wholly and exclusively to his service as their *principal* occupation. The structure of the emergent dynastic political formation, and indeed the entire character of the culture in question, very largely depended on the sources from which he drew such assistance. The need to do this was felt above all in those political associations which constituted themselves politically as (so-called) 'free' commonwealths through the complete abolition, or extensive restriction, of princely

[8] The reference is to councillors who did not live at court and who only took part in meetings of the prince's council when it met in their own area.
[9] The *curia regis* was an assembly which met wherever the king was in residence.

power – 'free', not in the sense of freedom from rule by force, but in the sense of the absence, as the exclusive source of all authority, of princely power legitimated by tradition (and mostly consecrated by religion). Such formations certainly had their historical origins in the West, and the germ from which they developed was the city as a political association. The city first emerged in this role in the cultural sphere of the Mediterranean. What did the '*full*-time' politicians look like in all of these cases?

There are two ways of making a vocation or profession out of politics. Either one lives 'for' politics or one lives 'from' politics. The antithesis is by no means an exclusive one. Generally one does both, at least spiritually and usually also in material terms. Anyone who lives 'for' politics 'makes this his life' in an *inward* (*innerlich*) sense, either enjoying the naked possession of the power he exercises or feeding his inner balance and self-esteem from the sense that he is giving his life *meaning and purpose* (*Sinn*) by devoting it to a 'cause' (*Sache*). In this inward sense probably every serious-minded person who lives for a cause also lives from this cause. The distinction thus applies to a much more weighty aspect of the matter, namely the economic aspect. The person who lives 'from' politics is one who strives to make it into an enduring source of *income*, whereas this does not apply to the person who lives 'for' politics. For anyone to be able to live 'for' politics in this economic sense, certain, if you like, very trivial conditions must obtain wherever the order of private property prevails. Under normal circumstances such a person must be economically independent of the income politics can give him. This means quite simply that he must be wealthy or have private means which yield an income from which he can live. At least this is the case under normal circumstances. Admittedly, the following of the war-lord is as little concerned with the conditions of normal economic life as is the following of the revolutionary hero on the streets. Both live from booty, robbery, confiscations, levies, the imposition of worthless compulsory forms of currency, all of which essentially amount to the same thing. Necessarily, however, such conditions are outside the everyday run of things; in normal economic life only private means can fulfil this function. Yet this alone is not sufficient. In addition, the politician must be economically 'dispensable' or 'available' (*abkömmlich*), which means that his income must not depend on the fact that he personally and constantly devotes all or most of his productive energy and thought to the task of earning a living. The person who is most unconditionally 'dispensable' in this sense is the *rentier*, that is, someone whose income is entirely unearned, whether, as in the case of a lord of the manor in the past or of large landowners and the higher aristocracy in the present, this income is derived from ground rents – in the ancient world and during the Middle Ages there were also rents for slaves and serfs – or whether it comes from securities or similar modern sources of investment income. Neither the worker, *nor* – a fact of great importance – the entrepreneur, and *particularly* the modern large-scale entrepreneur, is able to make himself available in this sense. The entrepreneur in particular is tied to his business and is *not* dispensable; this applies very much more to the industrial or commercial entrepreneur than to the agricultural entrepreneur, given the seasonal nature of agricultural work. It is usually very difficult for the entrepreneur to allow anyone to deputise for him, even temporarily. The same applies to doctors, for example, and the more eminent and busier a doctor is, the less easy is it for him to absent himself from work. Things are easier for the advocate, for technical reasons connected with the organisation of his work, who for this very reason has played an incomparably greater role as a professional politician, indeed often a dominant one. Rather than pursue this casuistry'[10] any further, let us consider some of the consequences of this state of affairs.

If a state or party is led by people who (in the economic sense of the word) live exclusively for politics and not from politics, this necessarily means that the leading political strata are recruited on a 'plutocratic' basis. Admittedly, this does not also entail the converse, namely that plutocratic leadership meant that the leading political strata did not also strive to live 'from' politics by exploiting their political rule to the benefit of their private economic interests. There is of course no question of that. There has never been a social stratum which did not do this in one way or another. It means simply that such professional politicians are not obliged to seek recompense directly *for* their political work, as anyone without means is bound to do. Nor does it mean that politicians without a private fortune are merely or

---

[10] Weber often refers to his clarification of conceptual distinctions as 'casuistry'; ch. 1 of *Economy and Society* is an example.

chiefly concerned with providing for themselves by means of politics, and that they are not, or not chiefly, concerned with the 'cause'. Nothing could be less correct. We know from experience that a man of property makes provision for his economic 'security' a cardinal point in his whole conduct of life, whether consciously or unconsciously. Unconstrained and unconditional political idealism is to be found, if not exclusively then at least to an unusual degree, precisely in those strata whose lack of means places them outside the circles of those who have an interest in preserving the economic order of a particular society. This is particularly the case during out-of-the-ordinary, which is to say revolutionary, periods. Rather, it means simply this: that any *non*-plutocratic recruitment of those with interests in politics – the leadership and its following – is tied to the self-evident condition that the business (*Betrieb*) of politics must produce a regular and reliable income for such people. Politics can either be conducted on an 'honorary' basis, which means by so-called 'independent', that is wealthy people, above all those with unearned income. Or access to political leadership can be given to people without private means, in which case it has to be remunerated. The professional politician living *from* politics can be a pure 'prebendary' or a salaried 'official'. Either he draws an income from charges and fees for particular services – gratuities and bribes are only an irregular and formally illegal variant of this category of income – or he draws a fixed remuneration in kind or a salary in money, or a combination of both. He can assume the character of an 'entrepreneur', like the *condottiere* or the holder of a leased or purchased office in the past, or like the American 'boss'[11] who regards his expenses as a capital investment from which he will derive a yield by exploiting his influence. Or he can draw a fixed wage, as does an editor or party secretary or a modern minister or political official. In the past fiefs, grants of land, benefices of all kinds, but above all, once a money economy had developed, fee-yielding prebends – these were the typical forms of recompense paid to their following by princes, victorious conquerors or successful party leaders. Nowadays the rewards bestowed by party leaders for faithful services are offices of all kinds in parties, newspapers, cooperatives, medical insurance schemes, municipalities and states. *All* clashes between parties are not only conflicts about

---

[11] Weber uses the word 'boss' here and in the rest of the essay in its American sense.

substantive (*sachlich*) goals; they are also and above all struggles for the patronage of office. All the conflicts between particularist and centralist ambitions in Germany also revolve around the question of which powers are to control the patronage of office: whether it is to be the powers in Berlin or in Munich, in Karlsruhe or in Dresden. Any diminution of their share of the offices available for distribution is felt by the parties to be a graver loss than actions directed against their substantive goals. In France a large-scale change in the party-political prefecture was always considered to be a greater upheaval, and generated more hubbub, than a modification in the government's programme, since this meant little more than a change of wording. Some parties, and notably those in America since the disappearance of the old conflicts about the interpretation of the constitution, have become simply parties of position-seekers which change their substantive programme according to the chances of winning votes. Until very recently in Spain, where 'elections' were manufactured from above, the two major parties simply had an agreement to govern by turns so as to provide offices for their following. In the Spanish colonies all so-called 'elections' and all so-called 'revolutions' are always concerned with the state trough at which the winners wish to be fed. In Switzerland the parties divide the offices peacefully amongst themselves according to the principle of proportionality, and a number of 'revolutionary' draft constitutions here in Germany (for example the first one proposed for Baden) sought to extend this system to ministerial offices, thus treating the state and its offices simply as an institution for the provisioning of prebendaries. The Centre Party in particular was enthusiastic about this proposal, even making it an item in its manifesto that in Baden offices should be distributed proportionally according to religious confession, which is to say, regardless of achievement. This tendency is growing amongst all parties, and in the eyes of their following the parties are increasingly regarded as a means to the end of being provided for in this way. The growth of this tendency is connected with the growth in the number of offices as a consequence of general bureaucratisation and with the growing appetite for such offices as a form of specifically *assured* provision.

There is however a countervailing tendency to all this in the development of modern officialdom into a body of intellectual workers highly qualified in their speciality by long years of preparatory training and with a highly developed sense of professional (*ständisch*) *honour* which puts a premium on integrity. Without this sense of professional honour it would be our fate to have hovering over us the permanent threat of terrible corruption and base philistinism. This would also threaten the purely technical performance of the state apparatus which has grown steadily in its importance for the economy, and will continue to grow, especially with increasing socialisation. In the United States, where professional officials with lifelong tenure were once unknown, amateur administration by booty politicians meant that hundreds of thousands of officials, right down to the postman, changed office as a result of the outcome of the presidential election; this system has long since been punctured by the Civil Service Reform. Purely technical, compelling exigencies of administration have determined this development. In Europe the division of official labour into specialist areas of competence is a development which has taken place gradually over a period of five hundred years. It began in the Italian cities and *signorie*,[12] while the first monarchies to take this course were the states of the Norman conquerors. The decisive step was taken in the area of the princes' *finances*. One can see from the administrative reforms of the Emperor Max[13] how difficult it was, even under the pressure of direst necessity and Turkish rule, for officials to dispossess the prince in this area, although this was the sphere which could least tolerate the amateurism of a ruler who at that time was still, first and foremost, a knight. The development of the techniques of warfare gave rise to the specialist officer, the refinement of legal processes did the same for the trained lawyer. In all three areas specialised officialdom was finally victorious in the more advanced states in the sixteenth century. Thereby two simultaneous processes were initiated: the rise of princely absolutism *vis-à-vis* the estates, and the prince's gradual abdication of personal rule to the specialist officials to whom he owed this victory over the estates in the first place.

Simultaneously with the rise of professionally trained *officialdom* there came about the development of the 'leading *politicians*', albeit by much more gradual stages. Of course, throughout the world there

---

[12] Weber discusses the *signorie* in *Economy and Society*, vol. II, pp. 1317–22. They were, in Weber's view, the 'first political power in Western Europe to introduce rational administration by officials who were (increasingly) *appointed*.'
[13] Maximilian I.

had always existed advisers to the princes whose word was in fact decisive. In the Orient the typical figure of the 'Grand Vizier' was created out of a need to exonerate the Sultan as far as possible from personal responsibility for the success of government. In the West diplomacy first became a *consciously* cultivated art during the reign of Charles V (the age of Machiavelli), particularly under the influence of the reports from the Venetian legates which were read with passionate interest in specialist diplomatic circles. The adepts of this art, most of them with a humanist training, treated one another as a specially educated stratum of initiates, much like the Chinese statesmen with humanist training during the last period of Warring States.[14] The necessity for a leading statesman to give formally unified leadership to the *entire* policy of a government, including domestic policy, only came about finally and compellingly as a result of constitutional developments. Until then there had of course always been individuals who advised or – in fact – actually led the princes. But the organisation of the administrative authorities had initially followed other paths, even in the most advanced states. The highest administrative authorities had been founded on the *collegial*[15] principle. In theory, and to a gradually diminishing degree in practice, their meetings were presided over personally by the prince who gave the decision. The prince, finding himself increasingly in the position of an amateur, attempted to free himself from the inevitably growing weight of the officials' specialist training and to keep supreme leadership in his own hands by means of this collegial system, which led to expert opinions, counter-opinions and reasoned votes of the majority and minority, but also by surrounding himself with purely personal confidants – the 'cabinet' – alongside the official highest authorities; he would then let his decisions be known, via these confidants, in response to the resolutions of the council of state (or whatever else the highest state authority was called). This latent struggle between professional officialdom and autocratic rule existed everywhere. The situation only changed with the advent of parliaments and the aspirations of their

---

[14] The period of the Warring States was 475–221 BC Weber's account of the nature of the Chinese state can be found in the essays translated under the title *The Religion of China. Confucianism and Taoism* (New York, 1951).

[15] The concept of 'collegiality' is discussed in *Economy and Society*, ch. 3, section 8. A contemporary example cited by Weber is the power of the German revolutionary 'councils of workers and and soldiers' to countersign official decrees.

party leaders to power. Yet the same outward result was produced by very varied sets of underlying conditions. Admittedly, there were certain differences. Wherever dynasties kept a hold on real power – as was the case in Germany in particular – the interests of the prince were now joined in solidarity with those of the officials *against* parliament and its claims on power. It was in the interest of the officials that the leading, which is to say, ministerial posts should be filled from their ranks, or in other words that such posts should be goals to which officials could aspire by the process of promotion. The monarch for his part had an interest in being able to nominate ministers as he thought fit from the ranks of the officials dedicated to his service. But both monarch and officials were interested in ensuring that the political leadership presented a united, closed front to parliament, which means that they both had an interest in the replacement of the collegial system by a unitary chief of cabinet. Furthermore, simply in order to remain above party struggles and party attacks in a purely formal sense, the monarch needed a responsible individual to give him cover, which meant someone who would confront and be answerable to parliament and who would deal with the parties. With all these interests pulling in the same direction, there came into being an official minister (*Beamtenminister*)[16] who provided unified leadership. The development of parliamentary power generated an even stronger impulse towards unitary leadership in places where, as in England, parliamentary power gained the upper hand over the monarch. Here the 'cabinet', headed by the single parliamentary chief or 'leader',[17] developed as a committee of that power which, although ignored by official laws, was in fact the sole decisive political power, namely the *party* currently in possession of a majority. The official collegial bodies were not, as such, organs of the power which really exercised rule (that is the party), therefore they could not be the bearers of real government. What a ruling party needed in order to assert its power in domestic politics and to conduct high politics in relation to other countries, was an effective organ, meeting in confidence and composed exclusively of the men who truly led the party, in other words, a cabinet. But it also needed a leader responsible for all decisions to the public, and especially to the public in parliament,

[16] The term *Beamtenminister* is an unusual one. Presumably it means the minister responsible for the civil service.
[17] 'Leader' is in English.

namely a head of cabinet. This English system was then adopted on the continent in the form of the parliamentary ministries. Only in America and in the democracies influenced by America was a quite different system developed in direct contrast to the English one. Here the chosen leader of the victorious party elected by direct popular vote was placed at the head of an apparatus of officials whom he nominated; he was tied to parliamentary approval only in budgetary and legislative matters.

The development of politics into an organisation (*Betrieb*) which demanded training in the struggle for power and its methods, as it has been developed by the modern party system, resulted in the division of public functionaries into two clearly, although not absolutely, distinct categories: specialist, professional officials (*Fachbeamte*) on the one hand, and 'political officials' on the other. The 'political' officials in the true sense of the word are usually outwardly recognisable by the fact that they can be transferred or dismissed at will at any time, or at any rate 'sent into temporary retirement', as in the case of the French prefects and officials of the same type in other countries, in sharp contradistinction to the 'independence' of officials whose function is a judicial one. In England this category includes officials who, in accordance with established convention, leave office whenever there is a change of parliamentary majority and thus of the cabinet. In particular, the officials who tend to belong to this category are those whose area of responsibility includes the general administration of 'home affairs'; the 'political' component of this responsibility consists above all in the task of maintaining 'law and order' in the country, which is to say, upholding the existing relations of rule. As prescribed by Puttkamer's edict,[18] these officials had the duty in Prussia, on pain of being disciplined, to 'represent the policy of the government', and were used, like the prefects in France, as an official apparatus to influence elections. Under the German system, admittedly, and in contrast to other countries, most 'political' officials shared the same quality as all other officials, in that these political offices, too, could only be attained on the basis of academic study, professional examinations and a defined period of preparatory service. In Germany only ministers, the heads of the political apparatus, lack

---

[18] When Minister of the Interior for Prussia, Puttkamer initiated a reform of the civil service. In January 1882 a royal edict announced that officials were bound by their oath of office to support government policy.

this specific characteristic of the modern professional official. Under the old regime it was possible to become Prussian Minister of Culture without ever having attended an institution of higher learning, whereas it was only possible for a candidate to become *Vortragender Rat* [19] on the strict condition that he had taken the prescribed examinations. The *Dezernent* [20] and *Vortragender Rat* with his professional training was of course infinitely better informed about the real technical problems in his specialist area than his chief (as, for example. when Althoff headed the Prussian Ministry of Education).[21] The situation was no different in England. Consequently the official was also the more powerful figure as regards all day-to-day needs. There was nothing inherently nonsensical about this arrangement. The minister was, after all, the representative of the *political* power constellation, and his task was to represent its political criteria and to test the proposals of the specialist officials under him against those criteria, or to give them appropriate directives of a political kind.

Things are very similar in a private economic organisation. The true 'sovereign', the shareholders' meeting, has as little influence on the management of the business as a 'people' governed by professional officials, and those who have the decisive say in the policy of the firm, the 'board of trustees' dominated by the banks, only give economic directives and select the men who are to carry out the administration, without having the technical expertise themselves to manage the business (*Betrieb*). In this respect there is nothing fundamentally new about the present structure of the revolutionary state which is putting power over the administration into the hands of complete amateurs simply because they have the machine-guns at their disposal, men who would like to use the trained, specialist officials merely as executive heads and hands. The difficulties in the present system lie elsewhere, but these are questions which shall not concern us today.

---

[19] The head of an administrative section in the Foreign Office who reported to a higher level.

[20] The head of a division in a ministry.

[21] F. Althoff (1839–1908), an academic turned civil servant who was responsible for higher education policy in Prussia from 1882 to 1907. This period was marked by both expansion and ministerial interference. Weber's attitude to, and dealings with, the 'Althoff system' are available in *Max Weber: On Universities. The Power of the State and the Dignity of The Academic Calling in Imperial Germany*, ed. E. Shils (Chicago, 1974).

Rather, we want now to ask what are the typical, distinguishing characteristics of professional politicians, both those of the 'leaders' and those of their following. These characteristics have changed over time, and even today they are very varied.

As we have seen, 'professional politicians' developed in the past as servants of the princes in their struggle with the aristocratic estates. Let us consider the main types briefly.

The prince drew support in his struggle with the estates from the politically usable strata who did not belong to the estates. To these strata belonged, firstly, the clergy; this applies as much to Western or Eastern India, to Buddhist China and Japan, and to Mongolia with its Lamas, as it does to Christian territories in the Middle Ages. The technical reason for this was the fact that the clergy were literate. Wherever Brahmins, Buddhist priests or Lamas were imported, or bishops and priests employed as political advisers, the reason was the need for literate administrators who could be used by the emperor or prince or *khan* in his struggle with the aristocracy. The cleric, especially the celibate cleric, stood outside the machinations of normal political and economic interests and was not exposed, as vassals were, to the temptation to compete with his lord for political power of his own, so as to benefit his descendants. By virtue of the peculiar characteristics of his own estate, the cleric was 'separated' from the means necessary to conduct the prince's administration.

A second stratum of this type was formed by men of letters with a humanist education. There was a time when one learned how to make speeches in Latin and verses in Greek in order to become the political adviser and above all the writer of political memoranda for a prince. That was the time when the first flowering of humanist schools and princely foundations of chairs of 'poetics' took place. In the case of Germany this epoch passed quickly, yet it had a lasting influence on our system of education, although it was without any more profound political consequences. Things were different in Eastern Asia. The Chinese Mandarin is, or rather was in his origins, approximately the same thing as the humanist during the Renaissance period here – a man of letters trained and examined along humanist lines in the linguistic monuments of the distant past. If you read the diaries of Li Hung Chang you will find that he was most proud of the fact that he wrote poems and was a good calligrapher. This stratum, with the conventions it developed on the model of the ancient Chinese past, has determined the entire fate of China. Our own fate would perhaps have been similar if, at the time, the humanists had had the slightest chance of establishing their influence with the same degree of success.

The third stratum was the court nobility. Once the princes had succeeded in taking political power away from the nobility as an estate, they drew them to court and used them in their political and diplomatic service. The major change in our educational system in the seventeenth century was conditioned, amongst other things, by the fact that professional politicians from the court aristocracy entered the service of princes, replacing the humanist men of letters.

The fourth category was a specifically English phenomenon, a patrician group embracing the petty nobility and the urban *rentiers*, known technically as the 'gentry'[22] a stratum of people whom the prince originally recruited as his allies against the barons and whom he made proprietors of the offices of 'self-government',[23] only to find himself becoming increasingly dependent on them later. This stratum retained possession of all the offices of local government by taking them over free of charge for the sake of its own social power. These people preserved England from the bureaucratisation that was the fate of all states on the continent.

A fifth stratum, that of jurists with a university training, was peculiar to the West, particularly the mainland of Europe, and was of decisive importance for its entire political structure. There is no clearer evidence of the powerful long-term effects of Roman law, as transformed by the late Roman bureaucratic state, than the fact that trained jurists were the main bearers everywhere of the revolutionary transformation of the conduct and organisation (*Betrieb*) of politics, in the sense of developing it in the direction of the rational state. This is also true of England, although the great national guilds of lawyers hindered the reception of Roman law there. One can find no analogy of any kind for this in any other part of the world: the beginnings of rational legal thought in the Mimamsa[24] school in India, and all the elaboration of ancient legal thinking in the Islamic world could

---

[22] Weber uses the English word.
[23] Weber uses the English word.
[24] Weber mentions the Mimamsa school in particular because it is an example of a rational method for achieving holiness. It 'acknowledged ceremonial good work per se as the holy path', Weber, *The Religion of India* (New York, 1958), p. 52.

not prevent rational legal thought being overgrown with theological forms of thinking. Above all, trial procedure was not fully rationalised. That was only achieved thanks to the adoption by Italian jurists of ancient Roman jurisprudence (the quite unique product of a political formation which rose from being a city-state to ruler of the world), the *usus modernus* of the late medieval pandect jurists and canon jurists,[25] and the, subsequently secularised, theories of natural law born from legal and Christian thinking. This legal rationalism had its great representatives in the Italian *podestat*,[26] in the French crown-jurists who created the formal means whereby the power of the king could undermine the rule of the *seigneurs*, in the canon lawyers and conciliar theologians who thought in terms of natural law, in the court jurists and learned judges of the continental princes, in the teachers of natural law in the Netherlands and in the monarchomachs,[27] in the lawyers of the English crown and parliament, in the *noblesse de robe* of the French parliaments and, finally, in the advocates at the time of the Revolution. Without this legal rationalism the emergence of the absolute state is as unthinkable as the Revolution. If you look at the remonstrances of the French parliaments or the *cahiers* of the French *états généraux* from the sixteenth century up till 1789, you will find the same thing everywhere: the mind of the jurist. If you survey the professions to which the members of the French Assembly belonged, you will find – although they were elected on the basis of equal suffrage – just one proletarian and very few bourgeois entre-preneurs, but masses of jurists of all kinds, without whose presence the specific spirit inspiring these radical intellectuals and their pro-posals would be quite unthinkable. Since then the modern advocate and modern democracy absolutely belong together – and advocates in our sense, as an independent estate, actually only exist in the West, having developed since the Middle Ages out of the spokesman

---

[25] For a comment on the 'pandects' see footnote 25 to 'The Nation State and Economic Policy' (p. 18 above).

[26] In Weber's view the institution of the *podestat* played an extremely important role in the development of law in medieval Italy. The term refers to 'an aristocratic profes-sional officialdom' which was elected from another community and given judicial power. See *Economy and Society*, especially pp. 1273–6.

[27] The term 'monarchomach' ('fighter against the king', sometimes translated as 'king-killer') was given by William Barclay, in his *De Regno et regali potestate* (Paris, 1600), to a diverse group of political thinkers in France who had argued for the right of resistance to the monarch.

(*Fürsprech*) of the formalistic Germanic trial procedure as trials became subject to rationalisation.

It is no accident that advocates have played a significant part in western politics since the rise of the parties. Party politics means quite simply politics run by interested parties; we shall shortly see what that entails. The effective conduct of a case on behalf of interested parties is the craft of the trained advocate. In this he is superior to any 'official' (a lesson we have been taught by the superiority of enemy propaganda). Certainly, a case (*Sache*) which is supported by logically weak arguments (a 'bad' case in this sense) can, in his hands, be brought to a successful conclusion, that is be conducted 'well' in the technical sense. But he is also the only person capable of conducting a case that can be supported by logically 'strong' arguments (a 'good' case in this sense) 'well', in the sense of successfully. When an official acts as a politician, his technically inept conduct of the case all too frequently makes a 'bad' case out of one that is 'good' in every sense – as we have had to learn from painful experience. The reason for this is that politics nowadays is predominantly conducted in public and by means of the written or spoken word. Weighing up the effects of words is pre-eminently the domain of the advocate, and certainly not that of the specialist official who neither is, nor is intended to function as, a demagogue, and who usually becomes a very bad demagogue when, despite this fact, he attempts to be one.

In terms of what he is really called upon to do (*Beruf*), the true official – and this is crucial for any judgement of the previous regime here in Germany – should not engage in politics but should 'administer', and above all he should do so *impartially*. This also applies, officially at least, to so-called 'political' officials (*Verwaltungsbeamte*), always provided there is no question of a threat to the *reason of state*, that is the vital interests of the prevailing order. The official should carry out the duties of his office *sine ira et studio*, 'without anger and prejudice'. Thus, he should not do the very thing which politicians, both the leaders and their following, always and necessarily must do, which is to *fight*. Partisanship, fighting, passion – *ira et studium* – all this is the very element in which the politician, and above all the political *leader*, thrives. *His* actions are subject to a quite different principle of *responsibility*, one diametrically opposed to that of the official. When, despite the arguments advanced by an official, his superior insists on the execution of an instruction which the official regards as mistaken, the official's honour consists in being able to carry out that instruction, on the *responsibility* of the man issuing it, conscientiously and precisely in the same way as if it corresponded to his own convictions. Without this supremely ethical discipline and self-denial the whole apparatus would disintegrate. By contrast, the honour of the political leader, that is, of the leading statesman, consists precisely in taking exclusive, *personal* responsibility for what he does, responsibility which he cannot and may not refuse or unload onto others. Precisely those who are officials by nature and who, in this regard, are of high moral stature, are bad and, particularly in the political meaning of the word, irresponsible politicians, and thus of low moral stature in this sense – men of the kind we Germans, to our cost, have had in positions of leadership time after time. This is what we call 'rule by officials'. Let me make it clear that I imply no stain on the honour of our officials by exposing the political deficiency of this system, when evaluated from the standpoint of success. But let us return once more to the types of political figures.

Ever since the advent of the constitutional state, and even more so since the advent of democracy, the typical political leader in the West is the 'demagogue'. The unpleasant overtones of the word should not make us forget that it was Pericles, not Cleon, who first bore this title. Lacking an office, or rather being charged with the office of leading strategist (the only office to be filled by election, in contrast to the others which, in ancient democracy, were filled by casting lots), Pericles led the sovereign *ekklesia* of the *demos* of Athens. Actually, modern demagogy, too, employs the spoken word, and does so to an enormous extent, if one considers the electoral speeches a modern candidate has to make. But it makes even more sustained use of the printed word. The political writer and above all the *journalist* is the most important representative of the species today.

Even to sketch the sociology of modern political journalism would be quite impossible within the framework of this lecture, for it is in every respect a topic in its own right. But there are a few things which must be mentioned. On the continent at any rate, in contrast to conditions in England (and, incidentally, also in Prussia in former times), the journalist shares with the demagogue, the advocate and the artist the fate of lacking any firm social classification. He belongs to a kind of pariah-caste which, in the eyes of 'society', is always gauged socially by those of its representatives who are of the lowest moral quality. Thus the strangest ideas about journalists and their work are widespread. Few people are aware that a really *good* piece of journalistic work demands at least as good a mind as that of any scholar, above all because of the need to produce the work immediately, to order, and because it has to be immediately *effective*, although produced under quite different conditions from those of the scholar. There is hardly ever any proper appreciation of the fact that the responsibility and the *feeling* of responsibility in every honourable journalist is usually not a whit lower than that of any scholar; indeed on average it is higher, as the war has taught us. This is because it is, of course, the *ir*responsible pieces of journalism which stick in our memory because of the dreadful effects they often have. And of course nobody believes that the discretion of reliable journalists is on average higher than that of other people. Yet this is indeed the case. The incomparably greater temptations inherent in this profession, as well as the other conditions of working as a journalist at present, produce those effects which have accustomed the public to regard the press with a mixture of contempt – and craven cowardice. This is not the occasion to talk about what should be done about this. What interests us here is the *political* fate to which journalists are exposed by their profession, their chances of attaining positions of political leadership. Until now the chances were favourable only in the Social Democratic Party. But within this party editorial posts predominantly had the character of posts for officials, and have not formed the basis for a position as *leader*.

In the bourgeois parties, taken as a whole, the chances of rising to political power by this path had got worse rather than better, compared with the previous generation. Of course, all important politicians needed press influence, and hence press connections. Contrary to what one might have expected, however, it was certainly exceptional for party *leaders* to emerge from the ranks of the press. The reason for this lies in the much diminished ability of the journalist to absent himself from his duties, particularly the journalist without private means who is tied to his profession. This is because journalism has become a much more intensive and up-to-the-minute kind of business. The need to earn money by writing articles daily or at least weekly is like a ball-and-chain round a politician's ankle, and I know of cases where this has been an outward and, above all, an inward impediment to natural leaders in their rise to power. The fact that relations between the press and the ruling powers in the state and in the parties under the old regime were as detrimental as they possibly could be to the quality of journalism is a separate problem. In the countries of our enemies these relations were different, but it appears that there too, as in all modern states, the same principle applied, namely that the political influence of the working journalist is steadily diminishing, while that of capitalist press magnates, like 'Lord' Northcliffe, for instance, is growing ever greater.

In Germany, admittedly, the big capitalist newspaper concerns which took control of the papers carrying 'small ads' in particular – the various 'General Advertisers' – have, typically, bred political indifference in most cases. For there was no profit to be made from an independent political line, and especially not the commercially useful goodwill of the ruling political powers. During the war, too, the business to be had from advertising was used as a means of exerting massive political pressure on the press, a practice which looks set to continue. Even if we may expect that the major newspapers will resist this kind of influence, the situation for small papers is much more difficult. In this country, at any rate, a career in journalism is not at present a normal path to political leadership, attractive as this career may be in other respects, and despite the possibilities for influencing and affecting politics and above all the degree of political responsibility it entails. Whether this is no longer, or whether it is not yet the case, we shall perhaps have to wait and see. Whether abandoning the principle of anonymity, as advocated by some but not all journalists, would alter the situation in any way is hard to say. The 'leadership' (*Leitung*) of newspapers by specially recruited personalities with a gift for writing, whose pieces always and expressly appeared under their own name, which was something we experienced in the German press during the war, unfortunately demonstrated in a number of the better known cases that it is *not* as reliable a means of breeding a heightened sense of responsibility as one might have believed. It was the worst sections of the popular press which, regardless of party alignment, both aimed for and achieved increased circulation by such means. The gentlemen concerned, publishers and sensationalist journalists alike, earned a fortune – but certainly no honour. This is no argument against the principle itself; the question is very complicated and that phenomenon is not generally the case. *Up till now*, however, this has not been the path to genuine leadership or the *responsible* conduct of politics. How the situation will develop in the future remains to be seen. Whatever happens, however, a journalistic career remains one of the most important paths to professional political activity. It is not a path for everyone. It is certainly not one for weak characters, particularly not for people who can only maintain their inner balance in a situation of social and professional (*ständisch*) security. Although the life of a young scholar involves taking a gamble, he is surrounded by the firm conventions of his social position which keep him from going off the rails. A journalist's life, however, is essentially a gamble in every respect, and, what is more, one that is made under conditions which put a person's inner security to the test as few other situations in life do. Bitter professional experiences are perhaps not even the worst thing about it. It is in fact the successful journalists who have to cope with particularly difficult inner demands. It is no small thing to frequent the salons of the mighty of this earth, apparently on an equal footing, often being flattered on all sides because one is feared, and, at the same time, to know that one will have hardly left the room before the host is perhaps having to make excuses to his guests about the need to consort with 'those rogues from the press' – just as it is no small thing to have to deliver prompt and convincing pronouncements, at the immediate behest of the 'market', on anything and everything, on every conceivable problem in life, and to do so without falling prey, not only to utter banality, but, above all, to indignity and self-exposure with all their merciless consequences. It is not surprising that there are so many journalists who have lost their way or their value as human beings. What is surprising, rather, is the fact that, despite everything, this section of society in particular contains such a large number of valuable and quite genuine people, many more, indeed, than outsiders tend to imagine.

If the journalist, as a type of professional politician, can already look back on a considerable past, the figure of the *party official* is one who has emerged from the developments of the last few decades or, in some cases, years. We must turn our attention to the party system and party organisation if we are to understand the position of this figure within historical developments.

The organisation of politics is necessarily an *organisation run by interested parties* in all political associations of any magnitude where the holders of political power are elected periodically, which is to say in all associations with a territory and range of responsibilities extending beyond those of small, rural cantons. This means that a relatively small number of persons with a primary interest in political life (meaning participation in political power) create a following by free recruitment, present themselves or those under their tutelage as candidates for election, raise funds and set about collecting votes. One cannot imagine how elections could be arranged properly in larger political associations without this organisation. In practical terms it means the division of all citizens entitled to vote into politically active and politically passive elements. As this difference is a voluntary one it cannot be abolished by special measures such as the obligation to vote, or representation according to 'occupational group', or other proposals of this kind which are aimed expressly or in fact against this state of affairs, which is to say, against rule by professional politicians. The leadership, active in recruiting the following, and the following who freely canvass the body of passive voters who will elect the leader, are necessary elements in the life of any party. The structure of parties varies, however. The 'parties' of medieval cities, say, like the Guelfs and the Ghibellines, were purely personal followings. If one examines the *Statuto della parte Guelfa*,[28] the confiscation of the estates of the *nobili* (which originally meant all those families living in the knightly manner and qualified for fief), their exclusion from offices and denial of their right to vote, or the inter-locality party committees and the strictly military organisations with their rewards for denunciations, one feels reminded of Bolshevism with its Soviets, its strictly sifted military and informant organisations (above all in Russia), its confiscations, the disarming and political disentitlement of the 'bourgeois', that is the entrepreneurs, traders, *rentiers*, clerics, descendants of the dynasty and police agents. The analogy becomes even more striking when one sees on the one hand that the military organisation of the Guelph party was a purely knightly army, formed on the basis of matricular lists, and that nobles occupied almost all the leading positions, while the Soviets for their part have retained the highly remunerated entrepreneurs, piece-work wages, the Taylor system, discipline at the workplace and in the army; or rather they are re-introducing these things and looking around for foreign capital – in other words, they have had to accept once more

---

[28] The *Statuto della parte Guelfa* was first published in 1335.

absolutely *all* the things they fought against as institutions of the bourgeois class, in order to keep the state and the economy going at all. In addition to all this, they have re-employed the agents of the old *okhrana*[29] as their principal instrument of state power. What concerns us here are not such organisations based on violence, but professional politicians whose aim is to achieve power by means of sober, 'peaceful' canvassing by the party in the electoral market-place.

Parties in our usual sense of the word also began, in England for example, as pure followings of the aristocracy. Whenever a peer changed his party allegiance, for whatever reason, all those who were dependent on him also changed to the opposing party. Until the Reform Bill the great aristocratic families, and the king not least of them, had the patronage of an immense number of electoral districts. The parties of local notables, which developed everywhere with the rise of the bourgeoisie (*Bürgertum*), closely resembled these aristocratic parties. Under the spiritual leadership of the intellectual strata typical of the West, those circles of 'education and property' split into parties which they led, dividing partly along the lines of class-interests, partly on the basis of family tradition, partly for purely ideological reasons. Clergymen, teachers, professors, advocates, doctors, apothecaries, well-to-do farmers, manufacturers – in England that whole stratum that considers itself 'gentlemen' – formed occasional associations in the first instance, or, at the most, local political clubs. In times of agitation the petty bourgeoisie would make its voice heard, and occasionally the proletariat, too, when men arose to lead it (although such leaders did not usually come from its own ranks). In the country parties simply do not yet exist at this stage in the form of permanent associations organised across local boundaries. Cohesion is provided solely by the members of parliament. Local notables have the decisive say in the nomination of candidates. Programmes are formed partly on the basis of the electoral appeals of the candidates, partly in accordance with assemblies of notables or decisions of the parliamentary party. The clubs are led on a part-time, honorary basis. Where no clubs exist (as was usually the case) the completely formless organisation of politics is led by the few men with a permanent interest in politics under normal conditions. Only

---

[29] The political police force of Tsarist Russia. It operated a network of secret agents whose task was to investigate the revolutionary movement.

the journalist is a paid professional politician, only the organisation of the press functions as a continuous form of political organisation. Apart from this there is only the parliamentary session. Admittedly, the members of parliament and the leaders of the parties in parliament know which local notables to turn to when some political action seems desirable. But only in the great cities do permanent party associations exist with modest membership subscriptions and periodic assemblies and public meetings to hear the member of parliament give an account of himself. Things only come to life during the period of an election.

The driving force behind the progressive tightening of party ties was the interest which the members of parliament had in possible electoral compromises between localities, and in the effectiveness of unified electioneering in the country and of unified programmes accepted by broad sections of the country. In principle, however, the character of the party apparatus as an association of notables remains unchanged, although a network of local clubs (now in middle-sized towns as well) and, additionally, of trusted local agents (*Vertrauensmänner*) extends over the whole country. A member of the parliamentary party acting as the leader of the central party office is in permanent correspondence with these bodies and individuals. Outside the central office there are still no paid officials. The local associations are still led everywhere by 'respected' people who take on this responsibility for the sake of the esteem they enjoy in other areas. These are the extra-parliamentary 'notables' who exert influence alongside that of the stratum of political notables who actually sit as members of parliament. The press and local associations are, however, increasingly provided with intellectual nourishment by the party correspondence which the party publishes. Regular subscriptions from members become indispensable, and a proportion of this money has to go to meet the costs of the central office. Until relatively recently most party organisations in Germany were still at this stage of development. In France, indeed, some places were still at the first stage, with a quite unstable coalition of the members of parliament, a small number of local notables out in the country, with programmes being drawn up by the candidates themselves or on their behalf by their patrons, in some cases at the point of recruitment, although those working in the localities did refer, to a greater or lesser extent, to the resolutions and programmes of the members of parliament. At first the erosion of this system was only partial, The numbers of those whose main occupation was politics were small and composed mainly of the elected representatives, the few employees at central office, the journalists and – in France – those position-seekers who were already in a 'political office' or who were currently seeking one. Formally, politics was a part-time profession in the vast majority of cases. The number of parliamentary deputies appointable to ministerial posts was strictly limited, but so too was that of the possible electoral candidates, given the character of a system dominated by notables. However, the number of people with an indirect interest, particularly of a material kind, in the conduct and organisation of politics was very great. For all measures taken by a ministry, and particularly decisions relating to personnel, were taken with an eye to the effect they would have on the chances of electoral success, and people sought to achieve all manner of wishes through the good offices of the local member of parliament. Whether he liked it or not, a minister was obliged to listen to the member of parliament, particularly if he belonged to his majority, which was therefore the goal pursued by everybody. The individual deputy had control over the patronage of office and indeed every kind of patronage in all matters concerning his constituency, and he in turn maintained relations with the local notables in order to secure his own re-election.

The most modern forms of party organisation contrast sharply with these idyllic conditions of rule by circles of notables and, above all, by the members of parliament. These new forms are the offspring of democracy, of mass suffrage, of the need for mass canvassing and mass organisation, the development of the strictest discipline and of the highest degree of unity in the leadership. Rule by notables and direction by the members of parliament comes to an end. 'Full-time' politicians *outside* the parliaments take the business (*Betrieb*) in hand – either as 'entrepreneurs' – which is in effect what the American 'boss' and the English 'election agent' were – or as officials with a fixed salary. Formally, a far-reaching process of democratisation takes place. It is no longer the parliamentary party which creates the authoritative manifestos, no longer the local notables who have control over the nomination of candidates. Instead, general meetings of the organised members of the party select the candidates and delegate members to the higher assemblies, of which there may be several, right up to the general party conference. But in fact, of course, power lies in the hands of those who do the work *continuously* within the organisation, or with those persons on whom the running of the organisation depends, either financially or in terms of personnel (for example wealthy patrons or the leaders of powerful clubs of vested political interests, such as Tammany Hall). The decisive fact is that this whole human apparatus – the 'machine', as it is revealingly called in English-speaking countries – or rather the people who control it are able to keep the members of parliament in check, and can even impose their will on them to a considerable extent. This is of particular importance for the selection of the *leadership* of the party. The person who now becomes leader is the one whom the machine follows, even over the heads of parliament. In other words, the creation of such machines means the advent of *plebiscitarian* democracy.

The party following, and above all the party official and party entrepreneur, naturally expect personal recompense to flow from the victory of the leader, either in the form of offices or other benefits. The decisive point is that they expect these things from him, and not, or not only, from individual members of parliament. Above all, they expect that the demagogic effect of the leader's *personality* during the election will win votes and mandates, and thus power, for the party, and will therefore maximise the chances of the party's supporters finding the rewards they are hoping for. On the level of ideas, one of the driving forces is the satisfaction to be gained from working for an individual, out of conviction and devotion to him, rather than for the abstract programme of a party composed of mediocrities; this is the 'charismatic' element in all leadership.

To very varying degrees, and in constant latent struggle with members of parliament and with local dignitaries fighting to preserve their influence, this form succeeded in establishing itself, first in the United States, amongst the bourgeois parties, and then in the Social Democratic Party, above all in Germany. Reverses constantly occur whenever there is no generally acknowledged leader. Even when such a leader does exist, all kinds of concessions have to be made to the vanity and vested interests of party notables. Above all, however, the machine can also fall into the hands of the party *officials* who do the day-to-day work. Some Social Democratic circles take the view that their party succumbed to this 'bureaucratisation'. Yet 'officials' submit fairly readily to a leader with a strong, demagogically effective personality, for their material and ideal interests are, after

339

all, intimately connected with what they hope the power of the party will achieve under his leadership, and there is inherently more inner satisfaction to be had from working for a leader. The rise of leaders is far more difficult in cases where (as is usual in bourgeois parties) the 'notables', in addition to the officials, influence the party. For they 'make a life' for themselves in an *ideal* sense out of whatever minor position they hold as members of the executive committee or one of its sub-committees. Their actions are dictated by resentment of the demagogue as a *homo novus*, by their strong belief in the superiority of party-political 'experience' (which is indeed of considerable importance) and by ideological worries about the breakdown of the old traditions of the party. They also have all the traditionalist elements in the party behind them. The rural voter above all, but also the petit-bourgeois voter, respects the name of the notable who has been long familiar to him and mistrusts the man he does not know. Admittedly, should the new man be successful, the allegiance of these groups to him is all the more unshakeable. Let us look at a few of the main examples of the struggle between these two forms of political structure and at the rise of the plebiscitary form as described by Ostrogorski.[30]

Let us begin with England. Party organisation there was almost exclusively an organisation of notables until 1868. The Tories relied in the countryside on, for example, the Anglican vicar, as well as on the teacher (in most cases) and above all on the large landowners of the county, while the Whigs relied mostly on such people as the nonconformist preacher (where one existed), the postmaster, blacksmith, tailor, rope-maker, in other words on those tradesmen who could spread political influence because they were the ones with whom one could have a conversation most frequently. In the towns parties divided according to party opinions which were either economic or religious or simply traditional in one's family. But in every case the organisation of politics was borne by notables. At a higher level there was parliament and the parties, with the cabinet and the 'leader' who chaired the council of ministers or led the opposition. At his side the leader had the most important professional political figure in the party organisation, the 'Whip',[31] in whose hands lay the

---

[30] M. Ostrogorski, *Democracy and the Organization of Political Parties* (London, 1902).
[31] 'Whip' is in English.

patronage of office. The place-seekers had therefore to turn to him, and he consulted the members from the individual constituencies on such matters. Amongst these people a stratum of professional politicians slowly began to evolve, as local agents were recruited who were unpaid in the first instance and whose position was roughly equivalent to our *Vertrauensmänner*. Additionally, however, there developed in the constituencies a type of capitalist entrepreneur, the 'election agent'[32] whose existence was inevitable under the modern legislation introduced in England to ensure the fairness of elections. This legislation sought to limit electoral expenses and to counter the power of money by obliging candidates to declare what the election had cost them. For in England, much more than was once the case here, the candidate, as well as straining his voice, had the pleasure of taking out his purse. The election agent received from him a sum of money to cover all expenses, from which the agent usually made a tidy profit. In the distribution of power between leader[33] and party notables, both in the country and in parliament, the leader had always had a very important position in England, for compelling reasons which had to do with the facilitation of large-scale and at the same time stable policy-making. Nevertheless, the influence of members of parliament and party notables still remained considerable.

This is roughly what the old party organisation looked like, something half run by notables and half by an enterprise in which paid employees and entrepreneurs were already playing a role. From 1868 onwards, however, there developed the 'caucus' system, firstly for local elections in Birmingham and then throughout the whole country. A nonconformist preacher and Joseph Chamberlain combined to inaugurate this system. It was prompted by the democratisation of suffrage. To win over the masses it was necessary to call into being an enormous apparatus of associations which were democratic in appearance, so as to create a voting association in each district of the town, to keep the organisation in constant operation, and to subject everything to tight bureaucratic control. Increasingly, paid officials were employed, while the formal bearers of party policy were chief negotiators with a right of co-option, elected by local electoral committees in which perhaps about 10 per cent of the voters, all in all, were soon organised. The driving force came from local people,

---

[32] 'Election agent' is in English here and subsequently.
[33] 'Leader' is in English.

particularly from those with an interest in municipal politics (the source of the richest material pickings everywhere), who were also primarily responsible for raising the necessary funds. This newly emerging machine, no longer directed from parliament, very soon came into conflict with the previous holders of power, above all with the Whip. Drawing its support from local interests, however, it was so successful in this struggle that the Whip had to submit to its power and seek compromises with it. The result was the centralisation of all power in the hands of a few people and ultimately of one person at the head of the party. In the Liberal Party the rise of this whole system had to do with Gladstone's rise to power. The fascinating thing about Gladstone's 'grand' demagogy, the firm belief of the masses in the ethical content of his policies and above all in the ethical character of his personality, was what led this machine so quickly to victory over the notables. A Caesarist plebiscitary element, the dictator of the electoral battlefield, entered the political arena. This very soon made itself felt. The caucus became active for the first time in national elections in 1877, and did so with brilliant success, for the result was Disraeli's fall from power at the height of his great successes. By 1886, when the issue of Home Rule was opened up, the machine was already so completely oriented on the charismatic appeal of the leader's personality that the entire apparatus, from top to bottom, did not ask, 'Do we share Gladstone's position in this matter?', but rather simply wheeled at his command, saying, 'Whatever he does, we will follow him.' In so doing, the apparatus simply left Chamberlain, the man who had created it, high and dry.

This machinery necessitates a considerable human apparatus. In England there are probably no less than 2,000 individuals who make their living directly from party politics. Admittedly, the number of those who play a part in politics merely in order to obtain an office or pursue some personal interest is much greater still, particularly in local politics. As well as economic opportunities, the useful caucus politician has opportunities to satisfy his vanity. By the nature of things, it is the height of (normal) ambition to aspire to the title of J.P. or even M.P., and this goal is attained by people of good upbringing, that is 'gentlemen'.[34] The highest prize of all, one particularly

---

[34] 'Gentlemen' is in English here and subsequently.

striven after by wealthy patrons (in a country where approximately 50 per cent of party finances took the form of contributions from anonymous donors), was a peerage.

What has been the effect, then, of this whole system? It has been to turn most English members of parliament into nothing better than well-disciplined lobby-fodder, the only exceptions being a few members of the cabinet and some mavericks. In our Reichstag it was customary at least to deal with one's private correspondence while sitting at one's desk in the house in order to give the impression that one was working for the weal of the nation. Such gestures are not required in England. There the member of parliament merely has to vote and to refrain from betraying his party. He has to appear when the Whips summon him, and to do whatever is decreed either by the cabinet or the leader of the opposition. When the leader is strong, the caucus-machine out in the country is almost wholly unprincipled and entirely in his hands. This means that above parliament there stands a man who is in fact a plebiscitary dictator, who rallies the masses behind him by means of the party 'machine', and who regards members of parliament simply as political prebendaries who belong to his following.

How, then, is this leadership selected? Firstly, on the basis of what ability is the selection made? Here what matters most – apart from the qualities of will which are decisive everywhere in the world – is of course the power of demagogic speech. Its nature has changed since Cobden's time, when the appeal was to reason, via Gladstone, a master of the technique of seeming soberly to 'let the facts speak for themselves', down to the present where purely emotive means, like those of the Salvation Army, are often deployed in order to stir the masses. The existing state of things well deserves the name of a 'dictatorship which rests on the exploitation of the emotionality of the masses'.[35] But the highly developed committee system in the English parliament makes it possible and indeed forces any politician who hopes to gain a share in the leadership to join in the *work* of committees. All ministers of note during the last few decades have undergone a very real and effective training in this form of work, while the practice of reporting and publicly criticising these delibera-

---

[35] Weber is presumably referring again to Ostrogorski's work but these particular words cannot be found there.

tions means that this school involves a genuine process of selection which excludes anyone who is a mere demagogue.

This is how things are in England. The caucus system there, however, existed only in attenuated form in comparison with party organisation in America, where the plebiscitary principle was developed unusually early and in a particularly pure form. As he conceived it, Washington's America was to be a commonwealth governed by 'gentlemen'. In America, too, a gentleman was in those days a landed proprietor or a man with a college education, and this is how things were indeed run at first. When parties were formed it was initially members of the House of Representatives who claimed the leadership, as was the case in England during the period of rule by notables. Party organisation was quite loose. This state of affairs lasted until 1824. The party machine was already coming into existence before the 1820s in some municipalities (which were the birthplace of the modern development here too). But it was the election of Andrew Jackson as president, the candidate of the farmers in the West, which first overturned the old traditions. The formal end to the leadership of the parties by leading parliamentary representatives happened soon after 1840 when the great parliamentarians – Calhoun, Webster – withdrew from political life because parliament had lost virtually all its power *vis-à-vis* the party machine out in the country. The reason for the early development of the plebiscitary 'machine' in America was that there, and only there, the head of the executive and – most importantly – the chief of official patronage was a president elected on the plebiscitary principle who, as a result of the 'separation of powers' was almost independent of parliament in the exercise of his office. Thus the reward of success in the presidential election in particular was the prospect of being able to distribute booty in the form of official prebends. The consequence of this was the 'spoils system'[36] which Andrew Jackson now elevated, systematically, to the status of a principle.

What does this spoils system – the allocation of all federal offices to the victorious candidate's following – mean for the formation of parties nowadays? It means that the contending parties are utterly unprincipled. They are purely and simply organisations for position-seekers, which draw up their changing programmes for each election

---

[36] 'Spoils system' is in English here and subsequently.

campaign according to the chances of winning votes. It also means that these programmes are changeable to a degree not found anywhere else, despite any other analogies which may exist. The parties are entirely tailored towards winning the most important campaign for the patronage of offices, namely the election of the President of the Union and the governorships of individual states. The programmes and the candidates are decided at the parties' 'national conventions'[37] without the intervention of the parliamentary representatives. These are party congresses to which people are sent, in a formally very democratic way, by assemblies of delegates, which in turn derive their mandate from the 'primaries',[38] the fundamental voting assemblies of the parties. Even at the primaries the delegates are chosen in relation to the name of the candidate for the headship of state; *within* the individual parties the fiercest struggle rages around the question of the 'nomination'.[39] The president has in his hands the power to name the holders of no less than 300,000 to 400,000 offices, and he alone carries out this task, consulting only the senators of the individual states. The senators are therefore powerful politicians. The House of Representatives, by contrast, has relatively little political power because the patronage of office is not in its hands, and because ministers, who are purely aides to a president whom the people have legitimated *vis-à-vis* everyone (parliament included), are able to exercise their office regardless of its confidence or lack of confidence. This is a consequence of the 'separation of powers'.

The spoils system based on these arrangements was technically *possible* in America because a purely amateur way of conducting business could be tolerated in such a young civilisation (*Kultur*). A state of affairs where there were 300,000 or 400,000 of these party men whose only demonstrable qualification for office was the fact that they had served their party well could not of course exist without enormous evils – unparalleled waste and corruption – which could only be sustained by a country with, as yet, unlimited economic opportunities.

The figure who now appears on the scene along with this system of the plebiscitary party machine is the party 'boss'. What is the boss?

[37] 'National conventions' is in English.
[38] 'Primaries' is in English.
[39] 'Nomination' is in English.

A political capitalist entrepreneur who supplies votes on his own account and at his own risk. He may have forged his first connections as an advocate or a pub-landlord or the proprietor of some such business, or perhaps as a creditor. From there he spins his threads until he is able to 'control' a certain number of votes. Once he has got this far he forges links with the neighbouring bosses, and, by his zeal, skill and above all his discretion, catches the eye of those who have already progressed further in their careers, and so he begins to rise. The boss is indispensable to the organisation of the party. This is centralised in his hands. Very largely it is he who procures the means. How does he come by them? Well, partly by subscriptions from party members; above all by taxing the salaries of those officials who came to office through him and his party. Then through gratuities and bribes. Anyone who wishes to break one of the many laws with impunity needs the connivance of the bosses and has to pay for it – otherwise things will inevitably be made unpleasant for him. But this alone does not suffice to procure all the operating capital. The boss is indispensable as the direct recipient of money from the great financial magnates who would not entrust money for electoral purposes to any paid party official or indeed to anyone presenting accounts in public. With his astute discretion in financial matters, the boss is of course just the man for the capitalist circles who fund the election. The typical boss is an absolutely sober man. He has no ambition for social honour; the 'professional'[40] is despised in 'polite society'. His sole aim is power, power as a source of money, but also for its own sake. He works behind the scenes, which is where he differs from the English 'leader'. One does not hear him speak in public; he suggests to the speakers what they ought to say to achieve their goals, but he himself remains silent. As a rule he accepts no office apart from that of a federal senator. For, as senators have a constitutional role in the patronage of office, the leading bosses often sit in this body in person. The allocation of offices is determined first and foremost by what an individual has done for the party. Frequently, however, they were also allocated in return for payments of money, and some offices have particular rates attached to them – a system of selling offices familiar from many monarchies, including the Papal States, in the seventeenth and eighteenth centuries.

[40] 'Professional' is in English here and subsequently.

The boss has no firm political 'principles'. He is entirely unprincipled and is only interested in the question of what will win votes. Not infrequently he is a man with a fairly poor upbringing. His private life, however, is usually correct and beyond reproach. Only in his political ethics does he adapt himself, naturally enough, to the average ethical standards of political conduct which are a fact of life, just as many of us Germans probably did in the sphere of economic ethics during the period of hoarding. The fact that he is socially despised for being a 'professional' politician does not trouble him. There is an advantage in the fact that he himself neither can nor wants to enter the great offices of the Union, namely the possibility that good minds from outside the party may be adopted as candidates, men of reputation rather than just the same old party notables as in our system, provided the bosses think they will win votes. The structure of this unprincipled party with its socially despised wielders of power has thus made it possible for able men to attain the office of president who would never have succeeded under our system. Admittedly, the bosses resist any outsider whom they perceive as a possible threat to their own sources of money and power. But in the competition for the favour of the voters they have been obliged not infrequently to condescend to accept precisely those candidates who were reputed to be opponents of corruption.

Thus in America parties are run on markedly capitalistic lines. They are tightly organised from top to bottom, and supported by extremely stable political clubs such as Tammany Hall which are organised almost like religious orders but which aim exclusively at making profits by exercising political control, above all over municipal governments (these being the most important object of exploitation here too). It was possible for party life to develop this kind of structure in the United States because of the high degree of democracy in this 'young country'. The connection between these things means, however, that this system is slowly dying out. America can no longer be governed on a purely amateur basis. If you asked American workers fifteen years ago why they let themselves be governed by politicians whom they themselves claimed to despise, you got the answer: 'We would rather our officials were people we can spit on, than be like you and have a caste of officials who spit on us'. That was the old standpoint of American 'democracy'. Yet the socialists already thought quite differently even then, and this state of affairs is no longer tolerated. Administration by amateurs is no longer adequate and the Civil Service Reform[41] is creating tenured, pensionable posts in steadily growing numbers. As a result, university-trained officials, who are just as incorruptible and able as our own, are entering these offices. Approximately 100,000 offices are no longer objects for booty when the election comes round, but are pensionable and tied to the candidate's ability to demonstrate his qualifications. This will cause the spoils system to lose ground slowly; the leadership of the parties will then transform itself accordingly. It is just that we do not yet know, how.

Up till now the decisive factors affecting the operation of politics in *Germany* have been essentially as follows: firstly, there is the impotence of our parliaments. The result of this was that no one with leadership qualities went into parliament for any length of time. Supposing one wanted to enter parliament – what could one do there? If a chancellery post fell vacant, one could say to the appropriate administrative head, 'I have a very able man in my constituency who would be suitable, why don't you take him?' This was granted readily. But that was more or less all a German member of parliament could achieve by way of satisfying his instincts for power – if he had any. Then there was the fact that trained professional officialdom in Germany was so enormously important (this second factor being a reason for the first). We had the best officials in the world. A consequence of this was that trained officials sought not only posts in the civil service but also ministerial posts. Last year, when 'parliamentarisation' was being discussed in the Bavarian Diet, it was argued that gifted people would no longer want to become officials if ministerial posts were given to members of parliament. Apart from this, the administration carried out by officials systematically escaped the kind of control that is exercised through the discussions in committee under the English system. This made the German parliaments (with few exceptions) incapable of training genuinely useful heads of the administration from within their own ranks.

The third factor was the existence of parties in Germany (in contrast to America) which were parties of political principle (*gesinnungspolitische Parteien*) which claimed, in what they at least felt was good faith, that their membership supported particular *Weltanschauungen*. The two most important of these parties (the Catholic

---

[41] 'Civil Service Reform' is in English.

Centre Party on the one hand and the Social Democrats on the other) were, however, born minority parties, as indeed they were deliberately designed to be. The leading circles of the Centre Party in the Reich never made any secret of the fact that they opposed parliamentary rule because they feared being in the minority, for the reason that this would make it much more difficult for them to accommodate position-seekers who, hitherto, could be found posts by putting pressure on the government. The Social Democrats were a minority party and an obstacle to the growth of parliamentary power as a matter of principle, because they did not want to be besmirched by contact with the established bourgeois political order. The fact that these two parties excluded themselves from the parliamentary system made that system impossible.

Given this situation, what became of the professional politicians in Germany? They had no power, no responsibility, and could only play a fairly subaltern role as notables, with the result that they were animated yet again by the instincts which are typically to be found in all 'guilds'. It was impossible for anybody not cast in the same mould to rise within the circle of these notables who made their life out of whatever little position they held. I could cite numerous names from each of the parties (and the Social Democrats are, of course, no exception), which represent tragic political careers because the persons concerned had leadership qualities and, for that very reason, were not tolerated by the notables. By taking this path, all our parties have turned into guilds of notables. Bebel, for example, was still a leader by virtue of his temperament and the purity of his character, however modest his intellectual gifts. The fact that he was a martyr, that he never betrayed the trust of the masses (in their eyes), meant that he had the masses absolutely behind him, so that no power within the party was capable of seriously challenging him. After his death this situation came to an end, and rule by officials began. Union officials, party secretaries and journalists were in the ascendant, the instincts of officials dominated the party, a most honourable body of officials (indeed exceptionally honourable, one may say, if one considers conditions in other countries, particularly the often corrupt union officials in America), but the consequences of rule by officials discussed above also affected the party.

From the 1880s onwards the bourgeois parties became purely and simply guilds of notables. From time to time, admittedly, the parties had to recruit minds from outside the party for advertising purposes, in order to be able to say, 'These famous names are on our side.' As far as possible, they tried to prevent such people standing in elections. This only occurred where it was unavoidable, because the person concerned insisted on it.

The same spirit was to be found in parliament. Our parliamentary parties were and still are guilds. Every speech delivered before a full session of the Reichstag is thoroughly censored in advance by the party. This is plain from the fact that they are unspeakably boring. An individual may only speak if he is a nominated speaker. A greater contrast to the English system – or to what (for quite opposite reasons) is the custom in France – is hardly conceivable.

At present a change may be taking place as a result of the mighty collapse that is customarily referred to as the revolution. Perhaps this is so – but it is not certain. The beginnings of new kinds of party apparatus began to emerge at first. Amateur apparatuses in the first place, very often manned by students from the various universities, who say to a man to whom they attribute leadership qualities, 'We will do what needs to be done if you tell us what it is.' Secondly, commercial apparatuses. There have been cases of certain people approaching a man they thought had leadership qualities and offering to take care of the canvassing of voters in return for a fixed sum for each vote. If you were to ask me which of these two apparatuses I honestly thought the more reliable from a purely technical-political point of view, I think I would choose the latter. But both types of apparatus were bubbles which rose quickly and disappeared just as quickly. The existing apparatuses restructured themselves, but continued operating. Those phenomena were only a symptom of the fact that new apparatuses would perhaps come into being if only the leaders were to be found. But the technical peculiarities of proportional representation were enough to preclude their rise. Just a handful of street dictators arose, who then disappeared again. And it is only the following of a street dictator which has a firmly disciplined organisation, which explains the power of these tiny minorities.

Assuming all this were to change, it has to be clearly stated in the light of the above that, when plebiscitary leaders are in charge of parties, this means a 'loss of soul' (*Entseelung*)[42] for the following,

---

[42] The problem of how to overcome soul-destroying 'dehumanisation' and 'capitalist mechanisation' was a central topic in contemporary political debate. It was discussed

what one might call their spiritual proletarianisation. In order to be a useful apparatus in the leader's hands, the following has to obey blindly, be a machine in the American sense, it must not be disturbed by the vanity of notables or by pretensions to individual opinions. Lincoln's election was only made possible by this kind of party organisation, and in Gladstone's case, as we have said, the same thing occurred in the caucus. That is simply the price to be paid for having a leader in charge of the party. But the only choice lies between a leadership democracy with a 'machine' and democracy without a leader, which means rule by the 'professional politician' who has no vocation, the type of man who lacks precisely those inner, charismatic qualities which make a leader. Usually this means what the rebels within any given party call rule by the 'clique'. For the time being only the latter exists here in Germany. The future continuance of this arrangement, in the Reich at any rate, is favoured by the likelihood that the *Bundesrat* will come into being again, which will necessarily limit the power of the Reichstag and hence the importance of the Reichstag as a place where leaders are selected. A further factor is proportional representation in its present form, a typical feature of a leaderless democracy, not only because it favours horse-trading amongst notables for the allocation of places on the lists, but also because it will in future make it possible for pressure groups to force the parties to include their officials in the lists, thereby creating an unpolitical parliament in which there is no place for genuine leadership. The only remaining outlet for the desire for leadership might be the office of *Reichspräsident* if the president were to be elected by plebiscitary rather than parliamentary means. Leadership based on proven ability for work could emerge and be selected if, in the large municipalities, plebiscitary city dictators were to come on the scene with the right to assemble their own administrative bureaus independently, as happened throughout the United States wherever a serious effort was made to stamp out corruption. The precondition for this would be a party organisation tailored to the needs of such elections. But the thoroughly petty bourgeois hostility shown towards leadership by all our parties, (including the Social Democrats in particular), means that there is no way of knowing what shape parties

at the cultural conferences held at Burg Lauenstein in May and October 1917 which Weber attended.

will take in the future, and therefore what the chances are of any of these things coming about.

Thus there is no way of foreseeing today what outward shape the business of politics as a 'profession' will take, and consequently, even less possibility of knowing how opportunities might arise for politically gifted people to be presented with satisfying political tasks. Anyone whose financial situation requires him to live 'from' politics will probably always have to choose between journalism or a post as a party official, these being the two typical direct routes, or to join one of the organisations representing special interests, such as a trade union, chamber of commerce, agricultural chamber, chamber of crafts, trades council, employers' association, or to seek a suitable position in local government. One can say no more about the outward aspect of things other than that the party official shares with the journalist the odium of being 'declassed'. Unfortunately, the former will always hear the name 'hired hack' and the latter 'hired orator' ringing in his ears, even if these words are never actually spoken aloud. Anyone who is without inner defences against such slights and is unable, in his own mind, to give his own, correct reply to them, should steer clear of this career because, quite apart from the severe temptations to which it exposes a man, it can be a source of continual disappointment.

What kinds of inner joy does politics have to offer, and what kinds of personal qualifications does it presuppose in anyone turning to this career?

Well, first of all, it confers a feeling of power. The professional politician can have a sense of rising above everyday existence, even in what is formally a modest position, through knowing that he exercises influence on people, shares power over them, but above all from the knowledge that he holds in his hands some vital strand of historically important events. But the question facing such a person is which qualities will enable him to do justice to this power (however narrowly circumscribed it may actually be in any particular case), and thus to the reponsibility it imposes on him. This takes us into the area of ethical questions, for to ask what kind of a human being one must be in order to have the right to seize the spokes of the wheel of history is to pose an ethical question.

One can say that three qualities are pre-eminently decisive for a politician: passion, a sense of responsibility, judgement. Passion in the sense of *concern for the thing itself* (*Sachlichkeit*), the passionate commitment to a 'cause' (*Sache*), to the god or demon[43] who commands that cause. Not in the sense of that inner attitude which my late friend Georg Simmel was wont to describe as 'sterile excitement'.[44] This is characteristic of a particular type of intellectual (especially Russian intellectuals, but of course not all of them!), and also plays such a large part amongst our own intellectuals at this carnival which is being graced with the proud name of a 'revolution'; it is the 'romanticism of the intellectually interesting', directed into the void and lacking all objective (*sachlich*) sense of responsibility. Simply to feel passion, however genuinely, is not sufficient to make a politician unless, in the form of service to a 'cause', *responsibility* for that cause becomes the decisive lode-star of all action. This requires (and this is the decisive psychological quality of the politician) *judgement*, the ability to maintain one's inner composure and calm while being receptive to realities, in other words *distance* from things and people. A 'lack of distance', in and of itself, is one of the deadly sins for any politician and it is one of those qualities which will condemn our future intellectuals to political incompetence if they cultivate it. For the problem is precisely this: how are hot passion and cool judgement to be forced together in a single soul? Politics is an activity conducted with the head, not with other parts of the body or soul. Yet if politics is to be genuinely human action, rather than some frivolous intellectual game, dedication to it can only be generated and sustained by passion. Only if one accustoms oneself to distance, in every sense of the word, can one achieve that powerful control over the soul which distinguishes the passionate politician from the mere 'sterile excitement' of the political amateur. The 'strength' of a political 'personality' means, first and foremost, the possession of these qualities.

Every day and every hour, therefore, the politician has to overcome a quite trivial, all-too-human enemy which threatens him from within: common *vanity*, the mortal enemy of all dedication to a cause and of all distance – in this case, of distance to oneself.

---

[43] In this instance Weber is using *Dämon* in the same sense as the English 'demon'; elsewhere he uses it without the sense of moral evil.

[44] This use of *Aufgeregtheit* as a derogatory term for revolutionary fervour was prefigured in Goethe's fragmentary satire on the consequences of the French Revolution, *Die Aufgeregten*.

Vanity is a very widespread quality, and perhaps no one is completely free of it. In academic and scholarly circles it is a kind of occupational disease. In the case of the scholar, however, unattractive though this quality may be, it is relatively harmless in the sense that it does not, as a rule, interfere with the pursuit of knowledge. Things are quite different in the case of the politician. The ambition for *power* is an inevitable means (*Mittel*) with which he works. 'The instinct for power', as it is commonly called, is thus indeed one of his normal qualities. The sin against the holy spirit of his profession begins where this striving for power becomes detached from the task in hand (*unsachlich*) and becomes a matter of purely personal self-intoxication instead of being placed entirely at the service of the 'cause'. For there are ultimately just two deadly sins in the area of politics: a lack of objectivity and – often, although not always, identical with it – a lack of responsibility. Vanity, the need to thrust one's person as far as possible into the foreground, is what leads the politician most strongly into the temptation of committing one or other (or both) of these sins, particularly as the demagogue is forced to count on making an 'impact', and for this reason is always in danger both of becoming a play-actor and of taking the responsibility for his actions too lightly and being concerned only with the 'impression' he is making. His lack of objectivity tempts him to strive for the glittering appearance of power rather than its reality, while his irresponsibility tempts him to enjoy power for its own sake, without any substantive purpose. For although, or rather precisely *because*, power is the inevitable means of all politics, and the ambition for power therefore one of its driving forces, there is no more pernicious distortion of political energy than when the parvenu boasts of his power and vainly mirrors himself in the feeling of power – or indeed any and every worship of power for its own sake. The mere 'power politician', a type whom an energetically promoted cult is seeking to glorify here in Germany as elsewhere, may give the impression of strength, but in fact his actions merely lead into emptiness and absurdity. On this point the critics of 'power politics' are quite correct. The sudden inner collapse of typical representatives of this outlook (*Gesinnung*) has shown us just how much inner weakness and ineffectuality are concealed behind this grandiose but empty pose. It stems from a most wretched and superficial lack of concern for the *meaning* of human action, a blasé attitude that knows nothing of the tragedy in which all action, but quite particularly political action, is in truth enmeshed.

It is certainly true, and it is a fundamental fact of history (for which no more detailed explanation can be offered here), that the eventual outcome of political action frequently, indeed regularly, stands in a quite inadequate, even paradoxical relation to its original, intended meaning and purpose (*Sinn*). That does not mean, however, that this meaning and purpose, service to a *cause*, can be dispensed with if action is to have any firm inner support. The *nature* of the cause the politician seeks to serve by striving for and using power is a question of faith. He can serve a national goal or the whole of humanity, or social and ethical goals, or goals which are cultural, inner-worldly or religious; he may be sustained by a strong faith in 'progress' (however this is understood), or he may coolly reject this kind of faith; he can claim to be the servant of an 'idea' or, rejecting on principle any such aspirations, he may claim to serve external goals of everyday life – but some kind of belief must always be *present*. Otherwise (and there can be no denying this) even political achievements which, outwardly, are supremely successful will be cursed with the nullity of all mortal undertakings.

Having said this, we have already broached the last problem which concerns us this evening, the problem of the ethos of politics as a 'cause' (*Sache*). What vocation can politics *per se*, quite independently of its goals, fulfil within the overall moral economy of our conduct of life? Where is what one might call the ethical home of politics? At this point, admittedly, ultimate *Weltanschauungen* collide, and one has eventually to *choose* between them. The problem has recently been re-opened for discussion (in a quite wrong-headed fashion in my view), so let us approach it resolutely.

Let us begin by freeing the problem from a quite trivial falsification. In the first place, ethics can appear in a morally quite calamitous role. Let us look at some examples. You will rarely find a man whose love has turned from one woman to another who does not feel the need to legitimate this fact to himself by saying, 'She did not deserve my love', or, 'She disappointed me', or by offering some other such 'reasons'. This is a profoundly unchivalrous attitude, for, in addition to the simple fate of his ceasing to love her, which the woman must endure, it invents for itself a 'legitimacy' that allows the man to lay claim to a 'right' while attempting to burden her not only with misfortune but also with being in the wrong. The successful rival in love behaves in exactly the same way: the other man must be of lesser worth, otherwise he would not have been defeated. The same thing happens after any victorious war, when the victor will of course assert, with ignoble self-righteousness, 'I won because I was in the right.' Or when the horrors of war cause a man to suffer a psychological breakdown, instead of simply saying, 'It was all just too much for me', he now feels the need to justify his war-weariness by substituting the feeling, 'I couldn't bear the experience because I was obliged to fight for a morally bad cause.' The same applies to those defeated in war. Instead of searching, like an old woman, for the 'guilty party' after the war (when it was in fact the structure of society that produced the war), anyone with a manly, unsentimental bearing would say to the enemy, 'We lost the war – you won it. The matter is now settled. Now let us discuss what conclusions are to be drawn in the light of the *substantive* (*sachlichen*) interests involved and – this is the main thing – in the light of the responsibility for the *future* which the victor in particular must bear.' Anything else lacks dignity and will have dire consequences. A nation will forgive damage to its interests, but not injury to its honour, and certainly not when this is done in a spirit of priggish self-righteousness. Every new document which may emerge decades afterwards will stir up the undignified squabble, all the hatred and anger, once again, whereas the war ought at least to be buried *morally* when it comes to an end. That is only possible through a sober, matter-of-fact approach (*Sachlichkeit*) and chivalry, and, above all, it is only possible where there is *dignity*. But it can never be made possible by an 'ethic' which in fact entails indignity for both sides. Instead of dealing with what concerns the politician (the future and our responsibility for it), such an 'ethical' approach concerns itself with politically sterile (because unresolvable) questions of past guilt. *This*, if anything, is what constitutes political guilt. What is more, in this process people lose sight of the inevitable falsification of the whole problem by very material interests – the interests of the victor in maximising the gain (whether moral or material), and the hopes of the defeated that they will negotiate advantages by confessing their guilt. If anything is '*common*' (*gemein*)[45] it is this, and it is the consequence of using 'ethics' as a means of 'being in the right'.

What, then, is the real relationship between *ethics* and *politics*? Have they nothing at all to do with one another, as has sometimes been said? Or is the opposite true, namely that political action is subject to 'the same' ethic as every other form of activity? At times people have believed that these two possibilities were mutually exclusive alternatives, and that either the one or the other was correct. But is it in fact true that any ethic in the world could establish substantially *identical* commandments applicable to all relationships, whether erotic, business, family or official, to one's relations with one's wife, greengrocer, son, competitor, with a friend or an accused man? Can the fact that politics operates with a quite specific means, namely power, backed up by the use of *violence*, really be a matter of such indifference as far as the ethical demands placed on politics are concerned? Have we not seen that the Bolshevik and Spartacist[46] ideologues, precisely because they use this political instrument, bring about exactly the *same* results as any militarist dictator? What, apart from the identity of the holders of power (and their amateurism) distinguishes the rule of the Workers' and Soldiers' Councils from the rule of any wielder of power under the old regime? What distinguishes the polemics directed by most exponents of the supposedly new ethics at the opponents they criticise from the polemics of any other demagogues? Their noble intentions, some will say. Very well. But the question under discussion here is the means, and their enemies lay just as much claim to noble ultimate aims, and do so with complete subjective sincerity. 'All they that take the sword shall perish with the sword',[47] and fighting is fighting everywhere. What about the ethics of the *Sermon on the Mount* then? The Sermon on the Mount, by which we mean the absolute ethics of the Gospel, is something

---

[45] For Nietzsche, as for Weber, *gemein* ('common', 'base', 'contemptible') was the antithesis of *vornehm* ('distinguished', 'noble'). Weber's objection to the (mis-)use of 'ethics' to prove one is 'in the right' echoes Nietzschean scepticism about the 'moral interpretation of phenomena'.

[46] The Spartakus League, led by Karl Liebknecht, was formed in 1916–17. A left socialist group opposed to war, it adopted the name of the Communist Party of Germany in December 1918.

[47] Matthew 26, 52.

far more serious than those who are so fond of citing its commandments today believe. It is not to be taken frivolously. What has been
said about causality in science also applies to this ethic, namely that
it is not a hired cab which one may stop at will and climb into or out
of as one sees fit. Rather, the meaning of the sermon (if it is not to
be reduced to banality) is precisely this: we must accept it in its
entirety *or* leave it entirely alone. Hence the case of the rich young
man: 'he went away sorrowful, for he had great possessions.'[48] The
commandment of the Gospel is unconditional and unambiguous –
'give all that thou hast' – *everything*, absolutely. The politician will
say that this is an excessive and socially meaningless demand if it is
not made to apply to *everybody*, which means taxation, expropriation
by taxation, confiscation, in other words, coercion and order applied
to *all*. The ethical commandment disregards such questions *completely* – that is its essence. The same applies to the injunction to
'turn the other cheek!' – unconditionally, without asking by what right
the other person has struck you. An ethic of indignity, except for a
saint. This is the heart of the matter: it is necessary to be a saint in
all things, or at least one must want to be one, one must live like
Jesus, the Apostles, Saint Francis and men of that kind; *then* this
type of ethic becomes meaningful and expresses a kind of dignity.
But not otherwise. For while it is a consequence of the unworldly ethic
of love to say, 'resist not evil with force',[49] the politician is governed
by the contrary maxim, namely, ' You *shall* resist evil with force, for
if you do not, you are *responsible* for the spread of evil.' Anyone
seeking to act in accordance with the ethic of the Gospel should not
go on strike, since strikes are a form of coercion; instead he should
join an unaffiliated trade union. Above all, he should not talk of
'revolution', for that ethic surely does not teach that civil war of all
things is the only legitimate form of war. The pacifist whose actions
are guided by the Gospel will refuse weapons or throw them away,
as we Germans were recommended to do, so that we might fulfil our
ethical duty to end the war, and thus to end all war. The politician
will say that the only sure means of discrediting war for the *foreseeable*
future would have been peace on the basis of the *status quo*. Then
the people of all nations would have asked what the point of the war

[48] Matthew 19, 22.
[49] Matthew 5, 39: 'That ye resist not evil: but whosoever shall smite thee on thy right
cheek, turn to him the other also.'

was. It would have been reduced to absurdity, which is not now possible. For the war will have proved to be politically profitable for the victors, or at least for some of them. The responsibility for this outcome lies with the behaviour which made it quite impossible for us to resist. What will now happen – once the phase of exhaustion has passed – is, that *peace, not war, will have been discredited* – and this will be the result of absolute ethics.

Finally, there is the duty to be truthful. For the ethic of absolute principles this is an unconditional duty.[50] Hence it was concluded that all documents should be published, especially those which placed a burden of guilt on our country, and that a confession of guilt should be made on the basis of these documents – unilaterally, unconditionally, regardless of the consequences. The politician will take the view that the upshot of this will not serve the cause of truth, but rather that truth will certainly be obscured by the misuse of the documents and by the passions they unleash. He will take the view that the only productive approach would be a systematic, comprehensive investigation, conducted by disinterested parties; any other way of proceeding could have consequences for the nation which could not be repaired in decades. 'Consequences', however, are no *concern* of absolutist ethics.

That is the crucial point. We have to understand that ethically oriented activity can follow two fundamentally different, irreconcilably opposed maxims. It can follow the 'ethic of principled conviction' (*Gesinnung*) or the 'ethic of responsibility'. It is not that the ethic of conviction is identical with irresponsibility, nor that the ethic of responsibility means the absence of principled conviction – there is of course no question of that. But there is a profound opposition between acting by the maxim of the ethic of conviction (putting it in religious terms: 'The Christian does what is right and places the outcome in God's hands'),[51] and acting by the maxim of the ethic of

---

[50] Kant's attempt to found ethics on the 'categorical imperative' led him to argue that there was an absolute obligation to tell the truth, even where to do so might lead to the loss of human life. See, for example, *The Metaphysics of Morals*, ed. M. Gregor (Cambridge, 1991), pp. 225–7. Kant's was one of the most influential voices arguing for 'anti-consequentialism' in ethics in Germany.

[51] Although an exact source for these words (used on several occasions by Weber) has not been traced, the editors of the new *Gesamtausgabe* believe they allude to a passage in Luther's lectures on *Genesis*, 'Fac tuum officium, et eventum Deo permitte', *D. Martin Luthers Werke. Kritische Gesamtausgabe*, vol. XLIV (Weimar, 1915), p. 78.

responsibility, which means that one must answer for the (foreseeable) *consequences* of one's actions. A syndicalist who is committed to the ethics of conviction might be fully aware that the likely consequences of his actions will be, say, increased chances for the forces of reaction, increased oppression of his own class, a brake on the rise of his class. But none of this will make the slightest impression on him. If evil consequences flow from an action done out of pure conviction, this type of person holds the world, not the doer, responsible, or the stupidity of others, or the will of God who made them thus. A man who subscribes to the ethic of responsibility, by contrast, will make allowances for precisely these everyday shortcomings in people. He has no right, as Fichte correctly observed,[52] to presuppose goodness and perfection in human beings. He does not feel that he can shuffle off the consequences of his own actions, as far as he could foresee them, and place the burden on the shoulders of others. He will say, 'These consequences are to be attributed to my actions.' The person who subscribes to the ethic of conviction feels 'responsible' only for ensuring that the flame of pure conviction (for example, the flame of protest against the injustice of the social order) is never extinguished. To kindle that flame again and again is the purpose of his actions, actions which, judged from the point of view of their possible success, are utterly irrational, and which can and are only intended to have exemplary value.

Yet we have still not reached the end of the problem. No ethics in the world can get round the fact that the achievement of 'good' ends is in many cases tied to the necessity of employing morally suspect or at least morally dangerous means, and that one must reckon with the possibility or even likelihood of evil side-effects. Nor can any ethic in the world determine when and to what extent the ethically good end 'sanctifies' the ethically dangerous means and side-effects.

The decisive means of politics is the use of violence. Just how great are the ramifications of the ethical tension between ends and means in politics can be seen in the case of the revolutionary socialists

---

[52] Fichte quotes such sentiments from Machiavelli's *Discourses* in 'Über Macchiavelli (sic!) als Schriftsteller', *Johann Gottlieb Fichtes nachgelassene Werke*, vol. III (Bonn, 1856), p. 420.

(the Zimmerwald faction).[53] Even during the war, as is generally known, they espoused a principle which one might characterise thus: 'If the choice lies between a few more years of war, followed by a revolution, and peace now but no revolution, we choose a few more years of war.' If then asked what this revolution might achieve, any scientifically trained socialist would have replied that there could be no question of a transition to an economy deserving the name 'socialist' as *he* understood the term. Rather, a bourgeois economy would arise again which would have shed only its feudal elements and the remnants of dynasticism. For this modest result they would accept 'a few more years of war'! In this instance it could well be said that even a person of very firm socialist convictions might reject the end if these are the means it demands. But this is precisely how things stand with Bolshevism and Spartacism and indeed every type of revolutionary socialism. Hence it is of course utterly ridiculous for such people to condemn *morally* the 'politicians of violence' of the old regime for using precisely the same means as they are prepared to use (no matter how justified they may be in rejecting the *aims* of the other side).

It seems that the ethics of conviction is bound to founder hopelessly on this problem of how the end is to sanctify the means. Indeed the only position it can logically take is to *reject any* action which employs morally dangerous means. Logically. In the real world, admittedly, we repeatedly see the proponent of the 'ethics of conviction' suddenly turning into a chiliastic prophet. Those who have been preaching 'love against force' one minute, for example, issue a call to force the next; they call for one *last* act of force to create the situation in which *all* violence will have been destroyed for ever – just like our military leaders who said to the soldiers before every attack that this would be the last, that it would bring victory and then peace. The man who espouses an ethic of conviction cannot bear the ethical irrationality of the world. He is a cosmic-ethical 'rationalist'. Those of you who know their Dostoyevsky will recall the scene with the Grand Inquisitor, where the problem is dissected very acutely.[54]

---

[53] In September 1915 a group of radical socialists held a conference in Zimmerwald (near Berne) with the aim of founding a new (Third) International. Despite further conferences in 1916 and 1917, they could not achieve unity.

[54] F. Dostoyevsky *The Brothers Karamazov*, Book 5, ch. 5.

It is not possible to unite the ethic of conviction with the ethic of responsibility, nor can one issue an ethical decree determining which end shall sanctify *which* means, if indeed any concession at all is to be made to this principle.

My colleague, F. W. Foerster,[55] a man I hold in the highest personal esteem because of the undoubted integrity of his convictions (although I reject him unreservedly as a politician), thinks that he can get round the difficulty in his book with the simple thesis that only good can flow from good, only evil from evil. Were this so, the whole, complex problem would admittedly not exist. Yet it is astonishing that such a thesis could still see the light of day 2,500 years after the Upanishads were composed. Not just the entire course of world history, but any unbiased examination of daily experience, proclaims the opposite. The development of all the religions in the world rests, after all, on the fact that the opposite is true. The age-old problem of theodicy is, after all, the question of how a power which is said to be both all-powerful and benevolent can possibly have created such an irrational world of undeserved suffering, unpunished injustice and incorrigible stupidity. Either that power is not all-powerful or it is not benevolent – or quite other principles of compensation and retribution govern life, principles which we may be able to interpret metaphysically or which will for ever elude our interpretation. This problem, the experience of the irrationality of the world, was, after all, the driving force behind all religious development. The Indian doctrine of *karma*, Persian dualism, original sin, predestination and the concept of the *deus absconditus*, all these notions have grown out of precisely this experience. The early Christians too knew very well that the world was governed by demons, that anyone who gets involved with politics, which is to say with the means of power and violence, is making a pact with diabolical powers, and that it does *not* hold true of his actions that only good can come of good and only evil from evil, but rather that the opposite is often the case. Anyone who fails to see this is indeed a child in political matters.

Religious ethics have adopted various strategies to come to terms with the fact that we are placed in various orders of life, each of

---

[55] F. W. Foerster (1869–1966) was a leading spokesman of the Society for Ethical Culture. His *Staatsbürgerliche Erziehung* (1910) ('Education for Citizenship', reprinted under the title *Politische Ethik und politische Pädagogik*) was a popular expression of the ideas of this movement for social reform.

which is subject to different laws. Hellenic polytheism sacrificed to Aphrodite and also to Hera, to Dionysos as well as to Apollo, knowing that these gods were often in conflict with one another. The Hindu order of life made each of the various occupations subject to a particular ethical law, a *dharma*, and forever divided them one from another into castes, setting them in a rigid hierarchy of rank from which there was no escape for the individual born into a particular caste, except through reincarnation in the next life; the different occupations were thereby placed at varying distances from the highest religious goods of salvation. Hinduism was therefore able to elaborate the *dharma* for each caste, from the ascetics and Brahmins down to the rogues and whores, according to the immanent and particular laws governing each occupation, including war and politics. How war is fitted into the totality of the orders of life can be found in the *Bhagavad Gita*, in the discussion between Krishna and Arduna. 'Do what is necessary', which means whatever 'work' is imposed as a duty by the *dharma* of the warrior caste and its rules, whatever is objectively necessary in relation to the purpose of war. According to this belief, acting thus is not injurious to religious salvation; indeed it serves this end. Admission to Indra's heaven had always been assured to the Indian warrior who died a hero's death just as certainly as Valhalla was to the Germanic warrior. But the former would have scorned Nirvana just as surely as the latter would have scorned the paradise of Christianity with its choirs of angels. This specialisation of ethics made it possible for Indian ethics to treat the regal art of politics quite without reservation or scruple, following the peculiar laws of politics alone, indeed intensifying them radically. Truly radical 'Machiavellianism', in the popular sense of the word, finds its classic expression in Indian literature in the *Kautaliya Artha-Sastra* (composed long before Christianity, allegedly in the time of Chandragupta), in comparison with which Machiavelli's *Principe* is harmless. In Catholic ethics, to which Professor Foerster is otherwise sympathetic, the *consilia evangelica* are, as is generally known, a special ethic for those gifted with the charisma of holy life. Here, alongside the monk, who may spill no blood nor seek material gain, there stand the pious knight and the burgher, the first of whom may do the former, while the second may do the latter. The gradations in this ethic and its integration within an organic doctrine of salvation are less consistent than in India, as was bound to be the case, given the assumptions of the Christian faith. Because the world was corrupted by original sin, it was possible to build violence relatively easily into ethics as a means of chastising sin and heretics who endangered the soul. But the unworldly demands of the Sermon on the Mount, which represent a pure ethics of conviction, and the absolute demand for religious natural justice founded on the Sermon, have retained their revolutionary force and come to the fore with elemental power in almost every period of social upheaval. In particular they created the radical pacifist sects, one of which experimented in Pennsylvania with a state that abjured force in its relations with other states. The outcome of the experiment was tragic, however, inasmuch as the Quakers could not take up arms on behalf of their own ideals at the outbreak of the War of Independence, although this was fought on behalf of those very ideals. Normal Protestantism, by contrast, legitimated the state absolutely (and thus its means, violence) as a divine institution, and gave its blessing to the legitimate authoritarian state in particular. Luther relieved the individual of ethical responsibility for war and placed it on the shoulders of authority, asserting that no guilt could ever be involved in obeying authority in matters other than faith. Calvinism in its turn recognised as a matter of principle the use of force as a means to defend the faith, in other words religious war, which, in Islam, was a vital element in religion from the very beginning. Plainly, the problem of political ethics is *not* just one that has been thrown up by the modern lack of faith engendered by the cult of the hero during the Renaissance. All religions have grappled with it, and with very varying degrees of success; in view of what has been said above, things could not have been otherwise. The specific means of *legitimate violence per se* in the hands of human associations is what gives all the ethical problems of politics their particular character.

Anyone who makes a pact with the means of violence, for whatever purpose – and every politician does this – is at the mercy of its specific consequences. This applies particularly to the man fighting for a belief, whether religious or revolutionary. Let us simply take the present as an example. Anyone wishing to establish absolute justice on earth by *force* needs a following in order to do so, a human 'apparatus'. He must promise these people the necessary inner and outward prizes – rewards in heaven or on earth – because the apparatus will not function otherwise. Under the conditions of modern class-warfare the inner rewards are the satisfaction of hatred and revenge, of *ressentiment* and the need for the pseudo-ethical feeling of being in the right, the desire to slander one's opponents and make heretics of them. The outward rewards are adventure, victory, booty, power and prebends. The success of the leader is entirely dependent on the functioning of his apparatus. He is therefore dependent on *its* motives, not his own. He is dependent also on the possibility of providing those prizes *permanently* to his following, the Red Guard, the informers, the agitators he needs. Given these conditions of his activity, what he actually achieves does not, therefore, lie in his own hands but is, rather, prescribed for him by the, in ethical terms, predominantly base or common (*gemein*) motives prompting the actions of his following. He can only keep control of his following as long as a sincere belief in his person and his cause inspires at least some of the group, probably never in this life even the majority of them. Not only is this faith, even when held with subjective sincerity, in many cases merely the ethical 'legitimation' of the craving for revenge, power, booty and prebends (and let no-one try to persuade us differently, for the materialist interpretation of history is not a cab which may be boarded at will, and it makes no exceptions for the bearers of revolutions!), but the emotionalism of revolution is then followed by a return to traditional, *everyday existence*, the hero of the faith disappears, and so, above all, does the faith itself, or it becomes (even more effectively) a part of the conventional rhetoric used by political philistines and technicians. This development comes about particularly quickly in a war of faith, because these are usually conducted or inspired by genuine *leaders*, prophets of revolution. For it is one of the conditions of success in this, as in any apparatus subordinate to a leader, that things must be emptied and made into matters-of-fact (*Versachlichung*), and the following must undergo spiritual proletarianisation, in order to achieve 'discipline'. This is why the following of a man fighting for a faith, when it begins to rule, tends to decline particularly easily into a quite ordinary stratum of prebendaries.

Anyone wishing to practise politics of any kind, and especially anyone who wishes to make a profession of politics, has to be conscious of these ethical paradoxes and of his responsibility for what may become of *himself* under pressure from them. He is becoming involved, I repeat, with the diabolical powers that lurk in all violence.

The great virtuosi of unworldly goodness and love for mankind, whether they came from Nazareth or Assisi or from the palaces of Indian kings, did not employ the means of politics, force. Their kingdom was 'not of this world' and yet they worked, and work still, in this world, and the figures of Platon Karatayev[56] and Dostoyevsky's saints are still the closest imitations of their lives. Anyone seeking to save his own soul and the souls of others does not take the path of politics in order to reach his goal, for politics has quite different tasks, namely those which can only be achieved by force. The genius – or demon – of politics lives in a state of inner tension with the god of love, and even with the Christian God as manifested in the institution of the church, a tension that may erupt at any moment into irresolvable conflict. Even in the days of church rule people were aware of this. Again and again the interdict was imposed on Florence (something which represented at the time a far greater power over men and the salvation of their souls than what Fichte has called the 'cold approbation' of Kant's ethical judgement),[57] and yet the citizens of Florence fought against the Holy See. Machiavelli had such situations in mind when, in a beautiful passage in his Florentine histories (if my memory does not deceive me),[58] he has one of his heroes praise those citizens who placed the greatness of their native city above the salvation of their souls.

To see the problem in its current guise, replace the terms 'native city' or 'Fatherland' (which may not strike everyone as an unambiguous value at present) with 'the future of socialism' or even 'the achievement of international peace'. The 'salvation of the soul' is endangered by each of these, whenever men strive to attain them by *political* activity, employing the means of violence and acting on the basis of an ethic of responsibility. Yet if the soul's salvation is pursued in a war of faith fought purely out of an ethic of conviction, it may be damaged and discredited for generations to come, because responsibility for the *consequences* is lacking. In such circumstances those engaged in action remain unaware of the diabolical powers at

---

[56] Platon Karatayev is a character in Tolstoy's *War and Peace*.

[57] 'Das System der Sittenlehre nach den Principien der Wissenschaftslehre', *Johann Gottlieb Fichtes sämmtliche Werke*, vol. IV (Berlin, 1845), p. 167.

[58] The reference is to Machiavelli, *Florentine Histories*, Book 3, ch. 7, p. 114: 'so much more did those citizens esteem their fatherland than their souls' (in the translation by L. F. Banfield and H. C. Mansfield, Princeton, 1988).

work. They are inexorable, bringing about the consequences of their actions, including consequences for their inner being, to which they will fall helpless victims if they remain blind to them. 'The devil is old, so become old if you want to understand him'[59] – the saying does not refer to one's age measured in years. I too have never allowed myself to be outdone in debate simply because of a date on a birth certificate; equally, the mere fact that someone is twenty whereas I am over fifty does not persuade me that this in itself is an achievement before which I must expire in awe. What matters is not age but the trained ability to look at the realities of life with an unsparing gaze, to bear these realities and be a match for them inwardly.

For truly, although politics is something done with the head, it is certainly not something done with the head *alone*. On this point the conviction-moralists are entirely correct. But whether one *ought* to act on the basis of an ethics of conviction or one of responsibility, and *when* one should do the one or the other, these are not things about which one can give instructions to anybody. There is just one thing one can say in these times of excitement – *not*, you believe, a 'sterile' form of excitement (although excitement is not always the same as true passion) – if, *suddenly*, conviction-politicians spring up all around, proclaiming, 'The world is stupid and base (*gemein*), not I. Responsibility for the consequences does not fall on me but on the others, in whose service I work and whose stupidity or baseness I shall eradicate', then I say plainly that I want to know how much *inner weight* is carried by this ethic of conviction. For it is my impression that, in nine cases out of ten, I am dealing with windbags, people who are intoxicated with romantic sensations but who do not truly feel what they are taking upon themselves. Such conduct holds little human interest for me and it most certainly does not shake me to the core. On the other hand it is immensely moving when a mature person (whether old or young) who feels with his whole soul the responsibility he bears for the real consequences of his actions, and who acts on the basis of an ethics of responsibility, says at some point, 'Here I stand, I can do no other.'[60] That is something genuinely human and profoundly moving. For it must be *possible* for *each* of us

---

[59] Goethe, *Faust*, Part II, lines 6817–18.
[60] Luther is reported to have said this at the Diet of Worms in 1521.

to find ourselves in such a situation at some point if we are not inwardly dead. In this respect, the ethics of conviction and the ethics of responsibility are not absolute opposites. They are complementary to one another, and only in combination do they produce the true human being who is *capable* of having a 'vocation for politics'.

And now, ladies and gentlemen, let us return to these questions *ten years* from now. If by that time, as I am bound to fear will be the case, an age of reaction has set in for a whole series of reasons, and little has been realised of all those things which many of you and (as I freely admit) I too have wished and hoped for – perhaps not exactly none of them but apparently only very little (this is very likely, but it will not break my spirit, although I confess that it is an inward burden) – then I would very much like to see what has become of those of you – what has 'become' of you in the innermost sense of the word – who at present feel themselves genuinely to be 'politicians of conviction' and who share in the intoxication (*Rausch*)[61] which this revolution signifies. It would be fine indeed if Shakespeare's Sonnet 102 fitted the situation:

> Our love was new, and then but in the spring,
> When I was wont to greet it with my lays;
> As Philomel in summer's front doth sing,
> And stops her pipe in growth of riper days.

But that is not how things are. What lies immediately ahead of us is not the flowering of summer but a polar night of icy darkness and hardness, no matter which group wins the outward victory now. For, where there is nothing, not only has the Kaiser lost his rights but so too has the proletarian. When this night slowly begins to recede, which of those people will still be alive whose early summer seems now to have flowered so profusely? And what will have become of you all inwardly? Embitterment or philistinism, sheer, dull acceptance of the world and of your job (*Beruf*) – or the third, and not the least common possibility, a mystical flight from the world on the part of those with the gift for it or – a frequent and pernicious variant – on the part of those who force themselves into such an attitude because

---

[61] In criticising the *Rausch* ('intoxication') of revolutionary enthusiasm, Weber is striking at the ready welcome given to the 'Dionysian' aspects of Nietzsche's thought by many German intellectuals at the time.

it is fashionable. In every such case I will draw the conclusion that they were *not* inwardly a match for their own actions, *nor* were they a match for the world as it really is, nor for their daily existence. Objectively and actually, they did not have the vocation they thought they had for politics in the innermost sense of the word. They would have done better to cultivate plain and simple brotherliness with other individuals, and, for the rest, to have worked soberly (*sachlich*) at their daily tasks.

Politics means slow, strong drilling through hard boards, with a combination of passion and a sense of judgement. It is of course entirely correct, and a fact confirmed by all historical experience, that what is possible would never have been achieved if, in this world, people had not repeatedly reached for the impossible. But the person who can do this must be a leader; not only that, he must, in a very simple sense of the word, be a hero. And even those who are neither of these things must, even now, put on the armour of that stead-fastness of heart which can withstand even the defeat of all hopes, for otherwise they will not even be capable of achieving what is possible today. Only someone who is certain that he will not be broken when the world, seen from his point of view, is too stupid or too base for what he wants to offer it, and who is certain that he will be able to say 'Nevertheless' in spite of everything – only someone like this has a 'vocation' for politics.

Glossary

This is a glossary of key words used in the translated texts. In most cases the reader's attention is directed to the glossary by the inclusion of the German term, in brackets, after its translation, at least on the first occurrence. Terms have been included in the list for a variety of reasons. Some have a range of meanings which require them to be translated differently in different contexts (e.g. *Politik, Sache, sachlich*); some have no satisfactory equivalent in English (e.g. *Bürger, Bildung, Machtstaat*) and in a number of cases have simply been adopted into English usage; some have a different semantic range from their seeming equivalent in English (e.g. *Kultur*); some are closely associated with the thought of particular writers (e.g. *Ressentiment, vornehm*); some are institutional terms which are often left untranslated in works on German history or politics (e.g. *Reichstag, Bundesrat*); some are technical terms for which Weber offers his own definitions (e.g. *Herrschaft, Verband*). In cases where the gloss includes Weber's own definition, this has been translated from volume I of *Wirtschaft und Gesellschaft* (WG); the reader is also referred to the corresponding passage in Roth and Wittich's translation of *Economy and Society* (ES).

One of the peculiarities of Weber's language is the application of apparently anachronistic terminology, usually of medieval or early Germanic provenance (e.g. *Pfründe, Gefolgschaft*), to modern phenomena. The effect, and presumably the intention, is to draw attention to continuities in social and political arrangements which might otherwise remain unnoticed thanks to the introduction of new vocabulary to describe the 'new' phenomena. Generally speaking, the translation tries to convey any single German term by a fixed equivalent (e.g. *Mittel* by 'means' or occasionally 'instrument'), even where some more concrete term might have seemed more natural in a particular context. Thus *Machtmittel* is translated as 'means of power' rather than, say, 'weapon' because Weber, who had *Waffe* at his disposal in German, clearly preferred to form a compound from two of his key terms, thereby creating semantic links between different areas of activity (e.g. with *Betriebsmittel* or *Arbeitsmittel*). Similarly, *Beamter* is rendered as 'official' in all contexts (including those, for example, where, in the equivalent English situation, one would use 'civil servant'), since Weber's intention is to indicate functional similarities in different forms of organisation (governmental administration, the army, non-governmental administration). The word *Stand* has been translated in almost every case as 'estate', despite the relative unfamiliarity of both word and concept in English, because simply to substitute something like 'status group' would be to shift Weber's writing into an alien discourse. The overall aim of the translation has thus been to remain as close as possible to the German and to Weber's own, at times somewhat idiosyncratic, use of language, in the hope of providing the non-German-speaking reader with a bridge *into* the traditions of thought, values and feelings in which Weber and his intended readership were immersed, in preference to any attempt to uproot and transplant Weber's thought from its native cultural environment into the idioms of the English-speaking world.

Abgeordnetenhaus: Chamber of Deputies.
Abgeordneter: Deputy (in parliament).
abkömmlich: available, dispensable. The word literally means 'able to come away', in the sense that a person can easily be dispensed from his business in order to make himself 'available' for other things, such as politics.
Amtsgeheimnis: official secret.
Arbeitsmittel: means of work.
Aufklärung: enlightenment.
Auslese: selection. For further comment, see note 5, p. 21.
Ausnahmegesetz: emergency law, exceptional legislation.

Beamtenherrschaft: rule by officials.
Beamtenschaft: body of officials.
Beamtentum: officialdom.

Beamter: official.

beherrschen: to have command of or over, to rule.

die Beherrschten: the ruled.

Beruf: occupation, profession, vocation. In this last, most 'inward' sense, secular activity, such as politics, becomes heir to the pathos which originally attached to the inner voice of a religious calling.

Berufsstand: occupational estate (see *Stand*).

berufsständische Vertretung: representative assembly based on occupational estates or corporations (see note 10, p. 88).

Berufsverband: occupational association.

Betrieb: enterprise, activity, operation, conduct, organisation, firm, business. Weber defines the term thus (WG, 28; ES, 52): 'Continuous purposive action of a specific kind will be called *enterprise*.' The need to translate this central term so variously arises from the fact that it can denote either the conduct of an activity e.g. *der Betrieb der Politik*, 'the conduct of politics' or a set of activities or practices (*der wissenschaftliche Betrieb*, 'the business of science'), or an institution or organisation in which such activity is carried out (*ein kapitalistischer Betrieb*, 'a capitalist firm'). The term is often used by Weber to refer simultaneously to an activity and to its framework, as when he describes party politics as an *Interessentenbetrieb*, which roughly means 'a form of political organisation run by and, at least in part, for the benefit of interested parties'. The generality of *Betrieb* provides Weber with a common denominator for a range of activities and forms of organisation.

Betriebsmittel: means of operation.

Bevollmächtigter: plenipotentiary, delegate (of individual state in *Bundesrat*).

bezaubern: enchant.

Bildung: education. The German term is loftier in tone than its English equivalent. Its root meaning is 'formation', from which it has been extended to mean the development of a rounded personality and a cultivated mind and sensibility.

Bund: union, federation, Federation (in reference to the states federated in the German Empire).

Bundesrat: The 'Federal Council' (with executive powers) in Germany during the Second German Empire, composed of the heads of state (or their mandated 'plenipotentiaries') of the individual states in what was formally at least a federal structure.

Bürger: citizen, member of the middle class, bourgeois. The English reader needs to be aware, however, that, far from having derogatory overtones of self-centred materialism (for which the imported word *Bourgeois* was usually reserved), *Bürgertum* and *Bürgerlichkeit* represented for many Germans (and certainly for Weber) a proud tradition of educated, civil and moral virtues which were not merely expressions of class interest.

bürgerlich: the adjective from *Bürger*, hence civil, middle-class, bourgeois.

Bürgertum: the collective of *Bürger*, the middle class(es).

Charisma: charisma. The quality in a person which gives rise to one of Weber's 'three *pure* types of legitimate rule'. Weber defines it as follows (WG, 140; ES, 241): 'By "charisma" is to be understood the quality of a personality, held to be out of the ordinary (and originally thought to have magical sources, both in the case of prophets and men who are wise in healing or in law, the leaders of the hunt or heroes in war), on account of which the person is evaluated as being gifted with supernatural or superhuman or at least specifically out of the ordinary powers not accessible to everybody, and hence as a *"leader"*.' Weber insists that this evaluation is specifically that of the person's *followers*, and does not necessarily implicate the user of the term in the same evaluation.

Couleurwesen: the institution of (frequently political) student clubs or fraternities (see note 27, p. 115).

Dämon: can either refer to an evil or harmful spirit, as in the English 'demon', or to the 'daimon' at the core of an individual's personality.

Deutschtum: the German people or race, or the German character (the quality of 'German-ness').

Dienstwissen: official information or specialist knowledge, access to which is restricted to particular groups of officials.

Dreiklassenwahlrecht: Three Class Suffrage (see note 6, p. 82).

Durchstaatlichung: the taking of an industry into state management (see note 11, p. 283).

Enquête: enquiry, investigation.
Entzauberung: disenchantment.
Erwerb: gain.
Erwerbskapitalismus: entrepreneurial capitalism.

Fabrikherr: factory owner, master.
Fachbeamter: trained, specialist official.
Führer: leader. In Weber's usage this term does not seem to be clearly
    distinct from *Leiter* and does not convey the negative overtones
    'Führer' has acquired since his time.
Fürsprech: spokesman (in early Germanic trial procedure).

Gebilde: formation.
Gefolgschaft: following. One of the terms used by Weber which now
    normally refer only to an earlier historical period and which
    therefore have an archaic flavour when extended, as in Weber's
    usage, to modern phenomena. In this case the historical referent
    of the word is the Germanic military following, bound to its
    leader by an oath of personal loyalty, hence roughly equivalent to
    English 'liegemen', while its modern referent in Weber's usage is
    the following of a leader, particularly the leader of a modern
    political party. The distancing or estranging effect of the
    German term in a modern context needs to be borne in mind,
    since the flavour is not adequately conveyed by 'following' but
    would be overstated if one substituted 'liegemen'.
Gehäuse: housing, casing, carapace. For detailed comments on this
    recurrent metaphor, see note 57, p. 68 and note 11, p. 90).
Geheimrat: 'Privy Councillor', permanent under-secretary, title given
    to the highest civil servants until 1918.
gemein: common, mostly with the derogatory sense of 'base'; the anti-
    thesis of *vornehm* (see note 45, p. 357).
Gemeinschaft: community.
Gemeinwirtschaft: communal economy (see note 14, p. 91).
Geist: mind, mentality, spirit.
Gesellschaft: society.
Gesinnung: deeply held convictions, principles, sentiment (as in *mon-
    archische Gesinnung*, 'monarchic sentiment'), moral quality (as in
    edle Gesinnung, 'nobility of mind').
Gesinnungsethik: ethic of principled conviction.

gesinnungspolitische Partei: party of political principle.
Gewalt: force.
Gewaltsamkeit: violence.
Gewinn: profit.
Grundherr: landlord (who frequently also exercised police authority).
Gutsherr: lord of the manor.

Herr: any person who exercises *Herrschaft* or 'rule' (see below). Hence, depending on the context, 'lord', 'master', 'factory owner' (*Fabrikherr*), 'head of the household' (*Hausherr*), 'warlord' (*Kriegsherr*).
Herrengewalt(-en): power(-s) of rule, prerogatives.
Herrenvolk: nation of masters (see note 42, p. 124).
Herrschaft: rule. Weber defines the term thus (WG, 28; ES, 53): 'By *rule* is to be understood the chance of having an order with a specific content obeyed by specifiable persons.' (To render *Herrschaft* as 'domination', as in an earlier translation, is to use an emotionally weighted word and to blur the distinction Weber drew between the exercise of *Herrschaft*, which is validated by a general context of assent, and the mere exercise of *Macht* (see below) which need not be so validated.
Herrschaftsverband: an 'association of rule', defined thus by Weber (WG, 29; ES, 51): 'An association shall be called an *association of rule* inasmuch as its members are, as such, subject to relations of rule by virtue of an order accepted as valid.'
herrschen: to rule or (metaphorically) to hold sway.
Herrscher: ruler.
Hörigkeit: serfdom.
Honoratioren: notables.

ideell: ideal, relating both to ideas and to ideals.
Innenpolitik: domestic politics, domestic policy.
innerlich: inward.
Innerlichkeit: inwardness. The value of 'inwardness', meaning the capacity for intense personal, mental or emotional preoccupation with something, was for long regarded as a central characteristic of German *bürgerlich* culture.
Instanz: authority, institution. In legal parlance the English equivalent is 'instance' (as 'in court of last instance'), but German usage is wider than this.

Interessent: interested party, person with vested interests.
Interessentenverband: interest group, lobby.

Jurist: covers a range of meanings including 'jurist', 'legal expert', 'writer on law', 'professor of law', 'student of law' or simply someone trained in law. In terms of the generality of its application, the nearest equivalent in English is probably 'lawyer', but it should be remembered that the two legal systems are very different, the one being deductive in its determination of what is lawful and the other inductive.

Kleinadel: minor nobility.
Kleinbürgertum: petty bourgeoisie.
kollegial: collegial. Although the English word is fairly rare, referring principally to the sharing by Roman Catholic bishops in the government of the church, it nevertheless conveys the correct sense of co-responsible government (see note 15, p. 323). Weber's highly differentiated definition of the term can be found in WG, 158–67 (or ES, 271–83).
Kontrolle: control, scrutiny, supervision.
Körperschaft: body, corporation.
Kronrat: Crown Council.
Kultur: culture, civilisation. In contrast to English usage, the German word encompasses not only 'high' and 'low' culture, but most of what comprises the content of people's everyday lives, as in *friedliche Kulturarbeit* (see note 8, p. 5).
Kulturpolitik: cultural policy, both in the narrower and wider senses of *Kultur*. Weber repeatedly contrasts this term with *Staatspolitik*.
kulturpolitisch: translated, for want of an equivalent concept in English, as 'cultural-political'.
Kulturstand: level of cultural development.
Kulturvolk: cultural nation (i.e. one which contributes to the advance of culture).

Landamman: cantonal president (in Switzerland).
Landrat: district superintendent (in Prussia); a type of magistrate and administrator.
Landtag: diet. The parliament in each of the federated states (*Länder*) in the German Reich.

Leiter: leader, manager.
Leitung: leadership, management, direction.
leiturgisch: liturgical (see note 33, p. 158).
Literat: man of letters, littérateur. Occasionally Weber uses the term
in its neutral, descriptive sense (of a *literatus* or 'lettered person')
to refer to the literate classes whose skills made them invaluable
as administrators and advisers. In the contemporary context,
however, Weber mostly uses it censoriously to refer to those
writers, frequently in academic positions, who seek to influence
political life by their writings although lacking, in his opinion,
the expertise to do so and shouldering no political responsibility
for the effects of what they write.
loyal: in good faith, fair.

Macht: power. It is defined thus by Weber (WG, 28; ES, 53): '*Power*
means every chance of imposing one's own will within a social
relation, even against resistance, regardless of what this chance
is based on.'
Machtmittel: means or instrument of power.
Machtstaat: As Weber uses the term in these essays, it means a state
competing for power in the international arena.
majorisieren: to outvote.
maßgebend: decisive, crucial, the ... that matters.
mediatisieren: mediatise (see note 65, p. 234).
Misere: misère. The term refers to deplorable political conditions.
Mittel: means, instrument, device.

Nationalstaat: nation state.
Notstandsgesetz: emergency law.

Obrigkeitsstaat: authoritarian state; a state entirely focused on its ruling
monarch or class.

Parlamentarier: member of parliament, parliamentarian.
Parlamentarisierung: the introduction of parliamentary government.
Parteiwesen: party system.
Phrase: empty phrase, empty rhetoric.
Pfründe: prebends. Originally the grant of an assured income, in
money or in kind, to the holder of a clerical post, but applied

by Weber to modern conditions where it refers to the benefits (salary, pension) granted to officials (*Beamte*), who were (and are) unusually well provided for in Germany. For Weber's distinction between 'fief feudalism' and 'prebendal feudalism' see WG, 151–3 (ES, 259–61).

Polentum: the Polish population, 'Polishness'.

Politik: politics, policy, policies.

politischer Verband: political association. Weber defines this sub-category of *Herrschaftsverband* thus (WG, 29; ES, 54): 'An association of rule shall be called a *political* association only inasmuch as its existence and the validity of its ordinances within a definable geographical *territory* are continuously guaranteed by the application and threat of *physical* compulsion on the part of the administrative staff.'

Präsidialstimme: presidial vote.

Rechtsordnung: legal order, law and order.

Rechtsstaat: state founded on the rule of law.

regieren: govern.

Regierung: government.

Reichstag: The German national parliament, elected (at the time Weber was writing) by universal male suffrage. It did not have executive power, which lay with the *Bundesrat*; the head of government, the *Reichskanzler*, was a direct appointee of the Kaiser.

Rentier: rentier. The term (now commonly used by English economists) refers to a person with an unearned income or pension (*Renten* or *Rente* in German).

Ressentiment: Left untranslated in order to indicate the link with the writings of Nietzsche, where the term (borrowed from Paul Bourget) refers to the vindictive feelings felt by weaker natures towards those who are 'born leaders' (see note 8, p. 135).

Sache: thing, matter, issue, also cause (as in *der Kampf für eine Sache*, 'the fight for a cause'), and case (argued by an advocate or politician), an area of competence or responsibility.

sachlich: means 'relating to a "Sache"', hence, depending on context, variously translated as objective, sober, technical, practical, substantive, material.

Sachlichkeit: the noun from *sachlich*, translated by the same range of equivalents, but extended by Weber to include the oxymoron *leidenschaftliche Sachlichkeit* ('passionate objectivity' or 'passionate concern with an issue').

Sammlungspolitik: policy of national solidarity (see note 67, p. 73).

Schicht: stratum.

Schicksal: fate.

Selbstherrschaft: autocracy.

Selbstverwaltung: self-administration, self-government (often in the context of local government).

Septennat: from 1874 onwards the seven-yearly estimates of expenditure for the peacetime strength of the army, for which the German government had to seek the approval of the Reichstag.

Sinn: meaning and purpose, intended sense. Weber emphasised the distinction between subjectively 'meant' (*gemeint*) and objectively 'valid' (*gültig*) sense (WG, 1; ES, 4): 'By "meaning" (*Sinn*) is to be understood here either A) the sense that is actually subjectively *meant* a) by an agent in a given historical instance or b) on average and approximately intended by agents in a given mass of instances, or B) in a conceptually constructed *pure* type the sense intended by the agent or by the agent considered as a type. Not any kind of objectively "correct" or metaphysically divined "true" sense.'

Spießbürger: philistine.

Staat: state. The state is defined by Weber as a particular category of 'political association', thus (WG, 29; ES, 54): 'An *institutionalised* political *organisation* is to be called a *state*, if and only inasmuch as its governing staff successfully claims the monopoly of legitimate physical compulsion for the execution of its ordinances.' This monopoly must also apply to a definable geographical territory.

Staatsbürger: citizen (of the state).

Staatsgewalt: supreme powers, the powers proper and peculiar to the state.

Staatsordnung: political order, order of the state, the form in which a state is ordered.

Staatspolitik: national politics, national policy, the politics of the state as a whole. See comments on *staatspolitisch*.

staatspolitisch: national-political, relating to national policy. The choice of 'national' rather than 'state' as an equivalent for *Staats-* is not ideal, but it has been made to eliminate a source of confusion. The term actually means 'pertaining to the political concerns of the state as a whole or as such', as opposed, say, to *kulturpolitisch*. In the case of Imperial Germany there is also an implied contrast to the political concerns and interests of the individual *Länder* ('states') composing the Federation.

Staatsrat: Council of State.

Staatsspitze: head of state, headship of state.

Staatsvolk: nation, more particularly the dominant national group(-s) which is the bearer of the state.

Stand: estate. This term can refer to the 'estates' in medieval society or, in modern society, a social group defined by specific characteristics *other* than the economic or other social criteria which define *class* membership. Weber defines *Stand* thus (WG, 180; ES, 306): 'By "estate" is to be understood a number of persons who, within an association, effectively lay claim to a) a special esteem as an estate, possibly also b) special monopolies of that estate.' Despite Weber's distinction of 'estate' from 'class', there are occasions when the translator has no practical alternative to the latter term, e.g. *mittelständlerische Experimente* ('middle-class experiments').

standesgemäß: appropriate to one's estate or social standing.

Standesherr: mediatised prince, member of the higher aristocracy.

Ständestaat: state structured in estates (see note 18, p. 95).

ständisch: the adjective or adverb from *Stand*, hence relating to a profession or estate(-s), as in *ständisch gegliederte Gemeinschaft*, 'community structured in estates'.

Stellenjäger: place-seeker, careerist.

Stichentscheid: casting vote.

tüchtig: able, vigorous, fit (see note 5, p. 134).

verantwortlich: responsible, accountable, answerable.

Verantwortungsethik: ethic of responsibility.

Verband: association. This is one of Weber's general categories capable of assuming many specific forms. He defines it thus (WG, 26; ES, 48): 'By *association* is to be understood a social relation regulating its external relations by restriction or closure, where the observation of its order is guaranteed by the conduct of particular persons which is specifically directed towards ensuring that this happens, these persons being a *leader* (*Leiter*) and, possibly, an *administrative staff,* which may also normally have the power to deputise for the leader.'

verdrängen: supplant, displace; one of the Darwinian terms adopted by Weber (see note 5, p. 2).

Verelendung: immiseration.

Verfassung: constitution (political), arrangement or system (e.g. of agricultural tenure).

Vergesellschaftung: taking into social control.

Verhältniswahlrecht: proportional representation.

Versachlichung: objectification.

Vertrauensmann: agent, spokesman. The term literally means a 'person in whom one places trust', for which there is no exact equivalent in English. In certain contexts it approximates to the English figure of the local political agent, in others the *Vertrauensmann* is a spokesman or negotiator.

vertreten: represent, advance (an argument).

Verwaltung: administration, government.

Verwaltungsöffentlichkeit: public scrutiny of the administration.

Volksabstimmung: referendum.

Volksstaat: democratic state.

Volksverband: association of the people.

Volksvertretung: popular representative assembly, parliament.

Volkswirtschaft: economy, national economy.

vornehm: distinguished, well mannered, chivalrous. This is a central evaluative term in Nietzsche's writings where it is applied to the qualities of those who constitute a natural elite; the antithesis of *gemein.*

Wahlmänner: delegates, electors (at second or subsequent level of election).

Wahlrecht: suffrage, franchise.

Weltpolitik: (participation in) world politics.

Werbung: recruitment.

Willensbildung: formation of the will. In modern English one might speak of the 'process of decision-making', but as 'will' is an important term for Weber, a literal translation has been preferred.

Wissenschaft: science, scholarship. It is a broader concept than modern English 'science', which mostly means the natural or physical sciences, and therefore has to be translated variably in different contexts.

Zensuswahlrecht: property franchise.
Züchtung: breeding.
Zwangsläufigkeit: inevitability.
Zwangsverband: coercive association.
Zweckverband: single-purpose association (see note 13, p. 91).

Index

Index

Index

Chamberlain, H.S., 269
Chamberlain, J., 153, 341, 342
charisma, 311, 363; *see also* leader(s)
citizen [*Staatsbürger*], 103, 105, 129, 226
Cleon, 331
communism, agrarian, 42, 54–60, 299–301
community [*Gemeinschaft*]: 'organic', 91; political, 21; and socialism, 286, 289; village, 39
competition: economic, 14, 185, 284, 285, 289, 290–3; between states, 187; for votes, 347
condottiere, 146, 282, 313, 320
conflict: of economic interests, 111–15; of irreconcilable gods, 363, 366; political, 127, 150, 167, 173–178, 184; Prussian Constitutional, 140, 242
Conservative Party, 119, 153, 167, 184, 190, 202, 209, 235, 240–61
constitution: Russian, 30–74; Wilhelmine, 140–271; Weimar, 304–8
Constitutional Democratic Party, 31–58
conviction, ethic of [*Gesinnungsethik*], xxi–xxii, 359–69
Cromwell, O., 69
culture [*Kultur*]: advance of western, 70; defence of, 16, 20; determination of future, 76; lack of in Russia, 77; of the nation, 128, 134; national and language, 82; and national politics, 108–9, 265–6; western individualistic, 60

Dante, 15n
Darwin C., xi; Darwinian vocabulary, 2n, 14n, 16n, 84n, 134n
Delbrück, H. von, 13n
demagogue(s): ambiguous social position of, 331; and charisma, 312; and democracy, 218, 219–20, 331; demagogic policies in Russia, 73; following of, 314; officials as, 330; and political leadership, 125, 176, 181, 182, 191, 228, 230, 313, 340, 343, 344, 354, 357
demagogy: and Bismarck, 80, 141, 142, 143, 209, 221; and democratisation, 233; Gladstone's, 342; littérateurs

and, 267–8; and the modern monarch, 163
democracy: in America, 121, 224, 277, 325, 347; and Caesarism, 220–1, 222, 229; danger of mass, 230; and demagogy, 228, 331; direct, 127; 'elective affinity' with economic development, 68–9, 159; fear of, 107, 241; in Germany, lack of orderly, 220; leaderless, 351; leadership with a 'machine', 351; and the *Machtstaat*, 76; meaning of 'social democracy', 143; and the modern advocate, 110, 217, 329; nature of modern, 275–6; negative form of, 106; 'of numbers', 102, 103; plebiscitarian, 226, 339; in Russia, 30–70; of the street, 231; 'without parliament', 222–4
democratisation: cultural, 108–9; and demagogy, 220; and evolutionary socialism, 297; and parliamentarisation, 126, 193, 206, 209; passive, 222; and political parties, 214, 215, 218, 338, 341; social, in Germany, 121–2, 129
demon: commanding a cause [*Sache*], 353; of politics, 366
dictatorship: military, 62, 127, 299; of the masses, 305; over the masses, 343; of the proletariat, 288, 290, 295–6, 298, 299
Dilthey, W. von, xii
discipline: of bureaucracy, 154, 225, 281, 330–1; of industrial production, 283–4, 335; party, 209, 338; and revolution, 302–3, 365
dispensable [*abkömmlich*], economically and available for political work, 110, 276, 318, 319
Disraeli, B., 342
distance [*Distanz*], inner, 122–3, 353
distinguished [*vornehm*]: ideal of conduct, 108–11, 278; no German form of conduct, 119, 122
Dolgorukov, Prince P., 58, 64
Dostoyevsky, F.M., 361, 366
duma, 30–66
Durnovo, I.N., 66

Eisner, K., 310n
Engels, F., xv, 287, 289

Index

Cambridge Texts in the History of Political Thought

Titles published in the series thus far